Hints & Kinks

16th Edition

Editor
Steve Ford, WB8IMY

Composition and Proofreading
Shelly Bloom, WB1ENT
Paul Lappen
Kathy Ford

Cover Design
Sue Fagan

Published by:

ARRL
225 Main Street
Newington, CT
06111-1494 USA

ARRLWeb: www.arrl.org/

Contents

Foreword

This 16th Edition of *Hints and Kinks for the Radio Amateur* represents both a continuation of tradition and a new approach. It upholds tradition by bringing together, in one convenient place, useful items published in *QST*'s most popular column, Hints & Kinks. (This edition covers two years, 2000 through 2002.) This edition also includes material from QST's "The Doctor is In."

Whatever interests you most about Amateur Radio—antennas, weekend projects, computers and other digital subjects, shack accessories or operating—you'll find something that will spur you on to learn more about a new mode, build an evening project or find a new approach to a thorny problem.

If you have a tip or technique you'd like to share with the amateur community, please send it to the Hints & Kinks Editor at ARRL Headquarters. It could wind up in an upcoming column—and in the next edition of this book. You can also use the handy feedback form at the back of this book to let us know what you like or don't like about the book or any ARRL publication.

We're looking forward to hearing from you!

73,
David Sumner, K1ZZ
Executive Vice President
February 2003

Acknowledgments

We are grateful to all the authors represented in this book. Without your willingness to share what you've learned with the Amateur Radio community, there would be no Hints & Kinks column in *QST*, and no book.

US Customary to Metric Conversions

International System of Units (SI)—Metric Prefixes

Prefix	Symbol			Multiplication Factor
exa	E	10^{18}	=	1 000 000 000 000 000 000
peta	P	10^{15}	=	1 000 000 000 000 000
tera	T	10^{12}	=	1 000 000 000 000
giga	G	10^{9}	=	1 000 000 000
mega	M	10^{6}	=	1 000 000
kilo	k	10^{3}	=	1 000
hecto	h	10^{2}	=	100
deca	da	10^{1}	=	10
(unit)		10^{0}	=	1
deci	d	10^{-1}	=	0.1
centi	c	10^{-2}	=	0.01
milli	m	10^{-3}	=	0.001
micro	μ	10^{-6}	=	0.000001
nano	n	10^{-9}	=	0.000000001
pico	p	10^{-12}	=	0.000000000001
femto	f	10^{-15}	=	0.000000000000001
atto	a	10^{-18}	=	0.000000000000000001

Linear

1 metre (m) = 100 centimetres (cm) = 1000 millimetres (mm)

Area

$1 \text{ m}^2 = 1 \times 10^4 \text{ cm}^2 = 1 \times 10^6 \text{ mm}^2$

Volume

$1 \text{ m}^3 = 1 \times 10^6 \text{ cm}^3 = 1 \times 10^9 \text{ mm}^3$

$1 \text{ litre (l)} = 1000 \text{ cm}^3 = 1 \times 10^6 \text{ mm}^3$

Mass

1 kilogram (kg) = 1 000 grams (g)
(Approximately the mass of 1 litre of water)
1 metric ton (or tonne) = 1 000 kg

US Customary Units

Linear Units

12 inches (in) = 1 foot (ft)
36 inches = 3 feet = 1 yard (yd)
1 rod = 5½ yards = 16½ feet
1 statute mile = 1 760 yards = 5 280 feet
1 nautical mile = 6 076.11549 feet

Area

$1 \text{ ft}^2 = 144 \text{ in}^2$
$1 \text{ yd}^2 = 9 \text{ ft}^2 = 1\,296 \text{ in}^2$
$1 \text{ rod}^2 = 30\frac{1}{4} \text{ yd}^2$
$1 \text{ acre} = 4840 \text{ yd}^2 = 43\,560 \text{ ft}^2$
$1 \text{ acre} = 160 \text{ rod}^2$
$1 \text{ mile}^2 = 640 \text{ acres}$

Volume

$1 \text{ ft}^3 = 1\,728 \text{ in}^3$
$1 \text{ yd}^3 = 27 \text{ ft}^3$

Liquid Volume Measure

1 fluid ounce (fl oz) = 8 fluidrams = 1.804 in^3
1 pint (pt) = 16 fl oz
1 quart (qt) = 2 pt = 32 fl oz = $57\frac{3}{4} \text{ in}^3$
1 gallon (gal) = 4 qt = 231 in^3
1 barrel = 31½ gal

Dry Volume Measure

1 quart (qt) = 2 pints (pt) = 67.2 in^3
1 peck = 8 qt
1 bushel = 4 pecks = $2\,150.42 \text{ in}^3$

Avoirdupois Weight

1 dram (dr) = 27.343 grains (gr) or (gr a)
1 ounce (oz) = 437.5 gr
1 pound (lb) = 16 oz = 7 000 gr
1 short ton = 2 000 lb, 1 long ton = 2 240 lb

Troy Weight

1 grain troy (gr t) = 1 grain avoirdupois
1 pennyweight (dwt) or (pwt) = 24 gr t
1 ounce troy (oz t) = 480 grains
1 lb t = 12 oz t = 5 760 grains

Apothecaries' Weight

1 grain apothecaries' (gr ap) = 1 gr t = 1 gr a
1 dram ap (dr ap) = 60 gr
1 oz ap = 1 oz t = 8 dr ap = 480 fr
1 lb ap = 1 lb t = 12 oz ap = 5 760 gr

Multiply →

Metric Unit = Conversion Factor × US Customary Unit

← Divide

Metric Unit ÷ Conversion Factor = US Customary Unit

Metric Unit	=	Conversion Factor	×	US Unit
(Length)				
mm		25.4		inch
cm		2.54		inch
cm		30.48		foot
m		0.3048		foot
m		0.9144		yard
km		1.609		mile
km		1.852		nautical mile
(Area)				
mm^2		645.16		inch^2
cm^2		6.4516		in^2
cm^2		929.03		ft^2
m^2		0.0929		ft^2
cm^2		8361.3		yd^2
m^2		0.83613		yd^2
m^2		4047		acre
km^2		2.59		mi^2
(Mass)		**(Avoirdupois Weight)**		
grams		0.0648		grains
g		28.349		oz
g		453.59		lb
kg		0.45359		lb
tonne		0.907		short ton
tonne		1.016		long ton

Metric Unit	=	Conversion Factor	×	US Unit
(Volume)				
mm^3		16387.064		in^3
cm^3		16.387		in^3
m^3		0.028316		ft^3
m^3		0.764555		yd^3
ml		16.387		in^3
ml		29.57		fl oz
ml		473		pint
ml		946.333		quart
l		28.32		ft^3
l		0.9463		quart
l		3.785		gallon
l		1.101		dry quart
l		8.809		peck
l		35.238		bushel
(Mass)		**(Troy Weight)**		
g		31.103		oz t
g		373.248		lb t
(Mass)		**(Apothecaries' Weight)**		
g		3.387		dr ap
g		31.103		oz ap
g		373.248		lb ap

Schematic Symbols

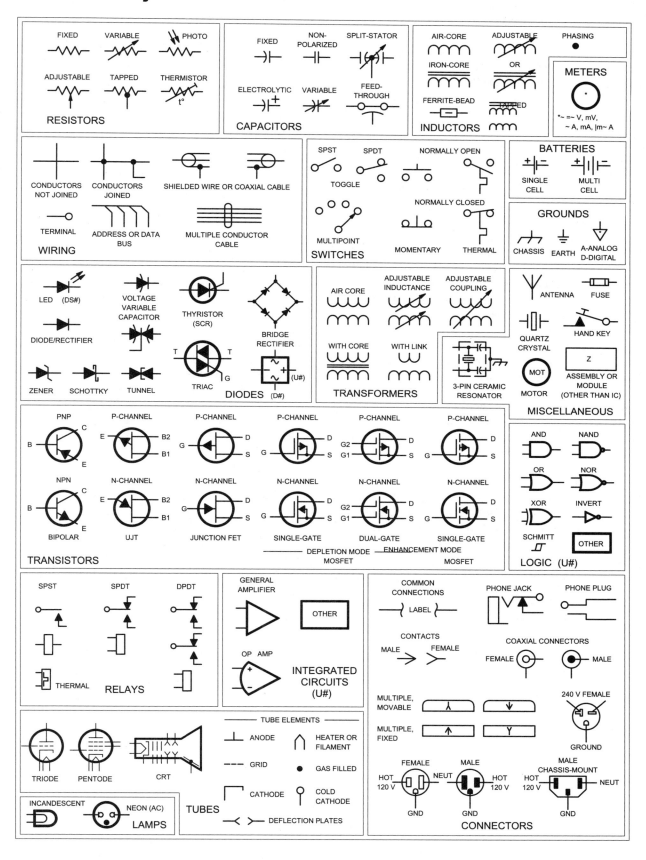

About the ARRL

The seed for Amateur Radio was planted in the 1890s, when Guglielmo Marconi began his experiments in wireless telegraphy. Soon he was joined by dozens, then hundreds, of others who were enthusiastic about sending and receiving messages through the air—some with a commercial interest, but others solely out of a love for this new communications medium. The United States government began licensing Amateur Radio operators in 1912.

By 1914, there were thousands of Amateur Radio operators—hams—in the United States. Hiram Percy Maxim, a leading Hartford, Connecticut, inventor and industrialist, saw the need for an organization to band together this fledgling group of radio experimenters. In May 1914 he founded the American Radio Relay League (ARRL) to meet that need.

Today ARRL, with approximately 170,000 members, is the largest organization of radio amateurs in the United States. The ARRL is a not-for-profit organization that:
• promotes interest in Amateur Radio communications and experimentation
• represents US radio amateurs in legislative matters, and
• maintains fraternalism and a high standard of conduct among Amateur Radio operators.

At ARRL headquarters in the Hartford suburb of Newington, the staff helps serve the needs of members. ARRL is also International Secretariat for the International Amateur Radio Union, which is made up of similar societies in 150 countries around the world.

ARRL publishes the monthly journal *QST*, as well as newsletters and many publications covering all aspects of Amateur Radio. Its headquarters station, W1AW, transmits bulletins of interest to radio amateurs and Morse code practice sessions. The ARRL also coordinates an extensive field organization, which includes volunteers who provide technical information and other support for radio amateurs as well as communications for public-service activities. ARRL also represents US amateurs with the Federal Communications Commission and other government agencies in the US and abroad.

Membership in ARRL means much more than receiving *QST* each month. In addition to the services already described, ARRL offers membership services on a personal level, such as the ARRL Volunteer Examiner Coordinator Program and a QSL bureau.

Full ARRL membership (available only to licensed radio amateurs) gives you a voice in how the affairs of the organization are governed. ARRL policy is set by a Board of Directors (one from each of 15 Divisions). Each year, one-third of the ARRL Board of Directors stands for election by the full members they represent. The day-to-day operation of ARRL HQ is managed by an Executive Vice President and a Chief Financial Officer.

No matter what aspect of Amateur Radio attracts you, ARRL membership is relevant and important. There would be no Amateur Radio as we know it today were it not for the ARRL. We would be happy to welcome you as a member! (An Amateur Radio license is not required for Associate Membership.) For more information about ARRL and answers to any questions you may have about Amateur Radio, write or call:

ARRL—The national association for Amateur Radio
New Ham Desk
225 Main Street
Newington CT 06111-1494
860-594-0200

Prospective new amateurs call:
800-32-NEW HAM (800-326-3942)

You can also contact us via e-mail at **hq@arrl.org**
or check out *ARRLWeb* at **www.arrl.org/**

CHAPTER 1

Equipment Tips and Mods

A QUICK, EASY MOBILE RADIO MOUNT

◊ Some vehicles have plastic boxes built into the dash to hold tapes, CDs and so on. I had a '92 Ford 150 pickup and a '96 Mercury Mystique that had them. Since most VHF-UHF transceivers will fit into these boxes, I developed a mounting system that works well. The boxes have small external ribs behind the instrument panel that snap them into place; they can be easily removed and replaced without any trouble.

I removed the backs of the boxes, so that the radio heat sinks and leads can protrude through the back. To hold the radios in place, I cut two three-inch-long pieces of ordinary automobile heater hose. I drilled two $1/4$-inch holes in each hose that engage the radio's two mounting bolts on each side (see **Figure 1.1**). With both hoses in place, the radio makes a good friction fit with the box. Radios mounted with this arrangement can be easily removed and replaced.—*Marland Old, W5LAN, Rte 1 Box 141b, Boston, TX 75570-9730;* **m.old@att.net**

SIMPLE EXTERNAL MIXER FOR THE HEWLETT PACKARD 8555A SPECTRUM ANALYZER

◊ Recently the HP-8555A spectrum-analyzer plug-in has become available as surplus at reasonable cost. It makes an excellent analyzer through 12 GHz and performs well. However, an external mixer is necessary to extend its range to 40 GHz. HP made a model-11517A external mixer that requires band-appropriate waveguide tapers to cover the 12-18, 18-26 and 26-40 GHz frequencies. The mixer is very sensitive to overloads and can be destroyed by power levels above 1 mW. Since the unit is sealed, it is very difficult to replace any internal components. Working mixers and tapers are very rare and dearly kept.

Briefly, in the external-mixer mode, the analyzer requires the normal input to be terminated with a 50-Ω load and a mixer connected to the "external mixer" connector. The first-LO signal, mixer dc bias and the returning IF signal are carried through coaxial cable to the mixer output. The input attenuator is out of the circuit.

In trying to find an alternate way to cover the 24-GHz ham band with the analyzer, it dawned on me that it would be possible to use other devices than the 11517A as mixers. I have found three techniques. The first unit I tested was a 24-GHz detector. It consists of a UG/595 flange and WR42 waveguide and a 1N26 diode mounted as a detector, with a coaxial output. With this detector connected to a very short piece of coax and the external-mixer bias adjusted for best signal, I was able to see signals from my Gunnplexer at 24 GHz at least 20 dB above the noise.

I also tried a Systron Donner mixer from an analyzer that used a similar arrangement. It also has a replaceable 1N26 mounted as a detector. It worked as well as the above unit.

A third method should work, but I have not tried it. It should be possible to use a waveguide-to-SMA adapter and put a coaxial detector in series between the adapter and the coax. The trouble with this arrangement is in finding components for this frequency range. Oddly, I have not found it difficult to obtain detectors.

The obvious advantages of these arrangements are that the 1N26 is relatively common, physically replaceable and cheaper than the HP part. The liability is that the arrangement is not very sensitive. However, there is enough sensitivity to do antenna alignment and signal analysis, which is its primary purpose.—*Doug Millar, K6JEY, 2791 Cedar Ave, Long Beach, CA 90806;* **dougnhelen@ moonlink.net**

◊ Here are some hints from the ARRL Lab: Andrew Pawl of ATP had WR-42 to SMA adapters at the last Hosstraders hamfest for $50 each. This is not a bad price, considering the cost of SMA connectors that work at 24 GHz. It may make sense to build your own diode detector with an inexpensive SMA connector on the output. This way, you don't need expensive coaxial connectors that can handle 24 GHz. You can reach Andrew at **ATP@worldnet.att.net**. I also found 24-GHz detector diodes at **www. shfmicro.com/diode.htm**. Look at the bottom of the page.—*Zack Lau, W1VT, ARRL Lab Staff;* **zlau@arrl.org**

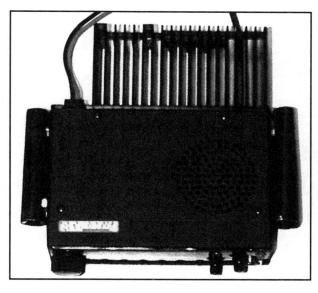

Figure 1.1—A photo of W5LAN's mobile radio mount, with the hoses on each side.

A 2-METER MEMORY PLAN

◊ If you have a 2-meter or dual-band transceiver with at least 100 programmable memory channels and you live in an area that uses 20-kHz repeater frequency spacing, there is an easy way to quickly access nearly every repeater pair in your part of the 2-meter world.

The repeater output frequencies in the 145.110 to 145.490-MHz segment of the band all have odd digits in the 10-kHz position. Therefore, they can be programmed into the odd numbered memory channels from 11 through 49.

The output frequencies for the 145.620 to 146.980-MHz segment all have even digits in the 10-kHz position. These repeater pairs can be programmed into the even numbered channels from 62 through 98.

The 147.020 to 147.380-MHz repeater output frequencies have even 10-kHz digits, and they fit neatly into the even memory channels from 2 through 38. The 147.000 output can occupy channel 100.

This pattern allows you to access each repeater by selecting the memory channel corresponding to its 100 and 10-kHz digits. For example, the 146.900 repeater is in channel 90, the 145.150 repeater is in channel 15, and the 147.140 repeater is in channel 14. Not only that, there are still left over channels for your favorite simplex frequencies (including channel 52 for the 146.520-MHz national calling frequency) and the few repeaters that may not fit the pattern.

Since my mobile radio (Kenwood TM-V7A) has an alphanumeric display, I program the CTCSS tone for each repeater into that area of the respective memory channels.

This is not a very technical hint, but it surely does make finding a repeater easy. It also allows me to use the memory scan and individual channel lock-out for listening to only selected repeater frequencies, rather than scanning a whole band segment on the VFO.—*Rick Melcer, N5KAO, 1103 S China St, Brady, TX 76825-6139;* **n5kao@arrl.net**

A CURE FOR INCOMPLETE AUDIO MUTING IN THE TS-430S

◊ The Kenwood TS-430S HF transceiver can exhibit incomplete audio muting of its internal audio stages while transmitting. This is particularly noticeable when the FM mode is selected and the squelch setting permits noise to pass through the audio chain. Before this modification, IC2 is only partially cut off, and receiver noise can sometimes leak through when transmitting.

This modification puts sufficient voltage on the section of IC2—the IC that's used as the audio preamplifier out of the detector stage—so that the IC will be completely muted during transmit.

The cure is simple. First, locate the TS-430 IF-unit board. It is the large circuit board that you see when you remove the top cover. Assemble a 2.2-kΩ, 1/4-W resistor in series with a 1N4148 switching diode and a piece of insulated wire with heat-shrink insulation to prevent inadvertent short circuits. (See **Figure 1.2A**.) The insulated wire should be long enough for you to install the new components between plug-in connector #10 pin 2 (TX +8 V dc) and the junction of diodes D25, D26 and D75 (also designated as TP3; see **Figure 1.2B**). The cathode of the new 1N4148 diode should point toward TP3. This junction of parts is located just to the right of connector #24.

If you'd like to do everything from the top of the board, the new diode's cathode can be soldered to the cathode of D25, D26 or D75—or to TP3. The cathodes are accessible at the top of the vertically mounted diodes. The other end of the extension wire can be spliced into the wire coming from connector #10 pin 2 (the top of R201 is a convenient point).—*Dave Miller, NZ9E, 7462 Lawler Ave, Niles, IL 60714-3108;* **dmiller14@juno.com**

A review of the IF-board schematic reveals that the TXB line also appears at the top of R201 and TP4, which are easily available from the top of the board. These may offer more con-venient connection points. Check to be sure that the voltage follows that of connector 10 pin 2 before using these alternate points—KU7G

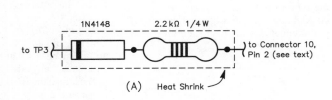

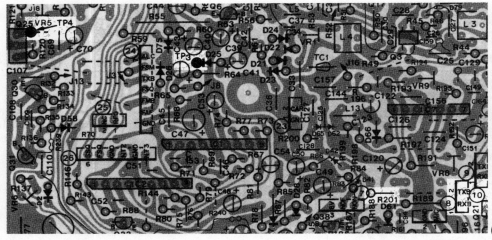

Figure 1.2—NZ9E's modification of the audio circuit of the Kenwood TS-430S for more complete audio muting while transmitting. (A) shows the added components. (B) is an enlarged portion of the IF board from the TS-430S Repair Manual.

HEATH SB-303 MODIFICATIONS

◊ The Heath SB-303 receiver dates back to 1970, but is still popular because of its good performance, low cost in the used equipment market and low power consumption. I modified my receiver for full break-in CW operation by adding a TTL- and CMOS-logic-signal compatible interface circuit for controlling the mute line, decreasing the RF-gain-control time constant and adding an AGC detector output buffer transistor. In addition, I cured a problem with the crystal calibrator.

QSK Muting

The objective of the full-break-in modification is to allow muting by means of a TTL- or CMOS-level logic signal from an electronic keyer while maintaining the original external mute control function and allowing normal receiver operation if the keyer was off or disconnected. Only two transistors are needed in the break-in interface circuit. The first transistor provides the logic interface and controls the second transistor connected to the receiver mute line. The +15 V source for the interface is taken from the receiver's regulated supply. To incorporate the interface circuit into the receiver, we need only break the connection from the mute line to the function switch (S704). Disconnect the purple wire from the mute line to the front panel **FUNCTION** switch at the switch and connect it to the drain of Q2 as shown in the schematic (**Figure 1.3A**).

The circuit is built on a small copper-clad board using insulated standoffs to mount the components. A wide range of silicon NPN switching transistors can be used for Q1 (eg, 2N2222, MPS2222, RS 276-2009, RS 276-1617), as long as the dc current gain, h_{FE}, is greater than 20. A MOSFET output transistor yields a lower mute-line operate voltage than the several hundred millivolts typical of a saturated collector-emitter voltage of a bipolar transistor. The measured Q2 sink current in the operate mode is 16 mA. The obsolete Siliconix VMP-2 that I used for Q2 has an *on* resistance of 2 Ω, resulting in a mute-line voltage of 32 mV. Newer devices such as IRFF110, IRFF210, 2N6659 and RS 276-2072A, have lower *on* resistances that will reduce the voltage further. Any N-channel enhancement-mode MOSFET with a turn-on gate voltage between 1 and 4 V and an *on* resistance below 4 Ω is suitable. The board is mounted on the

Figure 1.3—K1MC's modifications for the SB-303. At A, keyer-logic driven muting circuitry. At B, QSK AGC control. At C, two red LEDs act as a shunt voltage regulator for the crystal-calibrator RTL circuits.

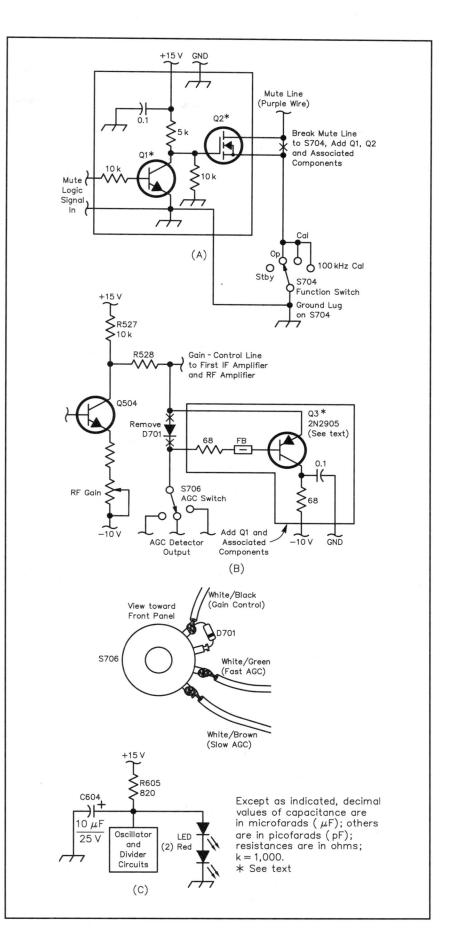

chassis left-side wall adjacent to the **FUNCTION** switch, on metal spacers. The power, logic-input and **FUNCTION**-switch signals are brought to the break-in circuit on twisted wire pairs. A small four-pin male connector for the inputs from the electronic keyer is installed on the receiver back panel in place of one of the spare phono jacks.

Operation of the interface circuit is straightforward. With the keyer input disconnected, Q1 is in the *off* state, which biases the gate of Q2 to +10 V to turn it *on*. In the **OPERATE** and **CALIBRATE** positions of the **FUNCTION** switch, the source of Q2 is grounded. The low *on* resistance of Q2 shorts the mute line to ground and allows the receiver to operate. In the **STANDBY** mode, the source of Q2 is floating, which mutes the receiver regardless of the logic input state. In the **STANDBY** and **MUTE** states, the mute-line voltage rises to +12.8 V. With the keyer connected, a high logic input signal turns Q1 *on,* which lowers the gate voltage of Q2 to 0.1 V, putting it into its high-resistance *off* state. A low logic input keeps Q1 in the *off* state to allow Q2 to be *on*. The original muting operation of the receiver is maintained with the break-in interface. With the receiver in the **STANDBY** mode an external relay can be used to short the mute line to ground, which puts the receiver in the **OPERATE** mode.

Fast QSK Gain Control

Modification of the RF gain control and AGC circuits was necessary to allow fast break-in CW operation. Grounding the receiver mute line takes the receiver from its **OPERATE** mode to its **MUTE** mode in under 10 ms. Fast break-in operation is limited by the transition time (several hundred milliseconds) from the mute to operate states.

A review of the receiver schematic reveals that the high value of R528 in the AGC summing circuit delays the mute-to-operate mode transition. The 1.5-MΩ value of R528 allows the AGC to control the RF gain of the receiver by overriding the manual gain-control voltage. The 0.05 mF decoupling capacitors in the amplifier gain-control circuits and R528 form a time constant of several hundred milliseconds that delays the mute-to-operate mode transition. The effect of this time constant is unnoticeable when going from operate to mute because grounding the mute line quickly disables the first and second mixer stages before the gain of the RF and IF amplifiers is reduced.

The solution to the timing problem is to decrease the value of R528 to 21 kΩ so that the mute-to-operate transition time is less than 10 ms. To allow the AGC to control the RF gain, a single-transistor emitter-follower amplifier is added to the output of the AGC detector (see **Figure 1.3B**). The amplifier provides the current gain needed to pull down the RF gain control voltage with a 30 kΩ source resistance without loading the AGC detector. The transistor base-to-emitter voltage drop matches that of the original silicon isolation diode (D701) to maintain the original AGC characteristics. A wide range of silicon PNP general-purpose small-signal transistors can be used in place of the 2N2905 I used for Q3, as long as the dc current gain (h_{FE}) is greater than 50. Suitable substitutes include the 2N2905A, 2N2907, 2N2907A and their plastic case PN-series counterparts The new value of R528 was determined by scaling the original value of 1.5 MΩ by the minimum transistor dc-current gain of 50 and subtracting the 10 kΩ value of R527. A 68 Ω resistor and ferrite bead in the base circuit of the emitter follower prevent parasitic oscillations. Another 68Ω resistor in the collector circuit limits current and forms a −10 V supply decoupling network with the 0.1 mF bypass capacitor.

The emitter-follower amplifier circuit is built on a small copper-clad board using insulated standoffs to mount the components. The board is mounted on the chassis right-side wall above the crystal filters, on metal spacers. The AGC output, buffer-transistor amplifier output and power signals are brought to the circuit on twisted wire pairs. Three changes to the SB-303 are needed to reduce the RF-gain-control time constant once the amplifier circuit card is installed. First, remove the IF/Audio circuit board and replace R528 with a 21 kΩ resistor. Second, remove the AGC switch (S706) from the front panel, disconnect the AGC summing diode (D701) and connect a twisted wire pair to the two switch terminals where the diode was connected. The connection of the gain-control line (white/black) to the anode of the diode is made on an unused terminal of the switch. Third, connect a twisted wire pair to the −10 V and ground terminals on the power-supply-board connector. Route the two sets of twisted pairs to the amplifier circuit card and connect them to complete the modification.

SB-303 Crystal Calibrator Cure

The built-in crystal calibrator runs at 100 kHz to provide band-edge markers and references for adjustment of the frequency dial. The receiver also has a 25-kHz-marker mode to identify subbands and improved tuning dial accuracy between the 100-kHz markers. The 25-kHz markers are derived from the 100-kHz oscillator output signal by blocking three of each four 100-kHz pulses, rather than by using two flip-flops to digitally divide by four.

The monostable timing for blocking out the correct number of pulses is critical to the proper operation of the circuit because longer timing periods increase the division ratio and shorter timing periods decrease the division ratio. The calibrator uses a resistor-transistor-logic (RTL) quad **NOR** gate IC. Two gates are used for the 100-kHz oscillator and two for the monostable-divider function. An explanation of the circuit is contained in a *QST* (July 1971, pp 48-52) review of the receiver.

I recently purchased a used SB-303 and found that the operation of the crystal calibrator in the 25-kHz mode was erratic. Operation was normal during first half minute after the power was switched on, with markers every 25 kHz. After this short warm-up period, the markers would shift down to a 20-kHz spacing—and then disappear. A quick check of the receiver showed that the +15 V supply to the calibrator is 0.5 V high. Reducing the voltage to its nominal value helped the problem a little, but did not fix it. The measured Vcc for the RTL IC was +4.0 V, well above the specified range of +3.0 to +3.6 V. As an experiment, I lowered the +15 V supply while monitoring the RTL logic supply with a DVM. The 25-kHz markers appeared when the RTL Vcc reached +3.6 V and remained down to +3.0 V. I chose lowering the supply voltage to the IC as the simplest solution.

The calibrator circuit uses an 820 Ω series resistor (R605) to drop the +15 V supply to the RTL operating voltage. The value of the dropping resistor in the circuit measured 854 Ω. With a series resistor already in place, my first thought was to add a 3.3 V Zener diode to form a shunt regulator. A quick check of my junk box and the local RadioShack found only 4.7 V and higher Zener diodes. From a previous digital clock project, I had learned that red LEDs have a junction voltage of about 1.6 V. I series connected two red LEDs and installed them in the calibrator circuit (see **Figure 1.3C**). The two LEDs glowed, and the calibrator 25-kHz markers appeared again as the IC Vcc dropped to +3.4 V.

A wide range of LEDs can be used in the circuit; power dissipation in each LED is about 0.8 mW. The computed LED current is 0.5 mA, based on the measured series dropping resistor value, the +15 V supply and the RTL Vcc. Use only red LEDs because other colors have higher junction voltages. An alternative solution would series connect five small-signal diodes to form a shunt regulator.

Increasing the value of the series resistor is not a practical method of lowering the RTL Vcc: The oscillator and monostable circuits draw approximately 13.1 mA and would require a precision resistor with a value of 885 Ω. In addition, increasing the resistor value would not compensate for variations in the +15 V supply that may create new operating problems for the monostable.

If your crystal calibrator operates consistently at 20 kHz, rather than 25 kHz, the problem is most likely the monostable resistor-capacitor time constant. The carbon-composite resistors used in the receiver increase in value as they age and gradually increase the monostable period until the circuit divides by five. Replace the timing resistor (R609) with a 22 kΩ stable metal-film unit to return the circuit to divide-by-four operation.—*Mal Crawford, K1MC, 19 Ellison Rd, Lexington, MA 02421*

SWEEP-TUBE REPLACEMENTS

◊ Here are a few thoughts regarding "A New Life for your FT-101," (May 1999, pp 68-69). I've done a fair amount of thinking and research about ways to solve the problem of the once common-and-cheap, but now scarce-and-expensive sweep tubes in HF transceivers and linear amplifiers. There are two categories of sweep tubes: small (about 18 W dissipation and 1.25 A heaters), and large (30+ W dissipation and 2.5 A heaters). The former include the 6DQ6B/6LQ6, 6JB6 and such (used in Drake equipment) and the latter 6JE6/6LQ6, 6JS6, 6KD6 and so on. Except for their bases, the 6146, 6146A (20 W CCS dissipation) or the 6146B (27 W CCS dissipation) match up closely to the smaller sweep tubes. The higher dissipation of the 6146B would be an obvious bonus. I would only use new-old-stock (NOS) 6146Bs; according to RF Parts, the current Chinese-made 6146Bs must be derated to 75% of published specifications.

For the larger sweep tubes, the current Svetlana EL-509/6KG6 is—except for its base—a close match in heater current, dissipation and interelectrode capacitances. According to Svetlana, it has a hard glass envelope, many other features of a transmitting tube and is usable at full ratings to 30 MHz. Svetlana Technical Bulletin 32 gives detailed instructions for conversion from 6KD6s to EL-509/6KG6s. "Evaluating the Svetlana EL-509/6KG6 Tube" (*Electric Radio*, Mar 1999; Svetlana Technical Bulletin 49) gives results of test-jig comparisons of an EL-509/6KG6 with a 6146B. (See References and **http://www.svetlana.com/docs/ TechBulletins/** for these articles.—*Ed.*)

I own two sweep-tube SSB rigs, a Drake T4XB and an EICO 753. There are many Drake rigs out there, and the con-

version would also apply to TR-series transceivers, which use three 6JB6 tubes. Unfortunately, I don't own any rigs that use the large sweep tubes. There are probably many sweep-tube SSB rigs and linears out of service due only to the cost and availability of the tubes.

Here are a few additional thoughts: The Chinese-made 6146B tubes, marketed under the Penta (and possibly other) brand names by several vendors, are priced substantially lower than NOS 6146Bs. Assuming the recommended 75% derating factor, their effective dissipation (27 W × 0.75 = 20.25 W) is still sufficient to directly replace American-made 6146 and 6146A (but not the "B") tubes and the smaller sweep tubes, with accommodation of the base differences. In addition to base changes, differences in interelectrode capacitances may require changes in tank and neutralization circuits.

You can expect reasonably close tube-to-tube uniformity between different Svetlana EL-509 tubes or among American-made 6146A/B/W-series tubes from the same manufacturer and with similar date codes. This may not be true for Chinese 6146B tubes.

Although the 6146W is a rugged variant of the 6146A, some vendors have claimed that their 6146W tubes were selected out of regular production runs of 6146B tubes. This may have been true of late-production tubes, but experimental evidence would be needed to confirm or deny this claim. If true, this suggests that sometime after the introduction of the 6146B (circa 1963) production was consolidated into one tube that had the increased dissipation and 1.125 A dark heater of the "B" variant as well as the "W" variant's ability to meet military specifications for vibration and shock. Such a tube could conceivably have been labeled as A, B or W.—*Bill Tipton, K5JRI, 1332 Pinewood Rd, Jacksonville Beach, FL 32250-2941*

References
G. Badger, B. Alper, and E. Barbour, Technical Bulletin, 32 (Huntsville, Alabama: Svetlana Electron Devices, 1997) "Save your Dentron GLA-1000 with the Svetlana EL-509."
Receiving Tube Manual (Harrison, New Jersey: RCA Corporation, 1973).
RCA-6146B/8298A Beam Power Tube (Lancaster, Pennsylvania: Radio Corporation of America, 1963).
Svetlana Technical Data: EL-509 Beam Tetrode (Huntsville: Svetlana Electronic Devices, 1997).
R. D. Straw, N6BV, Ed. *The ARRL Handbook* (Newington: ARRL, 1999) Order No 1832, $32. ARRL publications are available from your local ARRL dealer or directly from the ARRL. See the ARRL Bookcase elsewhere in this issue or check out the full ARRL publications line at **http://www.arrl.org/catalog**. See the Chapter 24 data tables for "Tetrode and Pentode Transmitting Tubes" and "TV Deflection Tubes."

TM-D700 (AND OTHERS) MIKE EXTENSION

◊ I recently did a mobile installation of my new Kenwood TM-D700 under the front passenger's seat and discovered that, while the control-head cable was plenty long enough, the mike cord was stretched uncomfortably. When faced with the $70 cost of a complete extension kit, I decided there had to be a better way. At the local electronics/computer discount store, I found a seven-foot Level 4 network patch cord. These cords contain four twisted pairs and they are terminated with the same connector as the Kenwood TM-D700 microphone cable. I also found a straight-through coupler for the cord (Fry Electronics #1727841 and 1794104). This makes a neat $6 alternative to the Kenwood extender kit, and it is long enough for any installation location using the standard control-head cable.—*Randy Thomson, K5MW, 4905 Westhaven Dr, Fort Worth, TX 76132-1522;* **k5mw@arrl.net**.

TS-850 VCO INSTABILITY

◊ I have a Kenwood TS-850SAT transceiver that has served me well, except for a problem it developed a while ago. Both the receive and transmit audio developed a raspy sound. It was very noticeable on SSB and CW, but nonexistent on AM. After much probing, I found it was due to instability of one of the voltage controlled oscillators (VCO).

There are three VCOs in the 850: a band-switched tuning VCO, the second-mixer VCO and a lower-frequency "carrier" VCO. The second-mixer VCO (64.22 MHz) in my radio was FMing. VCO2 is located on the PLL board (X50-3130-00).

Tapping the body of trim capacitor TC-1 caused it to worsen. The VCO controlling voltage on test point TP-2 was 3.1 V dc. The service manual calls for it to be 5.0 V dc. Adjusting the TC-1 trim cap would not raise this, only lower it until PLL lock was lost, at about 2 V dc.

With some finesse, it was possible to remove VCO2 with its shield can, along with the daughter-board. Touching up the TC-1 solder joint(s) did not improve the situation. I believe the sliding joint within the trim cap was intermittent.

I went looking at the local electronics shop to search for a decent 10 pF air-dielectric trimmer to replace the intermittent TC-1. They had to order it, so for the time being, I purchased a fixed value 8.2 pF monolithic capacitor to pop in there and try it. This was a stab at a ballpark, workable value. With 8.2 pF, the controlling voltage is now 5.9 V dc. Not perfect, but closer than could be achieved with that faulty trimmer. The raspiness (FMing) is gone and the rig is running well until the replacement trimmer comes in.

I have heard some other signals on the air that have the same raspy sounding signal. Perhaps they have the same condition and this repair might cure the problem.—*David Steels, VE3UZ, 444 Jellicoe Crescent, London, ON, Canada, N6K 2M5; dsteels@odyssey.on.ca*

MORE ON REPAIRING OLD HEADSETS

◊ Regarding those wonderfully flexible (but impossible to solder) metal-on-nylon cords which are found in headsets and some telephone cables, here's a hint that I've used for years. As N7OJ mentioned,[1] reconnecting them is a pain. A close examination of a typical connection on one of these will usually show that the original connectors have tiny teeth which went through the insulation.

Go to your local RadioShack and pick up their part number 64-3070, insulation-piercing telephone spade lugs (see **Figure 1.4**). A pack of 24 is about $1.49. These are perfect for this task.

Leave the outer insulation intact on your disconnected wires, trimming off any exposed metal conductor. Then carefully crimp one of those lugs onto the stub. The teeth poke through and make contact with the conductor, while the insulation keeps the foil/metal conductor in place and provides a bit of strain relief. Now you've moved from tinsel wire to real metal (tada!) and can trim/solder the spade lug as needed.

I've fixed headsets and other flimsy things for quite some time with this method, and I'm amazed that RadioShack still carries the lugs. They're vital when you need them, but can't be a big seller.

Here's another, newer solution: I told a friend about this headset-cord tip. He has a pile of antique headsets with cloth cords that are either missing or rotted. Therefore, he asked me to surf the Web and see what I could find. I found Phoneco Inc, 19813 E Mill Rd, PO Box 70, Galesville, WI 54630; tel 608-582-4124, fax 608-582-4593; URL **www. phonecoinc.com/**. They sell old telephones, reproduction and novelty telephones, miscellaneous parts and memorabilia. The cords shown on their Web pages might not be original-equipment headset cords, but they look awfully close.—*Jim Tolson, KF9CI, 4934 Dobson St, Skokie, IL 60077; jtolson777@aol.com*

[1]B. McCaffrey, N7OJ, "Don't Throw Away Those Old Headsets," *QST*, Feb 2000, p 61.

MORE ON D-104 MODS FROM W1AW

◊ In Steven Fraasch's, KØSF, article "Adapting the Astatic D-104 Microphone for Use with Modern Transceivers," (*QST*, Aug 1999, pp 34-36) he suggests that an Archer TLC274 op amp can be used in place of the LPC662AIM.

Here at W1AW, I have an Astatic D-104 (with the UG8 base) and decided to modify it for use with our Kenwood radios.

Because I couldn't find the LPC662AIM chip locally, I opted to use an Archer TLC274 single-supply quad op amp. Unlike the 8-pin LPC662AIM, the TLC 274 is a 14-pin DIP. The pin locations for the first op amp in this package almost match, except for ground and V_{dd}. On the TLC274, pin 4 is V_{dd} and pin 11 is ground. The TLC274 is a quad op amp, so the other three op amps are unused in this application. I tied the unused op amps together in the same fashion as the unused one (U1B) in the LPC662AIM circuit.

Since the original three-conductor (with ground) mic cable I had was rather old, I replaced it with a new four-conductor (with ground) cable. This allowed me to pull +8 V dc from the Kenwood microphone connector without using the dc power insertion circuit as shown in the article.

I didn't want to produce a printed circuit board, so I decided to fuse a 14-pin wire-wrap socket and perfboard for the circuit. Even with this high-profile socket, the board fits nicely in the UG8 base.

Figure 1.4—Insulation-piercing spade lugs, as sold by RadioShack.

I wired up an eight-pin mic plug for our Kenwood TS-950 and tuned to 20 meters. Although I did need to crank the mic gain down a bit, on-the air tests proved quite favorable.

The Astatic D-104 is a nice addition to the equipment complement here at the station. This microphone now sits proudly in one of our W1AW visitor-operating studios.—*Joe Carcia, NJ1Q, ARRL Staff*

DOX CONTROL FOR A YAESU FT-847

◊ I enjoy operating PSK31 with my FT-847, but I need the two serial ports on my PC for a packet modem and computer-control of the receiver, so I don't have a spare RTS or DTR line to key the transmitter, as is common with most PSK31 interfaces. The FT-847 does not have VOX, but it does have a data AFSK port that can be used to key the transmitter by pulling the transmit line low with a 22 kΩ (or lesser value) resistor. Keying the data port also disables the mike, an ideal situation for simple data-mode operations. To interface the PC to transceiver, I designed the *DOX* (data-operated transmit control, similar to VOX—*Ed.*), a minimum-component-count interface that keys the transmitter from the AFSK signal produced by the PC audio card. (See **Figure 1.5**) Although I have tried the interface only for PSK31, it should also work with other modes that use sound-card AFSK modulation.

Audio from one PC speaker output is stepped up by a reverse-connected speaker output transformer (T2, RS #273-1380) to approximately 30 V (P-P) and peak rectified by D1, D3, C2 and C3. The rectified positive voltage is applied to the gate of a 2N7000 MOSFET (Q1), which then appears as a low resistance to ground. The peak detection is very effective because the FET gate impedance is nearly an open circuit. Peak detection with a long discharge time constant is required because PSK31 data goes through a null with each phase reversal. The discharge time constant (C3-R5, approximately 0.1 second) is long enough to smooth ripple in the rectified voltage. The Zener diode (D2) provides protection for the 2N7000 gate in the event the input voltage is too high; as a bonus, the LED (DS1) in series with the Zener indicates that data is detected and the transmitter is keyed.

The combination of R1 and R2 reduces the 30-V audio to the approximately 30 mV (P-P) required by the transceiver data input. To adjust the transmit level, I connect the transmitter to a dummy load, set the PC software to the transmit mode and adjust the PC

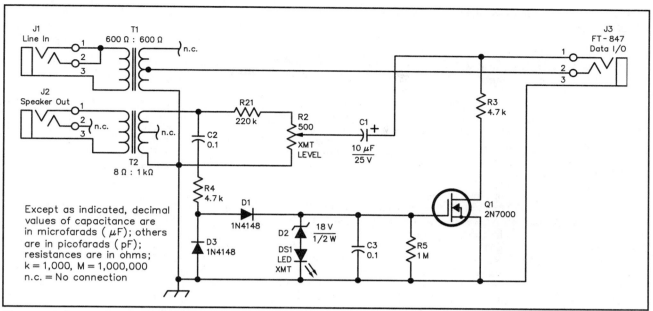

Figure 1.5—Schematic of AD6KI's DOX interface.

sound card software sliders so that the LED just lights. Then, adjust R2 so that the ALC meter barely indicates.

All component values are relatively noncritical. Diodes D1 and D3 may be any small-signal silicon diodes. Zener D2 may be any 18-24 V, 500 mW device. The LED may be omitted if desired. The time constant (C3-R5) may be varied; the values I use do not produce any relay chattering in the FT-847. This interface has no hysteresis (snap action)—as would be required in a VOX circuit—because the input data signal has constant amplitude while transmitting.

On the receive side, the center-tap of a 1:1 transformer (RS #273-1374) provides a 2:1 voltage step-up to the sound-card line input. This interface was constructed in a small metal enclosure and only the transceiver side of the circuit is grounded to the case. *The leads on the PC side are shielded and the shields grounded to the case only at the PC*; this is important to prevent any possibility of line-frequency hum being introduced into the low-level signals. I constructed the cables by cutting a shielded stereo patch cord (RS #42-2387) in half. —*David Smoler, AD6KI, 19982 Charters Ct, Saratoga, CA 95070-4458;* **ad6ki@earthlink.net**

MODIFICATION TO KENWOOD MC-53 MICROPHONE

◊ **Figure 1.6** is a drawing I made in order to explain a modification needed to most Kenwood MC-53 microphones commonly used with Kenwood TM-742 transceivers. If any of you proud TM-742

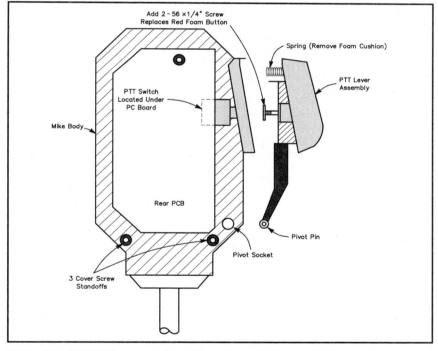

Figure 1.6—KC6NXZ's remedy for PTT problems in Kenwood MC-53 microphones.

owners have found your backlit-microphone PTT going away or becoming intermittent, the solution is at hand! Simply remove three screws holding the microphone's back cover, then remove the PTT lever. Remove and discard the foam-rubber cylinder from the lever. Now remove the small foam piece within the return spring. Next, install a #2-56× ¹/₄-inch screw where the first foam-rubber piece was glued into the hole in the plastic lever. Adjust for proper action on the PTT switch. Finally, close the microphone and perform a final check attached to the transceiver. This mod should give you a positive feel when the PTT switch transfers. I am told it did wonders for Carl, KE6JQL, who had lost some of his finger strength due to a stroke.—*Tom Caudle, KC6NXZ, PO Box 711825, Santee, CA 92072-1825;* **kc6nxz@ tns.net**

KEYER PTT CONTROL FOR SUPER CMOS KEYERS

◊ I like my station TR control closely linked to my CW keying. This function is present in N6TR's *TR Log* and K8CC's *NA* contest logging programs. Each accepts paddle input and keys the transceiver with variable PTT onset and delay. Nonetheless, it's awkward to have a station set up for the contest logging software PTT, but use the rig VOX (which doesn't track the sending speed) for an external keyer.

Keying-derived TR control is not a new idea with me, but I couldn't find any example of an external PTT-control circuit done well with a keyer. After some thought, I decided to add the function myself—just to see if I could do it. That's why I used junk-box discrete components rather than drive to town for Schmitt-trigger ICs.

Figure 1.7 shows the circuit I cooked up. It works well in my LogiKeyer K-1 (Super CMOS II). U1's oscillator turns off (enters sleep mode) 1.5 baud after the last character is sent, and its dc level changes at that time. The oscillator starts about 8 ms before the keying output becomes active, so it's a good event to use for PTT control. It lets all the radio TR events complete before the keying starts, but you must be careful not to load the resonator too heavily.

The turnoff timing (1.5 baud) is too quick though. If I were doing this in software, I'd set the total delay to 3 or 4 bauds, so it would follow the keyer speed. Unfortunately, I didn't find any output from the CMOS II chip that was delayed more than 1.5 baud after the end of the last character. For this junk-box project, I use a fixed delay equivalent to about four bauds at the keying speeds I use. The result is a little pulse stretcher that adds 90 ms to the turnoff delay in the keying circuit. This five-minute job, as always, took 24 hours, but it works fine.

The combination of 1.5 baud delay plus fixed time delay gives some tracking of code speed, although it's not as good as if nearly all the delay were in bauds.

The timing is set by a 47-kΩ resistor (to +5 V) and a 4.7-μF capacitor (to ground) at the collector of Q2. This time-constant circuit is followed by a discrete-transistor Schmitt-trigger circuit (Q3-Q6) that sharpens the switching time, so there's no chirp from a slow TR transition. The turnoff time with this circuit is still a bit fast; you can increase the delay by increasing the value of the resistor, capacitor or both.

This circuit conducts current through the input transistor of the Schmitt circuit even when it's off. Thus, it continually draws a little over 100 μA. This makes for poor battery life, but I only use a battery for backup power, so I don't worry about current drain. The whole thing can probably be done better with a low-drain Schmitt-trigger IC.

I really like the way the keyer feels with the PTT control, although it takes a bit of getting used to—sort of like an open mic. Whenever you key anything, it is sent! The PTT delay tracks keying very naturally, it's a wonder I waited so long to do this! This modification should apply to other keyers too. Bob, W9KNI, says it should work on the all Super CMOS 2, Super CMOS 3 and Logikey keyers.[2,3]

[2]Idiom Press, PO Box 1025, Geyserville, CA 95441; tel 1-707-431-1286; e-mail **Sales @IdiomPress.com**; **www.idiompress. com**.

[3]J. Russell, K0CQ, and C. Southard, N0II, "The CMOS Super Keyer" QST, Oct 1981, p 11-17.

J. Russell, K0CQ, and C. Southard, N0II, "The CMOS Super Keyer II" QST, Nov 1990, p 18-21.

J. Russell, K0CQ, "The CMOS Super Keyer 3" QST, Aug 1995, p 26.

Again, I think there's a better solution if someone has access to the code for the microcontroller. There seem to be plenty of unused I/O ports. An output with a programmable four- or five-baud delay that keys a simple NPN transistor would do this job properly. Tom Rauch, W8JI (**w8ji@contesting.com**), who is interested in the keyer/PTT area, suggests that some small additional fixed turn-off delay might be necessary for QSK PTT configurations.

My goal here is to encourage discussion of PTT control by modern keyers. For example, a series of inexpensive keyers offered by Steve Elliott, K1EL seem like a real step forward. He mentions PTT control on his Web site, but I'm not sure if it's timed to the data rate. I suggest you visit **members.aol.com/ k1el/**. If there is enough interest, I'd hope the function can be included in keyer chips.—*Dave Leeson, W6NL/HC8L, 15300 Soda Springs Rd, Los Gatos, CA 95030-8621;* **leeson@earthlink.net**

MORE ON TS-570 BATTERY PROBLEMS

◊ I noticed a piece on battery replacement for the TS-570 in the November 1999 Hints and Kinks. The piece is accurate regarding mechanics, however, Kenwood has a known problem with many of these radios discharging their batteries in about six months—well in advance of the expected life.

If you press them, Kenwood will install a diode in the line that prevents the battery from discharging through the ac power supply when the supply is turned off.

Read all about it at my Web site: **www.al-williams.com/wd5gnr/ kbatt.htm**—*Al Williams, WD5GNR, 310 Ivy Glen Ct, League City, TX 77573;* **alw@al-williams.com**

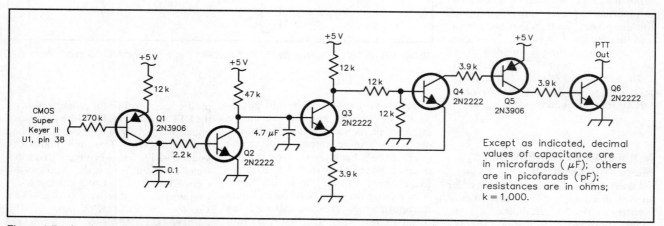

Figure 1.7—A schematic of W6NL's PTT-control circuit for Idiom Press Logikey and CMOS Super Keyers.

YAESU FT-847: A SEPARATE RECEIVE ANTENNA; BAND SWITCHING VIA MEMORY

◊ I recently purchased a Yaesu FT-847 transceiver after using an FT-767GX for many years. My station is in an extremely high-noise location: an industrial area surrounded by power lines. Receiver noise is a major problem, especially on 160 meters, so I use a six-foot tuned coaxial-loop receive antenna made out of 3/4-inch CATV Hardline hung inside the back wall of our building. The loop reduces "20 dB over S9" power-line noise to about S1. I connected the loop to the separate receive-antenna jack on the FT-767.

The FT-847, however, has no provision for a separate receiver antenna, so I improvised the circuit shown in **Figure 1.8**. My coax relay requires more current (600 mA) than the FT-847 standby transistors can handle, so I added a second relay (K1) to switch the coax relay.

The 47-Ω resistor in series with relay K2 works in conjunction with the 1N4007 to help suppress arcing across the contacts of K1 when keying K2, yet still passes enough current to operate the coax relay reliably. (I've been using this circuit for two years with no problems at all.) For coaxial relays requiring much less current, the 47-W resistor could be omitted.

The FT-847 has no VOX, so the relays are only active during PTT operation. My circuit has a 13.6 V dc, 4 A power supply, but something less would suffice.

Last night, I was talking to Morton Howard, W2ATO, who also has a Yaesu FT-847. He was complaining about needing to change out of the "fast tune" mode every time he wants to change bands. I told him that I stored CH1 in the memory at 160 meters and three or four frequencies in memory for each band up to 10 meters. With a few more frequencies for 6 meters and VHF and UHF, all 78 memories are used.

To change bands, simply change the VFO/M switch to memory and use the MEM/VFO CH switch to select the band. As soon as you move the tune dial, the rig is in the memory-tune mode. To change bands again, just hit the VFO/M CH switch and repeat the process in the memory mode. W2ATO and I prefer the fast-tune mode and don't need to leave it when switching bands in this manner. —*Gene Fisher, W9MZH, 1815 Taylor St, Fort Wayne, IN 46802;* **w9mzh@ juno.com**

RUBBER SKIRTS FOR SMALL KNOBS

◊ Fat fingers skinny knobs. For years, smaller radios with closely spaced knobs and the size of my fingers have formed a dilemma. To make matters less friendly, many knobs are now concentric, with a smaller inner knob that stands away from the front panel and a slightly larger knob that is set back against the radio face. The setting of the inner knob often gets disturbed when I try to turn just the outer knob.

My ICOM IC-746 fits this category. The radio is super in my estimation, but only when I don't try to turn just the outside knob in a concentric set. What I needed was a simple fix that could be undone so that another user or future owner would not have to be a part of my fix.

The solution is easy! I built a skirt for the outer knob using rubber washers! Every water faucet uses rubber washers, every garden hose as well. A trip to the local hardware store will uncover storage drawers of small parts, including rubber washers of every imaginable size. You need only measure the outside diameter of the knob closest to the radio face, and measure what you would like to have as its new outside diameter. I picked a size that is about the same as the printed dial markings on the radio.

At the hardware store, get to the rubber-washer drawer and match up your measured knob outside diameter with the inside diameter of the washer, and your desired outside size with the outside diameter of the washer. There are rubber washers available that are round like an inner tube (O-rings) and some that have flat faces with a sharper edge for your fingers. I prefer the latter.

With a trip to the local hardware store, I found that Servolite faucet adapters were available and that washer number FAWD 10 was right for my use. It is 3/16-inch thick with flat faces, a 5/8-inch ID and a 13/16-inch OD. You may choose

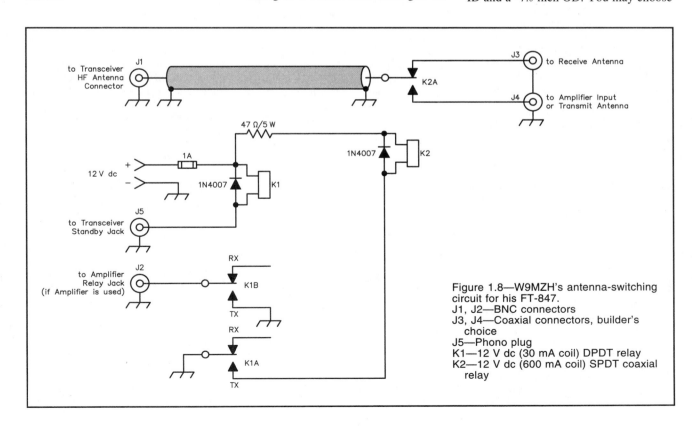

Figure 1.8—W9MZH's antenna-switching circuit for his FT-847.
J1, J2—BNC connectors
J3, J4—Coaxial connectors, builder's choice
J5—Phono plug
K1—12 V dc (30 mA coil) DPDT relay
K2—12 V dc (600 mA coil) SPDT coaxial relay

another size. The size you need varies for different radios or manufacturers.

I used just a touch of White Out on the surface to make a pointer. Then, I slipped the washers into place over the outside knob. Now I can turn the small inner knob, or widen my grip and turn the larger skirted knob. My problem is solved, for this radio anyway. To change the marker position or remove the modification, simply slide the skirt off the knob. **Figure 1.9** is a picture of my dime-a-piece solution.—*David B. Perrin, K1OPQ, 1161 Penacook Rd, Contoocook, NH 03229*

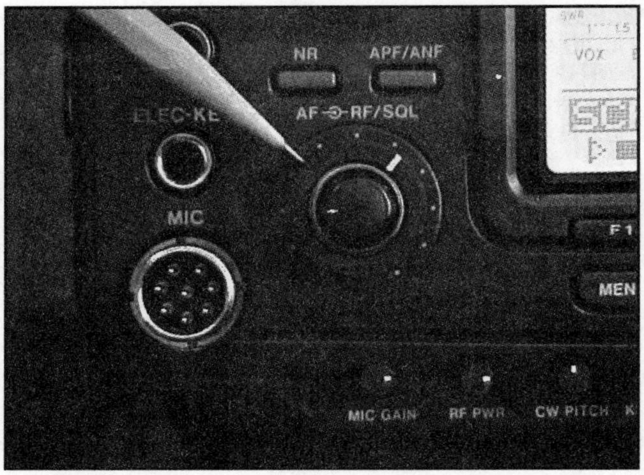

Figure 1.9—K1OPQ uses washers to make concentric controls easier to handle.

EXTERNAL KEYING LINE FOR THE ICOM IC-706 MKII

◊ I was tired of the fast hang-time drop on my old RF-Concepts 2-315 brick amplifier when on 2-meter SSB; setting the hang time to the maximum available still isn't quite long enough for us Southern folk. Therefore, I decided to make a connector for the brick's external keying line to use with my IC-706 MkII.

At first, I thought of switching the amplifier from the default positive keying to negative keying, but this caused more problems than it solved. So I reverted to the negative keying position, and after a little trial and error came up with the circuit in Figure 1.10.

This circuit inverts the output of the IC-706 MkII **VSEND** line (Pin 7 on the Accessory socket). My trusty DMM says this will only draw 1 mA from the +8 V reference regulator in the radio, which is rated at a maximum of 10 mA.

All parts for this circuit can be obtained from RadioShack, and assuming that you still have the pigtail connector that came with the radio, you can build this for about $5.—*James D. Bryant II, KC5VDJ, 8409 Farley St, Overland Park, KS 66212; kc5vdj@swbell.net*

YAESU FT-920 AUTOMATIC-TUNER TRICKS

◊ About two years ago, I traded for a Yaesu FT-920 that was in excellent condition, except for its automatic antenna tuner. I went to each band and started the matching process by holding the TUNER button in, and the tuner arrived at a good match on all the bands my antenna covered (40 through 6 meters). The next day, the match was gone on some bands.

Trying to tune those bands ended in a match failure, even with a dummy load!

I first suspected a relay or some mechanical failure, so I opened the transceiver and tried to determine the problem. There seemed to be no mechanical problems; everything was secure but to be sure, I went through the Antenna Tuner Adjustment procedure in the Service Manual. Everything seemed to work for a couple of days, and then the problem started again. I dug into it again and tapped on all the relays as it was tuning, hoping to find one that was sticking or making erratic contact—none found!

I decided to watch the tuner as I went through all the bands and noticed that one of the stepper motors had turned its variable capacitor beyond the fully unmeshed position. Normally the home position for these guys is fully meshed; there is a mechanical stop at this position. Looking from the front of the radio, the stepper motors turn the capacitors clockwise, to the fully unmeshed position at most. There is no stop at this unmeshed position and no feedback to the controller indicates whether this position—or any for that matter—has been reached. This time one capacitor was beyond the unmeshed position, and I thought that one of the stepper motors had a problem, so I replaced it. I should have watched it more closely, because that wasn't the case. The problem returned, and with it continued slipping of my sanity. I had about decided that this was a "return to Yaesu" problem and connected a manual tuner. However, the thought that a tuner was there but not working was driving me crazy.

I opened the radio up again, started the tuner on each band and noticed this time that *both* of the stepper motors had gone beyond the unmeshed position! Normally when you first turn the transceiver on, these capacitors go to the home position (fully meshed) and then go to the saved position for the current particular frequency. After one or both of the capacitors have gone beyond the unmeshed position, however, the home-position reference seems to be lost. When you move to another band, the controller takes the stepper-motor positions and relay sequences from memory and acts accordingly. However, the motor-position information is referenced from the home position, which has now changed. Since there is no positional feedback, the capacitor settings are completely wrong. If you try to tune again, the controller thinks the capacitors are somewhere within that

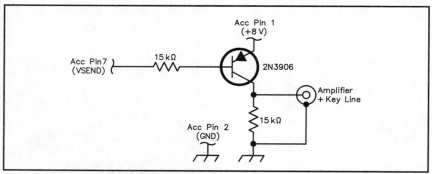

Figure 1.10—A keying-line inverter for the IC-706MkII transceiver for use with RF-Concepts style external keying circuits. ICOM rates the +8 V line at 10 mA, maximum. This circuit draws only 1 mA. Acc pin numbers refer to the pins on the accessory socket (13-pin DIN) on the radio rear panel.

180° arc from meshed to unmeshed, but instead one or both of them is beyond 180°. Therefore, the capacitance increases, rather than decreases with clockwise rotation. That's why no match could be achieved, even with a dummy load. If you turn the radio off and back on, the motors will turn (counterclockwise) for the length of time they are programmed to turn, but will not go fully home if they're beyond 180°. If you do this several times, they eventually get to the home position. Then, the positional information for most bands is correct again. When you go to one of those bands, everything works again.

I eventually discovered that doing a warm reset (pressing GEN and ENT on the keypad while turning the radio on) would clear the problem for a while, but it kept returning—usually every few days. I knew I shouldn't need to reset the radio that often.

Then one afternoon it was doing this wonderful thing again. Everything was fine on all bands until I went to 6 meters. The match was fine there, but when I went back to 10 meters, I heard a dip in the signal level and then it came back up a little. I knew the capacitors were in the wrong place. I opened it and that was indeed the case. I kept it on 10 meters, turned the radio off and on enough times to get to the home position and started the tuner. It did its thing and achieved a match. I went to 6 meters; the capacitors moved to the new location. Then I went back to 10 meters, and both capacitors went beyond 180°. I went through the off-on-tune thing several times, and each time I went to 6 and back to 10 the capacitors went past 180°. The only way to clear it was to do a warm reset and retune on each band.

It then dawned on me what the problem could be. The tuner uses a serial EEPROM to store values. This EEPROM and the microcontroller are powered from 5-V dc from a regulator on the Tuner Control Board. This 5-V line also goes to the Main Tuner Board for the relays, coils, capacitors and so on. Having had some experience with EEPROM devices, I surmised that noise/RF could be getting into them via this 5-V line and causing erroneous values to be written into memory. There are a couple of 1 mF electrolytic and 0.01 mF disc capacitors along this line, but with as much RF as could be running around in there, I thought it needed more. I took the board out, fired up the soldering iron and added a couple of parts. With these additions, I've had *no* problems with the tuner at all over the last two years. In fact, it seems to tune faster and smoother than before. I added two capacitors: a 330-mF 16 V

electrolytic. This could probably be much smaller and work as well, but this is what I had on hand: a 0.047-mF ceramic disc. I wanted a 0.1-mF disc, but this is what I had on hand. Here's the modification procedure:

1. Very carefully unplug all cables from the Tuner Control board. Don't jerk them or you might pull a wire out or break it. Gently rock them from side to side until they come loose.

2. There's a white (at least on mine) flat cable that comes up from underneath the transceiver and slides into a connector on the Tuner Control Board. Don't force this one free. Pull up the small clips on each side to release pressure on the cable so it will come out correctly.

3. Remove the four screws that hold the board in place.

4. There is a screened position on the board marked "C5547." There is no part in that position on my board, nor is there a part on the schematic with this designation. This is where I placed the 330-mF capacitor. Please note that the negative connection is marked with a dot on the board—at least on mine—please verify that on yours!

5. The 0.047-μF capacitor should be soldered as close to pin 8 of JP5004 as possible and ground. I traced the 5-V line and found a spot on the board where I was able to get to a ground connection that already had solder on it.

I also redressed the leads going to this board somewhat. Especially those going to the stepper motors. They seem three times longer than necessary. I bundled them with a wire tie.

That's it! Put the board back in place and replace all the connectors. Be sure to get the right connector to the right socket for each stepper motor.

Several people on the Internet reflectors reported problems similar to mine, even with multiband antennas such as a five-band vertical. At least five of them (the ones who contacted me) tried this modification and it solved the problem. In the real world, there are many variables. Perhaps Yaesu designed the tuner in a lab environment, then problems resulted outside that environment.

Other notes for FT-920 owners

The automatic tuner in the '920 "gives up" quickly if the SWR is high. In addition, if the SWR is more than 1.5:1, the settings will not be saved. A trick I've used is to turn the RF power to minimum and start the tune cycle. When it starts to tune, raise the power a little at a time so a rough match is attained, then turn it up completely near the end of the cycle. I have been able to get a good match on 40

through 6 meters on a half-length G5RV. The only thing I had to do was to increase the length of the feedline a little.

I've also seen that at certain frequencies the tuner will refuse to tune at all and give a "High SWR" indication. I found a way to get around this problem. Like before, turn the RF power all the way down, then start the tuning cycle. Now instead of gradually increasing the power, quickly rock the power control up and down until the tuner starts the sequence. Then like the other instance, increase the power a little at a time until it's at full power. This will take a few tries. You are really tricking the tuner because there's a slight dip that it sees.—*Anthony Bowyer, NT4X, 113 Cliffwood Rd, Bristol, TN 37620;* **adb1x1@yahoo.com**

◊ Have you read the notes at the end of every Hints and Kinks column? Some Hints are useful, but not necessarily safe in all situations. The important part of Anthony's advice is that stray RF can cause automatic tuners to malfunction. If you experience this problem, first do everything you can to remove the RF: Is the antenna too close to the operating position? Are you using a shield choke at the back of the radio? Is the station properly grounded?

For example, when operated at any SWR greater than 1:1 there are periodic voltage maxima and minima that develop along a feedline. RFI problems sometimes result when a maximum occurs near the affected equipment. Such problems may be reduced or cured when the feedline length is changed by ±1/8 on the problem band, so as to move the voltage maximum away from the equipment. Of course, changing the feedline length may create a problem on another band, so it may take several iterative adjustments to reach a cure.

Once you have exhausted other possible remedies, consider whether you feel comfortable modifying your equipment and with the possible consequences.

In the "Other Notes," Anthony is fooling the tuner into functioning with SWRs beyond its design specifications (greater than 3:1). Although the tuner might be persuaded to match the impedance, there is a concern that the higher RF voltages associated with the higher SWR might exceed tuner-component specifications. (The component specifications presume that the tuner will *not* try to resolve higher impedances.) Perhaps the increased voltages contribute to the need for additional bypassing in the tuner? So, as with all the Hints and Kinks, this technique is definitely "at your own risk."—*Bob Schetgen, KU7G, Hints and Kinks Editor*

CURE IC-707/FL-53A AUDIO HUM

◊ If you are a CW addict like me, a perfect audio tone with no background "hum" is essential. So for me, the following hum-reduction modification for the IC-707 turns a great CW rig to a super CW rig! I purchased an IC-707 new in July 1997 and performed the following modification shortly thereafter.

Since CW is my main mode of operation, I purchased and installed ICOM's 250 Hz FL-53A filter. The FL-53A operates at a center frequency of 455 kHz. It is electrically connected by plugging it into a PC board and soldering the four terminals. Once this was accomplished, a test on several CW bands indicated that this filter did indeed provide the kind of filtering needed for day-to-day DXing.

However, I soon noticed that upon "cranking up" the audio gain about halfway on weak but noise-free DX signals, there is a background hum. The frequency of the hum was about 125 Hz. At the wider bandwidth settings, no hum was discernible. This was somewhat disappointing since everything else about the 707 seemed to work perfectly.

After all the usual internal checks for possibly leaky capacitors and such, I discovered that the hum disappeared completely when the cooling fan rotation was manually stopped. I decided that the mechanical fan rotation modulated the dc fan voltage, which in turn made its way back to the 455-kHz amplifier containing the 250-Hz filter.

I found that 9400 µF across the fan dc line eliminated the hum. Fortunately, it's easy to come up with a couple of 4700 mF (35 V) capacitors from RadioShack at only modest cost. So I wired two such capacitors in parallel and installed them within the cabinet. (There is more than enough room in the 707 for these capacitors across the fan-motor dc power line.)

The IC-707 has run with this minor modification for several years now and I've noticed no side effects other than hum elimination. I sent the ICOM Service Department a summary of my experience at the time of the original modification.—*Paul E. Schmid, W4HET, PO Box 939, Vienna, VA 22183-0939;* **w4het @aol.com**

AN ADDITION TO THE KENWOOD TM-261A MANUAL

◊ The popular Kenwood TM-261A mobile 2-meter transceiver allows the user to assign names to channels. That is, the location or call sign of a repeater can show up on the display instead of just the frequency, but the manual leaves out a vital step in explaining how to do this.

As I found out from other hams, the way to assign a name to a channel is to:

1. Select the channel
2. Switch the power off;
3. While holding down the MN button, switch the power on again;
4. Immediately press the REV button (the step omitted in the manual);
5. Choose letters or digits with the tuning knob, pressing MN after each character;
6. Press the F button to exit.

The manual also omits the "wireless clone" feature that allows you to transfer the entire memory of a TM-261A to another TM-261A. However, that is documented online at **216.133.235.165/Amateur/AmateurApplicationNotes/ AAN0019.JPG**. During cloning, the "master" radio sends DTMF tones to the others for about five minutes. Using a dummy load on the transmitter is recommended because a range of only a few yards is generally sufficient.—*Michael A. Covington, N4TMI, 285 St George Dr, Athens, GA 30606-3943;* **Michael@ CovingtonInnovations.com**

ELIMINATING KEY-CLICKS IN MFJ-93XXK QRP-CUB TRANSCEIVERS
[This item was first published by QRP ARCI in the July 2000 *QRP Quarterly*. Thanks to Craig Behrens, NM4T, for permission to use it in Hints and Kinks.—*KU7GJ*]

◊ I noticed with interest the comment about the possibility of key clicks in Rich Arland's review of the MFJ-9340K (*QST*, Sep 2000, p 74). I built the 15-meter version of the kit and did indeed notice some key clicks when monitoring the output on another receiver. Looking at the Cub's output on a 'scope, it was immediately obvious that the keying-envelope rise time was much too fast—about 0.1 ms. After a little experimenting, I came up with a simple modification that fixes the problem. The keying rise and fall times are now about 2 ms, resulting in very nice keying.

The modification consists of adding a 0.22-µF capacitor between the base and collector of Q8 and a 2.2 kΩ resistor between the base and emitter of Q8 (see **Figure 1.11**). The two added components are highlighted in the accompanying figure. Don't be intimidated by the small surface-mount components in the Cub; the modification is actually quite easy to perform. First, solder a 2.2 kΩ resistor between the front of R28 and R29 (immediately to the left of C27). The pads to which you will solder the resistor are the ones that connect to Q8. The resistor should be positioned on top of R28 and R29 with the leads bent to touch the two solder pads. A $1/8$-W resistor works best for this, but a $1/4$-W resistor could also be used. Be careful not to heat the pads too long and keep the solder neat. When you have the 2.2 kΩ resistor in place and the leads trimmed, locate the two feed-through holes between R19 and C27. The hole nearest R19 (just to the left of C28) connects the "+T" line from the top to the bottom of the board. Solder one lead of the 0.22-µF capacitor to this feed-through and the other lead to the front pad of R29 (the same one to which the 2.2 kΩ resistor is attached).

Check your work to make sure the resistor and capacitor are installed correctly and that there are no solder bridges. Now, no more key clicks!—*Larry East, W1HUE, 1355 S Rimline Dr, Idaho Falls, ID 83401;* **w1hue@arrl.net**

MODIFYING THE YAESU FT-1000/ 1000D FOR DIGITAL MODE USB/ LSB OPERATION

◊ For a while now I have wanted to operate USB and LSB for computer-generated RTTY, PSK31, MFSK and such, without using the microphone connector on my FT-1000. As supplied by the fac-

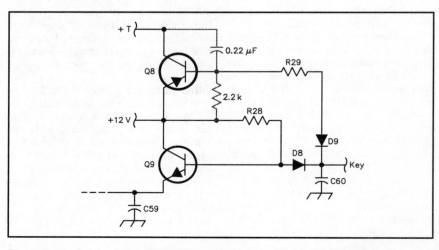

Figure 1.11—A schematic of W1HUE's cure for key clicks in the MFJ Cub transceiver.

tory, it can operate in either USB or LSB in the RTTY mode but only using the internal tone generator. In the PKT mode, back-panel external audio is used, but only LSB and FM can be selected. That leaves the voice modes for what I want, but I would have to swap microphone connectors or use an interface box to switch between voice and digital modes. This is not an elegant solution, and I want to continue to use the back panel interface to my PC and leave the microphone where it is.

I solved this by doing a simple, reversible, modification to the P36 connector to the audio board that does not involve circuit-board removal or modification. Now when in the RTTY mode, audio presented to the PKT back panel connection is used for transmitting in either LSB or USB. In addition, the VOX operates with the external audio, eliminating the need for a separate PTT signal from the PC. This is a real plus if you use a laptop with a single serial port that is dedicated to another function.

To make this modification, turn the FT-1000 over and remove the bottom panel. On the audio board (located at the rear of the rig), find 8-pin connector J3019 and carefully remove the corresponding plug, P36, from the connector. Then *carefully* (read on) remove female pins 6 and 7 of the plug and move pin 6 to the slot pin 7 previously occupied. (Pin 1 of P36/J3019 is closest to the 7-pin connector J3014.) It's best to remove the terminals using the appropriate extractor tool. It can be done with careful use of a

jeweler's screwdriver, but it's more tedious and risky to you, the terminals and the fragile wires!

This modification enables the audio transmission path for the PKT rear-panel input when in the RTTY mode and disables the RTTY audio transmission path, including the built-in RTTY tone generator. Reconnect the plug to the connector and isolate the pin-7 wire and terminal to keep it from touching anything. Alternatively, the pin-7 and pin-6 terminals of plug P36 can be interchanged, but when in the PKT mode, the RTTY tone generator will be enabled during transmit, which may not be desirable. After reassembling the rig, connect your PC to the PKT jack as described in the Yaesu manual (using the PTT connection is optional, since you can now use VOX). Now, to operate using the PC, set the rig for RTTY and either USB or LSB can be selected by repeatedly pressing the RTTY mode button.—*Scott McLellan, W3WT, 40 White Oak Ct, Kempton, PA 19529;* **smclellan@agere.com**

MORE ON THE ASTATIC D-104

◊ The D-104 microphone possesses many attributes not fully understood by most amateurs. Its crystal (or ceramic) element has a smooth frequency-response slope approaching a 3-kHz peak, yet it looks electrically like a 0.0015 mF capacitor. Therefore, the load impedance into which this mike is connected has a great effect on its output level and low-frequency contour.

If an unamplified D-104 feeds a typical transceiver directly, it sees less than 50 kΩ. The result is audio that sounds weak, high pitched and tinny, lacking adequate frequency response. If the load is above 1 MΩ, there are proportionally too many lows for good communications punch.

The ideal impedance is largely a matter of personal preference, plus such factors as voice and transmit characteristics. There is agreement, however, that 100 kΩ to 200 kΩ, or so, produces a modest rising-frequency response, yielding crisp, highly intelligible speech. To *reduce* the high-frequency response, add 200-2000 pF across the microphone.

QST articles (August 1999, p 34, and March 2001, p 59) use circuitry that allows the D-104 to be properly loaded while driving a rig from an appropriately low source impedance.

Many of today's transceivers have sensitive, high-gain microphone amplifiers that start showing signs of overload in the range of 100 to 200 mV (P-P). A close-talked D-104 can put out up to 1 V (P-P) or more into a reasonable impedance! Unfortunately, the referenced buffer-amplifier does not provide easily variable attenuation to prevent potential overdrive of the radio's first transmit-audio stage. (A mic-gain control usually follows the first stage.) Addition of an output potentiometer can provide protection needed by most rigs. (Ten-Tec radios may not need the extra attenuation.)

Figure 1.12 shows K0SF's op amp circuit with added output-attenuation pot. Adjust this pot for the correct range, after set-

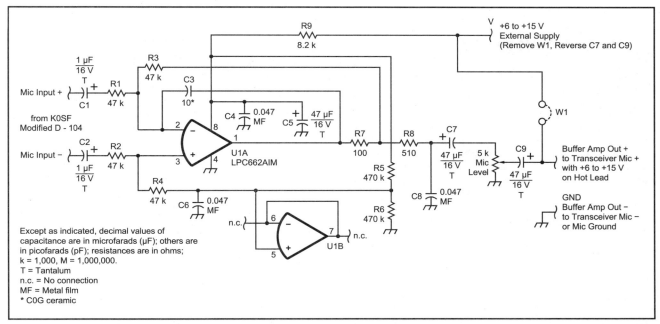

Figure 1.12—Schematic of a mic preamplifier suitable for adapting a D-104 mic to many modern rigs. The pot at the output can be adjusted to prevent the microphone from overdriving the audio-input circuit.

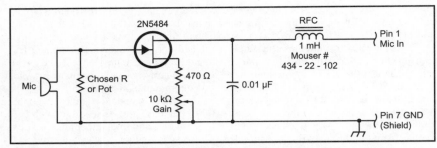

Figure 1.13—A circuit suitable for adapting a D-104 microphone to an ICOM transceiver with dc available on pin 1 (mic in) of the mic connector.

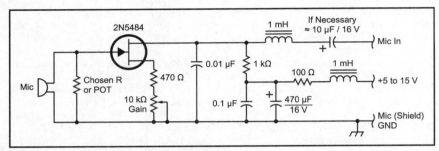

Figure 1.14—A circuit suitable for adapting a D-104 microphone to transceivers with dc available on a pin other than that carrying the audio.

ting your rig's mike gain at least as high as it is when used with the stock microphone.

Some transceivers have appropriate input impedance and gain, so that they can be fed by the D-104 through a simple series resistor of 100 kΩ, or so. Yaesu radios and some others may need the addition of a 10 kΩ shunt resistor across the mike input to avoid overload. Undesired response could result on rigs with very large values of input RF-bypass capacitance.

ICOM radios have input impedances that are too low to derive enough audio from the resistor-coupling method. One possible solution is the schematic in **Figure 1.13** with dc fed from the transceiver on mic pin 1.

This circuit may be adapted for other rigs that provide dc on a separate pin (see **Figure 1.14**). For best results, select a 2N5484 that draws close to 1.5 mA (1.5 V across the 1-kΩ resistor, or about 0.75 V across the 470-Ω resistor). Be sure the pot is well shorted out when making this measurement. In the ICOM version, look for about 0.66 V across the 470-Ω resistor. Power is fed over the audio conductor in the ICOM circuit. In the other hookup, dc can usually be obtained from the mic power pin or from elsewhere in the radio. Make sure the rig's mic-gain control is set high enough.

The element of the D-104-M6 handheld mike has roughly twice the impedance and half the capacitance and output of a D-104. To use it with these circuits, put 220 Ω in series with 10 mF across the 470-Ω resistor if needed for higher output.

Thanks to Rob Sherwood, NCØB, of Sherwood Engineering, Mike Tracy, KC1SX, of the ARRL lab for running rig tests and to the manufacturers for their assistance.—*George Heidelman, K8RRH, 8757 Brittany Dr, Cincinnati, OH 45242-7958*

The Doctor is IN

Q Charles, K2MZ, asks, "I'm considering a narrow band CW filter for my transceiver. The manufacturer offers 250 or 500 kHz filters. Do these frequencies refer to the bandwidth of the filter or the frequency of the CW audio tone heard? If it is bandwidth, why would I not want the narrowest possible? Does it matter whether it is in the 9 MHz or 455 kHz IF?"

A The frequencies indicate the width of the filter; the tone heard is the same as the rig's "offset" (typically 700-800 Hz).

The advantage of the 250 Hz filter is selectivity, but the disadvantage is in the increased tuning sensitivity (it makes tuning touchy). Also, many folks find 250 Hz filters impart a hollow sound to the rig's audio. For trying to pick out a signal from a pileup or working a contest in crowded band conditions, however, the narrower width can be really helpful.

If you are only going to install one filter, put it in the higher IF. If you want to be able to pick your selectivity, install a 500 Hz filter in the high IF and a 250 Hz filter in the lower IF.

Q Jim, WA2DMP, writes: I volunteer at an infirmary for the indigent. Recently a Realistic DX-302 communications receiver was donated to the Volunteer Department. The facility presently has PCs installed so that those who are able may access the Internet. I'm planning to install a dipole on the roof of this building (10 stories) so they may listen to worldwide shortwave and demonstrate the operation of a ham station at some time. What antenna would you recommend for this range of frequencies and what precautions must I take since there are fire and emergency communication antennas on the roof?

A If you are interested only in shortwave/ham listening to start with, I recommend a random, single wire as long as possible—RadioShack even sells such a complete kit (278-758, $9.99).

If you feel that the building wiring and lighting might cause some RFI with a single wire snaking through the walls to get to the roof (possibly the fluorescent lights interfering with the AM broadcast short-wave stations), then run coax—RG-58 will do nicely—and continue with a single wire once you get to the roof. The coax need only be "grounded" at the connection to the receiver.

Place any antenna as far as possible from the other antennas on the roof. There should not be much interference from the VHF/UHF antennas when you are receiving.

Q DJ Leiser, NH7NV, has a common problem. "I recently purchased an ICOM IC-V8 and need help programming this HT. The manual is not clear enough and I would like to get information on programming the scan edge channels."

A You should start by asking for help where you purchased the radio. If that isn't fruitful, read the manual carefully. It's technically true that "everything is in the manual," but it's not always easy to understand. Perhaps you can ask for help from an owner of a similar radio at your local radio club. The manufacturer may also offer software to program your radio with a more user-friendly interface than that of the radio itself. In fact, ICOM offers the CS-V8 software (www.icomamerica.com) for just that purpose, as well as cables that allow more than one radio to be "cloned" from one programmed rig.

Q Neal, AA5QP, asks about amplifiers: I am looking for an amplifier for SSB and CW and want one that will put out 800-1500 W. I see both solid-state and tube amps on the market. Can the advantages and disadvantages of each be succinctly stated? What are the advantages of one over the other?

A The primary advantage of solid-state amplifiers is the convenience of "no-tune" operation— the output network of the amp does not need to be retuned for different bands. Tube-type amps tend to be less expensive, but are bulkier and usually noisier because of the cooling fan. Solid-state amplifiers operate at low-voltages (12-48 V) while tube amplifiers use voltages in the 1000-3000 V range. Some of the fancier tube amplifiers that feature auto-tuning (such as the ACOM 2000A or Alpha/Power 87A) are in the same price range as the solid-state models, but also offer more output (1500 W instead of 1000 W).

Q Carl, W3MAO, asks, "My Kenwood TS-570D transceiver has a 13-pin receptacle for accessories. They provide a 13-pin DIN plug with the radio. This plug has 13 stubs on the wiring side that do not appear to be meant for soldering. Is there some kind

of adapter that I can use with this plug to make an otherwise difficult solder job easier?"

A Through the years, I have encountered DIN plugs like the ones you describe. MFJ sells their 5213 open-end-adapter for $9.95, but if you opt to make your own, *careful* soldering is required.

If the wire is thin enough, and you are not connecting to adjacent pins, you can form a small loop at the tip of the wire, bend it 90° and slide it onto the pin for soldering. More often than not you are forced to "tack" solder the wire on, and when you are done, "pot" the connector with silicon rubber or another sealing compound to insulate the wires and pins from each other.

Q Brad, KE4XJ, has a good question about transverters: I will shortly be purchasing a new HF rig. I thought about using transverters to enjoy my new rig's features on the VHF/UHF/SHF bands, but covering those wide bands seems to be a problem. For example, the 10-meter band covers 1.7 MHz, while the 2-meter band is 4 MHz wide. How do others get around this problem? Do they use multiple LO frequencies in a transverter?

A Most hams only use an HF rig and transverter for SSB and CW VHF/microwave work—when it is only necessary to cover a small portion of each band. For instance, tuning from 144.000 to 144.300 MHz is plenty, even in populated areas. In some parts of the country, nearly all the activity occurs around 144.200, despite efforts to get people to spread out. Most hams just use a separate rig for FM. This avoids the need to automatically switch antennas when switching modes—by convention, SSB/CW weak-signal work is usually horizontally polarized while FM is vertical.

Q Walt Martin, KB5HOV, of Dallas, Texas writes: Older communications receivers (tube type) had front panel antenna trimmers. What function did these trimmers serve and why don't we have them on current model (solid state) receivers? Yes, I know we manipulated them while listening for a peak in white noise, but was the trimmer matching impedance between the feed line and the receiver input or was it a frequency matching function?

A Those little trimmers were intended to function as very crude antenna tuners. They essentially tuned the antenna system to be resonant, forming a series resonant circuit with the antenna. This created a low impedance point at

the receiver input, ensuring the best transfer of received-signal power from the antenna to the receiver, whose input impedance was typically low.

The trimmers are no longer useful, as tuning them for maximum noise would degrade sensitivity. Modern receivers often have impedances that are significantly mismatched from 50 ohms. Power matching with a tuner typically results in degraded signal to noise ratio, despite the higher noise level coming out of the receiver. Chapter 6 of *Introduction to RF Design* by Wes Hayward explains how increased sensitivity can be obtained by mismatching the receiver to 50 ohms. Most hams prefer increased sensitivity to low receiver input SWR. Tuning a matching network for best signal to noise ratio on SSB or CW signals is difficult.

Q Sam, KC8IHE, asks, "My transmitter requires a high impedance microphone. I have a large collection of microphones, but I have no way of knowing if they are high or low impedance. Is there an easy way to determine this?"

A A "quick and dirty" way of determining if a particular microphone is high or low impedance is to connect it to something that requires a low impedance. If the resulting audio is very low, this suggests an impedance mismatch and will indicate that the mike is of a much higher impedance than the device you are driving. Note that most newer ham rigs—excepting Kenwoods—are low impedance input whereas simple audio devices, like inexpensive tape recorders, are often high impedance input.

Q I left my H-T exposed to sunlight for several hours. When I finally retrieved it, I was horrified to see that the LCD (liquid-crystal display) was completely black. However, after it cooled for a few minutes, the display returned to normal. What happened to the display, and how did it recover?

A Liquid crystals used in most LCDs are long, straight molecules that tend to line up with each other, and anything else that's nearby. If you sandwich a film of liquid crystals between glass plates that are ridged like a miniature corrugated roof, the molecules will line up with the ridges. If you rotate one plate by 90° the molecules near that plate will orient themselves at right angles to the molecules near the other plate. Between these plates, the rest of the crystal lattice forms a smooth one-quarter twist. This twist rotates the polarization of light by 90° as it passes through the liquid crystal.

The liquid crystals used in displays are electrically unbalanced: one end of the molecule is slightly negatively charged, the other end slightly positively charged. So applying a small voltage across the glass plates causes all the molecules to "stand on end," and the liquid crystal loses its ability to twist the polarization of light. Switch off the voltage, and the lattice returns to its previous state.

To create a display, the glass plates are replaced with polarizing filters, also out of alignment by 90°, and a reflecting surface is put behind them. Incoming light is polarized by the first filter, twisted 90° by the liquid crystals, passes through the second filter, is reflected and reverses its journey.

Apply a voltage, however, and the incoming light passes unchanged through the liquid crystal and so can't pass through the second polarizing filter. Consequently, the display goes black. By using segmented electrodes, letters, numerals and other shapes can be displayed.

The liquid crystal state is a phase between solid and liquid—cool it and it solidifies; heat it and it melts. Melted liquid crystals lose their ability to change the polarization of light, becoming ordinary liquids. That's when you see the display going completely black or blue. When cooled, it returns to the liquid crystal phase and reflects light again.

Don't make it a habit to leave your rig in the sunlight for prolonged periods of time. Repeated abuse can, over time, permanently alter the chemical properties of the display and render it inoperable.

Q Steven M. Kent, WB6QQR, of Long Beach, California writes: What is a CW filter? Will it help my TS-520S with the transmission or reception of CW signals?

A When someone says "CW filter," they are usually referring to a filter in one of the receiver's IF stages, although there is such a thing as an external audio-frequency CW filter. In any case, in the IF stages of a receiver, a filter serves to limit the bandwidth of a received signal. Most radios have some built-in filtering, but adding an additional optional filter often improves performance greatly. IF filters can be the crystal type (made up of a series of quartz crystals), mechanical (a series of precision cut metal disks), or ceramic. The type using quartz crystals is the most common in optional filters; hence the often-used name "crystal filter."

Quartz is a material that is piezoelectric—a mechanical input causes an electrical discharge, and vice-versa—an electrical input causes a mechanical movement. Like a tuning fork, a crystal can be manufactured to mechanically

vibrate naturally over a narrow range of frequencies. An electrical input to a crystal so made will tend to either be dampened or not, according to how well the frequency of that electrical input matches the mechanical resonance. Thus, the filter effect—if a crystal is resonant at 9 MHz, an applied electrical signal of 7 MHz will be attenuated at the other side of the crystal, whereas a 9 MHz signal will pass through with very little attenuation.

Crystal filters are available in many different bandwidths. The bandwidth is the range of frequencies over which the energy is minimally attenuated. If the bandwidth of a filter is 2 kHz (± 1 kHz) and its center frequency is 9 MHz, that means it will minimally attenuate frequencies from 8.999 MHz to 9.001 MHz (9 MHz ± 1 kHz). On the output of the receiver, that translates to the range of audio frequencies that you would hear—in the case of a 2 kHz filter, the audio output might be 500-2500 Hz.

A CW signal takes up a relatively small amount of spectrum—typically only a couple hundred Hz at the most. So if you have a receiver with a 2 kHz filter, you may find that you will sometimes hear several CW signals at the same time, making it somewhat difficult to follow a particular signal. Of course, the human brain acts as quite a good filter in itself, but that is a skill that requires time and practice to develop to a high degree.

So, a "CW filter" then, is one optimized for receiving narrow bandwidth CW signals, as opposed to 2 kHz wide SSB signals. Most hams use a 400 or 500 Hz bandwidth filter. Narrower filters may be useful for contesting on bands where signals are closely packed together, but tuning in signals gets more difficult, particularly when using vinatge radios.

Q Michael D. Downey, K7MXB, of Bothell, Washington writes: Can the Yaesu FT-7100M be used for satellite communication? I plan to purchase equipment in the near future and the Yaesu unit appears to be an excellent buy at this time. I have only used HF to this point.

A The FT-7100 only offers FM, so that rules out the satellites that require SSB and PSK. However, that leaves three satellites that operate on FM voice and a couple that operate 9600-baud packet.

In general, to operate via satellites, your radio needs to be able to switch between one band on transmit and receive on another. Fortunately, most dual-band transceivers offer this feature. Another feature that is helpful for satellite operation is to be able to listen on one band while transmitting on the other so that you

can monitor your own signal as it is being sent back from the satellite. The FT-7100 offers this feature, so it should be a good choice for the FM-only satellites.

For current information on the status of the various amateur satellites, see **www.amsat.org/amsat/news/wsr.html**.

Q Don, W9DEW, asks, "I have owned an ICOM IC-720A and a Kenwood TS-450S for several years and have never really understood when to use the attenuator as opposed to simply turning the RF Gain control down. I think I understand the difference, but the result seems to be the same. Is there any real difference?"

A In a practical sense, there is no difference. However, at high levels of attenuation the RF gain control may be hard to set, so the fixed attenuator is easier to use. Under some circumstances you might even need both. When band noise and signals are both over S 9 with the RF gain up all the way, the attenuator will bring them down to where the RF gain can be used for "fine tuning" the level.

Q Ron Kosinski, N9KSG, of Cecil, Wisconsin, writes: I'm planning to use an ICOM IC-2800 dualbander as a base unit. I had decided to use a Diamond X200A antenna until I saw something unusual in last summer's AES catalog—an antenna by Comet called a dualband base *repeater* antenna. Do I need to use such a beast to do full duplex crossband repeat with this ICOM, or is the Diamond antenna sufficient?

A The only thing that would make an antenna a "repeater" type is that it would be designed for physical and mechanical ruggedness so as to provide a longer service without requiring any maintenance (or at least very little). From an electrical standpoint, there is no difference between that and a "regular" antenna.

Keep in mind that any crossband repeat operation has to meet certain legal requirements, and chief among these is the issue of control. Some means of controlling the transmitter in the event of a failure must be included. According to the rules, this type of control must be handled by "wire" (think telephone line) or by a separate radio "control link" on 222.15 MHz or above. The link must also be identified per the FCC rules, too.

Q Lionel, F5APZ, asks, "When I attempt to use my old Gonset linear amplifier with my ICOM IC-751 transceiver, there is a 3:1 SWR between the radio and the amp. Of course, this causes the 751 to fold back to only 50% output. What could be causing this?"

A My guess would be a problem with the amplifier-input circuit. A lot of older amps used tuned inputs that were switched as you changed bands. Over time, the values of the coils or capacitors can change, resulting in the input impedance changing. If you have the manual for the amp, take a look at the schematic. If the input circuit has adjustable coils or capacitors, you can try tweaking them for a better match. You could also use an antenna tuner between the rig and the amp, although you may still experience some power loss in the input circuit after the tuner. (Remember: An antenna tuner does not change the SWR at its output. See **Figure 1.15**.)

Although Gonset is long out of business, you might still be able to obtain a copy of the manual if you need one. To find a source for old equipment manuals, access the Web and go to the ARRL Technical Information Service page at: **www.arrl.org/tis/** and click on the TISfind link.

Q Allan F. Falcoff, K3YZ, of Chadds Ford, Pennsylvania, writes: Last week I bought a new IC-756PRO and was amazed to note that the rig will allow you to transmit quite a bit outside of US band limits even though the unit was purchased from a US dealer. Investigating further, I downloaded an expanded tech evaluation ARRL performed several years ago. You documented the very broad transmitting range that my rig also has:

Freq (band)	Frequency Limit (MHz)	
	Low	High
160	1.800.000	1.999.999
80	3.400.000	4.099.999
40	6.900.000	7.499.999
30	9.900.000	10.499.999
20	13.900.000	14.499.999
17	17.900.000	18.499.999
15	20.900.000	21.449.999
12	24.400.000	25.099.999
10	28.000.000	29.999.999
6	50.000.000	54.000.000

The rig has provision for a band edge beep that goes off at the edges of the above limits. There doesn't seem

any way to modify the beep to US edges. Unfortunately, ICOM does not provide documentation to modify band limits either by software or hardware modification to ensure legal transmission. I was under the impression that a rig had to be limited to transmit within US band limits if sold commercially within the US. Am I wrong?

A HF amateur transceivers do not go through the certification process, as it is not required for the Amateur Service (with the exception of amplifiers and the receiver portion of VHF/UHF transceivers). That is why individuals are free to build and sell as many HF transceivers as they might wish.

There are no particular rules governing the transmit range of amateur equipment, but all of the commercial manufacturers restrict the output to ranges only slightly larger than the amateur bands because of the possibility of misuse in other services where certification is required. One of the reasons ham rigs often transmit somewhat outside the ham bands is to accommodate MARS operation. It also tends to simplify the design of the transceiver, helping keep the cost reasonable.

Note that it is perfectly legal to own a transmitter capable of operation on frequencies outside of the bands, but is not actually legal to use them there (unless you are a MARS operator participating in that operation).

As far as I can determine, the "beep" in ICOM transceivers is intended to indicate the limit of transmit range, rather than the amateur band limits. This has been the case for about a decade.

Even if you are using equipment that does have transmit range limits set to the edges of the amateur bands (in 7 years of testing, I have seen perhaps a half-dozen such rigs), however, you still have to be alert to your operating frequency. Consider a radio set to 7.300 MHz (carrier frequency), operating in LSB. Although theory states that all of the transmit energy would be within the band, practical circuit design precludes this, so it is wise to stay a kHz or 2 below the band edge. If you are using CW, you could probably get much closer. For this reason, it isn't really practical to depend on the radio to

keep the operation legal. To operate legally, of course, you'll need to stay within the limits of your class of amateur license.

Q Jim, KI7AY, asks, "I have an ICOM IC-706 MkII and I would like to know what I need to interface an Electrovoice Model 664 dynamic cardioid microphone to it."

A With modern rigs, especially mobile rigs, the audio response is often limited by the mike amplifier and modulation circuitry, so there is a limit to what you can do with an external microphone to improve the situation over a stock mike.

If your desire to use the 664 stems from its appearance and feel to the hand, you honestly may well be better off replacing its older internals with a modern electret element.

However, if you really want to use the mike as-is with a modern rig, there are two things you'll need to determine: the mike's impedance and its voltage output. If the impedance is in the neighborhood of 100 kΩ, then you can probably adapt the circuit for the Astatic D-104 that was shown in August 1999 *QST*. As to the voltage, most modern rigs are looking for a maximum of 200-300 mV peak to peak. If the 664 puts out more than that, you'll need to attenuate it to a level in this range to prevent overloading the mike-input circuitry.

Q Bill, N3SNU, asks, "The display malfunction on my ADI-146 is definitely temperature-dependent. During summer, and to a lesser extent during spring and fall, all the segments of the LCD display activate so it is impossible to tell what frequency the radio is on, or any other displayed parameters. The radio apparently still works fine. Transmitting, especially on high power, causes heat to build up faster and the display to go haywire sooner, but in hot weather just having the radio on receive during a long drive will eventually bring on the problem. This is a mobile radio, installed in the family car, and taking it out whenever the car is parked is not a practical solution. If I had to resort to that I might as well go back to carrying a handheld

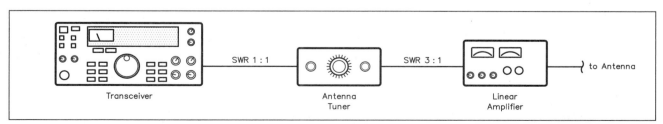

Figure 1.15—An antenna tuner installed between a transceiver and amplifier will provide a 1:1 SWR for the transceiver to prevent power foldback. However, the tuner does nothing for the SWR between the tuner and the amplifier.

and plugging it into an external antenna. Any troubleshooting suggestions?"

AThis problem crops up in many LCDs in conditions of extreme heat. Typical problem conditions include the obvious (when the car has been sitting in the sun on a 90° day with the windows closed) and the not so obvious (on a moderately warm day with the radio mounted on top of the dash in direct sunlight, or mounted in the dash without ventilation space around it). The ideal mounting position is under the dash where the rig would get some shade, but adding a small 12V fan helps in installations that are less than ideal.

If the display is failing under more normal conditions, then the LCD itself or the display driver circuit is very likely defective. If the radio was purchased recently, I would suggest asking the dealer for an exchange. If the dealer can no longer exchange it, then having ADI repair it may be your only option. This is not a problem that can be easily tackled on the typical workbench.

QGary, KD4SRX, asks, "I read the product reviews in *QST*, talk with other hams and radio dealers, and I'm still very much confused about handhelds (H-Ts). I'm not sure what model would suit my needs. To be more specific, I like working various ham events, as well as taking my handheld on Amtrak train trips along the Northeast Corridor. With all these various models to choose from, which features are the most important?"

AI'd suggest that you look for an H-T with a large battery pack (you may have to purchase this separately). Choose a pack that has enough capacity to last through a daylong hamfest or public-service event. I would suggest looking for one that has at least 600-m/Ah capacity.

Also, although 5W output is not a must, having at least 2^1/$_2$ to 3 W helps when trying to work someone (via simplex) who is on the other side of the hamfest grounds (for an outdoor hamfest). Higher output power will also be helpful when attempting to work stations from a moving train. Most modern handhelds will receive the 160-161 MHz Amtrak frequencies in the Northeast Corridor, but check the specs to be sure.

Concerning battery life, consult the *QST* Product Reviews and refer to the power requirements section. This will tell you the maximum receive and transmit current drawn for each handheld under consideration.

Ease of programming is another thing to consider, but there is a mitigating factor. If your H-T has a lot of features that you won't use, it doesn't matter if you can't remember (or figure out) how to program them. I prefer H-Ts with the most frequently used functions marked on the buttons (like switching between memory and VFO mode, setting PL tones, etc.). Failing that, you can make up a small (2-inch square) "cheat sheet" with the most important functions written on it.

Unless you plan on carrying the manual with you everywhere, direct keypad frequency entry is practically a must. Also convenient is automatic repeater offset, although that is more of a luxury than a necessity (if "-" doesn't bring up the repeater, just switch to "+" —assuming you don't need to consult the manual to remember how).

Don't forget audio quality. You want to be able to understand what is being said, even when you are in a noisy area.

QBob Evinger, WD9EKA/AAR5MG (Army MARS operator), of Marhsall, Illinois, writes: I have an Alinco DJ-V5. While changing the battery packs, I noticed a sticker that I had not seen before. It puzzles me and seems to contradict what I thought were the rules concerning type acceptance. Inside on the back plate is the standard Part 15 device warning that claims this radio is covered under Part 15 and must not cause harmful interference. What gives? I have never seen this on any of my other commercial ham gear.

AThe FCC's regulations require that most intentional radiators —translation: transmitters—be *Certificated* before they can be marketed in the US. This provision does not apply to Amateur Radio transmitters, except for linear power amplifiers that operate on 6 meters and below. However, other portions of the rules require that some receivers also be Certificated or authorized under a Declaration of Conformity, another FCC authorization procedure. The various FCC authorizations, mostly found in Part 15, are a very interesting set of regulations, with many subtleties and nuances.

Many of the devices must have some sort of label, which is what you read on your Alinco. The provision that the device not cause harmful interference applies only to the operation of the receiver. The transmitter is governed by Part 97, which stipulates absolute maximum spurious emissions levels and a requirement that spurious emissions that are below those levels not cause interference to authorized radio services.

For information about the Part 15 rules, see **www.arrl.org/tis/info/part15.html**.

CHAPTER 2

Batteries and Other Power Sources

SOLAR-POWER TIPS

◊ I've been running things from solar power for years—my shack, Field Day site, RV, campsites and so on. Many of these are mobile systems, from pocketsize QRP solar panels with 1.2 Ah batteries to a typical Field Day system with a couple hundred watts of solar panels and 400 Ah of batteries. In my shack and my RV, controllers (Trace C40s) are used for "set it and forget it" ease, but at portable sites I keep it really simple and use nothing but a voltmeter.

Battery Charging

When you attach a solar module to a battery and check the system voltage, the voltage usually approximates that of the battery. Most good solar modules are rated 17.5 V (or more) and have open-circuit voltages of around 22 V. When they're connected to a reasonably sized battery (say 2 Ah, or more, of battery per watt of solar panel) it takes a long time for the battery voltage to reach harmful levels. Check the specifications on the battery and radio, but up to 15 V is usually fine and sometimes necessary. If you are using the system to concurrently power your equipment, you'll probably never see a voltage that high. If you do, just disconnect the solar module for a while.

If the modules come with a diode, you can leave that in place and not worry about discharging at night. If there's no diode, just disconnect the modules when there's no sun on them. Remember, however, that they do work (but at reduced current) even on cloudy days.

Storage Batteries

Car batteries are not good storage devices for solar systems. They are designed to deliver large amounts of current for short periods and then recharge immediately. A good solar storage battery (deep-cycle battery) is designed to deliver a relatively small amount of current for a long period and be discharged somewhat before being recharged. Neither battery will last long in the wrong environment.

If you want to put together a 14 V system, a reasonable battery pair would be the Trojan T-500 (8 V, 190 A) and T-890 (6 V, 165 A). Keep the ampere-hour ratings of the batteries equal if possible, so you don't cook the smaller battery while the larger one is still charging. Keep an eye on the electrolyte levels in these mismatched systems, and select your solar modules for high voltage ratings so they are likely to charge the 14-V battery under most (cloudy) conditions.

Solar Modules

Solar-module output voltage varies with temperature, as do battery characteristics. A typical temperature coefficient would be around −0.38% per °C from a 25°C nominal cell temperature: On a very hot day, your 18-V module could struggle to charge a 12-V battery.[1] Remember you need about 15 V for a good charge, more to equalize, and there are diode and cabling losses to consider (which are significant in a 12-V system). What about using 16-V modules on a 14-V system? Forget about it. That voltage won't even do a good job on a 12-V system under all conditions.

Good solar modules are generally made up of 36 cells in a 12-cell series/parallel combination; they put out between 17.5 and 19 V. There are also 30-cell modules that put out between 15 and 16 V. These were designed for use without a controller. If an appropriately sized battery is used with these 16-V systems, it usually won't overcharge. No guarantees; on a cold, bright day the module voltage output can be high and

---

[1] I would not be surprised to find a module temperature (not ambient air) of 65°C on the right (wrong?) day. Consider a 16-V module (some of which only put out 15.5 V or less). At 65°C it will have an output voltage of 13.57 V (even at 45°C, it still only has 14.78 V). That's if the module output was actually 16 V in the first place. Now, throw in losses for the diode and cables (most people use cables that are way too small) and you can't even charge your HT.

---

the battery capacity low. That combination makes an overcharge likely. On the other hand, the module voltage on a hot day will probably be insufficient to charge the battery well.

Some amorphous thin-film modules don't appear to have "cells" at all. Just look at the "operating" or "rated" voltages to see how much electrical pressure you have available. If you measure module voltage, do so under load. Open-circuit voltages don't tell you much and are almost always over 20 V.—*JC Smith, K0HPS, 1249 Dewing Ln, Walnut Creek, CA 94595;* **k0hps@amsat.org**

MORE ON SOLAR-POWER TIPS

◊ I read the hint entitled "Solar-Power Tips" in *QST* (March 2000, p 61) and noticed that the author talks about a 14-V battery pack. He created this pack by combining a three-cell (6 V) and a four-cell (8 V) battery. This pack will indeed produce about 14.3 V under discharge conditions, but there weren't any cautions about using this battery during charging! An approximate "float" voltage for this battery would be 16.1 V (at 2.3 V per cell) and a "max charge" or equalize voltage would be 16.8 V (2.4 V per cell). The equivalent voltages on a 12-V battery would be 13.8 V and 14.4 V, respectively.

I realize that much modern 12-V equipment can operate at 16+ V, but this does exceed their ratings in most cases. Almost every radio I've seen is rated at 12-15 V dc. I think that a cautionary note is appropriate when talking about such a battery.—*Hartley Gardner, W1OQ, 3602 N 31st St, Phoenix, AZ 85016-7009;* **w1oq@arrl.net**

JC addresses the output voltages of solar modules and conditions where the charge for 12-V batteries may exceed 15 V under "Battery Charging." He recommends that we "Check the specifications on the battery and radio, but up to 15 V is usually fine and sometimes necessary."

I've operated a modern 100-W transceiver from a vehicle battery on Field Day and found that output was down about 30%

unless the alternator was charging. Therefore, I think the 14-V battery suggestion is a good one. Nonetheless, I can see that there may be problems when the load current is not much greater than the charge current (as when receiving). Thanks for the cautionary note, Hartley.—*Bob Schetgen, KU7G, Hints and Kinks Editor*

SAVE NiCdS FROM OVERCHARGING

◊ As we all know, nickel cadmium (NiCd) battery packs for H-Ts and other equipment can be very expensive to replace. They're also rather difficult to repair by replacing bad cells, because they are usually glued into nonserviceable plastic cases. I have successfully performed surgery on many such cases, but it is tedious and time consuming.

One way that cells in a pack can go bad is by overcharging. One mechanism appears to be the breaching of the cell vent, which allows the electrolyte in the cell to dry up. I understand that this can result from oxygen gas generated at the anode, or may be due to electrolyte expansion from heat build up. Whatever the mechanism, it has been my experience that cells can go bad this way, or their life can be shortened.

The standard charge rate for NiCds is 10% of their rating (often expressed as 0.1 C) for fifteen hours. Many specially designed cells can be charged at much faster rates because they have special oxygen-absorbing anodes and perhaps other design improvements, but the tradeoff can be a somewhat shorter life span. In any event, overcharging fast-charge NiCds can be even more disastrous to cell life. Some better packs include technology to reduce the charge rate if overcharging is approached, but why depend on failsafe mechanisms that may not be perfectly failsafe when you can easily resolve the problem?

I have a problem remembering when the pack should be removed from the charger after 15 hours, or whatever amount of time the manufacturer of the charger/battery pack recommends. I have put a charger on a 24-hour timer, but sometimes forget to remove it—even after a day or two. The resulting double or triple overcharge can cause cells to go bad. I have also thought of designing a suitable one-shot circuit, but why go to all that trouble when you can purchase a solution inexpensively at your local department store!

The Intermatic #TN711 24-hour timer is ideal for charging NiCds! It can be purchased for less than $10 at many stores.This and many similar timers use removable pins to set the start and stop times on the timer. The procedure for failsafe recharging is very easy: Insert the green (start) and red (stop) pins into the dial face to set the correct charge-time duration. (Insert the pins fully or they may not activate the ac switch. If a stop pin is not fully inserted, the timer will not switch off!) Then plug the charger into the timer and the timer into an ac outlet. Turn the timer face until the start pin just clicks the switch on; this enables 120 V ac to the charger. Now immediately *remove* the green start pin entirely, but leave the red stop pin in the timer. You now have a one shot timer that will run the required time to charge your batteries and shut off at the required time. It will *never* switch on again, no matter how long you forget about it! It is impossible to overcharge your expensive NiCd battery pack by this method!

I set the green (start) pin at 12 AM and the red (stop) pin at 3 PM, for a 15-hour charge. I turn the timer dial until the green pin just trips the switch, then remove the green pin. Fifteen hours later, my NiCds are perfectly charged, even if I go away on vacation for a week and forget to remove them from the charger. This means I have no more overcharged cells. Now battery-pack surgery is only needed when a cell fails from old age!

Remember! Don't leave those little green and red pins lying around if you have small children in the house, as the pins could be easily swallowed. Place your timer out of reach of small children (they could also turn the dial and switch it off prematurely).

I hope this technique helps you avoid the frustration of NiCd overcharge and get the maximum use out of your rechargeable batteries. Except for long-term storage, *always* keep your NiCds charged! Charge them as soon as they are fully discharged. Never leave uncharged NiCds lying around, and don't overcharge them. That way you should get the maximum life from your batteries. Best of luck.—*Owen O'Neill, N2IWN, PO Box 222, Clarksburg, NJ 08510;* **wilycoyote@juno.com**

POWER ATTACHMENT TO GM SIDE-TERMINAL BATTERIES

◊ At Dayton, I've seen GM representatives distributing brochures on how to attach radios to the automotive batteries with the GM side-terminal design. Connections to these batteries are not quite as easy as they were to standard top-terminal batteries, where one may attach directly to the bolts on the terminal clamps. GM offers an attachment terminal for adding radio equipment, but I found it cost over $70 for the necessary hardware. There had to be a less expensive way that would still provide a good connection, and I found it.

Realizing that custom audio installations in vehicles must require lots of current to get that bass to thump so annoyingly, I stopped at a car-stereo installation shop. After a few minutes of discussion with the installer, I had two threaded brass terminal bolts to replace the stock bolts. The difference is that these have an additional threaded stud on the top, where radios can be connected easily. The total cost is under $10, and the resulting connections have proven durable. Be sure to know how many connections are currently on each of your car's battery terminals as that determines the length of each bolt. Happy mobiling! *Duane A. Calvin, AC5AA, 4102 Everest Ln, Austin, TX 78727;* **ac5aa@earthlink.net**

ADDING A TRICKLE-CHARGE MODE TO KENWOOD'S WALL-TRANSFORMER CHARGER

◊ Kenwood TH-215 and TH-26 H-Ts come with wall-transformer 45-mA battery chargers that recharge the 500-mAh battery pack in about 14 hours. The manufacturer cautions against prolonged overcharging at this rate.

Sometimes, however, an H-T must be kept on trickle charge to guarantee that the batteries are always fully charged for use in an emergency. In addition, you sometimes don't know the state of your batteries' charge and would like to "top them up" without endangering them.

A safe trickle-charge rate for a NiCd battery is about $C/30$ mA, where C is the capacity in milliampere hours. At this rate, a full charge would take days, but the charger can be left connected indefinitely without overheating the batteries. The batteries should still be cycled occasionally—that is, discharged and then recharged at the normal 14-hour rate—to prevent loss of capacity.

Adding a trickle-charge mode to Kenwood's "wall wart" is remarkably simple—put a 330-Ω resistor (R1) in series with the charger. (That's a $1/4$-W resistor—*Ed*) If you add a switch too, you can bypass the resistor for normal 14-hour charging (see **Figure 2.1**). I built the switch and resistor into a 35-mm film can. The LED on the Kenwood charger glows when charging at the normal rate but not at the reduced rate.

Other chargers can be modified similarly; you can find the appropriate resistance by experiment or as shown in the "The Math is Easy!" sidebar. For example, I've modified the charger for my Skil Twist power screwdriver so that it delivers a 20-mA trickle. Because the screwdriver is only used occasionally for brief periods, keeping it constantly "topped up" is much more important than obtaining maximum battery performance.—*Michael A. Covington, N4TMI, 285 St George Dr, Athens, GA 30606*

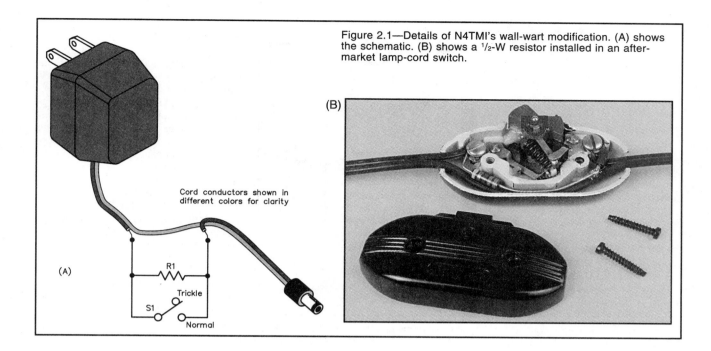

Figure 2.1—Details of N4TMI's wall-wart modification. (A) shows the schematic. (B) shows a ¹/₂-W resistor installed in an after-market lamp-cord switch.

Cord conductors shown in different colors for clarity

(A)

R1

Trickle

S1

Normal

(B)

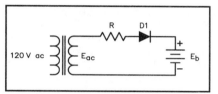

Figure 2.2—A schematic of a simple wall-wart NiCd charger.

MORE ON "THE MATH IS EASY" AND WALL WARTS

◊ This message is a comment about "The Math is Easy!" sidebar in the March column (p 58). While I cannot fault the arithmetic, I believe the assumption concerning how these chargers work is off base. It seems to me that battery resistance is independent of the charger rating.

Most of the chargers that come with the radios are simple: a transformer and full-wave rectifier. There may be a regulator in the radio, but here I address only the simple type.

A charged NiCd battery will reach about 1.4 V/cell and will exhibit a low resistance. Current will flow into the battery when the voltage at the transformer exceeds the battery voltage plus two diode junction-voltage drops. The current flow is determined primarily by the transformer impedance, which is usually high enough to prevent a fire in case the wall wart output is shorted. From this explanation, the charge current flows in pulses. The calculation might result in the correct resistor value, but that would

seem to be accidental.

Further, the power-dissipation calculation will always be low unless the current is pure dc. Ripple, or a pulsed charging current, will result in greater dissipation. For example, consider a rectangular wave with 50% duty cycle. The actual power dissipation is twice that calculated by considering the average value.

For many years, I have trickle-charged auto batteries while the vehicles are stored. I use wall warts and series resistors determined by trial and error. It works!—*Gene Pentecost, W4IMT, 42 Maximo Way, Palm Desert, CA 92260-0361;* **gene.pentecost@ieee.org**

◊ I stand corrected. The General Electric *Nickel-Cadmium Battery Application Engineering Handbook* (second edition, General Electric, 1975) explains the situation. For a half-wave supply, as shown in **Figure 2.2**, the charge current and I_{RMS} depend on the battery voltage (E_b) diode junction drop (E_d) and the transformer output voltage (E_{ac}). E_{ac} increases as the charge current lessens, requiring much more resistance than pre-

dicted in "The Math is Easy." The General Electric book addresses this by means of two coefficients determined by a nomograph based on $(E_b+E_d)/E_{ac}$.

Easy math doesn't work in this case because this is not a simple resistive dc-supply feeding a load. The transformer output voltage is influenced by the charge current. The result of my calculation is only coincidentally close to the value the author found by experimentation.—*Bob Schetgen, KU7G, Hints and Kinks Editor*

TS-570 BATTERY FEEDBACK

◊ My article, "TS-570 Battery Replacement," appears in the November 1999, issue of *QST*. When writing the piece I had forgotten to include the following. Before removing the old battery, 13.8 V dc must be applied to the power connector on the rear panel. To protect the equipment, the radio should not be turned on during this procedure.—*Harold Kane, W2AHW, 326 NE 45th St, Pompano Beach, FL 33064;* **HAROLDKANE@ worldnet.att.net**

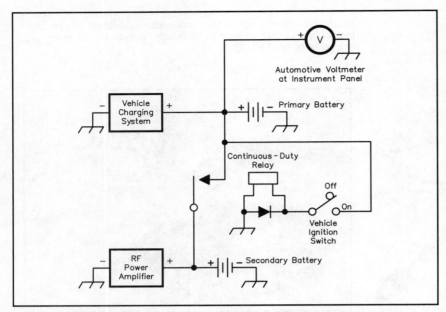

Figure 2.3—WK5S uses a continuous-duty relay to connect a second vehicle battery and a high-power amplifier to the vehicle primary battery and charging system only when the ignition is on.

A TWO-BATTERY SOLUTION FOR MOBILES

◊ Many of us use an RF high-power amplifier while operating mobile. In my case, I run an MFJ ALS-500 in my 1996 Chevy Suburban truck. Until recently, I operated with two batteries separated by a 160-A battery isolator. Over two years, I had the alternator and the battery isolator fail twice. Let me tell you, this gets expensive!

I believe I have found the perfect solution! My friend Steve, at Texas Alternators of Austin, Texas (tel 512-836-6601) introduced me to an automotive continuous-duty relay. It looks very much like a starter solenoid, but it is designed for continuous duty—that is, *on* for *long* periods.

This relay is energized only when the engine is running. It then connects a second battery in parallel with the main engine battery. (See **Figure 2.3** for a schematic.) The beauty here is that when the engine is off, the secondary battery is disconnected from the main battery; the batteries cannot discharge one another. When the engine is running, the alternator is in control and keeps current flowing to both batteries. The magnitude of the charge current depends on the charge level of each battery, current demands of the vehicle system and the alternator output limit. The point is that current flow is *into* the batteries, not *out* of them, unless there is a super-high demand by the system being supplied (the RF amplifier on speech peaks).

I have used this system for a while now and it seems to work perfectly. It is

a lot less expensive than an isolator and far more reliable. The continuous-duty relay that I use is built by Accurate Parts Co of Kokomo, Indiana.[2] I understand from Steve that this system is being offered in the latest two-battery vehicles. This system does require that the engine run for both batteries to be connected while you are using your RF power amplifier—which is always the case for me. Hope this helps other QRO mobile operators!—*Steve L. Sparks, WK5S, 2701 High Country Blvd, Round Rock, TX 78664-6204*

A BATTERY-SAVING TIMER CIRCUIT

◊ My shack is cluttered with homebrew projects and helpful little gadgets that operate from 9-V batteries. Most consume only a few milliamperes and operate for only a few minutes at a time. Theoretically, an alkaline battery in that kind of application should last for years—unfortunately this theory does not consider forgetfulness. If I don't remember to turn off the power switch, the battery is stone dead within a day or two. It happens with every piece of battery-

[2]I was unable to locate contact information for Accurate Parts, but I found a Web site for Electro Automotive **www.electroauto.com**. Electro caters to persons building electric-powered vehicles and sells a 12-V contactor (electrician talk for a power relay).

powered gear I have, eventually. Besides the cost factor, I don't like the idea of picking up a piece of equipment, finding that the battery is dead, looking around the house in vain for a fresh one and finally robbing one from another gadget.

The simple circuit in **Figure 2.4** takes care of my memory problem by providing a few minutes of operation and then automatically putting the circuit to sleep. With the component values shown, pushing S1 gives two or three minutes of operation, which is often as long as the circuit is needed. If a good-quality tantalum capacitor is used for C1, the time can be extended considerably; for example, increasing C1 to 100 mF provides an operating time of approximately 20 minutes. Capacitor leakage eventually becomes a problem, so I would not use a simple circuit like this if longer operation is required. Nevertheless, as long as you push S1 before the timeout has expired, operation can be extended until your finger gets tired or the battery goes dead, whichever happens first.

One CMOS integrated circuit, a garden-variety PNP transistor and a few other components make up the entire circuit. Operation of the circuit is very simple. When the normally open pushbutton switch S1 is pressed, it discharges C1, bringing the input of gate U1A near 0 V and causing its output to go high. U1B is also an inverting stage, so its output goes low, pulling down the voltage on R2 and turning on Q1. After S1 is released, C1 charges slowly until the gate threshold voltage on U1A is reached, at which point the output of U1A goes low and the output of U1B goes high, turning off the PNP transistor.

R3 and D1 are not essential to circuit operation, and their purpose may be a little obscure. The CD4093 is a Schmitt trigger with hysteresis. This means that even if the gate voltage is changed very slowly, the output will change state abruptly as soon as a threshold voltage is reached; it does not hover in indecision between "high" and "low" states. However, the CD4093 continues to draw current even after the output has changed. On the chip I used, the "excess" current isn't very high, starting at about 100 mA and decreasing gradually to essentially zero. This probably would not have any noticeable effect on battery life, but it bugged me, so I added R3 and D1 to reduce the transition time by forcing C1 to charge rapidly once the threshold is reached.

In applications requiring only a few milliamperes, there will be very little voltage drop across Q1 when it is turned on. For higher current applications, the value of R2 should be decreased proportionally. For example, if the circuit being

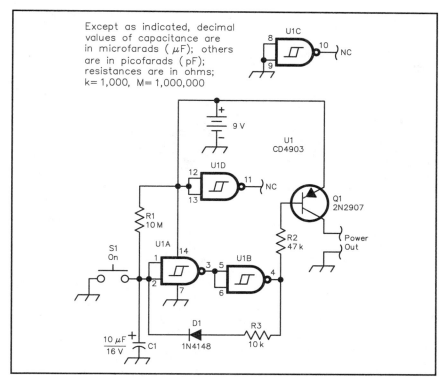

Except as indicated, decimal values of capacitance are in microfarads (μF); others are in picofarads (pF); resistances are in ohms; k= 1,000, M= 1,000,000

Figure 2.4—KØLR's battery-saver provides an automatic-power-off function for low-power accessories. Mouser Electronics, 958 N Main St, Mansfield, TX 76063; tel 817-483-4422, fax 817-483-0931; e-mail **sales@mouser.com;** Web **www.mouser.com.** RadioShack, National Parts Department, 900 E Northside Dr, Ft Worth, TX 76102; tel 800-442-2425, fax 817-870-5751, Tech Assistance 817-878-6875; **www.RadioShack.com**

C1—10 μF tantalum capacitor, RadioShack #272-1436 or Mouser #80-T350E106K016

D1—1N4148 diode, RadioShack #276-1122 (10-pack) or Mouser #78-1N4148

Q1—2N2907 or equivalent PNP transistor, RadioShack #276-2023 or Mouser #610-PN2907A

R1—10 MΩ resistor, RadioShack #271-1365 or Mouser #291-10M (10-pack)

R2—47 kΩ resistor (see text), RadioShack #271-1342 or Mouser #291-47K (10-pack)

R3—10 kΩ resistor, RadioShack #271-1335 or Mouser #291-10K (10-pack)

S1—Pushbutton switch, normally open, RadioShack #275-1547 (4-pack) or Mouser #103-1012

U1—CD4093 IC, RadioShack #RSU 11482239 (special order) or Mouser #511-4093

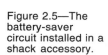
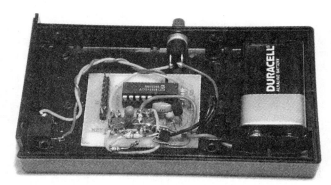

Figure 2.5—The battery-saver circuit installed in a shack accessory.

controlled by the timer requires 20 or 30 mA, R2 should be reduced to something like 10 kW. This battery-saver circuit can also be used at other voltage levels from less than 5 V to about 15 V, as defined by the operating voltage limits of the CD4093. Circuits drawing much more than 30 mA would require a beefier transistor for Q2 and a smaller resistor for R2. If necessary, the drive current capa-bility of U1 can be increased by putting the unused sections U1C and U1D in parallel with U1B. (This circuit could also be used to power a relay that acti-vates high-power devices, too.—KU7G.)

Figure 2.5 shows the battery-saver cir-cuit installed in the ICOM direct-fre-quency-entry keypad described by John Hansen in QST.[3] This is an extremely use-ful accessory for my IC-706, by the way. The CD4093 is installed dead-bug fashion on an unused portion of the main circuit board with double-stick tape, with the rest of the components suspended from the IC's pins. The toggle switch that was previously used to turn the unit on and off has been replaced by a pushbutton, and the battery-power leads have been routed through the timer circuit.—*Lyle Koehler, KØLR, 30141 Oriole Ave, Aitkin, MN 56431;* **k0lr@ arrl.net**

RADIOSHACK HTX202 AND HTX404 RECHARGEABLE-BATTERY REPLACEMENT

◊ Thousands of HTX202 and HTX404 H-Ts have been sold by RadioShack since they were introduced in the 1990s. The rechargeable batteries cost around $50 new. The 7.2 V battery can be re-placed with two RadioShack #23-193 3.6-V, 700-mAh telephone batteries for $20.

The old battery case comes apart eas-ily. Two screws in the top correspond with two screws in the bottom, and the case splits in the middle. Identify the screws as you remove them from the top and bottom so that they can be replaced accurately. Unsolder the four wires of the old battery, two from the positive and negative connections at the top and two from those at the bottom.

Now remove the plugs from the tele-phone batteries, keeping the black and red wires as long as possible. Solder the batteries in series, with the black lead from one battery soldered to the red of the other battery, and tape the connec-tion. This leaves a black lead from one battery and a red from the other supply-ing 7.2 V. A slight modification to the inside of the case lets both new batteries lie in like the original pack. Solder the red lead to the positive case terminal and the black lead to the negative terminal. (The terminals at the case bottom were never used.)

Some HTX202s experience "ER-2" problems even before any attempts to replace their batteries. I have a solution and I've notified the Tandy engineers of it: While the battery is apart, cut a piece

[3]J. Hansen, W2FS, "A Direct Frequency Entry Keypad for ICOM Transceivers," QST, Dec 1999, pp 38-39.

of insulated #22 AWG wire 12³/₄ inches long. Solder one end of it to the negative battery terminal (where the black wire was soldered) and coil it along the inside of the battery case next to the new battery. This wire does several things: (1) It acts as a counterpoise and serves as the second half of the "rubber duck" antenna.

(2) It lowers the SWR so the radio performs better, and (3) it helps keep RF out of the PLL circuit to help prevent ER-2 problems.—*David P. McDaniel, AB5UE, 412 Cedar Pl, Boerne, TX 78006*

The Doctor is IN

QDonn, WB4ZWT, asks, What's the difference between a regulated and unregulated power supply?

AAn unregulated supply is the most basic form of power supply possible. It consists of a transformer, rectifier and filter (plus a case with a switch and a fuse, of course!). Lacking any kind of regulator circuit, the output voltage can change quite a bit from a small load to the rated load. For example, if you have a supply that is rated as "12 volts, 3 amps, unregulated," that means that the voltage is 12 V at the rated current of 3 A but can be higher (perhaps 15 V or more) with a small load like 0.5 A.

A regulator circuit keeps the output voltage of a supply to a nearly constant level over a wide range of loads. A typical regulated supply for amateur use is rated for 13.8 V at 20 A. At 1 A or less, the voltage may still go up, but only by a small amount, such as to 14.2 V. How much of a swing depends upon the type of regulation circuit used. "Precision" or "Lab" type power supplies typically keep the output voltage within a ¹/₁₀ of a volt over the full range of loads the supply can handle.

So why would anyone want an unregulated supply? The reason is cost, but your device being powered must be able to handle a wide range of voltages. In addition to the basic cost of the parts, there is also the cost of designing the regulator circuit and the additional cost (labor) in manufacturing.

Many types of devices are designed to be powered off batteries. Since batteries change voltage quite a bit from full charge to discharge, the devices attached to them have to be able to handle the change. These same devices can often be powered by an unregulated supply.

Radios designed for mobile use can be powered by unregulated supplies, but many folks prefer to use regulated supplies since radios will often have reduced output at lower voltages. Also, as the total cost of a power supply increases, the regulator circuit becomes a smaller fraction of that cost. So although there is a substantial difference in the cost of a 12 V, 3 A regulated supply compared to an

unregulated one, there is very little difference when the supplies are 12 V, 10 A models. That's why most high current supplies are regulated.

QBill Schmidt, KC5JHW, asks: I have set up a 115 A/h, deep-cycle, lead-acid battery as my station's emergency power source. I charged it with my car battery charger and now have a 12 V dc, 1 A wall power supply charging it. The voltage rose to 14 V and it is drawing 38 mA. How do I know when it is fully charged? Is it safe to leave the wall power supply connected all the time? After discharging the battery, can the wall power supply eventually recharge it or do I need to use a car battery charger?

AThe battery is fully charged if monitoring the voltage shows no change over a long period of time. Most manufacturers state that you can continually supply a battery with a very small amount of current ("trickle" charge) indefinitely without harm as long as the battery is in good shape and the electrolyte hasn't evaporated. The small power supply will eventually recharge the battery, but it will take a long time and it will likely be heavily loaded if connected to a discharged battery of that size. A quick recharge on the car battery charger followed by trickle-charge is the best option.

If something happens to the battery or power supply, an unprotected connection could cause trouble and even be hazardous in some situations. Add a fuse or circuit breaker to the wall power supply output and also attach a thermal fuse to the battery case itself (on the side) to assure that the battery isn't overheating during charge. Your battery manufacturer may have a recommended maximum temperature.

QVern Koepke, NT9N, inquires: I'd like to operate portable with my ICOM IC-706, carrying a separate battery in a cart on wheels. What kind of battery should I use? A deep cycle

marine battery? I would operate only about 40 minutes or so, 5 days a week. The battery can be recharged at home.

ATo minimize the battery size required for the short-term use you describe, the deep-cycle type is recommended. Assuming you transmit 10% of the time, you will need a battery with a capacity of 20 A × 6/60 + 2.5 × 54/60 = 2 + 2.25 = approximately 4.5 A/h. If you figure as much as 30% on the transmit (very little time listening!) that would be 6 + 1.75 = approx 8 A/h. If you want some overhead and time to operate longer, a 10 to 12 A/h rating would be recommended (and the size is still reasonable). Before choosing a battery, it's a good idea to check the manual for the requirements of your transceiver.

QClif Inabinet, Jr, KF4UOR, of St Matthews, South Carolina writes: I want to use a 100 A/h deep-cycle marine battery for emergency radio operation during electric power outages. Is there a danger of hydrogen gas buildup if I keep it under the operating table inside my home? What about using it in the home when there is no power outage and the central heat and air is available for circulating the air in the room? I will not be charging it inside.

AWhile batteries normally give off hydrogen gas while charging, they can also release low levels of gas while being discharged. As the battery nears low voltage, the cells with more charge remaining will begin to charge the cells with lesser charge, so good ventilation is still very important when using lead-acid batteries inside. A good Web site reference on deep-cycle batteries is **www.uuhome.de/william.darden/dcfaq.htm**.

QClayton, KE4RTM, asks, "I have a simple question regarding a 5-V Lambda power supply. On the output side there are –S and –V, ground, and +S and +V terminals. The V terminals are reading +5 volts. What are the S terminals for?"

A On a power supply with +/−V and +/−S terminals, the S terminals are very likely "sense" inputs. In circumstances where the current draw might cause a significant voltage drop in the cable you are using to connect the power supply to the load, you would connect the sense terminals to the load via separate wires. The sense terminals would read the voltage at the load and relay that information back to the regulator circuit. If the voltage at the load drops, the sense circuit detects this and adjusts the output of the supply to a higher voltage so that the voltage on the load comes back up to the proper supply voltage.

Because there is very little current draw in the sense circuit itself, the wires connecting the S terminals to the load can be small gauge, even if the wires that supply power from the V terminals are quite large.

For many applications, the voltage drop is not so critical, so the manufacturer often includes shorting bars that connect the V and S terminals together at the supply.

Q Paul, AD4IE, writes: I powered up my IC-706MKIIG on 2 meters at full power using a fully charged 7 amp-hour Yuasa battery, the radio's original power cord, and with a voltmeter across the battery terminals. Each time I transmitted, the reading on my voltmeter dropped to about 5 V and then returned to 13 V when I switched to receive. I only made a few short transmissions with good reports. This voltage reading has me concerned. My thoughts are that although the battery could deliver 13 V, it wasn't made to supply the 20 A draw.

A The Doctor is never drained by battery questions. You are correct about the battery. According to a Yuasa data sheet, the battery will only supply 8.4 V with a 14 A load, far too little for most ham rigs. If you need to power a 20 A radio with a small and light battery pack, you should investigate NiCd batteries. They are ideal for high current transmit applications. Don't forget that the power cord may drop another volt—it is a good idea to measure the voltage at the radio. The Yuasa Web site is at **www.yuasabatteries.com.**

Q I would like to save money and use 12-V car and motorcycle batteries as power supplies for my camera and radio modules which require 7 to 8.5 V dc at a current of 1200 to 1800 mA. Can a simple circuit be recommended to drop the battery voltage?

A You have two choices of voltage regulator—linear and switching. A linear regulator is a simple circuit and does not create any switching noise, but dissipates a lot of your battery capacity as heat. Essentially a "smart resistor," the regulator will dissipate 4 W when dropping 12 V to 8 V at a load of 1 A—one-third of the total power! A switching regulator, while slightly more complex, is also much more efficient—80 to 90%—which will extend battery life. If you choose to use a linear supply, three-terminal regulators such as the LM350 (**www.national.com/pf/LM/LM350.html**) can be used alone or with external pass transistors to boost current capacity. The *ARRL Handbook* also has a 28 V dc linear power supply design from which the regulator circuit can be adapted.

Building a switching regulator is much easier than you might think. The LM2596 (**www.national.com/pf/LM/LM2596.html**) can handle up to 3 A and uses only a handful of components. There is even a design tool at the National Web site to help you select your component values. The July 1997 issue of *QST* also has an article on a general-purpose dc-dc converter switching supply.[4] OEM dc-dc converters can also be found at retail and surplus electronics dealers.

Q Martha Colburn, K4VM, writes: My new motor home has a Trace Engineering converter to charge the batteries from ac power. This converter is creating severe interference from the broadcast bands up through 20 meters. I have looked through the owner's manuals and on the device itself and find nothing about interference. Does the FCC have any jurisdiction over this device? Do I have any grounds to insist that the manufacturer fix this "transmitter"?

A The legal part of this issue is very clear. The converter is in violation of FCC Part 15 Rules and Regulations that state that the operator of the device must correct any harmful interference that is being emitted, or cease operating it if so ordered by the FCC. Unfortunately, in this case you are the operator and your only recourse is through your dealer and/or the manufacturer. You can show or refer them to relevant sections of Part 15, which can be found at **www.arrl.org/tis/info/part15.html.** If your motor home is under warranty and the converter is original equipment, you may be able to pursue a warranty claim.

---

[4]S. Ulbing, "My All-Purpose Voltage Booster," *QST*, Jul 1997, pp 40-43.

Q Paul, W5PDA, asks "I have an HTX-202 hand-held transceiver. I would like to rebuild the battery pack, but I'm not sure how to go about doing it. Can you give me some advice?"

A Speaking as one who has rebuilt several battery packs (mostly for laptops), I have to caution against attempting it unless you have no other option. (Keep in mind that replacement packs are available from several aftermarket manufacturers. See the ads in this issue of *QST*.) If you choose to go ahead, proceed with caution.

The pack was assembled in such a way as to prevent disassembly. In order to disassemble it, you have to break it—there's just no way around this. However, if you are very careful, you can break it in such a way that reassembling the pack is still possible, and with a reasonable appearance to boot. Start by studying the pack carefully. Try to figure out what holds it together. Come up with an idea of how to take it apart, then try to come up with reasons why that won't work very well. When you have an idea with the least "won't work" reasons, that's the one you should use.

Once you have the case apart, the rest is fairly easy. You will find multiple NiCd cells connected together with thin metal strips, usually spot-welded to the cells. Your next task is to find cells of the same size (typically nonstandard, but usually obtainable—try Digi-Key for one source). There is a caveat here: the original cells were probably matched according to their charge and discharge characteristics. If you buy unmatched cells, you won't get as much use from a rebuilt pack because you'll have the "weakest link in the chain" effect.

Once you have the replacement cells in hand, you have to connect them together in some fashion. You can do this with wire and solder, or you can use the original strips if you can yank them off the old packs without cutting yourself (been there...).

To solder the wire or strips to the new batteries is a difficult task because solder doesn't like to stick to stainless steel or shiny aluminum (which is what most new batteries use as contact plates). First, warm up your soldering iron to its maximum temperature (if you have a 300-W iron, use it, although 60 W will do). Sandpaper or file the contacts on the new batteries to rough them up a bit so that the solder has a place to stick. Take your iron and heat the contact plate up as quickly as possible—a 3-second or longer "dwell" time will probably damage the battery, so keep it shorter than that. Apply solder to the contact to make sure it sticks. Once you get the solder to stick to the contact, add your wire/metal strip and "reflow" the solder.

Of course, when you do this, you also have to make sure that: (1) the new cells go together with the exact alignment of the old cells and (2) that the solder you added doesn't cause the resulting pack to be too big to fit back in the old case.

Assuming you are able to connect all of the cells in a way that allows them to fit in the battery pack case, you'll have to find a way to get the pack back together (glue, small screws, etc).

If this sounds like a lot of work, that's because it is, but it is the cheapest way to get close to your original pack capacity.

There is a much cheaper and easier alternative, but the price is in time per charge. Buy a battery case for the rig (made for alkalines) and just put NiCds in it. The capacity (and possibly the voltage) will be less than your original pack, but it is definitely a cheap and sweat-free alternative.

Q Phillip Shelton, K4RCE, of Lafayette, Georgia, writes: I've selected a 2.3 Ah 12 V sealed lead acid battery to power an APRS tracker project. The batteries are both inexpensive and readily available. I have tried to research the proper charging methods but only become more and more confused. I know that they last for years in many applications such as emergency lighting and alarm systems with little or no maintenance. How is this best accomplished in both the home (115 V ac) and mobile (12 V dc) environments?

A The charging circuits in lighting and alarm systems are intelligent units costing many times what the batteries go for. The charging circuitry detects when a full charge is reached and then switches over to a float charge mode to keep the battery topped off. When the battery is discharged by an event, the charging circuit switches over to a fast charge mode to prepare the batteries for service again as soon as possible.

Intelligent charging circuits (examples of which have been featured in *QST*) cost upwards of $70-$100 for the parts alone. If this is what you are looking for, take a look at "An Automatic Sealed-Lead-Acid Battery Charger," May 2001 *QST*, p 43. However, if you don't care how long it takes the battery to recharge, there are much less expensive alternatives.

First, let's cover some battery basics. A new, fully charged 12 V lead-acid (sealed or not) will have a resting voltage somewhere between 13.2 and 14.4 V. The resting voltage, what the battery terminal voltage will read a couple of hours after the charger is disconnected, is said to have nominal value of 13.8 V. As bat-

teries age, the resting voltage drops. Most manufacturers consider a battery to be at the end of its useful life when the resting voltage is only 11.5 V. Some equipment (alarm and lighting systems for instance) are designed around a higher minimum voltage—hence the large number of "pulls" being sold at hamfests. Anyway, for the sake of this discussion, you can consider 13.8 V to be the resting voltage of new batteries. Let's say you will be allowing them to discharge down to 11.5 V.

Batteries last longer when the charge and discharge currents are lower. Since the discharge current is set by your application, the main way of changing the discharge rate is to operate multiple batteries in parallel. However, assume for now that you have a single battery. Charging is where we have some control—currents as low as 1/1000th the battery capacity (C) would be ideal. However, since it would take a very long time to recharge at 1/1000 C, a more reasonable rate is 1/20 C.

The challenge is providing a charging rate of 1/20 C without investing in an expensive charging circuit. Since the resting voltage on a new battery can easily be anywhere between 13.2 V and 14.4 V, a supply voltage of 13.8 V could either overcharge or undercharge the battery. That is, with a supply of 13.8 V, a battery of 13.2 V would be constantly charging. Likewise, a battery with a resting voltage of 14.4 V would never reach its full charge.

Lead acid batteries have a temperature coefficient of about -4 mV/degree Celsius per 2-V cell. This means the charging voltage will vary by 0.5 V when charging 6 cells if the temperature changes 20 degrees. Thus, as it overheats, the battery voltage drops, increasing the charge current with simple voltage chargers.

The simplest, least expensive approach to bringing the battery to full charge while limiting the charge to 1/20 C is to use a resistor between the supply output and the battery. What value and wattage? Assuming a charging voltage of 13.8 V, if the battery is discharged down to 11.5 V, the voltage across the resistor will be 2.3 V. The current through the resistor is set by the desired charge rate. For a 1/20th rate on a 2.3 Ah battery, that would be about 0.1 A. Ohm's Law gives 23 W and 0.23 W. The nearest standard value is fine and going up in wattage is probably a good idea.

So how long will it take to charge? A fairly long time—if the charge current was constant, it would take about 20 hours. Since the current goes down as the battery voltage goes up, it will probably take several days. However, since you can leave the supply connected indefinitely, it doesn't really matter. Alternatively, you can in-

crease the initial charge rate by switching to a resistor with lower resistance and a correspondingly higher power rating.

A few safety measures deserve mentioning here. Since batteries can short, adding a fuse in series with the resistor is a good idea. Batteries can also overheat, so check the battery case temperature several times early in the charging to check this—the thermometer tapes are an easy way to visually monitor temperature. Finally, non-sealed acid types should only be charged in a well-ventilated area to prevent risk of explosion.

Q When a resistor is connected to a battery, do the electrons flow from the positive terminal of the battery through the resistor to the negative terminal, or vice versa?

A Electrons flow from the negative terminal to the positive terminal of a battery, without question. However, there are two different points of view on the direction of *electrical current* flow, and the division between them is such that you will even find some books written with two different versions to accommodate both points of view.

One camp prefers to discuss electrical current in terms of *hole flow*. So what is hole flow? When an electron leaves an atom, it creates an electron deficit, or "hole," thereby creating what is known as a *positive ion*. This change-of-state progresses from one atom to another in bucket-brigade fashion, which can be considered hole flow. This is most often called *conventional current*.

The opposite view contends that electrons do indeed flow, not holes. The hole-flow proponents counter that free electrons don't travel fast enough in a wire to create the behavior we observe. On the other hand, the propagation of hole states is extraordinarily fast. Therefore, they believe hole flow must be correct.

Valid arguments can be made on both sides as to which concept is "correct." I strongly suggest not taking sides, but instead acknowledging the validity of both points of view and just keep in mind which convention is being used when discussing a particular circuit.

Q Every day I see old computers discarded such as old 486s that have operational power supplies. Many of these supplies can provide 200 to 250 watts at +12 volts, more than enough current capacity to supply much amateur gear such as 2-meter mobiles. The problem is that 12 V is a bit low. I have been unable to find diagrams for these common switching supplies and thus

have been unable to figure out how to raise the voltage to 13.8 V.

A In a computer, the biggest consumer of power is the microprocessor and the voltage on that is 5 V. Here's an example of the outputs from a 200 W power supply in a 486DX2/50 we have here:
5 V, 20 A (100 W); 12 V, 8 A (96 W) –5 V, 0.3 A (1.5 W); –12 V, 0.3 A (4 W)

While the supply could be modified to alter these outputs, the voltages and currents are determined by the transformer and the output circuitry, so it would all have to be replaced. As you can see, getting 200 W out of the 12-V output isn't quite so easy.

Computer supplies are switching supplies rather than linear. The near square-wave switching waveform creates a significant amount of RF. While it is possible to build an RF-quiet switching supply (witness the recent ham radio market switchers), it isn't necessary on a computer so the PC supplies are unfiltered and therefore unsuitable for use with radios in their "stock" form. To get an idea of the kind of filtering needed to produce "RF clean" output from a switching supply, you might want to take a look at the switching supply in Dec 1999/Jan 2000 *QST* (and *The ARRL Handbook* from 1999-present).

As you mentioned, schematics are not readily available for these supplies. Unlike a complex system such as a complete computer, it isn't cost-effective to have a technician (at a corporate rate of $15/hour or more) spend a couple of hours troubleshooting and fixing supplies that only cost (wholesale) $10-20 to replace. So, the foreign companies that build the supplies don't have a reason to include schematics. Pretty much the only recourse here would be to attempt to "reverse-engineer" the schematic from the components and circuit board in the supply. Even then, it may not be completely possible due to the use of specialty ICs that no data can be found for.

Now, with these points having been made, it still should be possible to use parts from several of these supplies along with some added filtering in order to produce something useful for the ham shack. However, if anyone has attempted it, they have not informed us of their work.

Q Brian, KA7KUZ, asks, "I am going to tour Australia. I know they use 220-V systems and all of my ham gear is 110 V. Do you know if the Australians also use 60 Hz for their ac mains? I can switch my rigs to run on 220 V, but I'm concerned about the frequency."

A Australia uses 220 V at 50 Hz. The 50-Hz power should not be a problem. Your power supplies may run a little hotter, but not dangerously so. And if you have difficulty converting your gear to 220 V, there are transformers available that will step 220 V down to 110 V. They are available from 50 to several hundred watts.

Q Keith, KF4BXT, asks, "What is a switching type power supply and what type is typically used and/or recommended for running a station? I think most of us, by now, understand that our power supplies should be regulated and filtered, but are there reasonable ways to add regulation and filtering to those that don't already have it?"

A In a linear power supply, the line voltage goes directly into a low-frequency transformer where it is stepped down to the appropriate low voltage before rectification, filtering and regulation. In a switching power supply, the line voltage is directly rectified and filtered to produce a high dc voltage. This voltage is then "switched" at a high frequency rate (not RF, but certainly higher than audio—perhaps 50 kHz, for example) by switching transistors. It is then fed into a high-frequency transformer and the output is rectified and filtered. Regulation can be done in the output stage, but more typically, the regulation is done at the switching transistor to allow the amount of energy fed to the transformer to be adjusted as needed.

One advantage of the switching technique is that higher frequency components are much smaller and lighter weight for the same power capability than their low frequency counterparts. Another advantage is that, since the transformer is the least efficient part of the supply, controlling its input power (as is done in a switching power supply) can provide much better efficiency. The power lost as heat in a linear supply is typically 40-60% of the output power. In a switching supply, that typically drops to 10-20%.

The disadvantages of a switching supply are the increased complexity (more likelihood of a component failure), increased cost (many more parts) and tendency to create radiated RF (the switching waveform is usually pretty close to a square wave, so it contains a lot of harmonics). This last item has been the main one that has kept switching supplies out of the ham market until recently. Current designs use an extensive amount of filtering and radiation suppression techniques to greatly reduce unwanted RF.

Adding filtering and regulation to a linear supply is a simple matter. Information on calculating filter component values for a particular desired ripple can be found in *The ARRL Handbook* chapter on power supplies. However, regulation will come at a cost in reduced output capacity—if you have an unregulated supply that puts out 15 V, you probably won't be able to get more than 13 V from a regulator system attached to it.

All switching supplies have some kind of regulation, although some designs are quite crude and could use improvement. I don't suggest trying to modify a switching supply unless you have studied switching power supply design extensively.

CHAPTER 3

Digital Modes

USE KENWOOD TS-570 OPTIONAL FILTERS FOR PSK31

◊ I have owned a Kenwood TS-570 for about four years and am generally pleased with it. I recently started using it on PSK-31 and soon discovered a problem with this usage. PSK-31 operation requires that the TS-570 be in SSB mode. The default IF filter for this mode has a 6-dB bandwidth of 2.2 kHz. This bandwidth is large enough to simultaneously include a substantial number of PSK signals. I found that if I was working a weaker station and a stronger station suddenly started transmitting on a nearby frequency, the weaker station would, in many cases, completely disappear from my *Hamscope* Version 1.4 waterfall display. After some puzzlement, I realized that this occurred because the stronger station "pumped" the receiver's AGC line and the resulting reduction in receiver gain equally affected both the strong interfering station and the weaker station I was working.

The solution is, of course, to filter out the stronger station. Unfortunately, the DSP filters included in the TS-570 are located in the audio section, after the AGC voltage is derived, so they are no help for this problem.

My TS-570 is equipped with an optional 500-Hz CW filter. Since this filter is located in the IF section of the receiver, it could, in principle, filter out interfering PSK stations. Unfortunately, the TS-570 is programmed so that this filter can only be used in CW mode, which means it is of no use for PSK reception in SSB mode. While looking at some material on the Web recently, I learned that certain older ICOM radios could be "tricked" to overcome a similar problem. I decided to try the same trick on my TS-570.

You tell the TS-570 what kind of optional filter is installed using Menu 46, which is accessed through the MENU key on the front panel. I selected Menu 46 and set the IF Filter Bandwidth to 1800 Hz rather than the true value of 500 Hz. I then found that in SSB mode, I could press the front panel FILTER button and select between wide and narrow filters, whereas previously I could only select the wide filter. The effect of selecting the narrow filter is dramatically evident on my waterfall display, where now only signals (or noise) in a 500-Hz bandwidth show. Furthermore, I discovered that this 500-Hz wide band could be moved around horizontally on the waterfall display by adjusting the IF SHIFT control on the front panel.

Now, I start in "wide" filter mode. Once I select an operating frequency and interference is a problem, I select the narrow filter and adjust the IF SHIFT control to place the filter over the signal I want. This removes as many interfering signals as possible. Using the approach, I am able to make and maintain more contacts with weak stations than before.

Kenwood produces an optional 270-Hz CW filter for the TS-570, which would presumably be even more effective for this application than the 500-Hz filter I own.—*Bill Kaune, W7IEQ, 111 Piper Ct, Richland, WA 99352;* **w7ieq @arrl.net**

IS YOUR TNC DRIVING YOU CRAZY?

◊ A few years ago I purchased a used PK-80 TNC. It was driving me crazy with very random and unpredictable behavior. Recently my Kantronics KPC-3+ started doing weird things. I spent about half of a day troubleshooting before finding the source of the problem. The keep-alive battery (a CR-2032) was going dead. None of the troubleshooting charts mention how to tell when this battery needs replacement. The symptoms I had were quite strange. The TNC would randomly reinitialize without any apparent pattern. After much troubleshooting, I discovered that the TNC was reinitializing each time a packet was received. My theory is that when a packet is received the TNC draws a bit more current for processing, and it was just enough that the keep-alive battery could not keep up and instead was loading down the power supply circuits.

The solution for my KPC-3+ was to replace the battery. I could not find a replacement battery for the PK-80, so I just operate without one. I could have replaced the battery with something of the correct voltage, but since most modern packet software packages load the parameters each time they are started, I never went to the trouble. Bottom line: Power is often a culprit in digital circuits when things seem to make no sense. —*Chuck Rexroad, N4HCP, 7511 Fairwood Ln, Falls Church, VA 22046;* **n4hcp@arrl.net**

A RADIO/DATA INTERFACE CONNECTION

◊ With the popularity of modes other than CW and voice, I have begun using the auxiliary connections on the back of my transceivers. In addition to using these connectors for connecting a PC to my radio, I also have used a variety of MCPs (Multimode Communication Processors). There is no connector standard for transceivers or MCPs. Whenever I acquire a new MCP, it seems like I have to build a new cable. When I'm fortunate enough to acquire a new transceiver, I have to build a new cable for each MCP I want to use.

In addition, switching among MCPs and the computer is a little tedious, requiring me to unplug one cable (which may go to multiple connections on the transceiver) and plug in a different one.

I've solved both problems by creating my own *standard*. I chose to use a DB9 connector for my standard. This allows for audio input and output lines with grounds for each, a common ground, PTT, FSK, CW and squelch. That seems to cover most common interface needs, but if you need more, you could use a DB15 or DB25. One advantage of using DB-style connectors is those connectors and cables are readily available and inexpensive.

To solve the problem of using multiple MCPs with a single transceiver, I connect the transceiver to a DB9 ABCD switchbox (see **Figure 3.1**). These boxes contain a 9P4T mechanical switch and usually have a metal cabinet. This allows me to leave up to four devices connected to the switchbox and easily switch among them.

To build the transceiver cable from a typical switchbox with an attached cable, I remove the DB9 connector and solder the wires from it to cables with the appropriate connectors for my transceiver. To avoid ground loops that might degrade the audio, I install 1:1 isolation transformers on both of the audio lines. If the transceiver has no way to adjust the audio levels, I install pots to do so (5 kΩ or 10 kΩ, the value is not critical). There's plenty of room for these in most switchboxes.

I install connectors on the back of the switchbox as needed to bring out any other useful signals that are carried by the cables between the switchbox and the transceiver. Usually, these are the CW keying input and a PTT output for a remote switch.

This makes connection of the MCPs a piece of cake. Start with a pre-made serial cable with DB9 male connectors on both ends (all switchboxes I have seen have DB9 female connectors) and cut it in half. This yields cables to wire two different MCPs.

When I do get that new transceiver with a different pin out, all I need do is adapt one new switchbox. I can use my existing MCP cables.

To connect a computer to the radio, you may need to translate EIA-232 levels to TTL levels for the radio. I do this in a small inline box between the switchbox and the computer. You might choose to build that interface inside the switchbox.

A note on PTT switching on Kenwood radios: The **ACC2** jacks on Kenwood radios have a signal labeled **MIC MUTE**. Connecting this line to ground mutes any audio coming from a microphone connected to the radio. This is a nice feature. I have worked with two Kenwood models (TS-940 and TS-870) and have found that the handling of this signal is different between them.

On the '940, grounding the **MIC MUTE** signal mutes the **MIC** input, but does not cause key the PTT line. Therefore, I connect a 1N4001 (or similar) diode between the **MIC MUTE** and PTT signals for the '940 interface, as shown.

The diode is necessary to prevent PTT activation from muting the mic when you do want to use the mic.

On the '870, grounding the **MIC MUTE** signal also keys the PTT line, so the diode is not required. I have discovered, however, that unless you cause the radio to transmit by grounding the **MIC MUTE** signal, audio supplied to the **ACC2** jack is not transmitted. I've not tried other Kenwood radios, but I suspect that one of these approaches should work.

A note on grounding: If your radio doesn't provide separate grounds for the audio lines, use the common ground instead. Also, if your MCP does not provide a separate audio ground, use the common ground instead. —*Mark Erbaugh, N8ME, 3279 Norton Rd, Grove City, OH 43123;* **mark@ microenh.com**

PSK31/PACKET SWITCHBOX

◊ I've been listening to PSK for several weeks now and have heard many operators complain about plugging and unplugging connectors in order to use the mode or change to another.

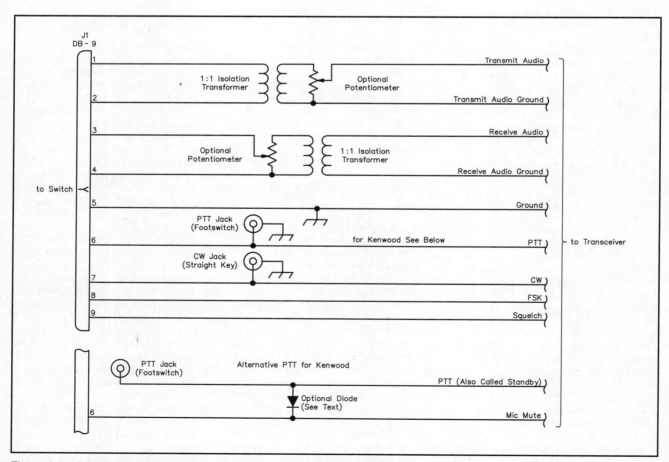

Figure 3.1—A typical radio/switchbox wiring diagram for N8ME's station.

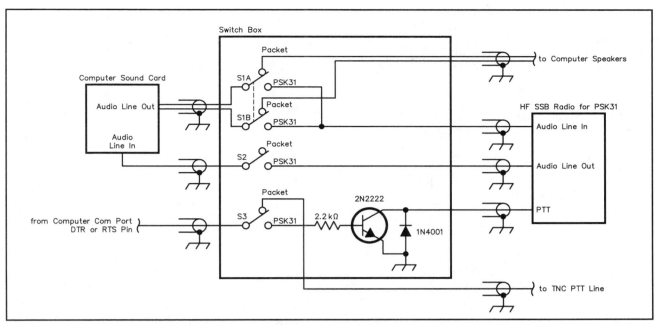

Figure 3.2—KN6TC's setup for switching between PSK31 and packet operation. If a 4PDT switch is available, S1, S2 and S3 could be combined.

I simply made a harness containing all the necessary cables, switches and enclosures to get around all the changing and fuss. **Figure 3.2** is a schematic of my harness. All parts are available from a junk box or your friendly local RadioShack and/or a retailer that handles computer accessories. For details of the radio and computer connections and operation, see "PSK31—Has RTTY's Replacement Arrived?" by Steve Ford, WB8IMY (*QST*, May 1999, pp 44). —*James H. (Jim) Walker, KN6TC, 211 East 22nd St, Owensboro, KY 42303-5110;* **kn6tc@freewwweb.com**

PSK31 AND NEWER KENWOOD RADIOS

◊ Ray Schneider, W6JXW, points out that Figure 1 in the November 1999 column (p 75) contained an error. The 100-Ω resistor should have been connected at the Mike end of the 10-kΩ resistor, not the sound-card end as shown. **Figure 3.3** shows the correct arrangement. Also, the text values for the resistors are incorrect. Those in the figure are correct.—*KU7G*

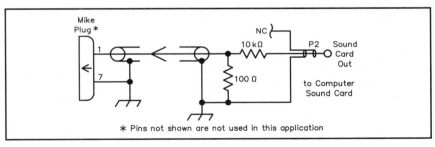

Figure 3.3—Corrected sound-card to Mike-plug circuit.

The Doctor is IN

Q Les, W2QHS, asks, "Recently I tuned through some PACTOR signals, but all I could copy were call signs being sent repeatedly. Were these stations attempting to link to BBSs? Is it possible to have just a casual conversation with a PACTOR station?"

A The PACTOR signals you've seen are indeed stations attempting to establish connections, often to automated BBSs or Internet e-mail gateways that are part of the Winlink2000 network. Winlink2000 in particular has become popular among sailing enthusiasts and others who wish to exchange e-mail from remote locations. It is certainly possible to enjoy casual keyboard-to-keyboard PACTOR QSOs, but these tend to be the exception rather than the rule.

For "live" HF digital conversations, most amateurs have chosen PSK31 or RTTY. You should be able to find someone to chat with on either mode on 20 meters between 14.070 and 14.099 MHz at just about any time. PSK31 predominates between 14.070 and 14.073 MHz, but in recent months activity has expanded to 15 meters (21.070 MHz) and 10 meters (28.120 MHz).

Q I'm just getting started with the HF digital modes, but I've run into trouble already. The "help" file in one of the software packages I recently downloaded from a source in Europe suggested an operating frequency on 160 meters between 1.838 and 1.840 MHz. I tried this and quickly discovered—the hard way—that I was in the middle of the 160-meter CW DX window. Was the software programmer mistaken in his choice of suggested frequencies?

A For the IARU Region in which he lives, I'm sure his suggestions make perfect sense. For amateurs living in Region 2 (North and South America), it will cause no end of headaches. See the ITU/IARU map in **Figure 3.4**.

You'll find a comprehensive chart of IARU Region bandplans on the Web at **www.iaru-r2.org/p11e.htm**. The chart is too large to publish here, but let's take a look at just the 160-meter portion. See **Table 3.1**.

As you can see, on 160 meters in Region 1 the recommended digital segment is 1838-1840, so 1838 is okay in that part of the world. For hams in Region 2, however, 1830-1840 is for intercontinental operating *only*. Routine domestic operation is 1800-1830, so Region 2 digital operators should be lower in the band. It pays to remember that our world is host to a diversity of bandplans; what works in one location may not be appropriate in another. When in doubt, double check.

Q In the "PSK31 2000" article in the May 2000 *QST*, there is a single-transistor circuit that is used for transceiver keying via a computer COM port. I've seen this circuit used frequently for other switching applications, but some versions add a diode between the base of Q1 and ground. Why is this?

A Radio designer Dave Benson, NN1G, provides the answer: "The diode (D2) between the base of Q1 and ground acts as a 'shunt diode' (see **Figure 3.5**). The RTS or DTR pins on COM ports can drop to about -10 V in the 'off' state, which may be sufficient to get Q1 to go into reverse breakdown. The results could be a rig that is locked in transmit, or otherwise be erratic in its keying characteristics. Adding the shunt diode will prevent this from happening."

Q Don, WB5UIA, asks, "Can I still find RTTY on the HF bands? What about VHF? What do I need to get started with this mode?"

A RTTY as a digital mode is still very much alive, although it is primarily used for DXing and contesting these days (PSK31 has taken over the lion's share of the "conversational" HF digital activity). You'll find RTTY on just about every HF band, but it is mostly heard on 20 meters between approximately 14.080 and 14.095 MHz. As far as VHF is concerned, RTTY was once heard on 2 meters—there were even "RTTY repeaters"—but VHF RTTY activity today has all but disappeared in the US.

To operate RTTY you have two options: purchase an external multimode interface for your computer, or purchase software that will send and receive RTTY signals using your computer's sound card. The external interfaces are still popular, but the software approach is gaining ground. (See our review of *RITTY 4.10* by Brian Beezley, K6STI, elsewhere in this issue.) Beyond that, all you need is an SSB transceiver and you're good to go.

To learn more I'd strongly recommend that you pick up a copy of the *ARRL HF Digital Handbook*. You can purchase this book at your favorite dealer, or order directly from the ARRL. See the ARRL Publications page in this issue.

Table 3.1

Region 1	Region 2	Region 3
1810-1838 CW	1800-1830 CW, digital	1800-1830 CW
1838-1840 digital	1830-1840 CW (DX window)	1830-1834 digital, CW
1840-1842 digital	1840-1850 phone, CW	1834-1840 CW
1842-2000 phone, CW	1850-2000 phone, CW	1840-2000 phone, CW

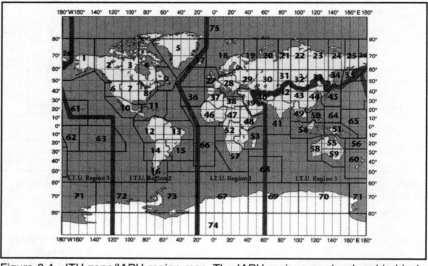

Figure 3.4—ITU zone/IARU region map. The IARU regions are bordered in black.

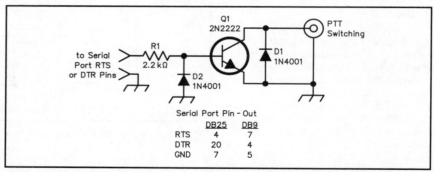

Figure 3.5—A COM port switching circuit modified with the addition of a shunt diode (D2) between the base of transistor Q1 and ground.

Q Dennis, AAØA, asks, "I'm attempting to run PSK31 with the *DigiPan* software, but I can't seem to get the waterfall display to function properly. I know that audio is getting to the sound card from my transceiver (I can even record the audio using *Windows Sound Recorder*). Any ideas?"

A This sounds like a display problem of some sort. Are you using the 256-color display mode? Check your *Windows* display properties under SETTINGS—CONTROL PANEL—DISPLAY. Make sure the SETTINGS are either 256-color or "High Color." See **Figure 3.6**.

Update: Success! I was running under the lowest color mode—16 colors. I changed the display setting to 256 colors and everything is working!—*AAØA*

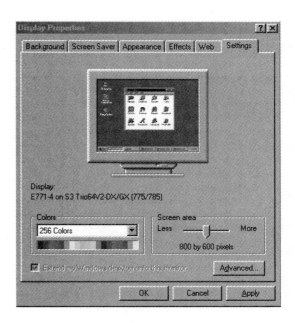

Figure 3.6—To change your display color settings in *Windows*, you need to access the DISPLAY window in CONTROL PANEL.

Q Larry, WA5MHE, asks, "When operating PSK31 I notice that some hams type their text in all uppercase letters, apparently unaware that the PSK31 code supports upper and lower case. Why do they do this?"

A I suspect that some of these operators may be RTTY veterans. The RTTY code used by most amateurs in the United States is known as ITA No. 2. With the limitations of a 5-bit code, ITA No. 2 can only support a relatively short list of characters. Therefore, RTTY text is in all-uppercase letters, rather than the mix of upper and lower case that we are accustomed to seeing.

There are three problems with sending text in all uppercase: (1) It is more difficult to read, (2) in the age of the Internet the custom is to interpret all-upper-case words as SHOUTING and (3) uppercase characters in PSK31 take longer to send. Internet-savvy hams (the majority of us, these days) are becoming more sensitive to the use of upper and lowercase in digital communication. I think this issue will resolve itself over time.

CHAPTER 4

Software and Computers

QUIKLOOP A LOOP-ARRAY MODELING AID

◊ For hams who love the lure of antenna designs, *EZNEC* by Roy Lewallen, W7EL, is a dream come true. I had in mind building a 2-meter loop array with circular elements and rather than guess, I wanted to design it on paper first. Fortunately, my loving daughter, Carolyn, saw *EZNEC* on my Christmas list one year, and there it was, under the tree.

Typical antenna-design programs require that we define the antenna as a series of straight segments, the ends of which must be identified by Cartesian (*X*, *Y*, *Z*) coordinates. Once you have these segment-end coordinates, they can be typed into the analysis program, and you can begin the analysis. For example, in a loop array with vertically oriented elements, *EZNEC* can use *X* for depth (toward the horizon—element spacing in this case); *Y* is the horizontal distance left or right from the centerline of the array; and *Z* is height.

Earlier experience with *MININEC* meant I wasn't a complete stranger to this process. For a simple dipole or long wire, it is a rather simple and quick description process. Thinking of a loop array in three dimensions—particularly one with circular elements—boggled my mind. Further, if I wanted to change or make a new antenna, I had to calculate and manually enter *all* those locations again. My design uses octagons to simulate circular loops—eight wires per element, three elements, three numbers for each point and two ends for each wire. That totals 144 numbers—and one mistake in manual calculation or data entry makes my work garbage!

An Easier Way

I learned from Roy that *EZNEC* can read a data file containing the information! So, into geometry, trigonometry and program writing I went. The result is *Quikloop*, an MSDOS (or DOS window) program.[1] *Quikloop* calculates each wire's endpoints for square, diamond or octagon (to approximate circles) element shapes in loop arrays and places the data

Table 4.1

A Square-Loop Yagi with Three 0.25-inch-diameter Elements

Element Number	Function (inches)	Circumference (inches)	Distance from Element 1
1	Reflector	86.84	0
2	Driven Element	82.78	20.5
3	Director	78.57	32

Contents of the resulting file "MYLOOP.EZA"

```
0 ,–.275717 , 5.820283 , 0 ,–.275717 , 6.371717 , .00635
0 ,–.275717 , 6.371717 , 0 , .275717 , 6.371717 , .00635
0 , .275717 , 6.371717 , 0 , .275717 , 5.820283 , .00635
0 , .275717 , 5.820283 , 0 ,–.275717 , 5.820283 , .00635
.5207 ,–.2628265 , 5.833174 , .5207 ,–.2628265 , 6.358827 , .00635
.5207 ,–.2628265 , 6.358827 , .5207 , .2628265 , 6.358827 , .00635
.5207 , .2628265 , 6.358827 , .5207 , .2628265 , 5.833174 , .00635
.5207 , .2628265 , 5.833174 , .5207 ,–.2628265 , 5.833174 , .00635
.8128 ,–.2494598 , 5.84654 , .8128 ,–.2494598 , 6.34546 , .00635
.8128 ,–.2494598 , 6.34546 , .8128 , .2494598 , 6.34546 , .00635
.8128 , .2494598 , 6.34546 , .8128 , .2494598 , 5.84654 , .00635
.8128 , .2494598 , 5.84654 , .8128 ,–.2494598 , 5.84654 , .00635
```

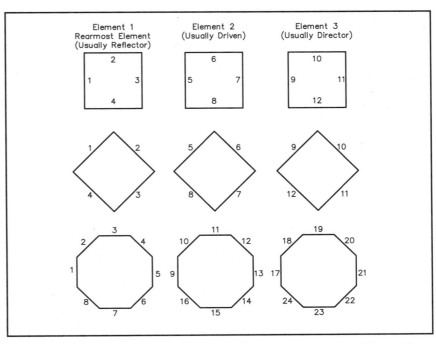

Figure 4.1—Wire numbering in antennas defined by *QuickLoop*. Numbering continues in similar fashion for additional elements. Use this diagram to determine the appropriate wire for source location in *EZNEC*.

in a file *EZNEC* can import. It can save you many hours of calculations and key-boarding.

It is convenient to load and run the program in the same directory where *EZNEC* looks for its antenna-description files. Once started, the program asks for the information that defines a loop array, in this sequence:

1. Number of elements.
2. Element circumference (in inches, for each element).
3. Element spacing from element 1 (in inches, for each element). For a three-element loop Yagi, element one is usually the reflector, element two is the driven element and element three is the director.
4. The element shape: square, diamond or circular (octagon).
5. Conductor diameter (the program assumes all elements have the same diameter, but you can change any element diameter once the data is in *EZNEC*).
6. A filename of your choice, but include no file extension. *Quikloop* automatically adds an "EZA" extension that distinguishes *Quikloop* files from other *EZNEC* files. If a file with the same name exists, it will be overwritten.

Quikloop asks for dimensions in inches and feet, but the wire-end locations are converted to meters, the default dimension for uploading into *EZNEC*. After you import the data into *EZNEC*, you can change to whatever units you prefer.

Getting the Data into *EZNEC*

Let's say you have just run *Quikloop* for a three-element loop Yagi described in **Table 4.1** and named the output file "MYLOOP." To get the data from "MYLOOP.EZA" into *EZNEC* follow these steps:

1. Start *EZNEC*.
2. Go to the Wires menu.
3. Type "I" to import wires data.
4. Choose the file "MYLOOP.EZA" from those shown.
5. When asked, hit "R" to replace any existing wires data.

You will see that the coordinates from MYLOOP.EZA (also shown in Table 4.1) have been imported, and you are ready to analyze the antenna. At this point, you may want to change *EZNEC*'s dimensions to those that are familiar to you.

[1]You can download this package from the ARRL Web site at **www.arrl.org/files/qst-binaries/**. Look for QUIKLOOP.ZIP. If you want QUIKLOOP on a 3.5-inch PC-format floppy, send your name and address and a check payable to Robert Patzlaff for $5 to W9JQT, 422 W Maple St, Hinsdale, IL 60521.

If analysis shows that the element circumferences are too short or too long, you can easily generate a new EZA file and import the new data. This process is much easier than manually recalculating all those wire endpoints.

Quikloop makes loop-array analysis as easy as that for any other wire antennas. I find analyzing loop antenna arrays is now fun, and I like using circular elements at VHF and UHF. The geometry used in *Quikloop* defines vertically oriented elements in a loop array. **Figure 4.1** shows the wire numbering plan used so you can pick your source wire location.

You can model other complex antennas by doing the geometry once and making a simple file to calculate the wire end coordinates. The *EZNEC* manual gives you criterion for the data file.—*Robert Patzlaff, W9JQT, 422 W Maple St, Hinsdale, IL 60521-3229;* **bobpatz@mediaone.net**

[W9JQT's great discovery is that we can import properly formatted text files into EZNEC. This means that we can model any antenna by using a spreadsheet or custom program to calculate segment endpoints and produce a file that EZNEC can import. QUIKLOOP .ZIP includes an example Excel spreadsheet (DeltaLoop.xls) that I created for a three-element array and EZNEC 3.0. W9JQT's instructions apply to DOS-based EZNEC versions; EZNEC 3.0 is written for Windows and has a File menu command to import Wires data from a file.—Ed.]

A UNIVERSAL LOGGING COMPUTER INTERFACE

◊ Would you like automatic entry of frequency and mode data to your logging computer even from a rig that's not computer controllable? I have modified the software for Neil Heckt's PIC-based frequency display[2] to provide a serial data port. All you need to do is replace the PIC16C71 chip with my modified version[3] and connect it to your computer via a TTL-to-EIA-232 level converter.

[2]N. Heckt "A PIC-Based Digital Frequency Display," *QST*, May 1997, pp 36-38.

The data port is RB6, pin 12 on the PIC16C71 (see **Figure 4.2**). This pin was formerly used for the **ZERO** switch, S1. With the new software, when S1 is closed the counter performs as before; that is, it will count and display. When S1 is open, the counter halts and waits for a serial command. The command can be any character; the software only looks for start and stop bits. On receipt of a command, the counter counts and displays the result, then transmits it to the computer. If the computer sends a command repeatedly, as most logging programs do in automatic mode, the display will be updated regularly. Otherwise, it will display the frequency and mode at the time of the last command or S1 closure. I inserted a 220 Ω resistor between S1 and ground to protect the chip if S1 is closed while it is transmitting.

The schematic in Figure 4.2 includes a circuit and PC board layout for a TTL-to-EIA-232 level converter. I built the level converter on a small PC board that can be mounted on the back of Neil's board. The display module is not essential and it may be omitted; the counter will still transmit data to the computer.

Ideally, the counter should be connected to the local oscillator and **MODE** switch of your rig, but I have used it with an antenna to pick up transmitted RF. I have also linked it to my transmission line via a toroidal transformer. The disadvantages of this method are that you must press the logging key when you are actually transmitting and no mode data is available.—*Dave McClafferty, VE1ADH, 28 Balsam Cir, Lower Sackville, NS B4C 1A9, Canada*

[3]I supply programmed chips for $25 US, contact me by e-mail: **at060@chebucto.ns.ca** by "snail mail" at the address shown on the hint or by telephone at 902-864-0268. Please specify the data rate, 1200 to 9600. I will send the .HEX file via e-mail to anyone wanting to burn their own chip.

Table 4.2—Displayed Mode versus MODE Resistor Value and RA3 Voltage

Mode	R(kW ±5%)	V at RA3
blank	OPEN	5.0
AM	65.0	4.3
FM	27.5	3.7
CW	15.0	3.0
USB	8.8	2.3
LSB	5.0	1.7
FSK	2.5	1.0
FAX	0.0	0.0

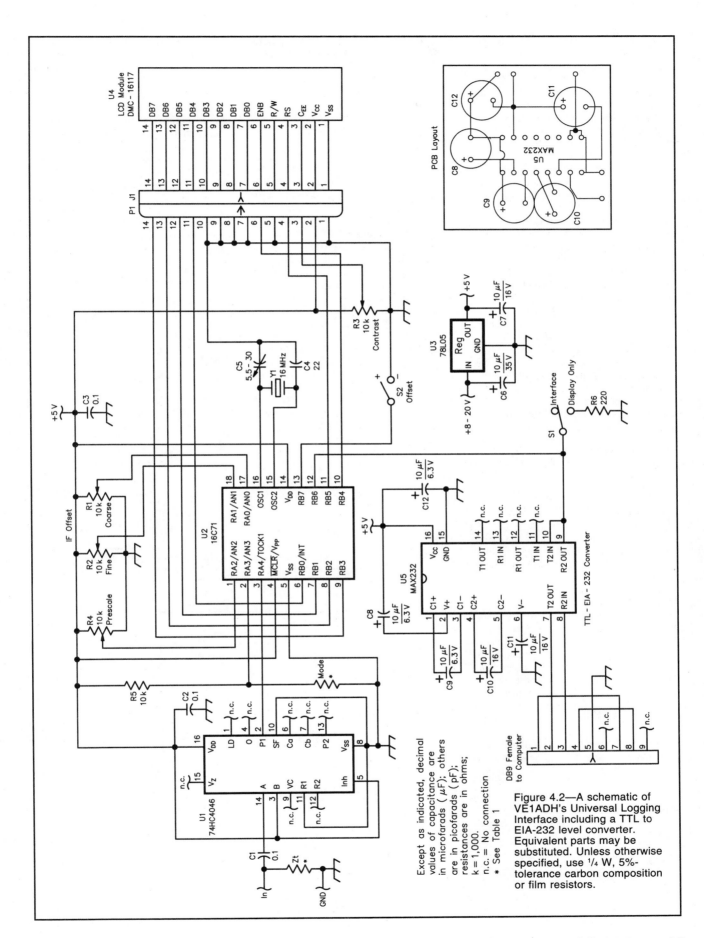

Figure 4.2—A schematic of VE1ADH's Universal Logging Interface including a TTL to EIA-232 level converter. Equivalent parts may be substituted. Unless otherwise specified, use 1/4 W, 5%-tolerance carbon composition or film resistors.

Except as indicated, decimal values of capacitance are in microfarads (μF); others are in picofarads (pF); resistances are in ohms; k = 1,000.
n.c. = No connection
* See Table 1

SCHEMATIC DRAWING SOFTWARE

◊ Readers occasionally ask me to recommend graphics software for drawing schematics. There are many answers to this question, so I think it's a good topic for Hints and Kinks. I'll give you some ideas this month, and collect what information you send me. I use Windows, so that's where I'm starting. We need to cover Mac and Unix/Linux based applications too. When there's enough material, I'll publish periodic updates.

After a couple years of making circuit boards in the ARRL Lab, I find dead-bug construction much more convenient. With no need to make circuit boards, I seek programs with simple drag-and-drop operation. *QST* described the simplest of these before,[4] but the necessary files fell through the cracks when we discontinued the dial-up ARRL BBS. I've posted them again as SCHEMAT.ZIP.[5] This Zip file contains Schemat.bmp, which may be opened in the Windows Paint accessory or any simple bitmap editor. To make schematics, simply open Schemat.bmp in one instance of Paint and your drawing in another. To place a symbol, select it in Schemat.bmp, copy it to the clipboard and paste it into your drawing. If you want a quick, inexpensive way to draw schematics, this setup is available right now and the price is right.—*Bob Schetgen, KU7G, ARRL Staff*

MORE SCHEMATIC DRAWING SOFTWARE

◊ CadSoft produces *EAGLE*, a schematic/PC-board-layout program. They have a Web site (**www.cadsoftusa.com**) and offer freeware trial versions of their software for DOS and *Windows*. I took a quick look at the *Windows* version. It appears to be of German origin, and it has been around since at least 1995. It uses European schematic styles (rectangular blocks for resistors and a single horizontal line for the ground symbol), but the program offers the ability to construct your own symbols. The program also allows the use of scripts and if you're fluent in *C*, you evidently can do some program customization.

The freeware version is limited to one schematic page and a PC board size of something like 4×3.5 inches, but that should be sufficient for many who build small projects. For current prices, visit their Web site or contact the US distributor: CadSoft Computer, Inc, 801 S Federal Hwy, Delray Beach, FL 33483-5185;

tel 1-800-858-8355, 561-274-8355, fax 561-274-8218; **www.cadsoftusa.com; sales@cadsoftusa.com; support@cadsoftusa.com**.

TurboCAD 4.0 and later (a generic CAD program) has some nice electrical symbol libraries, but I doubt that it's as well integrated as dedicated schematic-capture/PC-board-layout programs. A free download version of *TurboCAD 2D V6* is available from the IMSI Web site.[6]

Circad is a schematic-capture/PC-board-generation package with auto-routing, netlists, etc. Holophase Inc (**www.holophase.com**) offers free size-limited downloads of *Circad* in 32-bit Windows and 16-bit MS-DOS versions (**www.holophase.com/dleval.htm**). Although it's not readily apparent at the Holophase home page, there's a **CIRCAD Library Exchange Project** page (**www.holophase.com/libexproj. htm**) from which user-generated libraries can be downloaded. Holophase encourages user library exchanges.

If one is not concerned with creating net lists, PC boards, and so on, just about any CAD program can be used to draw schematics, but they'll likely lack the smoothness of dedicated programs. —*Paul Pagel, N1FB, ARRL Staff*

◊ Free schematic drawing software can be found at **hometown.aol.com/ KQ6QV/index.html**. The program, which I wrote, can be downloaded in a few minutes. Enjoy!—*Ken Nist, KQ6QV, 22001 Scenic Heights Wy, Saratoga, CA 95070;* **KQ6QV@aol.com**

◊ I saw the December hint about schematic drawing software. I use the drawing facility of Microsoft *Word97*. The later versions of MS-*Word* have a pretty good drawing package and most folks that have purchased computers in the last couple of years have *Word*. (This is *Draw98*; *Office97* users can upgrade to *Draw98* from **download.microsoft.com/download/office97std/Update/1/WIN98/EN-US/draw98.exe** —*Ed.*)

Figure 4.3 is a little sketch I made some time ago that was used to describe a temporary construction power arrangement. **Figure 4.4** is a small symbol library.[7] Notice that the sample is not an

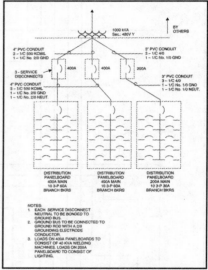

Figure 4.3—A sample diagram drawn with Microsoft's *Draw98* facility of *Office97*.

[6]IMSI Corporate Headquarters, 75 Rowland Wy, Novato, CA 94945; tel 415-878-4000, fax 415-897-2544; **www.turbocad.com**.

[4]K. Schofield, W1RIL, "Schematics at Your Fingertips," *QST*, Oct 1993, pp 39-40.
[5]You can download this package from the *ARRL Web* **www.arrl.org/qexfiles/**. Look for SCHEMAT.ZIP.

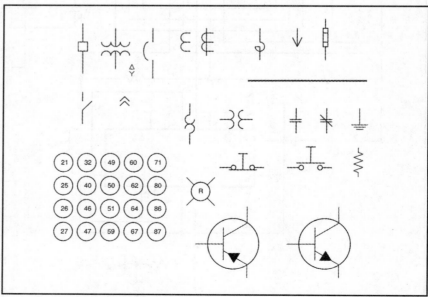

Figure 4.4—A simple *Draw98* symbol file.

electronics drawing but the principles are the same. You can create your own symbol library with capacitors, transistors and so on. I am an electrical engineer (power) and these are some of the symbols I used most often. A professional draftsperson I am *not*.

Start by opening MS-*Word*. I find that using a 200% or 300% Zoom factor, you can nudge the symbols into line effectively. Be sure to set the **GRID** command so the objects are snapped to each other. (If you don't do this, you will have one heck of a time.) Open the symbol library file. Leave the library image displayed and click on **FILE NEW** to get a new page in front of you. (As you probably know if you use Word, you can cascade the two files—or you can switch between the files by clicking on **WINDOW**.) Click on **VIEW TOOLBARS, DRAWING** to get the drawing toolbar on the screen. To make a line, select the line tool by clicking on the line button (to the right of **AUTOSHAPES**, indicated by a line segment). Next, click on the page where you want the line to begin and drag the line to where you want it to end. Right click on the line (or any other object) and click **FORMAT AUTOSHAPE**. Then, you can set the line width of the object.

The *Draw98* Help file is fair, but most of the commands are intuitive. Text boxes can be created, moved, resized and the text font can be changed. The **SNAP** function is good, but if you look closely at Figure 4.3, you will find some dis-

[7]This symbol file has been added to SCHEMAT.ZIP as DRAW98.DOC. You can download this package from the *ARRL Web* at **www.arrl.org/files/qst-binaries/**.

jointed lines and symbols.

When I start a drawing, I throw all symbols that I think I might need in the corner of my clean sheet and then drag them around or copy/paste them where I need them. I was trained on *AutoCAD*; it is an expensive (but good) program. When I worked in the field at construction sites, however, I did not always have *AutoCAD* program available. *Word* is, for better or worse, usually available. Drawings are printed in the same way as a text document. By the way, *Draw98* is also accessible from *Excel*, the spreadsheet program.

Earlier versions of *Draw* were—in my opinion—very unstable and in general, very primitive. I struggled with it on an overseas project where I had to make some sketches and was very unhappy. My employer later upgraded with later versions of Word and the new versions were much improved. One function that is very helpful is **GROUP**. Using the "select" arrow on the draw toolbar, you can enclose several objects and group them together. Sometimes I will make an entire section of a drawing, group it, copy it, move it, ungroup it and modify it. (That's a trick I learned with *AutoCAD*.)—*John Hudelson, K5DL, PO Box 21, Carmine, TX 78932-0021;* **k5dl@arrl.net**

ONLINE GRID-SQUARE RESOURCES AND UTM COORDINATES

◊ When I visited the TopoZone site, I found that the coordinates associated with the cursor were given in UTM coor-

dinates, not degrees. UTM stands for "Universal Transverse Mercator," a coordinate system used by the military and others for local navigation. The UTM system divides the world into 60 zones (each 6° of longitude wide, extending from 80°S to 84°N latitude) and superimposes a rectangular grid over each zone. A position is specified by its zone number and Cartesian coordinates (in meters) from a point on the equator 500,000 meters west of the zone center. The first coordinate is an "Easting" and the second a "Northing" (in the Northern Hemisphere, I saw no mention of a "Southing" for the Southern Hemisphere). With the cursor on the ARRL HQ building, UTM 18 688945E 4620367N shows in the status window of the map page. (For an explanation of the UTM system, visit the Map Tools Web page at **www.prusik.com/maptools/UsingUTM/** or the USGS Fact Sheet 157-99 at **mac.usgs.gov/mac/isb/pubs/factsheets/fs15799.html**.) Clicking on the QUAD INFO link at the upper right of the map takes you to a page of information about the USGS map that you are viewing. There, you can read the HQ position as latitude 41.7146°, longitude –72.7288°, where the negative sign indicates west longitude.

Many Web map sources include latitude and longitude information. I often use MapBlast (**www.mapblast.com/myblast/index.mb**). There, you simply enter an address, click the CREATE MAP button and read "Lat: 41.716905, Long: –72.727083" above the map's upper-right corner. MapBlast doesn't give topographic information.—*Bob Schetgen, KU7G, Hints and Kinks Editor*

The Doctor is IN

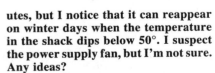

Q I have a large number of 3.5-inch diskettes—almost all of which appear to be defective! I don't see how this is possible, but recently when I needed to back up some log files on my station PC I kept getting "defective disk" messages. I've been storing the disks properly, and I haven't exposed them to magnetic fields. Do you have any idea what might be causing this?

A If you have been carefully storing your diskettes, there is one culprit you may have overlooked: your disk drive. The Doctor is willing to bet that you have a flaky 3.5-inch drive. The read/write head could be dirty, or the tracking mechanism could be faulty. These drives

are so inexpensive (less than $20 in some stores), I'd suggest replacing the drive entirely. If that isn't the problem, hang onto your receipt and take the drive back.

By the way, consider adding a CD-R or CD-RW drive to your station computer. It is *much* easier to do backups when you can dump 650 Mbytes of data at a time! The CD-ROMs are more durable and reliable than diskettes, too.

Q My station computer makes a terrible noise when I first turn it on. It is a loud screeching and grinding sound. It stops after about 2 or 3 min-

utes, but I notice that it can reappear on winter days when the temperature in the shack dips below 50°. I suspect the power supply fan, but I'm not sure. Any ideas?

A A defective bearing in the power supply fan is usually the cause of the noise you've described. There may also be a tiny fan on your CPU, but it is usually silent.

Not only is the fan noise annoying, it is a harbinger of danger for your computer. Some computer manufacturers cut corners by installing low-cost power supplies. These power supplies are assembled with the cheapest components possible, including poor-quality cooling fans. The Doc's suggestion is that you replace your power supply as soon as possible. Don't wait for the fan to fail outright. The supply could overheat and break down catastrophically, sending a voltage surge directly into the mother-board and other components. You can pick up a good-quality 250-W supply for about $50, and they are relatively easy to install.

Q A traveling reader writes: The car adapter for my laptop computer can also be used onboard an airplane. It is a four-pin connection. I could use this type of plug in my shack to power all my 12 V equipment. But where can I get this type of plug and does it have a special name? How are the connections arranged?

A This is known as the Aerospace Operations EMPOWER In-Seat System. A list of authorized manufacturers can be found at **www.rocket.com/adapter.html**. However, it is a 15 V standard, too high for some amateur equipment to handle without expensive damage. The once-popular ICOM IC-2AT would only handle 12 V maximum, and included a warning about hooking it up to automotive systems. The Doctor feels it is unlikely that manufacturers will sell this plug inexpensively to hams.

Q I've been shopping for a new station computer and recently I've seen advertisements in the newspaper for Pentium III PCs selling at $600 or less. I knew computer prices were falling, but this seems incredible. What am I missing?

A You're missing that famous axiom: "If it sounds too good to be true, it probably is."

Yes, prices have been falling and will continue to fall. Basic Pentium III systems hit the market initially at about $2500, but they've since dropped to around $1500 at the time this column was written (late 1999). So how can someone advertise an $600 Pentium III without violating truth-in-advertising laws? There are a number of ways to do this, all of them devious.

The PC in question may have a Pentium III processor, but what kind of motherboard is it using? Chances are the seller has installed the processor in an "older" 66-MHz motherboard, which effectively chokes off any speed advantage you would gain from the Pentium III processor! A 100-MHz motherboard is the only way to go with a Pentium III, but they cost more, of course.

What sort of memory is on the motherboard? I'm willing to bet that the seller has installed older (read: "slower") chips that are not compliant with 100-MHz boards.

What about the video card? You'll be lucky if you get more than a megabyte of video card memory. That's way too low for many modern software applications.

The hard drive may be an off brand that offers slow-as-cold-molasses access at best.

Finally, does the PC come with *Windows* installed? If it's *Windows 98* you can count on finding the less-stable first edition.

Bottom line: You get what you pay for. What you save in cash you may pay for later with severe buyer remorse. Whenever you purchase a complete PC system, Pentium III or otherwise, examine the specifications carefully and ask plenty of probing questions before you decide to buy.

Q When talking about computers, what does SCSI mean?

A SCSI is an abbreviation for Small Computer System Interface. Pronounced "scuzzy," it is a parallel interface standard used by Macs, PCs and many Unix systems for attaching peripheral devices to computers.

SCSI interfaces provide faster data transmission rates (up to 40 Mbytes per second) than standard serial or parallel ports. In addition, you can attach many devices to a single SCSI port, so that SCSI is really an I/O bus rather than simply an interface.

Although SCSI is an ANSI standard, there are many variations of it, so two SCSI interfaces may be incompatible. For example, SCSI supports several types of connectors.

While SCSI is the only standard interface for Macintoshes, PCs support a variety of interfaces in addition to SCSI. These include IDE, Enhanced IDE and ESDI for mass storage devices, and Centronics for printers. You can, however, attach SCSI devices to a PC by inserting a SCSI board in one of the expansion slots. Many high-end PCs come with SCSI built in. Note, however, that the lack of a single SCSI standard means that some devices may not work with some SCSI boards.

The following varieties of SCSI are currently implemented:

SCSI-1: Uses an 8-bit bus, and supports data rates of 4 MBps.

SCSI-2: Same as SCSI-1, but uses a 50-pin connector instead of a 25-pin connector for 16-bit transfers, and supports multiple devices. This is what most people mean when they refer to plain SCSI.

Wide SCSI: Uses a second cable (called a B-cable) to support 32-bit transfers.

Fast SCSI: Uses a 16-bit bus, but doubles the clock rate to support data rates of 10 MBps.

Fast Wide SCSI: Uses a 16-bit bus and supports data rates of 20 MBps.

Ultra SCSI: Uses an 8-bit bus, and supports data rates of 20 MBps.

SCSI-3: Uses a 16-bit bus and supports data rates of 40 MBps. Also called Ultra Wide SCSI.

Ultra2 SCSI: Uses an 8-bit bus and supports data rates of 40 MBps.

Wide Ultra2 SCSI: Uses a 16-bit bus and supports data rates of 80 MBps.

Q I've been connecting to the Internet with my shack PC at 28.8 kbps. Just this week I received word that DSL will soon be available in my area and that it would greatly accelerate my Internet access. What can you tell me about DSL?

A DSL stands for stands for digital subscriber line, and it takes advantage of the fact that the total capacity of the telephone line coming into your home is vastly under-utilized. Simple voice communication uses only about 1% of the available bandwidth, leaving huge amounts of unused capacity that can support digital transmissions.

DSL uses your telephone line by skipping analog conversion. That is, there is no digital-to-analog conversation process like you see (and hear) in conventional modems. Instead, DSL keys digital data directly on the line. The result is mind-boggling speed—theoretically as high as 8 mbps (megabits, or millions of bits, per second), which is more than 250 times the rate you get at 28.8 kbps. And because the analog voice signal and digital DSL signals use different frequencies, they can be transmitted simultaneously. So not only do you get much higher transmission rates, you can leave your computer connected to the Internet 24 hours a day and still receive telephone calls—all over a single copper phone line.

Of course, there is a catch. (Isn't there always?) DSL signals attenuate rapidly with distance. For most DSL technologies, the signal is only viable for 18,000 feet. In other words, if you don't live within about 3½ miles of your phone company's central office, you can forget about DSL. That excludes something in excess of one-third of all homes in the United States.

DSL actually comes in a number of flavors. One of the most common is ADSL (asymmetric digital subscriber line). Most home and small office computer users download a lot of data off the Web, but send relatively little data in the other direction. ADSL makes use of that by reserving more bandwidth for downstream data flow—from the Web to your computer—than upstream. With ADSL, downstream speeds of up to 6 mbps are possible (although 1.5 mbps is more typical); upstream tops out at 640 kbps. ADSL requires the installation of a voice/data splitter at your home. A slightly slower version, called DSL Lite, does the splitting at the phone company. Other varieties include HDSL (high bit-rate DSL) which carries equal amounts of data in both directions and has a maximum rate that is lower than ADSL; RADSL (rate-adaptive DSL), which analyzes the capacity of a customer's phone line and adjusts the rate accordingly; and VDSL (very high data rate DSL), which can send data at an astonishing rate of 55 mbps, but only for about 1,000 feet.

Q **I recently purchased a CW send/ receive program. It is *DOS* software, but I can run it under *Windows* in a "*DOS* window." The software processes the receive audio through the soundcard and uses DSP to filter and select the signal you want to decode. It does this remarkably well, but the problem is that I can't seem to get the CW keyboard function to work. According to the documentation, you're supposed to be able to build a simple single-transistor keying interface to key your transceiver through a COM port. I built the interface and I'm trying to use it with COM 2, but nothing works. Can you help?**

A I suspect that *Windows* has "seized" control of COM 2 and is reluctant to give it up! Even though you're running the software in a *DOS* box, *Windows* is still in control of the COM ports. To allow your software to control COM 2 in *DOS*, you need to disable the port in *Windows*.

Click on your START button, then SETTINGS, followed by CONTROL PANEL. Double click on the SYSTEM icon, then click on the DEVICE MANAGER tab.

Device manager will list all of your computer's "devices." Look for the PORTS label. Double click on it and you'll see a line for COM 2. Double click on this and you'll see the "properties" display for COM 2 (see **Figure 4.5**). *Uncheck* the box marked "original configuration." This should disable COM 2 in *Windows*, although you may have to reset your PC for it to take effect. Of course, you must remember to re-enable COM 2 if you want to use it for any *Windows*-based applications.

Q Scott H. Schau, NØNAB (scotschau@worldnet.att.net), of Prairie Village, Kansas, writes: Is there a way to listen to shortwave broadcasts/live HF ham radio on the Internet? If so, what are the sites?

A Yes, radio can be "broadcast" over the Internet. If you are using a PC with Windows, you already have a "window" onto the world. Open Windows Media Player (this is located at Start/Programs/Accessories/Entertainment). Click on Radio Tuner on the left hand side. Now, depending on the Version of Windows/Media Player, use the Station Finder to locate the type of commercial listening you want—these stations are from all around the world.

For ham radio "broadcast" on the Internet, check out the TIS Internet Ham Radio page: **www.arrl.org/tis/info/ internet.html**

In addition, using your Web browser and a search engine such as Google (**www.google.com/**) you can find more. Some examples:

windowsmedia.com/radiotuner/ default.asp
www.virtualtuner.com/
www.rac.ca/swl.htm

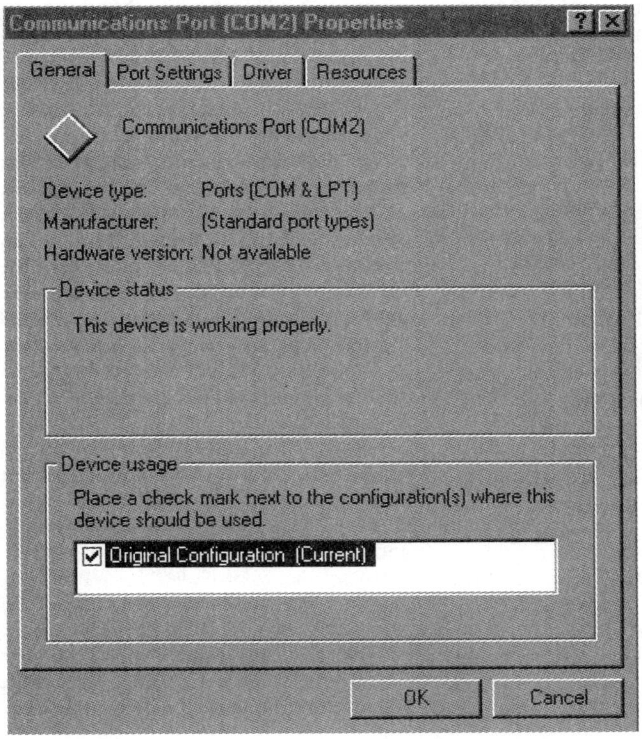

Q I own a Packard Bell SVGA monitor that has been giving me fits. It generates interference that just happens to fall on several of my "favorite" frequencies. I've tried every RFI suppression technique known—short of installing the monitor in a copper cage. Do you have any other tips?

A I'd suggest that you try changing your display settings. Going to a higher or lower resolution display may at least shift the interference away from your favorite frequencies. Frankly, you may want to consider shopping for a new monitor. You may discover that other brands offer better shielding. If you can get your hands on a portable shortwave receiver, take it to the computer stores and use it to check the various monitors. Obviously you want to find the monitor that generates the least amount of interference, if any at all, on the frequencies or bands you use most often.

Q I am running *Windows 98* on my station computer. Is it possible to digitally record small portions of my received audio (say, a minute or less) using my PC's sound card? Do I need special software to do this?

A Yes, you can digitally record your receive audio directly to your hard drive—and you already have the software to do so!

In *Windows*, click on your START button, then click **ACCESSORIES** and **ENTERTAINMENT**. That's where you'll probably find a neat little application called *Sound Recorder*. (*Sound Recorder* is also available on *Windows 95* and *ME*.) If you can connect an audio cable between your transceiver (at the accessory jack or external speaker) and the

Figure 4.5—Once you've reached the COM 2 properties under Device Manager in *Windows* just uncheck the Original Configuration box to disable the port.

line or mike input of your sound card, you should be able to use *Sound Recorder* to grab brief audio files up to about 60 seconds in length. For *Sound Recorder* to work, however, you may need to go into your audio mixer record settings (not the volume controls!) and make sure that the line or mike inputs are enabled. Just be aware that the resulting audio "WAV" files could be quite large. You'd better set aside a folder on your hard drive just for them.

Sound Recorder is nice for brief audio sampling, but you'll find more extensive audio recording capabilities in many of the Amateur Radio logging programs available today. See the advertising pages of *QST*.

Q My current shack PC is a 333-MHz Pentium II with 64 Mbytes of RAM and a 3-Gbyte hard drive. My son wants to run sophisticated gaming software on the computer when I'm not using it, and my wife would like to do a few things on the machine with *PhotoShop*. I'm considering the idea of pulling the motherboard and replacing it with a new 133-MHz bus board and 1 GHz CPU. Is this the most cost-effective approach?

A Motherboard and CPU prices have been plunging lately, but you'll still shell out about $600 for a good-quality 1-GHz motherboard/CPU combo. You can probably save more than $100 by purchasing a 933-MHz package. Believe me, you won't notice the performance differential between 933 MHz and 1 GHz. Clock speed isn't everything!

Here's another motherboard tip: the Intel 440BX motherboard chipset is "old" as far as the PC market is concerned, but I've measured it to be as fast, if not faster, than the newer 815E chipset. Go with a 440BX-chipset motherboard and you'll save a little cash without sacrificing performance.

You might consider expanding your memory to 256 Mbytes to accommodate future needs. Beware of cheap memory, however. You can find 256-Mbyte SDRAM for under $100, but there is memory and there is *memory*. Bargain-basement memory can drop data when you're cycling it at 133 MHz on your new motherboard. Just one dropped bit is enough to corrupt data and possibly trigger the dreaded "blue screen of death." This is the last thing you want to see, say, in the middle of a contest!

Definitely upgrade your hard drive. With drive prices falling through the floor these days, you have no excuse. You can find 30-Gbyte drives for less than $125. Stick with the high-speed (7200 RPM) drives and your programs will load at the speed of thought!

Q Madhu, VU2MUD, writes: I am interested in joining any discussion groups on antenna topics. I am new to the Internet. Can you provide some guidance for me?

A There are several mechanisms for discussion on just about any topic on the Internet. The most popular are probably chat rooms, reflectors and newsgroups. Each has its advantages and disadvantages.

Chat rooms are live discussions with a group of people keyboarding back and forth. All the comments appear on the screen as they are sent. AOL has an easy to use chat room mechanism, as does Microsoft's MSN. The disadvantage is that there is no record of what has gone on before. Most chat rooms are populated by folks who just want live conversation. The subject matter often strays from the posted subject.

Reflectors are e-mail based groups. An e-mail sent to the reflector is automatically sent to all its members. These groups tend to stay on topic and some very good information is exchanged. Another advantage is that (as opposed to chat rooms, where everything is "on-the-fly" whizzing by as fast as people can keyboard) you have the luxury of being able to digest a message and formulate a response or addition if you are so inclined. The down side is that your e-mail In-box can be filled with messages almost every day. Most e-mail programs contain filtering protocols that allow you to have e-mail from the reflector automatically go to a separate folder in your In-box. This makes your regular e-mail easier to manage. **mailman.qth.net/** is a place to look for active reflectors. A drop-down alphabetical list contains many reflectors, including those covering Antennas.

Newsgroups can be compared to the bulletin board at work or school. They are also divided into special interests on almost every topic on (or off) the planet. It is very simple to "subscribe" to a newsgroup. The advantage over the reflector is that nothing is sent to your computer. Subscribing means only that of all the thousands of newsgroups (there are upward of 45,000) only the ones you "subscribe" to will appear on your newsreader when you open it. Most e-mail programs have a newsreader included.

You access a newsgroup of choice and see a list of messages posted by Subject, Date, Sender, etc. Clicking on the subject line will open the individual message for reading (much like reading e-mail). Individuals can post a reply to a message, thereby creating a "thread," or you may post new messages. Newsgroups are an excellent resource for obtaining "how-to" information because they have the widest audience. Instruction on accessing newsgroups is best

obtained by contacting the Tech Support for your ISP (the company that provides your access to the internet; if you are in a university or a corporation, contact your network administrator).

The newsgroup for antenna discussions is **rec.radio.amateur.antenna**.

A word of caution: You're likely to find language that can best be described as "no holds barred." Those who post messages to newsgroups often express strong opinions.

Q Richard Klinman, W3RJ, from Coopersburg, Pennsylvania writes: Is the *ARRL Radio Designer* manual and software still available? I own the original 1994 version and would like to know if there is an updated version that will run on Windows 2000 Professional (Windows NT-5)? I can't find the software in the on-line catalogue.

A The *ARRL Radio Designer* software was dropped about two years ago when a free program with more capabilities became available. *Radio Designer* can't be updated to a new operating system because the source code is no longer available. The *Radio Designer* software was created for the ARRL by Compact Software, owned by Ulrich Rohde, KA2WEU. Ulrich subsequently sold the company to Ansoft Corporation, which introduced a new package called *Serenade. Serenade SV* is a free, downloadable, limited version of their commercially distributed *Serenade 8.5*. The 20 MB *Serenade SV* program, which runs under Windows 95/98/Me/NT4/2000, is available for download on their Web site (**www.ansoft.com/**). *Serenade* is a very capable superset of *Radio Designer*.

Q Edward Jones Jr, WB2DVL, of Highland Park, New Jersey, writes: An article in *Consumer Reports* magazine indicates that computers can be harmed by "hackers" and computer viruses. If state-of-the-art transceivers are computer-controlled, can the transceivers also be harmed by "hackers" or computer viruses?

A Computer viruses today are transmitted in primarily two ways—installing it from an infected disk, or via the Internet/LAN/e-mail. If you do not use the Internet or your computer is not connected to a wired or wireless network, and you only load disks from reputable software dealers in your computer, it's not very likely that you will be affected by a virus.

An important consideration is that most viruses are written to perform a specific function on a specific microprocessor-operating system—application combination. A standard computer virus designed to infect, say, Microsoft Word on a Windows PC, even if you could get it into your radio somehow, would have no place to go and nothing familiar to attack. It's virtually impossible for a computer virus to do anything to your standalone radio.

It is possible, but highly unlikely that someone could write a virus that would enter your computer via the Internet or infected disk, that would attach itself to your radio controlling/logging software and then find its way into the radio. But hackers are interested in causing the most visible and widespread damage possible. Introducing a virus that will attack the millions upon millions of common Pentium PCs on the planet is a lot more fun than one to attack the few hundred Yaesu FT-1000MP MARK-Vs that might be connected to a PC that in turn might be connected to the Internet. When it comes to viruses and ham radios, you have very little to worry about—much, much less than a direct lightning strike.

Q I operate slow-scan TV (SSTV) using sound card software. Last week I upgraded my PC to the *Windows ME* operating system and now my SSTV software is acting up. According to what I see on the display, I am grossly overdriving the sound card input. Reducing the LINE INPUT volume control on the sound card mixer helps, but I have to practically take the level to zero (and it is very touchy). Is this a problem with *Windows ME*?

A In an indirect way, yes. If you did a full installation of *Windows ME* (not just an upgrade), chances are it loaded a Microsoft sound card driver automatically. Depending on the type of sound card you own, the Microsoft driver can cause some strange behavior. If you still have your original sound card software, I suggest that you reinstall the original drivers. If not, go to the Web site of the company that made your sound card and download the drivers from there.

Q Jack Ward, K9ZQJ, writes: The cheapest "dime store" watch would keep better time than the clock in any computer I have ever owned. I just purchased another computer, better-than-ever model, but it too gains

about 3 minutes a month. Is there any way to adjust the computer clock so it will keep accurate time?

A There probably never will be an accurate on-board computer clock and there is no "faster" or "slower" adjustment. But there is a painless way to correct the time as often as you wish. There is a free program called *NistTime* available at: **www.freedownloadscenter.com/ Business/Time_and_Clock_Tools/ NistTime.html**.

NistTime sets your system time to the atomic clock in Boulder, Colorado via the Internet. No setup is required and it uses your registry settings for time zone information. It runs in the background and takes only a few seconds to complete its task and works well using the *Windows* scheduler. In *Windows 98*, the scheduler's icon (a little calendar and clock) is at the right of the task bar near the clock—setting the scheduler is simple and very intuitive.

If you use a cable modem or DSL and are therefore connected at all times, and you leave your computer on, you can set your scheduler to update the clock nightly while you sleep. If you turn your computer off when not in use, you can simply put *NistTime* in your StartUp folder so it will update when you turn on your computer.

If you use a dial-up modem, you can place the icon on your desktop and when you connect, just give the icon a click and it's done, in the background, without distracting you from your task.

I have been using *NistTime* under all the above conditions for several years and it really works!

Q Arnie, N1SZS, asks, "I would like to run my TNC and ICOM IC-737 transceiver simultaneously utilizing software that controls both devices. How do I configure my computer's two serial ports using *Windows 98*?"

A From the *Windows* START button, select **Settings**, then **Control Panel**, then double-click on **System**. Select the **Device Manager** tab, then click (once) on the "+" next to the Port item. You should see lines for both COM1 and COM2. Click on COM2, then click the **Properties** button. Next, click the **Resources** tab. If you need to change the settings shown, you will have to click on the "Use automatic settings" box to clear

the check mark. Next, select the "Interrupt Request" line or "Input/Output Range" line and click the "Change Settings" button to change the setting to whatever you need it to be.

Q Peter Jacqueline, WH6BDO, writes: Where can I obtain a satellite tracking program that will run on my Casio Cassiopeia Pocket PC, Model E-125. This unit runs Windows CE Version 3.0.9348 with a MIPS VR4122 processor. I've already found a program called *pTrack* but have been unable to get it to run—I believe it was developed for an earlier model.

A You may want to try *TrackSat/ CE* by ZL3TPL. You'll find it on the Web at **www.qsl.net/zl3ad/tracksat. htm**. If this doesn't do the job, join the AMSAT e-mail reflector and post a message asking if other programs are available. You can join the reflector at the AMSAT site at **www.amsat.org**.

Q David L. Muse, KD4FEB, writes: I have an older computer that I would like to use for HF digital communication like PSK31. The computer is an IBM with a 133 MHz processor. I am having trouble with it shutting down on its own while it is running. It used to momentarily shut down and then reboot by itself. I changed the hard drive in hope of fixing this problem but now it just shuts down by itself like it's turned off. Would changing the processor in it fix this problem?

A Phantom shutdown can be caused by several things-the hard drive and CPU being near the bottom of the list. If you are running *Windows*, try a format of the hard drive and reinstallation of *Windows* (this you may already have done when you replaced the HD).

Look for a thermal problem-the fan on your CPU has failed or your power supply fan has failed or insufficient ventilation around your computer. Overheating will cause the computer to shut down as a self-protection scheme.

Determine that your computer is not loaded with more cards and drives, etc. than your power supply can handle. Some older computers came with a 150-200 W PS that may not be adequate if you have added several components.

CHAPTER 5

Troubleshooting

PC BOARD VIEWS

◊ When troubleshooting electronic equipment, we are fortunate to have the service manual. These manuals often have pictorial layouts of the circuit boards, complete with component designations and the printed wiring pattern. Usually, these images are the view from the component side.

Sometimes, only the opposite side is accessible. While probing the circuit board, one must form a mental mirror image of the component side to find the appropriate points. Recently, while troubleshooting a transceiver under these conditions, I decided to use my computer to ease the task. I scanned the service manual picture, then flipped the image electronically and printed it. Presto! The resulting image matched the pattern on the solder connection side. Probing was now much easier. Of course the component designations were now backwards, but that was a small price to pay.—*Gene Pentecost, W4IMT, 2017 Cedarmont Dr, Franklin, TN 37067-4019;* **gene. pentecost@ieee.org**

HUM CURED

◊ Thanks to W4HET for his suggestion in the March 2002 Hints and Kinks column about the hum problem in the IC-707. It brought to mind the hum problem I experienced with an IC-735, a FL32 filter and an Astron RS-35A power supply.

The hum was about 120 Hz, similar to that experienced by W4HET. It was noticeable on voice and serious enough on CW signals to be very annoying. After some analysis, I traced the problem to the proximity of an Astron RS-35A, which sat on the desk to the immediate right of the IC-735. Moving the Astron to a different position on the desk solved the problem. As far as I can determine, there are no problems with either the IC-735 or the Astron; they just work better when they are separated by several inches.—*Harlow Beene, W5ZSL, PO Box 348, Glorieta, NM 87535;* **w5zsl@ arrl.net**

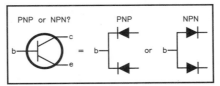

Figure 5.1—A bipolar transistor appears to an ohmmeter as a pair of diodes.

DETERMINING TRANSISTOR AND DIODE LEADS WITH AN OHMMETER

◊ This old technique bears repeating: Garden-variety bipolar transistors act like diodes when connected to an ohmmeter, and most modern multimeters have a diode-check function. The diode-check function typically applies a small, current limited voltage to the probes. By repeated tests, you can find which transistor lead is common. (See **Figure 5.1**.) This is the base lead. If the meter's positive lead is on the base, the transistor is NPN; if the negative lead is on the base, its PNP. This check can usually be made without unsoldering the transistor from the PC board. A transistor that passes this test is usually good—but not always. —*Bert Kelley, AA4FB, 2307 S Clark Ave, Tampa, FL 33629-5707;* **aa4fb@ mindspring.com**

FINDING A BREAK IN MULTICONDUCTOR CABLE

◊ Sometimes there is a break in a conductor of a multiconductor cable. Such breaks are usually near one of the cable ends. Here is how to locate the break without disassembling the plugs at both ends: First, disconnect the cable and determine which conductor is broken with an ohmmeter. Use a capacitance meter to determine the capacitance between two of the cable's good conductors. Then measure the capacitance of the broken wire to the same good conductor. The end with very low capacitance has the break. A break that is not at either end can be approximately located by measuring the capacitance from each end. Divide the capacitance from one end by the total capacitance and multiply the result by the cable length. This gives the approximate distance from that end to the break (see **Figure 5.2**).—*Bert Kelley, AA4FB, 2307 S Clark Ave, Tampa, FL 33629-5707;* **aa4fb@mindspring.com**

CURE A COMMON HP COUNTER PROBLEM

◊ I purchased a used Hewlett Packard 5334B counter with the oven-controlled oscillator option. Unfortunately, its crystal oven was not working. In the process of troubleshooting the problem, I found that this is common in the HP 10811-series of oven-controlled oscillators. The oscillator's oven-temperature control circuit has a thermal fuse that may fail to open, although there is nothing wrong with the circuit.

Complicating the problem, the HP (Agilent) parts department was unable to

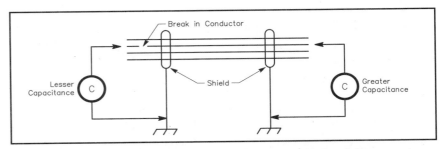

Figure 5.2—AA4FB's setup to estimate the location of a cable break by measuring capacitance between conductors.

find the part number of the fuse. After I found a replacement on my own, they determined that the original 108°C unit had been updated to 115°C. The new part is HP #10811-80008. The price was $10.50 plus tax. I plugged it into my counter's oscillator, and it has been working perfectly for over two months.

Before I obtained the correct part, I experimented with makeshift fuses. NTE Electronics has an NTE8115 "Thermal Cut-Off," rated at 117°C. RadioShack has a #270-1322A thermal fuse rated at 128°C. Both of these are physically larger than the original, and their leads are too thick to plug into the oscillator's fuse socket. To mount them, I extended the fuse leads with some cut from a resistor. Heat sink the fuse leads before soldering to prevent the soldering process from ruining the fuse. The assembly is a tight fit that required some insulating tape, but I was able to fit the larger fuse in place of the original.—*Fred McKenzie, K4DII, 2867 Epp Bivings Dr, Titusville, FL 32796;* **fmmck@aol.com**

The Doctor is IN

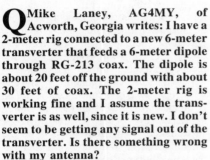

Q Mike Laney, AG4MY, of Acworth, Georgia writes: I have a 2-meter rig connected to a new 6-meter transverter that feeds a 6-meter dipole through RG-213 coax. The dipole is about 20 feet off the ground with about 30 feet of coax. The 2-meter rig is working fine and I assume the transverter is as well, since it is new. I don't seem to be getting any signal out of the transverter. Is there something wrong with my antenna?

A There are several possibilities. You may not be switching the transverter between receive and transmit properly. Some transverters require a connection to the PTT (push to talk) line. Some need an external relay to perform antenna switching. Improper adjustment of transmit power level can also keep a transverter from working. Too much power from the 2-meter radio can actually damage the transverter while not enough results in a weak output.

Check your antenna wiring to be sure one half of the dipole is connected to the coax center conductor and the other half to the shield with no connection between them. Have you checked the SWR with a wattmeter or SWR bridge? Use an ohmmeter to be sure the coax is not shorted. If all seems to be working well, remember that 6 meters is an unpredictable band—you can listen for some time without hearing anything in some parts of the country. Try a QSO on a local FM repeater or calling frequency to check your equipment. The following Web page lists the band plans for all amateur bands: **www.arrl.org/FandES/field/regulations/bandplan.html**.

Q Frank, NI9W, asks, "Is there a simple way to measure the resistive product of a matched antenna? In other words, if the X_L and X_C components cancel, the antenna is resonant, but how about the resistive component to insure that there is a proper, in most cases 50-Ω, resistance?"

A One of the more accurate ways to measure both the resistive and reactive components of an antenna is to use one of the antenna-impedance analyzers. Several companies advertise these in *QST* magazine.

If you know an antenna is resonant, you can use an SWR meter to get an indication of the resistive component. If there is no reactance and the SWR is 2:1, then the resistive component of the antenna would be either 25 Ω, or 100 Ω if the measurement equipment is calibrated for 50 Ω. In the real world, things aren't usually this clean—the point of best SWR may contain some reactance. What really counts, though, is that the SWR on the feedline is low enough that it isn't too lossy (usually about 5:1 for coax is okay, depending on the coax type and length) and that the transmitter sees a reasonable load. Most rigs today will operate into a 1.5:1 to 2:1 load, although some fold back power at SWRs greater than 1.5:1.

Q I have a 10-year-old Realistic 13-inch color TV that I use with my ATV station. Recently the TV went completely dead. It won't turn on when I press the ON button on the front panel, or when I try to turn it on from the remote. I checked the power supply fuse and it is okay. The power supply appears to be working as well. Any ideas?

A Many TVs operate in what you might call a "sleep" mode. That is, there are circuits within the TV that are active continuously—even when the rest of the TV is off. Usually the primary micro-processor is always active, waiting for the command to switch on the rest of the set. If the microprocessor isn't responding to manual or remote "on" commands, the microprocessor could be defective. If you have a volt-ohm meter and a schematic diagram, measure the voltage at the V_{cc} pin of the microprocessor. Is it receiving power from the power supply (probably 5 V)? If so, find the microprocessor pin that produces the output signal to turn on the rest of the TV. Do you get a reading at this pin when you press the TV's "ON" button? If not (and I suspect you won't), the microprocessor is probably dead. On the other hand, if you do get a reading, it's time to troubleshoot the rest of the circuit that is responsible for switching on the set. This is likely to include a couple of switching transistors and possibly an optoisolator.

Q Brian Lakner, ABØSD, of Exline, Iowa writes: I have a really good question for you. Once in a while I notice that the 2 meter band has much less noise on it than is normal. I turn the preamp on, and still do not hear a difference. The effect is across the entire SSB subband. It is as if there is an AM carrier, as I spoke with another ham during this phenomenon and could barely hear him. Is this a weather affect, as a large front is passing through, or is it something else?

A It sounds like there is a very powerful signal near the 2-meter amateur band that is densensing your receiver. This often occurs with RF preamplifiers—a powerful near-band signal saturates the preamplifier, leaving less gain for the signals you want to hear.

Q Bob, N7PTM, writes: I have an ICOM IC-706 in my van. It is connected directly to the battery. If I start scanning the memory channels before I start the engine, the scanning stops when I start the engine. I think the radio briefly shuts down when the engine is being cranked. Why is this happening when I'm connected directly to the battery (it's not only the 706 that does it; other radios have, too)?

A First, you should turn off all your radio equipment (and anything else possibly plugged into the cigarette lighter, like a GPS unit, portable CD player, etc.) before starting the engine. There are spikes produced by the electrical system at this time that could severely damage your power supply.

The reason your ICOM stops functioning properly is because there is a tremendous voltage drop when the starter motor draws almost all the available current from the battery to turn the engine. Since the resulting voltage is below the minimum required by the radio, it momentarily stops functioning. Remember, when your radio is connected directly to the battery, it is in parallel with the rest of the car's electrical system.

Q Juan, KB3CJG, asks, "I have a problem with my dual-band (VHF/UHF) mobile FM transceiver, a Yaesu FT-8100. When I install it in my car I cannot transmit. The voltage of my car battery appears to be a bit low (around 12 V, as reported by the rig's built-in voltmeter) and the FT-8100 manual recommends 13.8 V. I have no problem operating at home using a 13.8 V power supply. How can I solve this problem?"

A It sounds like you have a bad battery, voltage regulator or alternator, or a "partial short" (a low resistance that shouldn't be there) in your automotive electrical system.

Take your car to a mechanic and have your battery system checked with your rig disconnected. If there is a problem, such as the battery not holding a charge, or a faulty alternator, get it fixed. My guess is that the mechanic will find a problem.

However, if everything is okay, then disconnect the automobile cables from the fully charged battery. Connect your rig to the battery and see if it operates. This will tell you if you have a "partial short" in the car.

If all of the above are good, then make sure that you have a good *direct* connection from your rig to the battery (no substitutes such as the fuse block or cigarette lighter!).

Q Bill Gier, KB0VYG, of Omaha, Nebraska, writes: I have been trying to figure out why I can't seem to make my 2-meter H-T work with any antenna other than the rubber ducky that came with it. The rubber ducky is fine, but when I hook a BNC adapter to receive a PL-259 from a 5/8 wave mag mount mobile antenna, or my 5 el Yagi

on the roof of my house, I get no reception and weak reports from a fellow ham who lives just a few miles away. I know he can hear me because I listen to him responding to my transmission on another 2-meter rig. I do know when I use the H-T on simplex (hardly ever visit the local repeater) when mobile at 5 W, my friend and I can usually maintain contact around the city. I wanted to use my H-T through my 5/8-wave 2-meter mag-mount antenna for better coverage.

A The only possible reason I can think of for this would be that you have some sort of problem with the adapter you are using. When I test radios in the ARRL Lab, I do not use the rubber duck antennas. We use cables with BNC connectors attached (or SMA connectors, if that is what the H-T has).

I will say that the mag mount *must* be used with something large and metal though—if you are using it indoors rather than mounting in on the car, try placing it on top of a stove or other large metal object. Of course, the Yagi should work fine as is.

Q WB6RLP/0 writes: As I recall, in the vacuum tube transceiver days, maximum power was determined during tune-up in the CW mode. I believed that the maximum peak envelope power at full modulation in SSB would be the same as the maximum power obtained during tune-up in the CW mode.

I purchased a 100 W transceiver and a 300 W tuner. It has worked fine for several months. Two weeks ago I purchased a linear amplifier. I assumed I could drive the amplifier to 300 W output in the CW mode for tune-up into the tuner and then switch to SSB. This seemed to work for about a week and then I noticed that if I kept the power at 300 W in CW the SWR would start to rise slowly, then more rapidly, and the meters would peg. This included the plate and grid current meters on the amplifier. I didn't hear arcing in the tuner. I eliminated the bad load as the problem. I called the tuner manufacturer and their technician said on CW you can input only 150 W and that 300 W was the PEP for SSB. He said he thought it was an arcing problem, but didn't know where it was originating.

As I understand the definition of peak envelope power, it is the average power of one RF cycle at the peak of the modulation envelope. If I am fully modulating, why isn't this average power for one cycle the same as the average power of a maximum power CW signal?

A The gradual change in SWR sounds more like an overheating than an arcing problem. Usually if a tuner arcs over, you can hear it and the SWR goes sky high while the arc is occurring. It is possible that continuous power of 300 W CW is causing one of the coils or capacitors in the tuner to overheat, and thus change value.

You are correct: PEP is the average power of a single cycle of RF at the modulation peak. Thus, a 300-W CW signal has a 300-W PEP. But any heating effects in the tuner will be dependent on the average power, with a time period based on the time it takes the overheating component to either change value or reach thermal equilibrium. So, with typical dit/dah ratios, a CW signal has an average-to-peak ratio of about 40%. An SSB signal can range from 10% to 30%.

For more info, see **www.arrl.org/tis/ info/pdf/9505088.pdf**. This *QST* article, "Power: Watts It All About" is from the May 1995 "Lab Notes" column.

Q My Radio Shack HTX-202 displays a "PLL Unlock" error occasionally. I have been fixing it by grasping the transceiver in my right hand and tapping it moderately into the palm of my left hand. Usually this fixes it and the radio works just fine. What causes this error?

A Phase-locked-loop (PLL) oscillators operate with a certain amount of frequency drift, over which the PLL stays within a given range, whereas if it goes outside that range, it will tend to stay outside that range. The term for this is "lock" since within the range a PLL tends to stay "locked in."

On computer-controlled rigs, there is a circuit that senses if the PLL is staying in lock. If the PLL unlocks, an error message can be generated. However, I've only seen this on rigs where the allowed tuning range exceeds the guaranteed range; e.g., a 2-meter rig that includes wideband reception to 900 MHz and the tunable frequency range goes up to 999 MHz, but the manufacturer only guarantees 930 MHz. Then, selecting something above 930 MHz might cause a PLL lock error.

Within the rig's normal operating range, this should not happen unless the PLL IC is defective, or there is a bad connection on the circuit board. Given that a mechanical input puts the PLL back in lock in your rig, I suspect the latter is most likely the case.

Another possibility is that the HTX-202 is out of alignment.

CHAPTER 6

Restoration

RESTORING PLASTIC WINDOWS ON RADIOS AND GEAR

◊ Most of us have purchased or owned gear that has developed those annoying scratches or haze on the plastic display windows. I have discovered an excellent product designed to remove these artifacts and make those windows look like new. It is a complete abrasive/polishing system made by Micro-Surface Finishing Products of Wilton, Iowa. (See **Figure 6.1**.)

The product is called Micro-Mesh; it is a series of special flexible abrasive sheets. These are supplemented by Micro-Gloss liquid polishes for that last bit of smooth flawless shine. Each abrasive sheet has a cloth backing for flexibility and a thin latex material coated with special abrasive crystals. The samples I have consist of nine sheets graduated from 1500 to 12000 grit.

By following the instructions carefully, I have restored several windows and displays on flea-market bargains to a perfectly brilliant transparency. Make no mistake about it, this is a professional product for restoring just about any unpainted plastic. The aerospace industry uses this product to remove scratches and haze from jet canopies, and as an avionics repairman I use it at work to fix

displays on very expensive cockpit instruments. You could use it to restore irreplaceable plastic windows on antique radios, or increase the value of equipment before sale. Clean, scratch-free gear always sells first at the flea markets! To select the product kits that best fit your needs, go to **www.micro-surface.com** or call 1-800-225-3006. It's great for plastic watch crystals, too! —*Tom Sherwood, W8AAZ, 324 Linton Dr, Wilmington, OH 45177;* **tsherwood @in-touch.net**

NEW LIFE FOR THE YAESU FT-200

◊ Since my article about Yaesu FT-101s was published in May 1999, I have been inundated with letters asking for copies of my similar modification for the FT-200 that was published in *Radio ZS* (October 1995). The cost of sending photocopies to the many amateurs who have written is prohibitive, so here is the FT-200 article. (Thanks to *Radio ZS— Ed.*) It shows how to modify the Yaesu FT-200 / Sommerkamp FT-250 / Henry Tempo One, to replace the 6JS6Cs with 6146B output tubes.

Remove the old 6JS6C output tubes and disconnect all wires from the 12-pin tube bases (sockets) taking care not to damage any of the decoupling capacitors,

which are used on the new bases. Remove the two 12-pin bases and using the same screws, install two octal tube bases as shown in **Figure 6.2**. Make sure that the locating keys are pointing in the position as shown. Cut short the orange wire that was used to supply the grid 2 (screen) voltage. This wire is no longer required.

Rewire the octal bases as shown. It may be easier to wire pins 1, 4 and 6 together before installing the bases. Make sure that each of these pins, which are the cathode and grid-3 (suppressor) connections, is decoupled to ground with a 0.01 µF ceramic capacitor, otherwise the output power will be low on 10 meters. Likewise, both screen grids, pin 3, on each socket must be decoupled as well as the heater pins.

The new screen-grid voltage is 250 V. Obtain this by wiring a 100 V, 5 W Zener diode in series with the 350 V line to the screen grids. (In the absence of a suitable Zener diode, use an OB2 neon regulator tube in series as shown in **Figure 6.3**.) We can take the 350 V from the dc supply to the choke feeding the cold end of the 12BY7A anode (plate) tuned circuits.

To change the neutralizing circuit for the lower interelectrode capacitance of the 6146Bs, connect an additional 200-pF 1-kV capacitor across the 200-pF capacitor shown as C40 on the original circuit diagram. C40 is the decoupling capacitor on the cold end of the 12BY7A plate tuned circuits.

In the early 1970s, I diagnosed an inherent fault with all FT-200s, FT-101s and FT-400/560 series: The 100-pF coupling capacitor from the plate of the 12BY7A to the grids of the finals becomes leaky or fails short. This places the full +350 V on the grids of the finals. Unfortunately, this normally occurs in receive mode when the meter is reading S-units and not PA current. This leaky capacitor immediately destroys the output tubes and—in some instances—the plate choke and power transformer. If this capacitor has not yet failed, it will. It is imperative that this capacitor be changed to one rated for at least 1 kV dc. In the absence of a replacement, install a 1000-

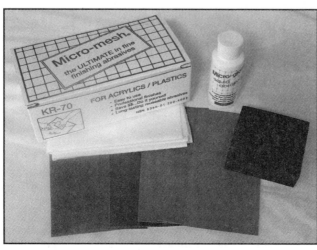

Figure 6.1—Micro-Mesh products for removing scratches.

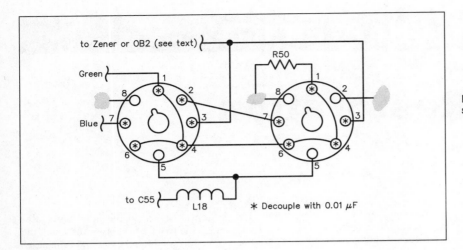

Figure 6.2—A pictorial diagram of the socket wiring for the 6146s.

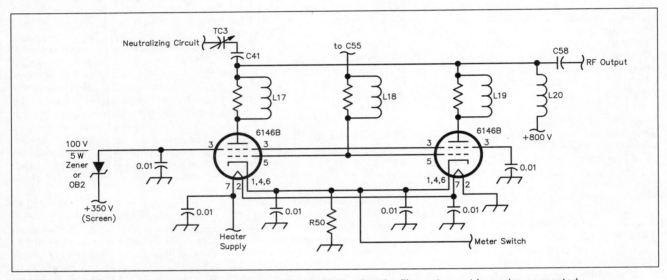

Figure 6.3—Schematic of two 6146 tubes in a Yaesu FT-200. Notice that the filaments must be series connected.

pF 1-kV unit in series with the old 100 pF unit as a dc blocking safety measure.

The final modification is to the power supply. Open the Yaesu power supply to expose the PC board with the high-voltage rectifiers on it. Once you have removed the four silicon rectifiers and the parallel resistors, you will see that the PC board is marked and drilled to take eight diodes and resistors. Fit eight 1N4007 diodes with eight 470 kΩ, 1/4 W resistors and then move the tap on the transformer from the 460-V position to the 600-V tap. (Modern diodes are sufficiently consistent that equalizing resistors are no longer needed or recommended.—*Ed.*) This will give a high voltage of 850 V.

When you are ready to test and align the set, switch on the transceiver and set its mode to SSB, meter switch to plate current and mike gain at zero. As soon as the rig is warmed up, key the microphone and quickly set the plate idle current to 50 mA using the bias control on the rear panel. Align the transceiver and neutral-ize the final amplifier stage in accordance with the original manual. RF output should exceed 100 W on all bands if modified and aligned correctly.

Should you attempt the modification with older 6146 tubes, you may find that the holes in the main upper chassis are too small to pass the tube bases. To make them fit, use a file to carefully remove the excess phenol from around the base of the 6146s until they pass through the holes. Older 6146 tubes work identically to those (6146Bs) with higher plate dissipation ratings in the FT-200. They yield a full 100-W output on all bands.

The modified set runs much cooler than with the original tubes, which were never designed for HF use.

Since publishing the original article, I have modified many FT-200s and have heard of many other amateurs who have undertaken the task with perfect results. This modification will give a new lease on life to the FT-200, which can still hold its own against many modern HF transceivers.—*Roger Davis, ZS1J, Whitewebbe Farm, PO Box 1660, Plettenberg Bay, 6600, South Africa*

GE MASTER-II REPEATER MODIFICATIONS

◊ Commercial crystal-driven FM radio equipment is proliferating at flea markets with attractive prices. GE Master-II mobile radios are available, not because they're inferior or lack performance, but due to the incessant desire for more channel capacity. In the 1950s, a two-channel radio was thought to be all the radio anyone would want; today 64 channels are not enough.

The Master II radio is user friendly, reliable and simple to service. To convert a mobile (with its original control head and accessory cables) into a repeater is simple and easy as this article shows. All one need add is a duplexer, a time-out timer board and a controller board if "bells and whistles" are required. A few

Table 6.1
GE Master II Frequency Ranges

Model # Digits 8 and 9	Frequency Range (MHz)	Model # Digits 8 and 9	Frequency Range (MHz)
12	25-30	66	150-174
33	42-50	77	406-420
56	138-150	88	450-470

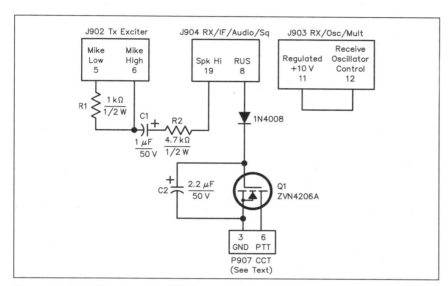

Figure 6.4—Modifications to a GE Master II land-mobile two-way radio for use as a repeater. In addition, two jumpers must be cut as described in the text. Unless otherwise specified, use 5%-tolerance carbon composition or film resistors. Equivalent parts may be substituted.

changes make the radio into a repeater with good audio and a dropout delay using very few components.

Table 6.1 explains the frequency ranges coded into digits eight and nine of the model number. If the radio frequency range suits your application, no tuning is necessary. If you need to shift the operating frequency range, there are several conversion articles on the Web.

First, obtain a service manual for the version of radio you have. You can find one at two-way service shops; GE radios are now serviced by Ericsson Inc, Private Radio Systems. A manual speeds up the conversion and is necessary to find the jumper connections (GE prefixes them with "H") on the systems board. Locate and cut the jumper between H95 and H96; this eliminates receiver muting when transmitting. Cut another jumper between H79 and H80 on the same board to isolate the receiver-oscillator control from the switched +10 V receiver power. Now install a jumper between pin 11 and 12 on J903 of the same board. This jumper keeps the receiver channel-element energized all the time, thus keeping the receiver operating while the transmitter is on the air.

The second modification phase is to route the received audio to the transmitter. Do so by installing a 1 μF capacitor in series with a 4.7 kΩ resistor from pin 19 of J904 on the receiver board (received audio) to pin 6 of J902 (microphone audio). In addition, install a 1 kΩ resistor between pins 5 and 6 of J902 to stabilize and improve the transmitter audio characteristics.

Next, we need to make the receiver key the transmitter when it hears a signal. This is accomplished by installing a diode, MOSFET and capacitor from pin 8 of J904 (see **Figure 6.4**) to pins 3 and 6 of P907, the connector to which a carrier-control timer board (CCT) mates. This CCT board is a factory timer that can be set to end transmissions after a fixed period. Suitable used boards are #19B226617G1 or #19C320134G1. Make the connections close to the systems board so that the CCT board can inserted without any obstructions. The capacitor and diode in conjunction with the MOSFET produce a transmitter dropout delay (hang time) of a few seconds. The length of this delay can be altered slightly by changing the value of the capacitor. If you substitute an LED for the diode, it serves as an on-board trans-

mit indicator.

The mobile radio control-head volume control adjusts the audio level going into the transmitter. Set this control so that the average deviation of the transmitter is high and set the deviation control so that the deviation does not exceed 5 kHz. If the speaker volume is too great, install a padder at the speaker to reduce it.

If your repeater will have a lot of users or long-winded operators, reduce the transmitter power output setting, which is controlled by a power control on the transmitter PA board. This will reduce chances of the PA overheating—these mobiles were not designed for continuous duty. A fan to cool the PA would also be helpful. This modification works well for me and the audio sounds great.

To go on the air, add an antenna duplexer and identifier circuit. Connect the duplexer transmitter port to the UHF connector on the radio front panel and the receiver port to J1 (phono jack) on the receiver RF/Mixer assembly. You can use a different controller to make the radio into a repeater, but the cost of the modification described here is easily less than $10. Have you seen a controller lately for this price?—*William Plante, K1PPN, 2 Debra St, Farmingdale, ME 04344;* **billplante@hotmail.com**

USE THE CRYSTAL CALIBRATOR TO ADJUST DRAKE R-4C OSCILLATORS

◊ The crystal-oscillator and BFO frequencies of an R-4C receiver can be adjusted without any test equipment. This method, which uses the 25-kHz crystal calibrator, is actually simpler than those that use test equipment.

Tune the receiver to the 28.0-MHz band. With the **MODE** switch in the **SSB** position and the calibrator on, tune the receiver to 28.225 MHz. Adjust C59 for a zero-beat note. This works because 28.225 MHz is the fifth harmonic of the 5.645-MHz crystal frequency.

Similarly, with the **MODE** switch in the **AM** position and the calibrator on, tune the receiver to 27.975 MHz and adjust C60 for a zero-beat note. The VFO should to tune to 27.975 MHz although it is outside the band.

To adjust the 50-kHz BFO, connect a 0.1 mF capacitor between pin 2 of V4 and the antenna input connector. Detune the preselector for minimum noise and adjust T11 for a zero-beat note. See the instruction manual for the locations of C59, C60 and T11.—*William J. Robertson, W9WJR, 11408 Brantford Ct, Fort Wayne, IN 46814;* **W.J.Robertson @worldnet.att.net**

Q John, W1CPW, writes: Can you give me some clues on how to fix my Johnson Viking Kilowatt Matchbox? It's a super tuner, but a problem has me baffled.

After turning on my amp (Heathkit SB-200) on 80 meters one night I heard some buzzing and figured there was some shorting. Before I shut it down I checked the SWR and it was quite high (don't recall the exact value, but well above the usual near 1:1 for my ladder line fed dipole). I guessed that I could later open it up (not an easy task) and find the traces of arcing. Once open, there were no arcing traces! I removed the coil and switch, cleaned the contacts and tightened the tension on the switch contacts (the pressure plate with fingers was moved closer to the stationary contacts). All paths were dc/ohmmeter checked for continuity. The SWR was checked with an MFJ analyzer and the SWR could not be brought within acceptable operating range.

I removed the feedthru insulators and cleaned them and the insulating washers, which seemed to have some corrosion on them. No luck. I bypassed the insulators. Still no luck.

With the help of a friend, I removed each of the capacitors in succession and cleaned them, checked the slip rings and contacts to the rotors and reinstalled them. The only change was that the SWR for all frequencies is at infinity on the analyzer or above, although changing the cap setting does change the resistance and slightly increases the SWR.

Finally we bypassed the input SO-239 with a new one, and still the same result.

It seems to be such a simple arrangement of robust hardware that any problem should be very obvious, but I can't seem to find it.

A It looks like the problem was never with your tuner, but the antenna. Remember that the tuner does nothing but match the impedance at the near end of the transmission line to that of the transmitter final output circuit—it does *not* tune the antenna or the transmission line—any SWR present there is still there! It seems that for a period of time, due to water or some other circumstance, the impedance at the near end of the transmission line exceeded that which the Johnson could handle and it did in-

deed arc. You instantly shut down the system, thereby preventing any damage and in fact preventing any evidence of arcing. If this happens again, check the antenna system for breaks or shorts, or perhaps the wind moved the ladder-line close to metal objects.

Q W. J. Stanley, W4RDG, asks, "My friends and I have been trying to apply crackle-finish paint to aluminum and steel panels, but with unsatisfactory results. Do you know of any method for producing a high-quality crackle-paint finish that does not require the use of expensive equipment?"

A Getting a good crackle finish is a two-step process with an interesting twist:

(1) Spray metal with a thin coating of zinc chromate primer. Apply the yellowish primer in an almost transparent layer and allow it to dry for at least an hour.

(2) Buy or borrow an infrared heat lamp for the next step. Spray on the crackle-finish paint, following the instructions on the can. Position the lamp about 2 feet from the painted surface and apply heat for 2 to 3 minutes. The paint should start to crinkle right before your eyes. Be careful not to overheat the metal, though.

This technique takes some practice to perfect. I'd suggest that you experiment on metal scraps until you get the hang of it.

Q My friend and I picked up an ancient General Electric "Prog" line FM mobile transceiver that we are going to convert to 2 meters and use as a base rig. Although the radio apparently operates on 12 V, it is full of vacuum tubes. I assume that it must convert the 12 V to higher voltages in some fashion, but that would involve changing the 12 V dc to ac before it could be stepped up by a transformer. We don't have a schematic diagram yet, so I am mystified about how the transceiver manages this trick. Can you enlighten us?

A The GE rigs, and quite a few other mobile radios of that era, relied on ingenious devices called *vibrators*. A vibrator is essentially an electromechanical switch. The switch opens and closes many times per second, making and breaking the 12-V dc line. By doing so,

the vibrator creates pulsating dc with a voltage that rises and falls rapidly. This isn't ac, but it is close enough to be fed to the primary winding of a transformer. The transformer responds to the pulsating dc just as it does with ac. As the dc voltage rises and falls, alternately expanding and collapsing electromagnetic fields form around the primary and induce higher voltages in the secondary windings, depending on the winding ratio, of course. Just pass the pulsating secondary voltage through a rectifier and filter and you have (drum roll, please) high-voltage dc for your vacuum tubes.

Vibrators tended to wear out (they also made quite a racket!), so they were designed to be easily replaceable. Look for a metal cylinder a few inches high and about an inch across. You'll probably find that you can easily remove the vibrator from its chassis socket. The trick is finding a replacement if you need one. Fortunately, you can find so-called "solid state vibrators" (the switching is done with transistors) at Antique Electronic Supply on the Web at: **www.tubesandmore.com/**.

Q I bought (at an on-line auction) a receiver built in the '60s. When it arrived it reeked of cigarette smoke. I tried to clean the radio, going as far as using gasoline to scrub the chassis. That didn't work. How can I get rid of the cigarette residue?

A That can be a tough nut to crack. Here's what I did about 10 years ago with two Yaesu units of 1980 vintage—hybrid units with plug-in boards—that I had acquired for my collection.

First I disassembled the units as much as I could. I removed all cabinet panels. I removed all the knobs from the front panel and removed all the tubes (driver and final tubes). I then removed all the plug-in/screw-down modules/boards. No wiring was disturbed.

The cabinet sheet metal, the knobs and the tubes were washed in the kitchen sink. I placed them in a plastic tub filled with Fantastic, 409 or a similar strong household product and individually scrubbed with a discarded toothbrush. The components were rinsed, dried with paper towels and set aside. I found that the smell and grunge on these parts were completely gone. Now for the guts of the radio.

From my experience in electronic manufacturing I knew I wanted a good cleaning solvent that would leave no residue. At a local electronics parts distributor I found a product in spray-can form called Freon TF Cleaning Solvent. It was somewhat expensive, about $10 per can as I remember, but I was cleaning a $400 vintage investment so I didn't mind. Although it came in a fairly large can (a little larger than your average spray paint size), I figured I would need more than one can to do the job—I ended up needing about 1½ cans per radio. I stress that whatever you use must leave absolutely *no* residue.

Working in a well-ventilated area (I worked in the garage with the door open and a cross draft to the garage door), I took each PC board, held it vertically, and sprayed it with copious amounts of the product until it was freely running and dripping off the board. Quickly, before it evaporated, I scrubbed it using the toothbrush—which was now thoroughly dry from the previous use (absolutely no water). I did this 2 or 3 times for each board. I propped up the boards on a dry surface and directed a fan at them (the component side) to make sure all nooks and crannies were perfectly dry.

Next came the chassis. I performed the same procedure as with the boards, making sure to get all corners. It's best to do this operation with the surfaces vertical so that the solvent drips off the chassis. I worked on one area at a time, starting at the top and working toward the bottom (both sides of the chassis—transformers, too). Again, I scrubbed with the toothbrush while it was still wet (this stuff evaporates in seconds). When done, I placed the chassis in front of a fan for several hours to make sure it was completely dry.

When everything was thoroughly dry, I placed the chassis and the boards in a cardboard box with some crumpled newspaper and several dryer sheets, closed the box and left it for about a week. The rig came out smelling like a proverbial rose!

You might contact the solvent manufacturer, which is still in business, for information on current, environmentally safe, products. I saw a product on their Web page called Safezone that might be "green," yet suitable.

Contact:
Miller-Stephenson
George Washington Hwy
Danbury, CT 06810
203-743-4447
www.miller-stephenson.com/main. htm

Q Tom, N8EUI, asks, "I recently purchased a used Heath HW-101 and matching HP-23C power supply from a ham friend of mine. Both units are in very good condition and operate like a champ. I purchased an Astatic 10-DA mike with the T-UP9 stand for the rig. The mike connector on the rig uses two pins, but the Astatic mike cable has five wires (yellow, white, blue, red and black) and a bare wire which must be ground. I'm confused. Can you please tell me the proper way to wire the mike to the connector?"

A The Astatic microphone is designed for modern radios. On most modern rigs, the mike connector has 8 pins and on Ten-Tec rigs there are 4 pins. Of course, some of the pins on both connectors are unused, but on the 8-pin connectors, two pins are used for ground—one for a PTT (push to talk) ground and one for the mike shield. In the Ten-Tec connector, a single pin is used for both.

On the old Heath connectors, the shell of the connector is actually the ground. The two pins are for mike audio and PTT. The pin with the 22-kW resistor connected to it (on the back of the connector) is the mike audio pin and the other is PTT.

Although I haven't seen your microphone, I assume it is somewhat similar to the Astatic D-104 from a wiring standpoint. Like the Heath radios, the Astatic mikes are a bit of an oddity. The mike element of a D-104 has separate wires for the high side and the low side (which is not internally grounded) and another wire provides a shield.

Also, in the D-104 the PTT switch is a DPDT affair, much more complex than the simple SPST (normally open) switch that most mikes have. The DPDT PTT switch has a section that is "break before make" and another that is "make before break" (that is to say, the wiper in one section momentarily connects both contacts while transitioning and the other momentarily floats while transitioning). Of course, none of this matters if you want to use the microphone with the Heath rig—it just gives the mike maximum flexibility to be used with all manner of systems (not just radios).

You should be able to get a schematic of the 10-DA from Astatic if you don't already have it. If not, try a Web search on **www.Google.com** for "Astatic 10-DA" and you'll find it there.

From the diagram, you should be able to identify the wires for the mike element, shield and switch sections. On the mike element, you want to connect the low side and shield wires to the ground (shell) of the Heath connector. On the switch, just pick one half, connect the wiper to the same ground and connect the wire for the normally open contact to the Heath pin for PTT.

Q I have a set of Drake Twins, 4C models, that I purchased new in 1977. They have not been used or plugged in since 1986 and I am concerned about electrolytic capacitors drying out and causing all kinds of problems when I try to use them. The local ham radio store says they can bring up the voltage "slowly" and let the capacitors "rebuild themselves." The cost will be a flat $200, not counting parts and labor if necessary. Do you have any suggestions on putting these back in service at a reasonable cost?

A Sure: Do the start-up yourself. Just borrow a variable transformer (Variac and Powerstat are two popular brands) from someone—maybe a member of your local club has one or you can borrow one. The most common ones are about the size of a small lunch box and have a knob at the top with which to vary the voltage.

Remove all the tubes from the rig.

Turn the knob on the autotransformer to zero.

Plug the autotransformer into the wall.

Plug your Drake into the autotransformer.

Turn on the radio.

Very slowly turn the knob on the autotransformer up until you get to 25 V ac.

As you turn, look and listen for smoke or sizzling.

Wait a few minutes.

Increase the voltage to 50 V.

Keep this up until you have full voltage on the radio.

Moderately slowly turn the autotransformer down to minimum.

Turn off the radio, unplug it and replace the tubes.

Perform the procedure again.

If you had no bad "special effects," you just saved yourself a bundle of money.

If you had any components act up, you know what needs to be replaced.

CHAPTER 7

Construction/Maintenance

A HOMEBREW ESD MAT

◊ Most semiconductor devices can be damaged by electrostatic discharge (ESD), but many hams do not take precautions to make their work area ESD-safe. This is probably due to the high price of ESD mats and other equipment.

A cheap ESD mat for almost any size bench top can be made in the following way. Cut a piece of Masonite to the desired size and coat it with a diluted India ink. This ink is available in art-supply stores and uses carbon as its pigment, so it is conductive when dry. I have used Rapidograph 3080-F ink since it is waterproof when dry. Dilute the ink with two parts rubbing alcohol to one part ink to thin it and make it soak into the Masonite more readily. Then spread the diluted ink around the surface of the Masonite with a piece of Scotchbrite, or other non-absorbing material, until the entire surface has an even black coating. Wear rubber gloves and protect your work surface because this ink stains whatever it touches! When dry, the surface of the board should measure between 100 kΩ and 10 MΩ between any two points on its surface.

One $^3/_4$-ounce bottle of ink is about enough to coat two square feet of Masonite when diluted. Since this ink is inexpensive (one or two dollars a bottle), even large mats can be made inexpensively.

Ground the mat at one corner by drilling a hole and securing a solder lug in firm contact with the black surface using a machine screw and nut. Run a wire from the lug to a good dc ground. A connection for a wrist strap can be made in the same way, but a wrist strap should *not* be directly connected to the ground lug, for safety. You don't want a low-resistance path between your body and ground when working with high-voltage equipment! If you don't have a wrist strap, a piece of wire with an alligator clip to connect to a ring or watchband will suffice.

For extra safety, mask a section of the Masonite before applying the ink and use that area to mount the main ground connection and then use a second lug (still on the isolated area) to attach the wrist strap. Then solder a 1-MΩ resistor between the ground and the wrist-strap lugs to make sure that you are isolated from ground. A third lug can be attached to the black area and grounded through a second 1-MΩ resistor, so that you and the mat are isolated from each other, while still providing a high-resistance path to drain off static charges.—*Bill VanRemmen, KA2WFJ, 104 Mitchell Ln, Hamlin, NY 14464;* **billy@frontiernet.net**; **www. frontiernet.net/~billy/**

DECAL LABELS MADE EASY

◊ Labeling home-built equipment has always been a challenge for me. Until now, all of the labels on my equipment *looked* homemade. Here's a technique I've found to remedy that situation.

1. Typewrite or print the labels on paper.

2. Photocopy the labels onto a transparency.

3. Trim the labels from the transparency.

4. Glue the labels to the equipment panel. (Be careful not to smear the letters)

5. Coat the panel and labels with clear spray varnish.

The finished panel has proper letter alignment and spacing, as if professionally printed.—*John Bandy, WØUT, 2810 Euclid, Wichita, KS 67217-1927;* **john. bandy@twsubbs.twsu.edu**

◊ There are more options. Some computer applications can print a mirror image of a document. By doing so, you can print a reversed image onto acetate or photocopy one from paper onto acetate. This places the printing on the rear of the plastic sheet to protect the printing and present a nice, finished appearance.

With a little planning, one could properly position all labels for a panel on a sheet of paper or acetate so that a single smooth plastic sheet would cover the whole panel. To add some color, use a sheet of colored paper or contact paper behind the plastic and affix the whole assembly to the project.

At a local model train show last spring, I saw blank decal paper for sale. It's available from Walthers (**www. walthers.com**) and other suppliers at hobby shops. According to the rec. models.scale FAQ, part 13 (**www. 1250fleets.com/FAQ/rmsfaq.13.htm**), modelers have had a little trouble using ink-jet printers directly on the decal paper, but they've had good results with laser printers and copying onto decal paper at local photocopy shops.—*Bob Schetgen, KU7G*

MORE ON DECAL PANEL LABELS

◊ A discussion of panel-labeling methods appeared in the September 2000 column.[1] Since then, I've received more information about decal paper for ink-jet printers. Here is an edited excerpt from a marketing e-mail on the subject:

At the time, we carried paper that could be used only with a laser printer or run through a color copier. That was then, this is now.

Bel Inc[2] is proud to announce the introduction of our new line of specialty papers specially formulated to be used with your ink-jet printer. This paper along with your printer and software will allow you to create the most spectacular decals you can image and then place them on plastic, metal, ceramic, candles, soap, wood and so on. You can order on-line from our Web page at **www.beldecal. com**. The prices for 8.5×11 sheets are as follows: 25 sheets, $31.25; 50 sheets, $57.50; 75 sheets, $78.75; 100 sheets, $100. Shipping and handling was $5 at the time of publication.—*Bob Schetgen, KU7G, Hints and Kinks Editor*

[1]J. Bandy, WØUT, "Decal Labels Made Easy," *QST*, Sep 2000, p 69.
[2]BEL Inc, 6080 NW 84th Ave, Miami, FL 33166; tel 305-593-0911, fax 305-593-1011; **beldecal@bellsouth.net**;

FIELD REPAIR OF RIBBON CABLE (KENWOOD TH-79A)

◊ A few weeks ago, I turned on my Kenwood TH-79A dual band H-T for a quick QSO. I was immediately greeted by two disturbing symptoms: a short beep and no receive audio. This had happened before, so I immediately knew the cause—the ribbon cable connecting the front and rear PC boards had one or more broken conductors. I also knew that the replacement part would take several days to arrive, so I was temporarily off the air.

I'm active in ARES, so this kind of failure could mean some serious problems, especially on an extended ARES callup. This particular TH-79A is my H-T, mobile and base station—a complete hamshack in one hand; I needed a quick solution.

A field repair turned out to be simple. It didn't restore the radio completely, but it would work well enough to do the job in an emergency. I opened the radio and removed the ribbon cable, which had four broken wires at one edge near the RF board. Peeling the foil from the cable bared the plastic insulation. I trimmed the damaged end to be as square as possible. To make a connector, I placed the cable on the bench (with the other connector facing upward) and shaved about $^1/_8$ inch of insulation from the upper side of the cut end. This exposes the flat conductors in the cable (see **Figure 7.1**). I had to do this twice, but I eventually got a clean square end with all 26 wires exposed.

Next, I inserted the new "connector" into the socket on the RF board. It was a reasonably good fit, but wouldn't stay in the socket or make reliable contact. A shim made from some plastic film and inserted behind the insulated side of the cable, holds the stripped conductors in place against the contacts. I connected the other end at the controller board and reassembled the radio. This took about half an hour, most of that spent shaving down the plastic. The only tool I needed was a trusty Swiss Army knife.

This repair restored all VHF functions, and all UHF functions but the S-meter. I received several encouraging signal reports on local repeaters, and everything worked well enough to trust. I recommend such repairs only in serious emergencies when you absolutely *must* get a radio working.—*Bruce Bostwick, KD5BIV, 9504 Oriole Dr, Austin, TX 78753;* **lihan@ccwf.cc.utexas.edu**

This idea can be used with any ribbon cable. If the conductors are stranded, as in Figure 7.1, be sure that they don't touch each other when inserted into the connector. It's wise to tin the wires or leave a little insulation in place to secure the strands.—KU7G

Figure 7.1—Standard ribbon cable prepared as described by KD5BIV. This is *not* the flat cable from a TH-79A.

CIRCUIT BOARDS FROM CARDBOARD AND COPPER TAPE

◊ Many experimenters have their own favorite means of putting together prototype circuits. "Ugly construction," printed circuit board and solderless breadboards all have their devotees. Here's another method for you to try.[3] It's both simple and cheap—no chemicals, circuit-board material or resist pen is needed. As the cost of each board is close to zero, you can simply throw away boards once you've finished with them.

Cardboard construction is ideal for low-power RF and audio circuits using discrete components only. If done with care, the results are even good enough for a permanent project—handy for those

---

[3]This method was previously described in the author's October 1997 Amateur Radio (WIA) article "Receive SSB on Your Shortwave AM Radio."

---

times when the prototype works so well that you're afraid to pull it apart.

The technique is based on using strips of self-adhesive copper tape stuck to pieces of cardboard (see **Figure 7.2**). This tape is used extensively by stained-glass craftspeople. Available on rolls of 30 meters (≈30 yards) length, the 5-mm ($^3/_{16}$ inch) tape can be cut with ordinary scissors. What makes the tape useful for our purpose, however, is the strong adhesive backing on one side of the copper. This backing can withstand high temperatures, such as applied by a soldering iron.

The cardboard acts as a nonconductive surface on which rectangles of copper foil are placed. Components are soldered directly to the copper: there is no need for holes to be drilled through the insulating material, as is the case with conventional printed circuit boards. Though cardboard from the side of an ordinary cardboard box is satisfactory, any rigid insulator, such as glass, wood or fiberglass could be used instead.

When building a cardboard circuit the first step is to look at the project's schematic diagram and estimate the size of the cardboard required. Then, working from the schematic, plan the position of each piece of copper tape. Cut the tape into rectangles of appropriate size (with a pair of household scissors) and peel off the paper backing. Pressing the tape tightly against cardboard with your index finger should result in a strong bond, able to withstand the heat of a soldering iron.

To form a right-angled bend, place one piece of copper strip over another, with their ends overlapping. For a good connection between the two pieces, solder the overlapping edges together.

Once the board has been completed, the components can be mounted: these are soldered straight to the copper tape. A blob of Blu-Tac adhesive[4] can be used

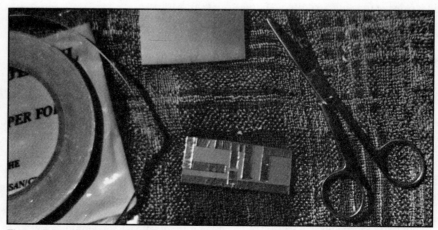

Figure 7.2—A photo of VK1PK's cardboard circuit boards suitable for AF test and experimental circuits.

to attach the cardboard circuit board to the interior of the case housing the project.

Because it is easy to add or remove components, experimentation is far easier than if you used an ordinary printed circuit board. As mentioned before, the cost of assembling circuits is very low, and the technique is ideal for simple school and club projects.

Self-adhesive copper tape is available from craft-supply stores. A 30-meter roll costs around $5. This amount should keep most experimenters going for months, if not years. Other uses for the tape include repairs to printed-circuit boards and window-mounted loop antennas.—*Peter Parker, VK1PK, 7/1 Garran Pl, Garran, ACT 2605, Australia;* **parkerp@pcug.org.au**

[4]Blu-Tac is apparently a tacky putty adhesive common in Australia and Europe. Suitable equivalent products are sold in stationery and department stores for mounting photos and posters.

nected it as a first-order low-pass filter with a gain of four at 500 Hz and a cutoff frequency of 1250 Hz. This reduces display jitter and provides enough control voltage. The time constant from a 100-kΩ potentiometer across a C5 of 22 mF steadies the display change but other values of C5 may be tried.

The average band noise in the receiver audio at first lit the bottom few LEDs all the time. By biasing pin 4 of the LM3914 with +0.3 V dc from a voltage divider across a 5.1-V Zener diode (see **Figure 7.3**) increases the display to a more useful range. In one application, I connected the input of the LED indicator in parallel with the speaker. The receiver volume control is then set for the desired speaker loudness and the pot adjusted to light eight or nine bargraph segments for the average talker.—*Jan K. Moller, K6FM, PO Box 2272, Grants Pass, OR 97528-0295;* **jankuno@internetcds.com**

EASY PROJECT LABELS

◊ I've used Clear Laser Labels by Avery to make panel labels for my projects. This lets me use the graphics capabilities of my laser printer. I use Avery #5664 (3$\frac{1}{3}$ by 4$\frac{1}{4}$ inches, but any size would work.)

Follow the supplied directions for setting up the printer. Only run the labels through the printer once. I've had them peel off the backing and stick in the printer, which is then very difficult to clean. Trim the labels to size while they're still attached to the backing. I recommend a paper cutter for nice straight cuts. Once they're trimmed to size, carefully separate the label from the backing and apply it to the panel. I use a Popsicle stick to burnish the bubbles out, but be careful not to scratch the printing off of the label!—*Dan Hinz, W6LSN, 1738 Manitou Ct, San Jose, CA 95120;* **w6lsn@arrl.net**

AN LED VU-METER

◊ Audio level indicators, like the old needle-pointer VU-meters in broadcast stations, are interesting to watch and useful around the station. The common 10-element LED bargraph makes a handy display. An LM3914 IC display driver will light all 10 LED segments with as little as 1.2 V of dc input.

Surprisingly, the audio voltage to drive 8-Ω speakers to comfortable loudness averages only 0.5 to 0.7 V. It was necessary to add a '741 op amp to get a meaningful presentation range. I con-

Figure 7.4— K6FM's VU-meter is mounted in the box with a CW decoder from an earlier *QST* article (F. Morgantini, IK3OIL, "A PIC16F84-Based CW Decoder," *QST*, Aug 1999 pp 37-39). The driver-gain control is to the right of the display; it's labeled SET. The VU-meter makes it easy to set the audio level for the CW decoder.

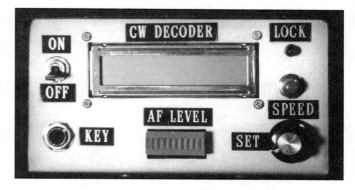

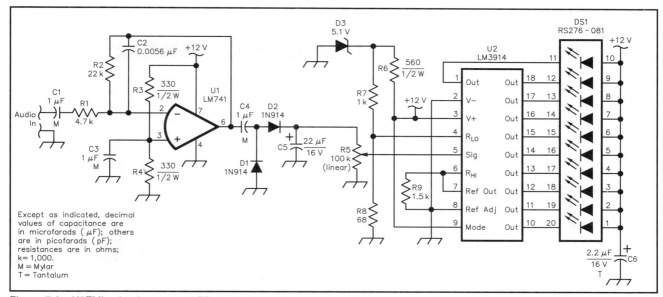

Figure 7.3—K6FM's circuit uses an LED bargraph and driver as a VU-meter.

SATURATING TOROID CORES

[This hint is part of a discussion I had with Mitchell Lee in 1997 about reports of possible balun-core saturation in RTTY applications.—*Ed.*]

◊ About saturating toroidal cores, I ran some numbers on my spreadsheet. I assumed a hypothetical coil of $4 \times 450\ \Omega = 1800\ \Omega$, or 41 µH at 7.05 MHz. A kilowatt across 450 Ω produces 671 V_{RMS}. As you can see in **Table 7.1**, the core loss is a meager 1 to 4 W, or 0.174 dB (4 W). Flux density, even for a bead, is only 150 mT. Considering that powdered iron can take 1 T, this isn't even near saturation. Temperature rise is the real limitation. A reasonable design is a T106-2 with a rise of 30°C. I think this analysis is valid in balun mode, but I'm not so sure about the transformer mode. I don't really know how transformers work.

If people burn up toroids with RTTY, my guess is that they either had too little inductance for the job (my example follows the $X_L = 4 \times RL$ rule), or perhaps the transmission line was not presenting 450 Ω, but rather some reactive load, across which the voltage could be much higher than what a resistive load would predict. The best way to handle that situation is to use a balanced tuner, then go through the balun.—*Mitchell Lee, KB6FPW, 686 N 21st St, San Jose, CA 95112*

Table 7.1—Calculated Core Losses

Core Number	OD (Inches)	Turns	Core Loss (mW)	Flux Density (Bpk, mT)	Temperature Rise (°C)	Series R (Ω)
T12-2	0.13	143.17	3831	149.7	2176.8	28.1
T16-2	0.16	135.51	3255	104.7	1015.4	23.8
T20-2	0.20	128.06	2784	72.8	654.1	20.4
T25-2	0.25	109.81	2887	52.8	451.1	21.2
T30-2	0.31	97.64	2577	36.6	295.3	18.9
T37-2	0.38	101.24	2768	33.1	243.9	20.3
T4-2	0.44	88.79	2547	24.4	173.3	18.7
T44-2A	0.44	106.71	2194	25.1	164.4	16.1
T50-2	0.50	91.47	2453	20.9	133.9	18.0
T60-2	0.60	79.42	2129	14.4	99.1	15.6
T68-2	0.69	84.81	2197	14.1	81.2	16.1
T68-2A	0.69	76.53	1921	11.6	66.3	14.1
T80-2	0.80	86.33	1895	10.7	54.8	13.9
T94-2	0.94	69.86	2050	8.5	43.7	15.0
T106-2	1.06	55.10	1838	5.9	30.0	13.5
T130-2	1.30	61.05	1749	5.0	22.3	12.S
T157-2	1.57	54.11	1690	3.7	15.4	12.4
T175-7	1.75	52.28	1529	3.1	11.8	11.2
T184-2	1.84	41.33	1710	2.8	11.7	12.5
T200-2	2.00	58.45	1482	2.9	10.2	10.9
T200-2B	2.00	43.36	1391	2.1	7.7	10.2
T225-2	2.25	42.68	2901	3.5	15.4	21.3
T300-2	3.04	59.97	1529	2.1	7.4	11.2
T300-2D	3.04	42.40	1245	1.3	4.2	9.1
T400-2	4.00	47.72	1348	1.3	3.5	9.9

L= 41 µH; f = 7.05 MHz; V= 671 V RMS; X_L = 1816.39 Ω;
I = 0.369414 A RMS
Resonating capacitance = 12.42698 pF; 03:48:29 02-12-1997

A COMPRESSION CAPACITOR FOR QRP TRANSMITTERS

◊ My favorite QRP transmitter generates enough power from a single IC to work plenty of 10-meter DX.[5] It, like many QRP circuits, uses a variable crystal oscillator (VXO). This allows operation over most of the 20-kHz region near the bottom end of the band, where the majority of the CW activity occurs.

Most VXO circuits specify a small air-dielectric variable capacitor. Unfortunately, these capacitors are becoming harder to find. When I recently rebuilt my QRP transmitter, I substituted a homebrew compression capacitor. The tuning range and resolution were significantly improved.

Construction is easy; there are no critical dimensions. (See **Figures 7.5 through 7.7.**) The PC-board pattern can be heavily scored with a sharp knife, and the unwanted copper foil can be peeled off after first heating it with a hot soldering iron. All parts except the PC-board material were purchased at my local ACE hardware store. (Choose the small screws and nuts to suit the tee nut available to you; then size the holes in the parts accordingly. Other fasteners such as anchor nuts or threaded

[5]L. Smith, N7KSB, "An Experimental ½-W CW Transmitter," *QST*, Nov 1994, p 84.

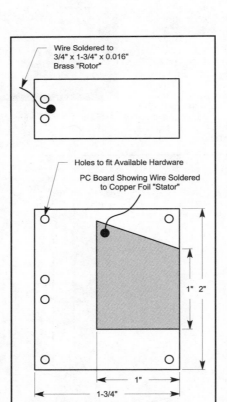

Figure 7.5—Cutting patterns for the circuit board and brass strip that form N7KSB's 4 to 75-pF homebrew compression capacitor.

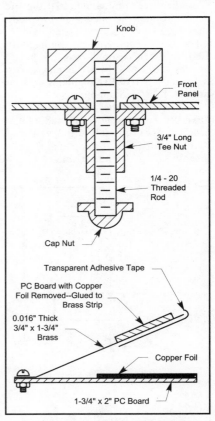

Figure 7.6—Mechanical details of the assembled compression capacitor. The spacers that hold the PC-board assembly approximately 1¼ inches from the front panel are not shown here. They are present in Figure 7.7.

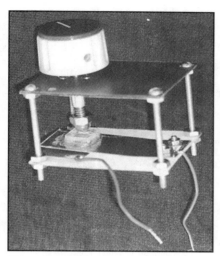

Figure 7.7—A photo of the prototype 2-pF (1×3-inch brass strip) compression capacitor.

inserts may be used in place of the tee nut if they are available to you.—*Ed.*)

I built two compression capacitors. The prototype was a 2-pF device using a 1×3×0.016-inch brass strip. It gave a 19-kHz range (versus a 12.5-kHz range for a conventional air-dielectric variable capacitor) for seven turns. A smaller, 4 to 75-pF, compression capacitor using a ³/₄×1³/₄×0.016-inch brass strip gave a 14.5-kHz tuning range for two turns. When limited to a single turn, the smaller capacitor had an 11.5-kHz tuning range. —*Lew Smith, N7KSB, 4176 N Soldier Trail, Tucson AZ 85749*

REDUCING HISS IN THE LM-386

◊ I know everyone is into direct-conversion receivers and digital VFOs, but there are still many AN602-LM386 low-budget receivers out here.

LM-386s have a bad reputation for hiss. I believe most of the hiss is not produced by the 386, but rather its wide gain bandwidth amplifies any noise from an IF section or 602 mixer stage.

My solution is to make the 386 into an active filter by adding series LC circuit[6] as shown in **Figure 7.8**. I figure the response of this filter peaks at about 800 Hz. My radio is an NW8020,[7] and the parts mount neatly on and beside the 386.—*James Graves, ex WA9RDT, 312 NW 12th St #317, Oklahoma City, OK 73103*

[6]Parts are from Mouser Electronics, 1000 N Main St, Mansfield, TX 76063; tel 800-346-6873, 817-804-3888, fax 817-804-3899; e-mail **sales@mouser.com**; **www.mouser.com**.
[7]EMTECH, 1127 Poindexter Ave W., Bremerton, WA 98312; tel 360-405-6805; **emtech.steadynet.com/qrpdesc.htm**.

FRONT-PANEL LABELS

◊ On a recent trip to the office-supply store, I discovered Avery number 5516 white weatherproof shipping labels and thought that I could turn my "drilling guides" into front-panel labels. (I am sure other label types and colors can be used, but I like the water-resistant feature. Unfortunately, the weatherproof labels are available in limited sizes and come only in white.)

Since the Simple Meter Tester has a simple panel, I used *Word* to make a drilling template, and then did a "Save As," and named the file "front panel." In the new document, I added text that would become the switch labels, and then deleted the guidelines and "holes."

Since the two "documents" are actually the same, the holes should always match the front panel exactly. Use a sharp knife or razor blade to cut the switch and control holes.

Voilá, a very nice, professional-looking cabinet, with legible legends and a very nice price.—*Wayne Yoshida, KH6WZ, 16428 Camino Canada Ln, Huntington Beach, CA 92649*

STARTING SCREWS IN TIGHT PLACES

◊ Often I need to replace a screw that is in between components and not readily accessible. I have a straight-blade screwdriver with a retaining device that works well, but nothing similar to that for use with Phillips screws. Sometimes it is necessary to place a lock washer with the screw, as well.

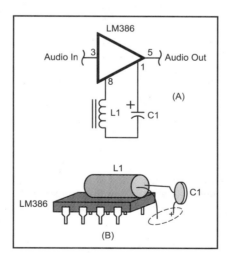

Figure 7.8—A shows the schematic. B shows how he mounted the parts in his NW8020 transceiver. Part numbers in parentheses are for Mouser (see Note 6).
C1—0.47 µF, 35 V electrolytic capacitor (#581-0.47K35V)
L1—82 mH inductor (R = 71 Ω, Q=100, #434-02-823J)

By securing the screw (and lock washer, if needed) to the end of the screwdriver with a small piece of adhesive tape, it's easy to start the screw on the first try. The tape gives a little, which makes a slight misalignment unimportant. After driving the screw, the tape breaks and comes away with the screwdriver. The same trick works with slotted screws and nuts on panels and in nutdrivers.—*Hugh Inness-Brown, WZ1B, 5351 State Hwy 37, Ogdensburg, NY 13669*

FINDING SMALL PARTS

◊ Lloyd G. Hanson, W9YCB, offered some good tips on finding small parts that have fallen to the floor ("Hints and Kinks," Aug 1999). My own solution is not to let the parts get that far. I added a very thin drawer to the knee opening in my workbench. It's an open wooden frame only ³/₄-inch thick, about 14 inches deep and the width of the knee opening. I stapled white cloth very loosely to the bottom of the frame. The cloth should sag about an inch in the center so it can't act as a trampoline. When I'm working with tiny things, I pull the drawer out over my lap to catch whatever I drop. This idea isn't original. Watchmakers and jewelers use similar drawers.—*Roy A. Raney, KØOVQ, 600 Jackson St, Denver, CO 80206*

HONEY SAVES SMALL PARTS

Here's a hint I received a while back. It gave me such a chuckle that I would like to share it with you. Sometimes it's good to remember that Amateur Radio is a hobby—a pursuit to bring us pleasure. Please don't take it seriously! **Figure 7.9** *is a picture of Earl with a future parts-storage jar.*—*KU7G*

◊ For those who are not ambitious enough to follow Lloyd Hanson, W9YCB's advice for finding small parts ("Hints & Kinks," Aug 1999) or either Roy Raney, KØOVQ's or Dan Trigilio, W6DAN's advice ("Hints & Kinks," Dec 2000), I offer an alternative method. This has the advantage that anyone not inclined to do all that sweeping and vacuuming is unlikely to expend much energy on doing dishes either; so we might as well kill two birds with one stone. I discovered it by the Eureka method.

I buy my honey in glass jars, which I use to hold the small parts for my projects after I've eaten the honey. Not having washed out the jars very well, the parts I drop into them stay put *real good*. I mean, I can tip the jar, shake it or watch the cat knock it over; those parts stay in it. When it comes time to install them in my project, I hold the jar up to the light until

Figure 7.9—N7NZ with a future parts-storage jar.

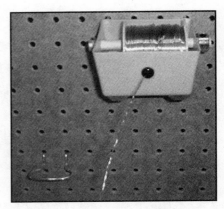

Figure 7.10—A front view of the solder-spool holder hanging on pegboard. Most construction details are visible.

Figure 7.11—A bottom view shows the stick-on feet in place.

I spy the part I want. Both the glass and the thin coating of honey are invisible, of course, but the curvature of the glass helps by magnifying small parts. Once I've located the part, it doesn't move as I turn or move the jar; it's quite stable. I then use my ball-point pen to tag it. It comes right out stuck to the pen. When I take it in my fingers, there's no danger of it being dropped. In fact, it will stick anywhere I place it.

Immediately before installing it, I give it a lick. I don't have any empirical data but I suspect the completed project will develop fewer bugs if we don't leave out this step. Just to be safe, though, I suggest treating button batteries differently, leaving them in their blister packages until ready for them.

This method has some fringe benefits. I find I have more energy when working on a long project, and I can complete it faster because I don't have to stop for a snack break. There is one problem I've encountered: The pen gets gummed up and won't write to check off the parts as they're installed. If that happens, I suggest moving the pen point rapidly back and forth on the paper until it starts writing again. Switching hands and using the soldering iron to pick up the parts is not recommended, for reasons I don't care to go into. It makes the difference between honeyed ham and smoked ham.

Of course, by now you've probably spotted the fallacy to this whole approach. The ham who is too lazy to sweep his floor or wash his dishes may lack the ambition to finish his projects quickly, and honey has a tendency to crystallize if it sits out too long. Not to worry. If that happens, pour some water into a pan, set the jar in the water and using a low

setting on your stove, put your project on the back burner.—*Earl Gosnell, N7NZ, Box 3492, Eugene, OR 97403; earl_gosnell@yahoo.com*

CIRCUITWORKS TOOLS FOR CIRCUIT REPAIR

◊ If you make or repair PC boards, visit the Hosfelt Electronics Web site (**www.hosfelt.com**) and look at the Circuitworks products page. You will find felt-tip pens that apply solder flux or remove it. The Gold Guard pen acts as tuner cleaner in pen form. It cleans and leaves behind a protective lubricant. A "conductive" pen draws "highly conductive silver traces," and an "overcoat" pen dispenses a tough conformal coating. A rubber-keypad repair kit puts a conductive coating onto worn carbon contacts. A second Circuitworks page shows connector lubricant in a tube, gelled cyanoacrylate adhesive (packaged with a bond accelerator) and two-part conductive epoxy.—*KU7G*

A SOLDER-SPOOL HOLDER

◊ I have been using this solder-spool holder for a while now. The holder keeps solder readily available and neatly packaged to keep your shack clean and orderly. The parts consist of a pegboard parts tray, a length of 3/8-inch dowel, a 3/8-inch washer-cap push nut, a 3/8-inch shaft collar, a rubber grommet and four stick-on rubber feet.

Construction of the project is easy! **Figures 7.10 and 7.11** show the finished project. Drill a hole in the parts box for

the dowel rod, approximately 1/2-inch down from the top edge of the box sides. Drill a hole for a rubber grommet in the front of the box, 3/4 inch down from top edge. Install a rubber grommet in the hole. Place the end-cap on one end of the dowel rod. Insert the dowel rod through one box side, the solder spool and the other box side. Place the shaft collar on the free end of the dowel and tighten it in place with an Allen wrench. Install the self-stick rubber feet on the bottom of the parts tray.

Once it's finished, you can either set the box on your desk or hang it on pegboard at your workbench. Pull out the solder as you need it and then roll the spool back up when you're finished. —*Dave Malara, KB2UBO/9, 40 E Field Stone Cir #5, Oak Creek, WI 53154; dmalarajr@wi.rr.com*

SOLDERING-IRON CONTROLLER

◊ I suffer from a common problem, forgetfulness. Some people call it "senior moments." I simplify it to "Oops!" Specifically, I'm talking about leaving my soldering iron hot and ready at the workbench for days or weeks without being touched. Before I designed and built this project, my iron was constantly wasting energy, or even failing with barely any real use.

When I learned about the BASIC stamp microprocessor, I thought a good first project would be a soldering-iron controller to turn off the iron when I'm not using it. As the project developed, more "features" came to mind and were added to the design. The current version (**Figure 7.12**) includes a warm-up timer, restart switch, shutdown warning and an on/off switch.

The on/off switch wasn't a necessity, since the controller will switch off the iron automatically after a predetermined time. I added the feature when I realized there was no way to manually switch off the iron, for those days when I "remembered."

The controller is basically a series of timers. A push of the start switch applies ac to the power supply, which powers the stamp. The start-up code of the stamp immediately activates the relay, latching the power on. A tone is sounded then the warm-up timer then starts; an LED flashing approximately twice each second indicates warm-up operation. Pressing the restart button during the warm-up cycle extends the cycle by two minutes.

When the warm-up cycle is complete, the unit sounds a few quick beeps to signal that the iron is "hot and ready." The LED then stays on constantly and a second timer starts. This is the "quiet" time, when I can use the iron.

When the second timer expires, about 30 minutes later, the unit flashes the LED and emits a short beep every second for a minute. This is the shutdown warning period. During this time, pressing the restart button will abort the shutdown sequence and restart the "hot and ready" cycle timer for another 15 minutes. If restart is not pressed before the shutdown warning timer expires, the unit will shutdown by deactivating the relay, removing power from the iron and the controller.

The total shutdown of power is one of my criteria for the project. When the controller is sitting there on the bench, it doesn't use *any* power. When activated, it only continues to use power as long as someone is around to press the restart button occasionally.

In the code, all timing parameters are set in the controller as constants, making it easier to change the timers to suit your preferences. Just make the appropriate changes, compile the program and install it in the stamp.[8]

[8]You can download the code from ARRLWeb at **www.arrl.org/files/qst-binaries/**. Look for 02HK09.ZIP.

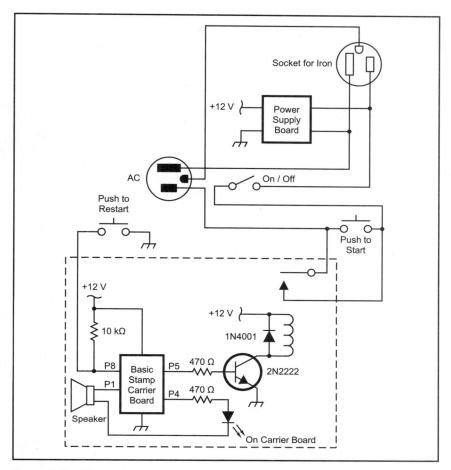

Figure 7.12—The soldering-iron controller.

From the code, you can see that the controller really is a series of timers. First we set the parameters for the warm-up timer, then call the timer procedure. When the timer procedure returns, we take action based on the result code, which indicates that either the timer expired or the user pressed the restart button.

After the warm-up timer has expired, we start the quiet-time timer. Again, we take action based on the result code, either starting the shutdown cycle or extending the quiet time.

The shutdown cycle includes sounding the tone every second. If the user presses restart, we jump back to the quiet-time cycle, extending it as designated. If the timer simply "times out," the processor deactivates the relay, which switches the unit off.

The timer procedure is the heart of the controller. It takes six input parameters, updating three of them as needed, and returns one output variable, TM_Result, which contains the reason that the procedure returned.

The input parameters include the length of the timer in minutes and tenths of a second. We use tenths because the timer uses a Pause command to pause for 0.1 second between button checks. Although it's a little inaccurate, it's close enough for this application. The timer deducts one tenth of a second from the count during every loop. When the count reaches zero, the routine checks the minutes remaining and either exits the procedure, returning "expired," or adds another minute to the tenths-of-seconds counter and keeps looping.

Other parameters control whether the time procedure will flash the LED, how fast to flash it and whether to sound tones. It's fairly simple code that could easily be modified for more accuracy or other features as desired.

Since building and using this project, I've never had to wonder if I remembered to turn off the iron. I always know it will turn itself off, saving irons, energy and money!—*Lawrence R. Houbre Jr, AA1FS, 63 Sycamore St, New Bedford, MA 02740; aa1fs@arrl.net*

INEXPENSIVE PROJECT BOXES AND CELL-PHONE BELT CLIP

◊ These days, homebrewers are faced with a very strange paradox: The enclosure or chassis box is often the most expensive part of a project.

For example, I built the Simple Meter Tester (*QST*, March 2000, p 41) with junk-box parts, and decided to see if I could use some old-fashioned ham-radio ingenuity to come up with a cheaper alternative to traditional electronic project boxes.

While browsing at the local hardware store, I noticed a variety of plastic and metal electrical boxes and covers. I selected a nice blue plastic electrical box for a very nice price—69 cents. I used a blank outlet cover to close up the back; however, a scrap piece of circuit board, masonite or other material would do just as well. (See **Figure 7.13**.)

Another item I use to make projects portable and handy is a replacement belt clip for cell phones, for less than five bucks.—*Wayne Yoshida, KH6WZ, 16428 Camino Canada Ln, Huntington Beach, CA 92649*

USING SURPLUS METERS

◊ Have you ever gone to a hamfest and found that you couldn't resist buying some of those small meters with special scales indicating VUs, battery level or whatever? I couldn't resist. After a few years of this, I discovered that I had quite a pile of small meters. Nevertheless, what could I *do* with them? I soon realized that these meters are not much use without characterizing them and knowing how to use them once their characteristics are known.

Meter Characterization

This is simple. Well, sort of. First, you measure the dc resistance of the meter. This is easily done with any ohmmeter. (This is true only for insensitive meters. Sensitive meters may be damaged by measurement with an ohmmeter. See page 26.4 of the *2002 ARRL Handbook* for a method that is safe for all meters —*Ed.*) For an example, let's say we find that the meter resistance is 370 Ω.

Next, we need to determine what current will make it read full scale. This is also reasonably easy, but a little more involved. The way I did it was to hook a variable power supply up through a variable resistance to the meter. Start with a very high resistance (that is, megohms) and a low voltage, then slowly change the combination until you get a full-scale deflection. See **Figure 7.14**.

Once you get that full-scale deflection, you simply measure the voltage across the meter with a dc voltmeter. As

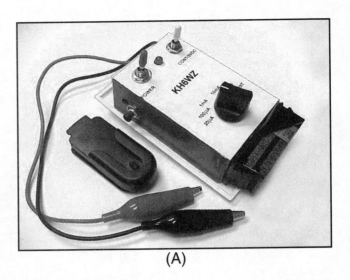

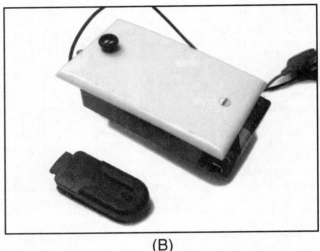

Figure 7.13—A meter tester built into a single electrical outlet box with an outlet cover for a rear panel. A shows the front view. (Yes, there is an "extra" hole on the side—that was a mistake: The solder tabs for the power switch and the "push to test" button interfered with each other.) B is the rear view showing the cell-phone button and belt clip.

an example, let's say we measured 85 mV across the meter. From Ohm's law, we get 0.085 V / 370 Ω = 0.229 mA full-scale reading. (See **Table 7.2**.)

Once you know the meter characteristics, how can you use it? Well, there are two basic ways to use your meter: as a voltmeter or an ammeter. Most projects use one or the other.

Making an Ammeter

The resistance of the coil in our example is 370 Ω. We already know that our meter measures 0.229 mA at full scale. It would be great if we had a special need that just happened to need a 0.229 mA full-scale meter, but that's not very likely. We need to add what is called a "shunt." A shunt diverts part of the current around the meter so that it will read full scale at some circuit current larger than 0.229 mA. A shunt is connected in parallel with the meter.

Let's say you were going to build a QRP wattmeter, ala Roy Lewallen's design. The circuit calls for a 1-mA meter.

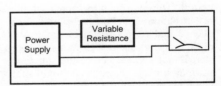

Figure 7.14—A test setup for measuring current at a meter's full-scale deflection.

Table 7.2—Surplus Meter Example

Coil Resistance	370 W
Measured Full-Scale Voltage	85 mV
Calculated Full-Scale Current	= 0.000229 A

This means that the full-scale reading of the meter needs to be 1 mA. You need to divert most of the current around the meter. In fact you need to divert (0.001 – 0.000229) 0.000771 A, allowing only 0.000229 A to go through the meter when 1 mA flows in the circuit.

We know that the voltage across our

example meter is 85 mV, so it's also across the shunt when the meter reads full scale. Therefore we calculate the shunt resistance as $R_s = 0.085 / 0.000771 = 110.24\ \Omega$. So, if we put about 110.24 Ω in parallel with the meter, we would get a full-scale reading of 1 mA. This same procedure applies for *any* full-scale current that you might want to read.

Making A Voltmeter

So we already have a great use for the surplus meter, now what about making a voltmeter from the same surplus meter? Let's say we want to make a meter to read 15 V from our surplus meter.

This might actually be a good example, as I bet many would like a small, inexpensive 15-V meter for their home-brew QRP rigs. We know that the maximum voltage that can be across the meter is 85 mV; we need to drop (15 V − 0.085 V) 14.915 V is across a series resistor.

We also know that the meter reads 0.000229 mA at full scale, so using Ohm's law, we get 14.915 V / 0.000229 A = 65,131 Ω. So if we put a 65.131 kΩ resistor in series with the meter, it would read full scale when the circuit voltage is about 15 V. (The 0.131 kW is insignificant compared to the 65 kΩ.) This method can be used for any voltage reading.

Once you start using surplus meters, you'll want to start changing the faceplate to reflect the new scale that you dictate; I leave that to artists. Good luck and have fun with meters.—*Brad Mitchell, N8YG, 148 Holley St, Brockport, NY 14420-1852; **n8yg@arrl.net***

A STICKY PAD KEEPS EQUIPMENT FROM WALKING

◊ Many methods have been described to hold keys and paddles, and prevent them from crawling about during a QSO. Sometimes, it is necessary to hold the device with one hand while sending with the other. In the past, I have screwed the key to the operating desk, which works very well, but it makes the key hard to remove when you need room. I have used double-sided adhesive pads, but they too can be difficult to remove when necessary. The top of my operating desk is covered with Formica, so it is very slippery, especially when it has been polished.

While getting some parts in RadioShack a few days ago, I came across an item called "Sticky Pad."[9] It is intended to hold items on the dashboard of a car (see **Figure 7.15**). The label says it "Magically holds cell phone, PDA,

[9]American Covers Inc, PO Box 987, Draper, UT 84020; **www.americancovers.com**. Their Web site shows Walmart, Best Buy, Comp USA, Staples and other nationwide distributors of their products.

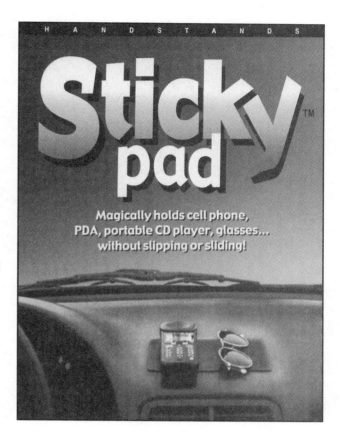

Figure 7.15—A photo of the Sticky Pad packaging shows its intended purpose: to hold handheld transceivers and such in place on automobile instrument panels. It also works well to keep keys and paddles in place on a desk.

portable CD player, glasses...without slipping or sliding!" The maker of this product claims that if the pad gets dirty, you need only wash it with soap and water, pat it dry and use it again—just like new.

Reasoning that if it would hold the things they claim, it would not be difficult for it to hold a key or paddle to the desktop; I got one. This pad turns out to be great for my use. It holds the key or paddle firmly in position but can easily be moved. It is almost exactly the right size and looks neat.

The substance feels like rubber and acts like the adhesive on Post-It notes. It easily peels off and leaves no residue. It is flexible and lies flat. The one I got is black, but I think there are other colors available. The only place I have seen this is RadioShack; the price is around five dollars.—*Hugh A. Inness-Brown, W2IB, 5351 State Highway 37, Ogdensburg, NY 13669; **w2ib@arrl.net***

ROTATING PEGBOARD STORAGE

◊ Would you like to store tools and hardware on pegboard, but you don't want to cover a wall with the stuff? Would you like to transport the pegboard and parts to wherever you're working? Why not build some space-saving, portable pegboard storage? You will need a few hand

tools (drill, wrench, saw, hot glue gun and glue) and the materials in **Table 7.3**.

The simplest way to construct this project is shown in **Figure 7.16**. (With precise cutting and fitting, craftspeople could produce smoother corners—*Ed.*) Cut four of the sticks to the length of the pegboard less the thickness of two plywood sheets ($24 - ^3/_8 - ^3/_8 = 23^1/_4$ inches). Hot glue two of the sticks to the long edges of one pegboard piece (A). The sticks should be flush with each long edge of the pegboard, and the pegboard should overhang the sticks by $^3/_8$ inch at each end to allow room for the plywood squares. Prepare a second pegboard piece (B) using the other two cut sticks. The $^3/_8$-inch square sticks will support the pegboard *from the inside* at each corner.

Drill holes in the centers of the three pieces of plywood for the threaded rod. Glue the edge of one plywood square (E) to the end of prepared pegboard piece (A). Glue the edge of another plywood square (F) to the opposite end of (A). Glue one of the remaining pegboard pieces (C) to plywood squares (E) and (F) and the stick at one edge of piece (A). Glue one stick of pegboard piece (B) to the free edge of piece (C) and the edges of plywood squares (E) and (F). This forms a pegboard U with plywood squares at both ends. Finally, glue the remaining pegboard piece to the plywood

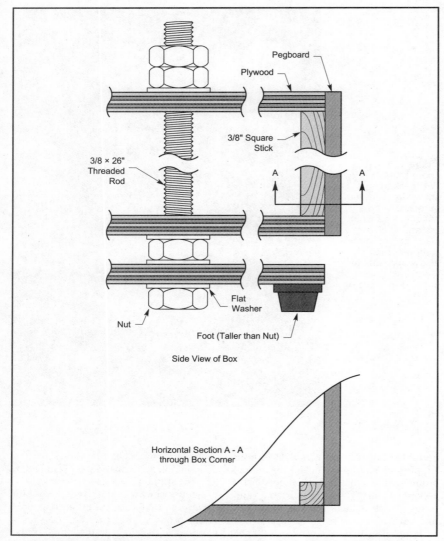

Table 7.3—Materials Required
1—24×48-inch piece of pegboard cut into quarters (4 pieces, 24×12 inches)
4—Wood sticks ³/₈-inch square by 36 inches long
1—³/₈-inch-diameter threaded rod, 26 inches long
4—Nuts and 4 flat washers to fit the threaded rod
3—12×12-inch pieces of ³/₈-inch-thick plywood
4—Rubber feet (high enough to clear the washer and nut)

Figure 7.16—A mechanical drawing of the rotatable pegboard storage assembly.

edges and sticks at the open side to finish the box.

Spin a nut and washer about one inch onto one end of the threaded rod and insert that end through the remaining plywood piece. Install a washer and nut under the plywood and tighten the first nut snugly against the top of the plywood. Place a flat washer on top of the nut and feed the end of the rod through the box. Install a flat washer and two nuts on the rod that extends from the top of the box. Tighten the upper nut against the lower one, as a jam nut, so that the box turns freely. Trim off any extra rod or install a cap nut as a safety measure. Add rubber feet on the bottom plywood piece to form a stable platform. Now you have space-saving rotatable pegboard storage (**Figure 7.17**) for your tools or electronic parts.—*Dave Malara Jr, KB2UBO, 40 E Fieldstone Cir # 5, Oak Creek, WI 53154;* **dmalarajr@wi.rr.com**

Figure 7.17—The author's finished pegboard carousel.

MAKING AN LED AUDIBLE

◊ I published an earlier solution to this problem in *Electronic Design* (May 28, 1992), but it required an LM3909 IC, which is no longer widely available.

Quite often, a piece of equipment contains an LED where an audible indicator would be handier. This audible alarm can be connected across any red or green LED and runs entirely on current "stolen" from the LED. The LED still lights with nearly full brightness.

Figure 7.18A shows the simplest solution. If the sound doesn't need to be very loud, you can connect a 3-V piezoelectric buzzer (such as RadioShack #273-074) across an LED and it will buzz faintly. **Figure 7.18B** shows how to get louder sound, although a lot more components are needed. Bipolar drive puts over 3-V (pk-to-pk) across the piezoelectric sounder. You can vary the resistors or capacitors to get the frequency that sounds best.—*Michael A. Covington, N4TMI, 285 St George Dr, Athens, GA 30606*

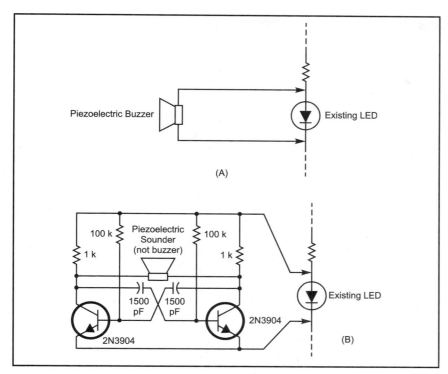

Figure 7.18—At A, a 3-V piezo-electric buzzer will sound faintly on power from an existing red or green LED. The circuit at B oscillates to place 3 V across a piezo speaker. Choose the resistors for the best performance with a particular sounder.

EASY CUSTOM METER FACES AT HOME

◊ Panel-meter faces have always been a problem for me in homemade projects that use an analog panel meter. Either the meter face did not have the correct scale or it needed some changes. I have used dry-transfer labels to add markings to existing meter-face graphics. Sometimes I have used a pencil eraser to lightly remove some markings before using the dry-transfer graphics. The results were usually functional, but lacked the professional look I desire. I wanted easily customized meter faces that look great and can be easily made at home at low cost. I never found a good method until I discovered the way Jim Tonne, WB6BLD, makes meter scales. Jim has written a meter-scale-drawing program that draws up to four scales on a meter face plate. This *Meter.exe* program is available from his Web site at **www. qsl.net/wb6bld/**. The program is offered at no cost for radio amateur use.

The program output may be customized to fit nearly any meter movement commonly available to radio amateurs (**Figure 7.19**). Just about every param-

Figure 7.19— Checking dimensions for a new meter face.

eter can be adjusted and the output (HPGL) can be sent directly to a PCL-5 capable printer (LaserJet III or later) or to an ASCII file. A variety of useful meter faces can be made by Jim's program as is. He is working, as time allows, enhancing the program, but in its current form, the program has some limitations. I'll describe a method that allows nearly any graphics printer to be used by the program, show how to substitute additional fonts, insert custom graphics, and add colors to the meter faces you generate using Jim's software.

The *Meter.exe* DOS-based program generates output files in HPGL and can add the required header and footer so a PCL-5 capable printer can accept the HPGL file. The HPGL format was developed by Hewlett Packard to allow standardized printing to their popular plotters. An HP device connected to the standard LPT1 printer port will print if that device can accept HPGL or HPGL plus the header/footer pair. If your printer can't respond to either of those formats, it won't print correctly. An inexpensive inkjet printer won't work and many non-HP laser printers won't work. The font generated by the program is suitable for many purposes, but since font choice is a personal decision, sometimes an alternate font would be useful.

I have a procedure that allows your existing graphics printer to work and allows any font handled by Windows to be printed on your custom meter. In addition, we'll see how to introduce custom graphics and colors to create truly custom meter plates.

Easy Steps to Success

We need to:
• Convert the *Meter* printer output to something compatible with your graphics editor
• Change fonts, add text, insert graphics and color with your graphics software
• Print the modified meter face with your existing Windows graphics printer

First, in *Meter.exe*, select the "write PCL5 data to file" option. This writes a file to your disk drive with a ".PRN" extension. Then use a file-conversion utility to convert this PCL data file to one that your graphics editor can read. Good results were attained with a shareware program called *View Companion*. The free download from **www. softwarecompanions.com** will give you a 30-day free evaluation of the program. This *ViewCompanion* software converts from the HP PCL-5 file format to about fifteen different raster file formats. This means that programs that use filename extensions of JPG, PCX, DXF, PDF, etc can now work with the *Meter* file output. I use *TurboCAD* for Windows (DXF file extension) for my changes. Another CAD drawing program may give you good results. After your changes are made, simply print to your printer using your graphics editor software.

While making changes to the meter scale using my CAD software, the thought occurred to me to just make the entire scale in CAD from the start. While it's possible to do this, I found that using Jim Tonne's software meter engine and importing the result to CAD software was easier. I just let the meter engine take care of the hard part. The only items I usually change in CAD are the font and perhaps the line thickness of an arc or a meter scale marker. These simple operations are relatively easy to learn in most CAD programs and won't require a long learning process.

For best results, use a high quality paper designed for your printer. Get paper with the highest brightness rating you can find. A rating of 100 is the whitest. The common papers have a rating of only about 80 or so. Since premium paper is more expensive, consider buying a smaller package. You can make your trial-and-error prints with common paper and switch to the premium material for your actual meter face. Select a clean work area since your internal meter movement will be open and exposed. Carefully cut the new meter face drawing from the paper sheet. Remove the original meter face and turn it over. Se-

cure the new face to the back of the original plate with adhesive. Do not use water-based glue because it may cause the paper to crinkle while drying. I have had good results using a spray adhesive made by Elmer's called "Extra-Strength Spray Adhesive." The orange and blue can is marked acid free, permanent bond, dries clear, no bleed through. I got a 10-ounce spray can at a Home Depot store.—*Bill Jones, K8CU, 5411 Spruce Ln, Westerville, OH 43082; k8cu@arrl.net*

IMPROVE AUDIO—AT THE *OTHER* END!

◊ Much has been done to improve transmit audio, from fancy microphones to speech compressors, but what about the receive end? With those itty-bitty speakers typical in modern radios, it seems like only a small percentage of the efforts put toward good transmit audio are realized at the received end. Through a bit of investigating, I found several solutions. They can be mixed and matched to suit the needs of the reader, or combined for an even better effect.

Initial experiments showed that even something as simple and minor as using a speaker larger than the one provided with the radio shows an improvement in audio response, but the effect is still relatively small. The biggest improvement came when the speaker was put inside of a baffle (for initial experiments, this con-

sisted of an empty tissue box—in addition to being low-cost, it also easily fit on the ham shack desk). The next step was a bookshelf-sized stereo speaker. When I hooked one of these up to my 220-MHz transceiver, the improvement was so great I told my friend Ken (N9HXD) that he sounds better through this speaker than in person! I found that a two-way (a three-way is overkill for speech, I noticed) car speaker intended for rear-deck mounting works equally well.

The received audio in my station has now improved to the point where working HF for hours is no longer a chore! Also, operating VHF opened up a totally new world—the differences in audio responses between repeaters became much more obvious, as every little nuance could be heard. With a little extra effort, I thought I could bring a level of consistency to what I heard—in addition to doing a bit of additional tweaking. To do this, I wanted to design an audio equalizer. Although there are units available commercially, they are too big and definitely overkill, since they are designed for use with stereos. At this point, I remembered the Heathkit "Microlizer" (microphone equalizer) that I had many years ago. Through some helpful hams on the Internet, I not only found out the model number (so I could order the manual), but a few folks actually sent their old manuals to me!

With schematic in hand, I set about to

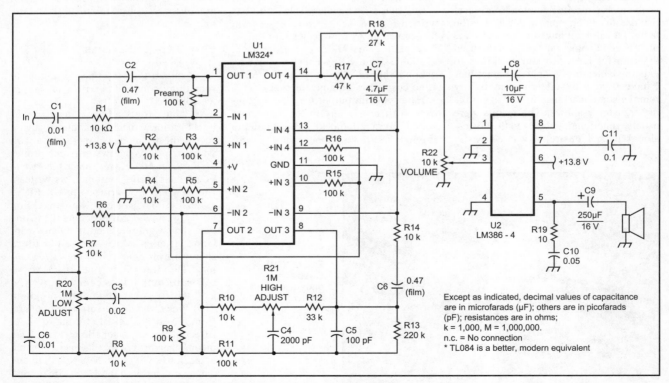

Figure 7.20—A schematic of an op-amp based AF equalizer from WB9YBM.

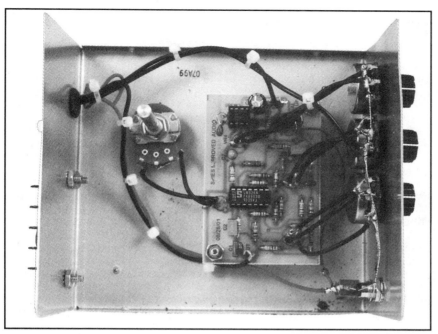

Figure 7.21—Here's a version of the AF equalizer built on a PC board from FAR circuits.[10] The preamplifier gain is set with the potentiometer inside the box. The front-panel volume control sets the gain of the 1/2-W AF amplifier.

[10]PC boards for this project are available from FAR Circuits, 18N640 Field Ct, Dundee, IL 60118; tel 847-836-9148; **www.farcircuits.net**. $4.50 plus $1.50 shipping and handling. $3 additional charge for credit-card purchases. Illinois residents add 6.5% sales tax.

modify the circuit for my needs. I no longer needed the switch. Since I am powering my circuit from the same 13.8-V supply that powers the transceivers, I didn't need the battery-saving LED "blinky" circuit either. I also updated the op-amp, in that I used a single IC containing four op amps. Also, the mic-gain control became the preamplifier gain setting. The resulting schematic is shown in Figure 7.20. (A few updates have been made as suggested by the ARRL Lab.—*Ed*)

No commonly available quad op amp can handle the higher power levels required by a speaker, so I needed a power amplifier after the equalizer output. I had no need of rattling the windows in my ham shack, so I picked another commonly available part: a 1/2-W AF amplifier. If you feel more power is needed, other amplifier ICs are available. Because of higher gain of these parts, however, I strongly recommend buying one as a part of a kit. Kits include a PC board that will minimize the chances of feedback that might occur with a homebrew layout.

Construction

To shield the circuit from stray RF in the ham shack, I enclosed the project in a metal box (RadioShack #270-253) and connected the electrical ground to chassis ground. Especially for the higher impedance of microphone cables, use a shielded cable with the shields grounded at both ends. Also, use bypass capacitors and/or ferrite beads on all leads entering the box; they are cheap insurance against potential problems. I routed all incoming and outgoing leads to terminal blocks at the rear of the cabinet (you can use plugs if you want), to minimize the chance of wires breaking inside the box from too much flexing. The three front-panel controls adjust the low-frequency gain, high-frequency gain and volume. I used very thin, shielded audio wire to avoid picking up any stray signals, either from inside the box or from whatever may have made it through the box. Some of this shielding might be overkill for normal operation, but it may be needed when you take this box out to Field Day and a few nearby people key up at full legal power. That is *not* the place to start troubleshooting a new squeal!

For a bit of final "dressing up," I added a professional looking equipment label. Some office-supply stores sell plastic nametags with two or three lines of inscribed print, like the call badges sold at hamfests. I get one without a clasp on the back and have a device description inscribed in the place of a name. A bit of double-sided tape affixes the label.

Operation

The only operating quirk I noticed

came from the radios. When the transceiver volume is set too low and most of the audio amplification is done by external circuitry, hum can become objectionable. To prevent this, simply leave the transceiver volume control at a normal setting, and use this circuit only to tailor frequency response.—*Klaus Spies, WB9YBM, 815 Woodland Heights Blvd, Streamwood, IL 60107-2029;* **wb9ybm @juno.com**

COILING WIRE OR ROPE WITHOUT KINKS

◊ I just finished reading a *Hints & Kinks* article by KB6FPW, about coiling and storing coax (*QST*, Aug 1992, p 60). The article contains many good tips, but states that coils of coax must be rolled and unrolled by turning them like a wheel to prevent kinks and tangles. Turning a coil of cable like a wheel to roll it up (without a reel) is a slow and rather inaccurate process and is unnecessary.

For years, it has amazed me that most people simply do not know how to handle cable without rolling it onto a form or rolling (and unrolling) by hand and putting twists into the cable.

Many years ago, as an industrial electrician, I rolled and unrolled thousands of feet of wire and cable. I noticed that my coworkers simply accepted frustrating twists and kinks as an inevitable part of rolling and unrolling cable. After a while, it dawned on me that the concept of phase cancellation (actually, *twist* cancellation) could easily be applied to everything that must be coiled: wire, cable, rope, hose, etc.

There are several easy and fast methods for rolling and unrolling that do not require a reel, do not require the roll to be turned like a wheel, do not impart twists to the material being rolled, and best of all, you eliminate tangles and kinks forever. "Impossible!" you say?

The basic idea is to develop the habit of always employing twist-cancellation techniques. As you read this article, practice with an extension cord. This will help you visualize and remember the techniques. A cord (or hose) with a stripe on it will make learning even easier.

Make rolls as large as possible. This is usually one full arm-span (about 6 feet), which will make a roll about 2 feet in diameter. Why? A large roll means fewer turns and less handling.

Basic Twist-Cancellation Technique

I call this method *left-five, right-five*. With it, I recently unrolled 300 feet of 1-inch black plastic irrigation pipe in less than five minutes without one twist, kink or tangle.

To unroll any roll you can carry, proceed as follows: Hold the roll in one hand and hold the current turn with the thumb and forefinger of the other hand. As you unroll, walking, circle the unrolling hand around the outside of the roll, Separating the turn from the roll before dropping the turn. Hold the roll loosely, allowing crossed turns to uncross and free the current turn.

Count five turns, then transfer the roll to the other hand and take five turns off the other side. *Do not* turn the roll around when you pass it from hand to hand (see **Figure 7.22**). Continue passing the roll back and forth, taking five turns off each side, until finished. Now stretch or simply drag the cable a bit. *Voila!* All those left-five and right-five twists will instantly cancel each other.

To coil a length, reach out a full arm span and bring in five turns. Twist the cable between the thumb and forefinger, once per turn, so the turn lays flat against the other turns. Now transfer the roll to the other hand and bring five turns onto the opposite side of the roll. Notice that the twisted turns are canceling, instead of flailing the tail of the cable into a wild Lissajous figure! The end of the cable doesn't need to spin around.

If you simply cannot roll or unroll with the "wrong" hand, employ this variation: Instead of passing the roll from hand to hand, keep it in the same hand but flip it on a vertical axis. (See **Figure 7.23**). Hold the roll one way and wind five turns forward, then flip it and wind five turns backward on its opposite side. Make sure you flip it back and forth, not the same way each time. Unroll in the reverse manner.

If the roll is too large or heavy to handle, simply lay it on the ground, pull in five turns, then flip it over and pull five turns into the opposite side. I have rolled industrial multi-conductor cables *800 feet long* in this manner, by myself.

Adjust the number of turns you pull in depending on the stiffness of the material being rolled. If a material is highly prone to kinks, take only one turn (not five) off each side of the roll at a time. Secure one end of the roll and keep a little tension on it as you walk and pay it out, alternating turns from each side. Flimsy light-duty cords may go 10 turns each way, while RG-8 or #2 AWG may tolerate no more than one or two turns each way. The only requirement is to maintain left-right turn equality.

Other Methods

Another method, which I always use for garden hoses, is called *figure-eight rolling*. Each half of the "8" cancels the other half.

For hoses or large cable, make the figure-of-eight roll on the ground. If you need precision, drive a couple of wood stakes. For antenna wire or small cords (say, 100 feet of THHN or a 50-foot extension cord), you can roll a figure-eight roll around your palm and elbow. The middle of the 8 crosses the forearm. You can convert the 8 into a regular roll simply by flipping one half over onto the other half. Wrap a band of tape around each end of the 8 to prevent mixing of the upper and lower loops so you can later "unflip" it back into an 8 for "twist-synchronous" unrolling.

To unroll, simply walk and pay it out. There is no need to alternate between sides, since the eight shape builds twist-cancellation into every turn. Be very careful, however, to maintain control of the 8 at all times to prevent a turn from pulling between other turns.

When paying out a large figure-of-eight roll that is on the ground (such as a garden hose, or say, 200 feet of RG-213), do not just walk off with the free end and expect the 8 to pay out properly. Turns will surely pull underneath other turns before you're done. Have a helper stand over the 8 and pay out from the top, as you walk out the tail.

Preventing Tangles

Most tangles occur because loops pass through other loops. It is important to unroll by passing the hand around the outside of the roll in a circular motion, separating a turn from the rest of the roll. Loops that crossed others must uncross as you go.

Other tangles occur because a line end passes through one or more loops. Control the ends by taping them to the first and last turns before storing the cable. If you don't want sticky tape "goo" on your cables, use bread-bag ties, pipe cleaners or cable ties. Don't use tie wire; it can gradually cut the insulation.

To "relax" a stiff antenna wire so it will not recoil itself, stretch it slightly. Tie one end to something solid. Wearing gloves, slick the wire out from the tied end to the free end several times to remove twists. Tie the free end to a suitable handle, like a piece of galvanized water pipe or a hammer handle. Place one foot well behind you, and "bounce" your upper body weight against the wire in tension. Start gently, then increase the effort until you feel the wire "give" a little. That's enough—once the wire gives, it will relax and lay flat. Steel and steel-core wire may require a fence-puller or come-along for sufficient pulling force.

Store patch cords and miscellaneous wires in a box without tangling: Simply place each one in a plastic bag. Freezer bags are stronger than others, last longer, and are well worth the extra price. The

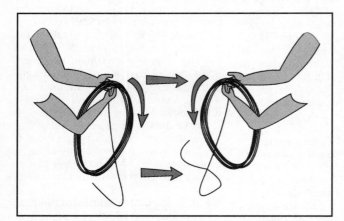

Figure 7.22—Ambidextrous hams can eliminate twists when coiling wire by periodically passing the coil back and forth between left and right hands. Don't rotate the coil when changing hands. See text.

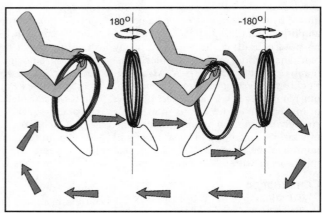

Figure 7.23—If you want to keep the coil in one hand, periodically flip it back and forth. (Wind five turns, rotate it 180°, wind five turns, rotate it the opposite direction –180° and repeat). See text.

one-gallon size will easily hold an 80-meter dipole. The two-gallon size will accommodate 100 feet of RG-58 or 8X.

N1FB stated in a related article that hose and cord reels are handy, and I agree. However, I advise against rolling large coaxial cable onto extension-cord holders. Their small diameters may be less than allowed by the cable's minimum bending radius. Bends that are too sharp may cause the center conductor to "cold flow" in the dielectric, particularly in long-term, possibly hot, storage.

Armed with knowledge of twist cancellation techniques, you can forever eliminate the frustration of kinked and tangled wires, cords, cables, ropes and hoses. Enjoy!—*Harold Melton, KD5IRR, 1822 County Rd 3618, Murchison, TX 75778;* **hmelton@ tvec.net**

WRIST REST CORRALS SMALL PARTS

◊ Here's a hint that I use both at work and on my home workbench. I use a simple wrist rest (the kind used to support wrists while typing at a computer keyboard) while I work at my bench. Not only does it support my wrists and forearms, but it also acts as a guard to keep small parts from falling off the bench. At work, where I repair medical equipment, I repair small devices that have tiny screws, springs and such. At home, it helps to keep surface-mount parts and other small parts from falling into the carpet. Since the rests are not attached to the bench, you can set it aside when you don't need it. Wrist rests can be purchased for a few dollars at ham-swaps and flea markets. I hope other readers find this a useful idea.—*Dan Trigilio, W6DAN, 948-A Kennedy Dr, Capitola, CA 95010-2317;* **danjt@cruzio.com**

painful to me, to the extent that the radio was of no use to me for HF reception. To remedy this, I came up with a clipper system that is quite effective, and makes a world of difference. I used two RadioShack #32-1031B line-to-voice-coil transformers. For the input and output terminals, I hooked the audio in and out between the C (common) terminal and the 4-W terminal. I wired the two transformer primaries together in parallel (using the 10-W and C terminals) and connected two strings of series connected silicon rectifier diodes across them. The two diode strings are oppositely polarized.

The circuit operation is simple: It transforms the low voltage audio from the receiver to a higher voltage (at 600 Ω). Two diode strings across the 600-Ω line clip both sides of the audio, and the clipped audio is transformed back to 4 Ω.

I used four series connected diodes for each string. Add more diodes if you want to increase the output volume. Check the clipping action by increasing the receiver volume until clipping starts, then back the volume down until it is clear. If it is not loud enough, add more diodes to the string. The NIR-12 is now extremely useful, thanks to this modification.—*William Bastian, N9BOE, 21226 Charcoal Ave, Warrens, WI 54666-8591;* **n9boe@mwt.net**

INSULATION HOLDS PROBES ON WIRES

◊ Performing a continuity check on newly constructed multiconductor cables and connectors can be most frustrating if no assistant is available. When confronted with these circumstances recently, I happened to notice a piece of insulation that had been stripped from

some #14 AWG wire. I cut two ³/₄-inch lengths of the insulation and forced all but ¹/₁₆-inch over each of my ohmmeter probe tips. The tubing is a great way to steady the probes on the tapered pins of the connectors. This simplified an otherwise difficult job. —*Charles Turner, KI7NW, 315 Center Ave, Bisbee, AZ 85603;* **cagt@theriver. com**

A BETTER SOLDER-REMOVAL TOOL

◊ I've recently done a lot of component changing on PC-board projects, and this involved a lot of solder removal. In some cases, I haven't had replacement parts for some of the things I was removing, so I couldn't employ the "sacrifice the component" technique (clipping the leads and then just desoldering the remaining stubs).

In any case, I've become very frustrated with the desoldering tools conveniently available to me. Desoldering braid works reasonably well most of the time, but doesn't always get all the solder out of a plated-through hole. "Solder-suckers" provide plenty of vacuum, but you must either remove the iron before applying the suction (so the solder cools some) or put the iron and suction device on opposite sides of the board. (This is somewhat difficult with a PC-board vise, very difficult without one.)

Another common method is a "bulb" type desolderer. These come in two varieties—just the bulb by itself and a version using a hollow-tip pencil soldering iron with a bulb attached. (Such as the RadioShack #64-2060.) Unfortunately, these do not produce very much vacuum, so they don't always get all the solder out of the "nooks and crannies." The second

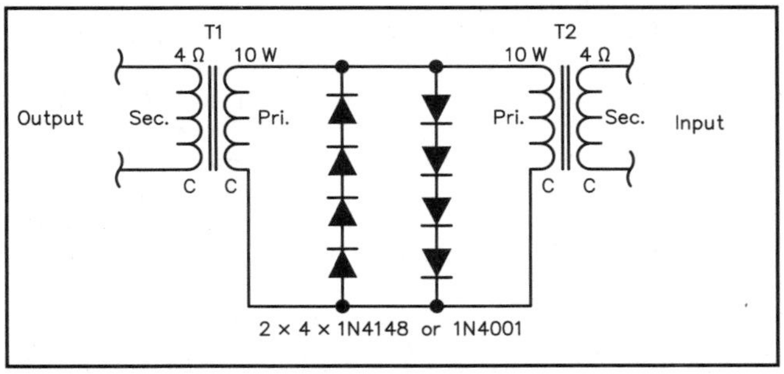

A MULTI-DIODE CLIPPER

◊ Several years ago, I purchased a JPS NIR-12 DSP unit. I have extremely tender ears, and impulse noise is extremely

Figure 7.24—N9BOE uses several diodes and transformers to expand the usefulness of a common diode-clipper circuit. T1 and T2 are RS #32-1031 audio transformers.

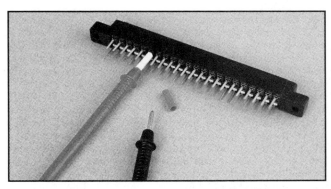

Fig 7.25—KI7NW slips some insulation over his probe tips to keep them on test points and prevent short circuits. This photo shows pieces of heat-shrink tubing used for the same purpose. Select the insulation diameter so that it holds the probe and test lead firmly together.

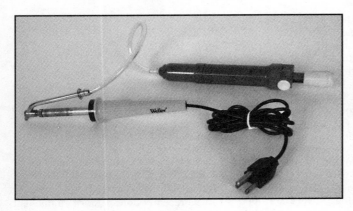

Figure 7.26— KC1SX's custom desoldering tool.

type does get heat and vacuum to the same point, however.

When I was in college, I was lucky enough to have a dedicated desoldering station available. These have heated hollow tips with a motorized vacuum pump. They're very nice indeed, but very expensive—the cheapest one I have seen along these lines is still about $100.

Since I've always been one to take something that needs improvement and tinker with it, I gave a little thought to the problem and came up with a reasonably priced solution that works quite well,

too. In essence, I combined two of the above-mentioned devices as you can see in **Figure 7.26**. I took a bulb-type desoldering iron, removed the bulb and replaced it with a solder-sucker (such as RadioShack #64-2120) connected via some flexible ¼-inch plastic tubing (plumbing supply, hardware stores or aquarium shops should have it). I'll be the first to admit that the result looks a little weird. It also makes desoldering a two-handed job. However, it really does work quite well.—*Michael Tracy, KC1SX, ARRL Lab;* **kc1sx@arrl.org**

MORE ON FINDING LOST PARTS

◊ Lloyd Hanson, W9YCB's "Recovery of Small Lost Parts" (*QST*, Aug 1999, p 65) is a very good article, and Mr. Hanson obviously has a lot of experience. Before sweeping with a squeegee, I sweep with a flashlight and my eyes. Lay a lit flashlight on the floor (or other flat surface where parts are lost) so that it shines across the area and look for shadows. A light source at the surface casts long, stark shadows even from very small parts. Sweep the light back and forth across the area and shadows will seem to jump at any object. I often find parts that I didn't know were lost!—*Roy Day, K4PXW, 3457 Glendale Ave, Louisville, KY 40215*

SALVAGE MONITOR TOROIDS

◊ Cut open the lumps in discarded computer monitor cables and you'll find great toroids for TVI suppression. They will slip over TV coax and act as a good shield choke to keep RF from coming down the lead-in.—*Rick Darwicki, N6PE, 17775 Elmhurst Cir, Yorba Linda, CA 92886;* **rickyd@deltanet.com**

The Doctor is IN

Q Dana, KD5PME, writes: I admit it, I am a packrat. I have several non-functioning VCRs that I cannot seem to throw away. Are there any parts that might be salvageable and of use to a ham? How about the tuners? Can they be used in a spectrum analyzer project?

A The Doctor is shocked—shocked!— to discover a packrat in the amateur ranks. In the best of amateur tradition (the Doctor still has parts he removed from TV sets in Junior High) old VCRs are chock full of useful parts. There are transistors and various other discrete components for starters. The tuners can indeed be used for the basis of a spectrum analyzer project. One such project appeared in Aug and Sep 1998 *QST*. If you do not have these issues, see "Projects for the Ham Shack" on the ARRL Technical Information Service pages (**www.arrl.org/tis**) for a copy. Another is a modular kit offered by a company called Science Workshop (**www.science-workshop.com/**).

Finally, some of the motors and drive

components can be useful in antenna tuners and small "magnetic" transmitting loops. If you have a steel workbench or filing cabinets, the magnets from the more unusual motors can be put to good use as note holders. The empty cases might be good as project enclosures or nice planters.

Q Walt Martin, KB5HOV, wonders, "When an air variable capacitor is mounted in a metal cabinet, how does the proximity of the cabinet affect its value? What is the effect on the rotor plates as they un-mesh and approach the top of the cabinet? Since all of the capacitor's plates, both stator and rotor, are in a plane that is at right angles to the cabinet panels I would assume stray capacitance would be minimal and any concern about cabinet proximity would be directed more toward arcing instead of stray capacitance."

A Your assumption is right on the money. The minimum capacitance

of large air-variables is usually a more limiting factor than the stray capacitance you get with the cabinet. Particularly in transmitting equipment, there must also be adequate clearance around the capacitor plates for the maximum voltage expected. In tuners, the maximum voltage may be considerably higher than at the transmitter output due to high impedance loads.

Q Jim Johnston, KØFNR, of Arvada, Colorado, writes: Is there any compilation of corrections to schematics published in *QST*—it would be handy to have some sort of reference so any corrections could be easily researched before a project is started (e.g., R10 should have been 10k not 10).

A If you go to the TIS Web Page (**www.arrl.org/tis/**), you will find that among all the useful information gathered there, is the *ARRL Periodicals Index Search* in the section available to members. This database contains the *QST* index from 1915 to the present and the *QEX* index from 1981 to the present. For *QST* issues from 1970 to the present, and some selected articles back to 1922 (when construction articles featuring tubes began in earnest), key words that help identify the article have been added. By entering key words (ANTENNA) or combinations (CONSTRUCTION ANTENNA VERTICAL HF) into the **Title words:** field, you will find all relevant technical articles and in fact create entire bibliographies on a particular subject.

Now, what does all this have to do with corrections? Well, Feedback items (corrections) in the database have the same title as the original article, and have been given the same key words. So if you search and find the article, any corrections will be listed right along with it. Or, simply search for the key word FEED-BACK.

Q Roger Brackney, K6ZTK, asks, "What is the meaning of 'DIN', the infamous multi-pin plug?"

A DIN is an acronym for Deutsche IndustriNorm, the standards-setting organization for Germany. A DIN connector (see **Figure 7.27**) is a connector that conforms to one of the many standards defined by DIN. There are many types of DIN connectors in addition to the familiar multi-pin circular types.

Q Rob Bennett, WD4DUI, writes: I am designing an active op-amp audio filter for my radio outputs. Is there any disadvantage to utilizing quad or dual devices that are contained in a single chip versus single

op-amp per package? Would there be crosstalk or other unwanted interaction between the sections? Is it worth the extra expense of using high performance devices compared to the more common/older devices such as an LM346 or TL084?

A You can get unwanted interaction between devices if the signal levels differ greatly—for example, using one section as an oscillator and another as a sensitive low-level preamp. It's also easier to get a clean circuit board layout with single or dual-section devices. For most communications applications, high-performance devices are not required except at very low signal levels, for very low distortion, or where power consumption must be minimized. Most op-amp are also unable to supply much output power for driving headphones or speakers cleanly. Audiophiles may be a useful resource—you might be able to find Usenet posts or Web sites that discuss the performance of op-amp in a highly discerning audio performance context.

Q I need a quick refresher on the meaning of Q. Can you help?

A Hmmm…I believe Q was the name of an omnipotent alien who appeared occasionally on *Star Trek: The Next Generation*. His "meaning" wasn't always clear!

But if you're talking about the ratio of an electronic component's ability to store energy to the sum total of all of its energy losses, I can help. That's Q in a nutshell and it is expressed mathematically as

$$Q = \frac{X}{R}$$

where:

Q = figure of merit or quality

X = X_L (inductive reactance) for inductors and X_C (capacitive reactance) for capacitors (in ohms), and

R = the sum of all resistances associated with energy losses in the component (in ohms).

The Q of capacitors is ordinarily high. Good quality ceramic capacitors and mica capacitors may have Q values of 1200 or more. Small ceramic trimmer capacitors may have Q values too small to ignore in some applications. Microwave capacitors typically have poor Q values (10 or less at 10 GHz).

Inductors are subject to many kinds of electrical energy losses including wire resistance, core losses and skin effect. As a result of inherent losses, inductor Q rarely, if ever, approaches capacitor Q in a circuit where both components work together.

Q Peter O'Connell, VK2EMU, writes: I am designing a two-tone oscillator for SSB testing and have been told that the frequencies used by the testing laboratories are 1000 Hz and 1600 Hz. All the books I have looked at (ARRL, RSGB, Bill Orr etc.) simply say any two "non-harmonically related frequencies." Are there specified frequencies and are not 1000 Hz and 1600 Hz both harmonics of 200 Hz?

A "Harmonically related" simply means that the two frequencies (as fundamentals) do not have any harmonics of themselves in common (such as if the 3rd harmonic of one were coincident with the 4th or 5th harmonic of the other). The reason this is important is that you want to easily separate the harmonic distortion from the intermoulation distortion products. It helps to spread out the frequencies so it is possible to deduce what is going on. Alternately, one could use a variable frequency oscillator and measure the velocity of the distortion products.

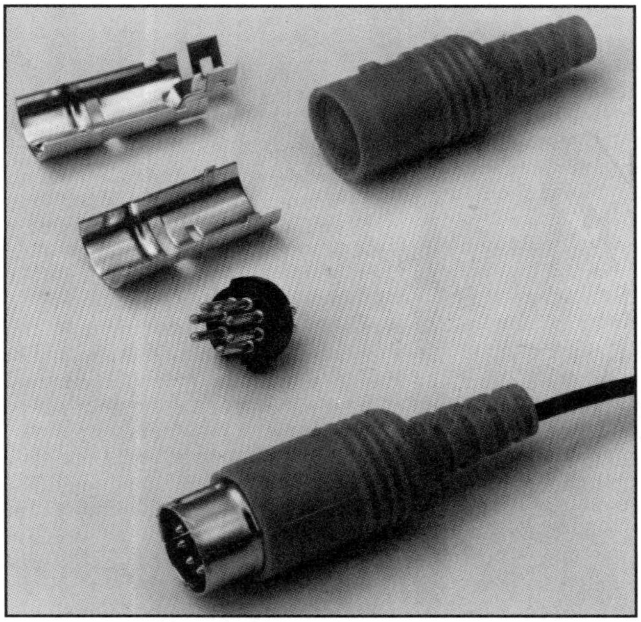

Figure 7.27—The ubiquitous DIN connector.

Q In *QST* I often see references to "ground plane" circuit construction. What does this mean?

A Ground-plane construction is a point-to-point technique that uses the leads of the components as tie points for electrical connections. You may also see it referred to as "dead bug" or "ugly" construction. (The term "ugly construction" was coined by Wes Hayward, W7ZOI.) "Dead-bug construction" gets its name from the appearance of an IC

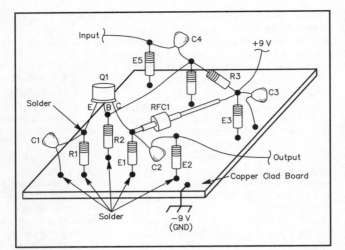

Figure 7.28—Typical ground plane construction. It may look ugly, but it is quick and easy.

with its leads sticking up in the air. In most cases, this technique uses copper-clad circuit-board material as a foundation and ground plane on which to build a circuit using point-to-point wiring, hence "ground-plane construction."

Ground-plane construction is quick and simple: You build the circuit on an unetched piece of copper-clad circuit board. Wherever a component connects to ground, you solder it to the copper board (see **Figure 7.28**). Ungrounded connections between components are made point-to-point. Once you learn how to build with a ground-plane board, you can grab a piece of circuit board and start building any time you see an interesting circuit.

A PC board has strict size limits; the components must fit in the space allotted. Ground-plane construction is more flexible; it allows you to use the parts on hand. The circuit can be changed easily—a big help when you are experimenting. The greatest virtue of ground-plane construction is that it is fast.

Circuit connections are made directly, minimizing component lead length. Short lead lengths and a low-impedance ground conductor help prevent circuit instability. There is usually less intercomponent capacitive coupling than would be found between PC-board traces, so it is often better than PC-board construction for RF, high-gain or sensitive circuits.

Q **Dick Keller, KF4NS, of St Petersburg, Florida, writes: I have one wish for the new year. After extensive searching I cannot come up with a decent electronic component identifier. I just returned a book that was nothing but a manufacturers' phone directory. It did nothing but tell you who made an item based on the stamped labeling on it.**

I wish someone would write a book that explains all the different components and what they look like as well as their recommended application. Take for example the capacitor; there are so many I can't remember them all. You have the electrolytic, the vacuum variable, the ceramic, the mica, feedthrough, etc, etc, etc. Resistors that I remember were all carbon or wirewound. If you look at a catalog like Newark, it blows your mind trying to differentiate the many types. Diodes are also a problem. There are so many, I can't determine which one is for what.

I am restoring some old (of course age is relative) tube rigs and would like to substitute state of the art components for resistors, capacitors and diodes. If you know of a book that will help me identify the components to use, please let me know.

A At first, we were at a loss and unaware of any one-stop book that goes into any detail on what specific component variety is good for a specific type of radio. You can usually glean this information from publications or articles on "How to"... build, design, restore, refurbish, etc, a variety of radio gear or test apparatus...

On component specifics, Chapter 10 in the current *ARRL Handbook* discusses the behavior of various components across wide ranges of frequency and temperature, and could give you a general idea of how to approach a given circuit. The rest of the *Handbook* has projects galore that list specific component types fitted to the application addressed by the specific project.

Other than that, the selection of, say, a metal film resistor for high stability and tolerance versus the older and more familiar carbon film, composition, or wire

wound variety is a decision that one could make based on studying and comparing the manufacturer's technical data sheets on the particular series of resistor, capacitor, inductor, etc, of interest.

There are, however, so many unexpected performance possibilities (and "exceptions to the rule") for such components in the actual applications in which they might be used. You almost always need to consider the specific circuit or project at hand, and the environment in which it must perform...

I've personally found that reading specific articles on, for example, amplifier construction, to be most insightful from others more knowledgeable and experienced than I on the subject. Often, they've done the grunt work of trial and error and can save you a lot of headaches!

If reading others' experiences or preferences does not fully answer your questions as a designer or restorer for a given area of interest, you can always experiment after viewing specific data sheets, performance curves, etc, provided by the component manufacturer. If you have access to the world wide web via your computer, you can also find a lot of useful information by doing component or subject-specific searches. The results—you must often review them considerably to find the exact area of relevance—are still mighty fast as compared to visiting a research library, for example.

A caveat (caution) to you according to one colleague regarding older radio component and wiring "layout": Typically, in older gear, the component size and wiring layout is such that there can be considerable interaction between stages/sections that is considered normal for proceeding with alignment at the factory when the gear was new. Altering the physical makeup or general interconnection/wiring layout as can occur with newer, smaller (or larger), different shaped components, etc, even with the best of restorative intentions, can change the operating characteristics of the circuit to varying degrees.

Nonetheless, regarding sourcing some guidance in the subject area you mentioned, try this: Go to **www.google.com** (an excellent search engine). Once there, in the search box, type in "Selection and Application of Electronic Components." Many of the first 10 (of approximately 418,000!) results appear quite relevant in the way of publications (Wiley, etc) that address the specific area of your interest.

I hope this helps you out, Dick. As a fellow homebrewer/restorer, it always helps to know a fair amount about the planned replacement component, as "trial and error" can be a tedious and frustrating experience.

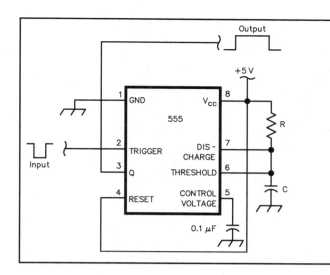

Figure 7.29—A simple one-shot multi-vibrator built around a common 555 timer IC.

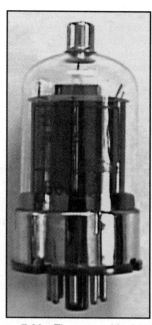

Figure 7.30—The venerable 6146 tube.

Q Many solid-state timers function by producing a logic "high" at the output within a specified time after the timer is triggered. For my application, however, I need a timer that "goes high" as soon as it is triggered and remains high for about 60 seconds before dropping back to zero. Can you steer me in the right direction?

A How about trying the one-shot multivibrator shown in **Figure 7.29**? This one uses a garden-variety 555 timer chip and a couple of components. The trigger pulse causes the output (Q) to go positive and capacitor C to charge through resistor R. When the voltage across capacitor C reaches $^2/_3$ of V_{cc}, the capacitor discharges to ground and the output returns to zero. You can calculate the values of R and C with the equation $T = 1.1(RC)$ where T is the duration of the output pulse in seconds, R is resistance in ohms and C is capacitance in farads. For a 60-second pulse, you'll need a 56-kΩ resistor and a 1000 μF capacitor. This works out to be about 61.6 seconds. Of course, you could use a potentiometer (a 100-kΩ pot, for instance) in place of R to tweak the pulse length and compensate for the tolerance range of the capacitor.

Q Peter O'Connell, VK2EMU, asks about connector designators. "In most magazines and catalogues, we see references to DB-9, DB-15, DB-25, etc. However, I have also seen references to DA, DC and DD, as well as DB. Which is correct?"

A The second letter in a D-style connector model number designates the shell size. For example, a 15-pin video connector has the same connector shell size as a 9-pin DB-9 serial port connector. The designations with the different second letters are the correct ones. The ubiquitous use of "DB" comes from a misunderstanding of the designation, but it is so prevalent now that most vendors use it for all sizes of D connectors.

Q Marvin Sackett, WA4WAY, of Largo, Florida writes: I have four tubes in my storage. All are 6146s finals. Two are RCA 6146A and two are Sylvania 6146W. Can you explain what the letter after the number means?

A The lineage of the 6146 (see **Figure 7.30**) is as follows: 6146—The original design with a plate dissipation of 25 W.

6146W—A ruggedized version of the 6146.

6146A—The first generation of improved 6146 design, also with a plate dissipation of 25 W.

6146B—A significantly improved tube design that offers 35 W of plate dissipation as well as an improved heater design that allowed much cooler operation. The 6146B was designed specifically for SSB service, and was used as a workhorse in many CW and SSB rigs.

In other words, the 6146W is not a replacement for the much more capable 6146B. If you must use a 6146, 6146A or 6146W, adjust your rig's final amplifier section so that the maximum plate dissipation rating isn't exceeded. A great Web site for detailed tube descriptions is **www.tube.be**.

Q Bob Appel, KE3VP, of New Berlinville, Pennsylvania writes: In old equipment and the old FCC regulations, power was expressed in input power to the finals (plate current times plate voltage). If the input power to the finals is 50 W, with a 1:1 imped-ance match to the antenna, what is the output power to the antenna? I'm guessing, half is dropped across the finals and half across the antenna (load) giving a maximum of 25 W to the antenna. If not, can you explain?

A Prior to 1983, the FCC power rules for the Amateur Radio service were based on dc input power to the final RF stage in the transmitter. In these rules, the power of an amateur transmitter was limited to 1000 W dc input to that final stage. To make this measurement, it was necessary to measure and monitor the dc voltage and current being supplied to the final RF stage. Many rigs of that day had built-in voltage and current metering.

The FCC changed its power rules in 1983. Modern ICs had made peak detection of voice signals quite inexpensive. The present rule permits 1500 W peak envelope power (PEP) RF output from transmitters used in the US Amateur Radio Service. Verifying compliance is as easy as connecting a peak-reading wattmeter to the output of the transmitter. Today, most rigs have some kind of built-in RF output measurement capability. In some rigs, possibly for cost containment, the meter is merely hooked up to the output of an RF detector, without any peak detecting or averaging circuitry. Normally, these radios are sufficiently low powered that the FCC does not require accurate power measuring.

In most cases, the final RF output stages in typical amateur transceivers use some variant of Class AB amplification, which provides around 50 to 60% efficiency under ideal conditions. In other words, the RF output from the amplifier is between 50 to 60% of the amount of dc power provided to amplifier from the power supply. Some FM or CW-only rigs use more efficient Class C amplifiers, which provide up to 70% efficiency under ideal conditions. Some special amplification techniques, such as Class E amplification, can achieve nearly 90% efficiency.

Power that isn't converted to RF energy appears as heat in the tubes or transistors and associated circuitry. As such, heat sinks, convection cooling, forced-air cooling and other methods of dissipating the heat must be employed to avoid premature failure of the amplifier. In reality, the ideal 1:1 impedance match is rarely achieved, resulting in decreased efficiency in the final amplifier stage.

The equations for calculating the loss in a feed line and antenna tuner are rather involved. The *TLW* program supplied with *The ARRL Antenna Book* will do these calculations.

Some articles that have featured high-efficiency final amplifier designs are:

Jan 2001 *QEX* "Class-E RF Power Amplifiers," p 9.

Jan 1998 *QST*, "Signal Envelope Elimination and Restoration in Class-E High Efficiency Linear RF Power Amplifiers" (Technical Correspondence), p 80.

May 1997 *QST*, "High-Efficiency Class-E Power Amplifiers—Part 1," p 39.

Jun 1997 *QST*, "High-Efficiency Class-E Power Amplifiers—Part 2," p 39.

Q Jon, W4BCT, asks, "I recently bought some radio crystals. Most are removed from 1940s Navy radios. When I was young my father had some of these, and I wanted to take them apart to see what was inside. Of course, he wouldn't allow this. Now I have some to play with, but I was wondering if you could explain how crystals work?"

A A number of crystalline substances found in nature have the ability to transform mechanical strain (movement) into an electrical charge, and vice versa (think of a tuning fork or a church bell which can transform mechanical strain into sound). This property is known as the piezoelectric effect. A small plate or bar cut in the proper way from a quartz crystal and placed between two conducting electrodes will be mechanically strained when the electrodes are connected to a source of voltage. Conversely, if the crystal is squeezed between two electrodes a voltage will be developed between the electrodes.

Crystalline plates also are mechanical resonators that have natural frequencies of vibration ranging from a few thousand hertz to tens of megahertz. The vibration frequency depends on the kind of crystal, the way the plate is cut from the natural crystal, and on the dimensions of the plate (like the tuning fork and the bell). The thing that makes the crystal resonator valuable is that it has extremely high Q, ranging from 5 to 10 times the Qs obtainable with good LC resonant circuits.

Since the crystal has a definite resonant frequency controlled by the crystal lattice, it can be used to "regulate" an oscillator to a high degree of accuracy.

The crystals we use most often resonate in the 1- to 30-MHz region and are of the *AT cut, thickness shear* type, although these last two characteristics are rarely mentioned. A 15-MHz-fundamental crystal of this type is about 0.15 mm thick. Because of the widespread use of reprocessed war-surplus, pressure-mounted *FT-243* crystals, you may think of crystals as small rectangles on the order of a half-inch in size. The crystals we commonly use today are discs, etched and/or doped to their final dimensions, with metal electrodes deposited directly

Q Ken, KE6ZWN, asks, "The material in an NPN transistor consists of a positive layer (the base) surrounded by two negative layers (the emitter and collector). How do the manufacturers build transistors so that the current flows correctly between layers while at the same time keeping them insulated from each other?"

A See **Figure 7.31**. Transistors are made up of layers of material that are "doped" with impurities so that they are either "P" type (positive charge) or "N" type (negative charge). Now, these charges aren't quite like the ones in a battery—they exist in the form of an occasional extra electron or positive ion (an atom with an electron deficit) that are available as "current carriers."

Where two different layers of material touch, an exchange of current carriers takes place and a neutral (or near neutral) "depletion region" forms (an area where the net charge is depleted). In a bipolar transistor, the base-emitter junction depletion region is fairly thin, whereas the region between the base and the collector is rather thick.

Q Dave, KO4KL, writes: I am confused by an apparent resistor value in an internet schematic provided by a Russian ham. The value given is 4K7 and another value for a different resistor is 3K which of course is 3000 ohms. What value in ohms is 4K7? I found this in several different locations in the schematic so it isn't a typo.

A The European standard for electronic component values is to list the multiplier in place of the decimal point. So a 4K7 is a 4.7 k ohm resistor. For values of a multiplier of one, the letter R is used (so 4R7 would be 4.7 ohms).

Q Putra Djaja, JZ9DEX, of Jakarta, Indonesia, writes: What is, actually, double, triple or quadruple conversion superheterodyne receiver, and what are the differences among them?

A In a superheterodyne receiver, the radio frequency (RF) signal is converted to another frequency prior to demodulation. This is typically the frequency of a band-pass filter, which removes as many offending signals as possible before they can cause

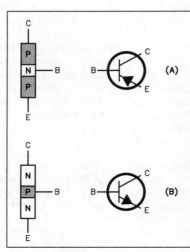

Figure 7.31—Bipolar transistors. **(A)** A layer of N-type semiconductor sandwiched between two layers of P-type semiconductor makes a PNP device. The schematic symbol has three leads: collector (C), base (B) and emitter (E), with the arrow pointing in toward the base. **(B)** A layer of P-type semiconductor sandwiched between two layers of N-type semiconductor makes an NPN device. Note that the arrow in the schematic points *away* from the base.

intermodulation distortion. This conversion takes place in the mixer stage of the receiver when the RF signal is mixed with another signal generated by the local oscillator (LO). This mixing process produces sum and difference signal frequencies. The difference frequency is amplified and becomes the intermediate frequency, or IF.

In a single-conversion superhet, there is only one IF. For example, let us say you have an IF of 4.9 MHz. So if you are listening to 40 meter CW on 7.040 MHz, this signal is mixed down to 4.9 MHz, where it is further amplified and filtered in IF stages of the receiver. After the IF, the signal goes to a detector stage, where it is turned into audio.

A dual-conversion superhet might use a first IF of 9 MHz and a second IF of 455 kHz. A triple conversion design would use three IFs, perhaps 60 MHz, 9 MHz and 455 kHz. A design in which the first IF is higher in frequency than any of the received frequencies is known as an "upconverting" type. Obviously, a quadruple conversion design involves 4 IF stages.

The advantage of more IF stages is that each one can provide less of the over-all gain ("better gain distribution" is the term for it), and additional filtering. The disadvantage is that more noise can be introduced at each stage.

Traditional thinking says that more conversion stages are better, although this has been proven to be wrong in some instances. One of the best receivers of the tube era is said to be the Hammarlund HQ-180, a triple conversion design. However, one of the best receivers of recent years is the Elecraft K2, which is a single conversion design.

The most common configurations are double and triple conversion.

CHAPTER 8

Test Gear

SWR ANALYZER CHECKS CRYSTALS

◊ I checked the antenna-analyzer article and found what I thought was a new discovery.[1] The other night, just out of curiosity, I tried measuring some crystals with my Autek Research RF-1 RF Analyst. Amazingly, I was able to get a low-impedance reading at the crystal frequency. How is this possible, when the VFO swings 10 kHz with slight changes of the dial? I listened to the oscillator with my rig and found that the oscillator actually locks to the crystal, allowing the crystal to take control. For a limited range of the tuning pot, the oscillator cleanly locks and the crystal frequency can be read rock-solid on the display. The "**Z Ohms**" numbers do not reflect the series resistance of the crystal, and shouldn't

[1]"SWR Analyzer Tips, Tricks and Techniques," *QST*, Sep 1996, pp 36-40.

be trusted. This technique was described the *QST* article on pages 39 and 40.
—*Mitchell Lee, KB6FPW, 686 N 21st St, San Jose, CA 95112*

RF-PROOFING PEAK-READING WATTMETERS

◊ Monitoring your peak power output is not only necessary to insure compliance with FCC power limitations but can provide you with invaluable information. However, my peak-reading meter uses an external power supply and was quite susceptible to RF, making its readings useless.

After considerable experimenting with several possible fixes, I found the following procedures to be quite effective:

1. Use a toroid core as a common-mode choke on the ac line of the dc supply used to power the meter (for example, a RadioShack 273-104 or 273-105).

Place the choke as close to the cabinet of the power supply as possible.

2. Place the meter as close to its power supply as possible and use shielded wire for the connection. I have tried both shielded microphone cable and miniature coax with equal success.

These procedures eliminated the RF effects on my meter. I also experimented with different methods of supplying power to the meter. I discovered that the best method was to use a "real" power supply, such as a 3 to 7 A regulated supply. The worst method, and most susceptible to RF, was to use an ac to dc wall adapter.

Being able to adequately monitor your peak power output can be an invaluable aid in setting your microphone gain and amplifier tuning. However, in order to use an externally powered peak-reading meter, it's a good idea to make its power leads "RF-proof."—*T. Stephen Thomason, W4IJ, 601 Black Oak Blvd, Summerville, SC 29485*

The Doctor is IN

Q Andy, KB1ETK, asks, "I have a question about an HF/VHF SWR/power meter I just purchased. I'm using an ADI AT600HP 2m/70cm hand-held transceiver. It generates 5 W output on the 'high power' setting when I use the 13.6-V battery. When I hook up my home-brew ¼-wavelength vertical the meter measures an SWR of 1.3:1 and the RF power measurements are correct: 5 W on high, 2 W on medium, 400 mW on low. But when I attach the rubber duck antenna that came with the radio (with the SWR/power meter in between), my measured power output shoots up to close to 10 W on high, 6 W on medium, and 3 W on low. How is this possible?"

A The power reflected at the rubber ducky is re-reflected back down the

coax from the transmitter to the antenna. When it reaches the antenna, the power again reflects and the cycle begins again. On each reflection, there is some power lost in the transmission line. However, the net effect is that both the forward and reflected powers will read higher than they actually are. The difference between the forward and reverse power readings is the actual net power. Thus, when the SWR is higher than 1:1, the forward power will rise, but so will the reflected power.

Here's a good case in point. I used to own an HF QRP rig that did not reduce power for high SWRs. Its maximum output was 2W. When I had a schedule with a station very close by and didn't have a tuner handy, I ran a random wire around the room and connected the rig directly

to it. The SWR meter said I had 10W forward and 8W reflected. The difference between forward and reverse powers was 10–8 = 2 W, just what it should have been.

Rubber ducks are poor antennas in all respects save one—portability. I wouldn't be overly concerned about the high SWR with your rubber duck. VHF/UHF equipment typically transmits into a 3:1 to 4:1 SWR without suffering ill effects. Further, a rubber duck uses the H-T (and the human body holding it) as its "ground plane." Putting a piece of coax between the rubber ducky and the SWR meter doesn't yield the same amount of ground-plane area and the feed-point impedance of the rubber ducky will change from when it is used in a more traditional fashion connected directly to the H-T.

CHAPTER 9

Antenna Systems

REPLACING BROKEN O-RINGS IN MFJ VERSA TUNERS

◊ Perhaps this will help many owners of MFJ Versa Tuner antenna tuners. As you may know, the digital readout for the inductor tuner coil is connected to the tuning knob by a very fragile O-ring. This ring always seems to fail during the heat of an SS contest; no fun! My solution is simple. Refer to **Figure 9.1** and read on.

Remove the top cover. Stuff a small rag under the inductor shaft to catch the filings, and use a hacksaw blade (blade only—no handle) to carefully cut through the shaft. With the shaft cut, you can pull the tuning knob out just far enough to slip a new O-ring through the gap in the shaft. Reconnect the two shaft pieces with a coupler. (I use a homemade brass coupler about one-half-inch long.) If your junk-box doesn't contain a suitable coupler, try the local hardware store or a fleamarket. You can buy replacement O-rings at hardware stores, but take the broken one along to check the size.[1] (If the exact size is not available, I have used rings that are one size smaller.)

I keep a spare O-ring stored inside the tuner so it's always available. In fact, I leave the tuner cover in place but unfastened. (The cover screws are in a small plastic bag right next to the spare O-ring.) Now I can replace a broken O-ring and be back on the air in less than 30 seconds.—*Don Miller, W2MQB, PO Box 3005, The Springs, NY 11937-0395*

ENGINE HOIST LIFTS TOWER EASILY

◊ About a year ago, I purchased an LM470 Tri-Ex motorized 70-foot tower, complete with a tilt-over fixture. I had planned to erect it at my new location in central Florida. I had purchased it from an old friend in southern Florida, rented

[1]William Wornham, NZ1D's article about drivebelts (*QST*, Apr 2001, p 83) tells how to calculate belt length.

a boat trailer and driven to his home to pick it up.

Quite a few local Ham Club members showed up to help get it on the trailer for us (I counted over fifteen). We pushed, pulled, shoved, lifted, slid, rolled and tried about everything in the book to get it up on my trailer—and we did succeed, but it took most of the morning.

This tower is massive to say the least, and it weighs in at over half a ton, not counting the separate tilt fixture that was over 200 pounds by itself.

After arriving at my new location, I had to return the trailer within 24 hours or pay a substantial premium. With two neighbors (we are each over 75 years of age), we began constructing a system of concrete building blocks and 4×4 planks under the extended end of the tower. Then, using two auto jacks, we lifted the tower and added more blocks and planks under each end until the trailer could be

Figure 9.1—A photo of W2MQB's Versa Tuner fix. The shaft coupler (right center) secures the inductor shaft that was cut to facilitate O-ring replacement. The tuner front panel is at left, with the turns-counter mechanism visible at lower left corner.

pulled out from under the tower.

This left me with a beautiful tower sitting in my backyard, but after all of this I began to have doubts about using the same technique to move the tower 70 feet to the spot I had selected for it. After I had admired it for some months, my XYL didn't, and I placed some ads for its sale.

A chap in the Miami area called and wanted to buy it and said he could bring a trailer and a helper.

About then, I recalled I had used a hydraulic automotive engine hoist to remove a ground post left over from an E-Z Way tower I had once owned. I checked around and found that one auto parts chain loaned them free of charge! The hoists are fully portable (on wheels), come disassembled and fit in my station wagon. They can lift up to 4000 pounds and have sufficient height that a tower could easily clear the top of a trailer. Moreover, one person, with one hand, can handle the entire operation with ease. The hydraulic cylinder has a handle that moves with very little effort.

My buyer came, but his helper bailed out at the last minute. By using the hoist, the two of us easily placed the tower on his trailer—not once but twice, because we decided it would ride better turned 180°. The whole operation took about an hour and he was on his way back for a successful 300-mile trip home.

I returned the hoist the next day and got my deposit (about $275) back. They did not charge me a penny. That was a lifesaver! Thanks to Discount Auto Parts.

In speaking with the people at our local branch, I was told that they still offer this at some locations, but each individual manager decides whether to rent the units.—*Stephen C. Taber W4ITD, 25 Cunningham Dr, New Smyrna Beach, FL 32168;* **w4itd@arrl.net**

A SIMPLE ANTENNA FLIPPER

◊ Make your Field Day or portable setup *faster* and *safer* with an inexpensive homebrew Antenna Flipper. One of my responsibilities as Field Day chairperson is to ensure the safety of participants and visitors at the site. After 30 years of Field Day operations, countless portable and rover expeditions, I became aware of a serious problem in partially elevating a tower to attach a beam antenna.

The Problem

The towers are propped up with stepladders or various other devices to facilitate attaching the beam to the mast. A lot of time is spent atop the props adjusting the level, tightening the U-bolts, installing feed lines etc. At tear down, the procedure is reversed. This part of the operation is great for action photos in *QST* (eg, June 1999, page 21), but it opens the door for accidents and possible damage to the antenna. Not only that, it takes too much time. There is a much safer and faster way to do it.

The Solution

You and your crew can keep your feet on the ground by building this simple hinge, which I dub the FD Antenna Flipper (see **Figure 9.2**). All antenna preparations and attachments are done at ground level. That way, more people can work on the setup at the same time. Sounds too good to be true?

How it Works

The hinge is made of two parts (see

Figure 9.2—Author N9KS with the FD Antenna Flipper ready for elevation.

Figure 9.3). One is attached to the mast and the other to the antenna boom plate. The two are joined with a bolt that is the hinge pin. As the tower is raised, the hinge closes, permitting the antenna to remain horizontal through the lift. The boom plate comes to rest on top of the mast end and the weight of the antenna keeps the elements horizontal. When the tower is lowered, it is very easy for helpers to grasp the element ends and guide the antenna back to the horizontal position (as the hinge opens) for disassembly. No ladder work or props are required, and in a matter of minutes, the antenna is disconnected from the mast.

The Hardware

The Field Day Flipper is made with two pieces of $4 \times 6 \times 3/16$-inch-thick flat

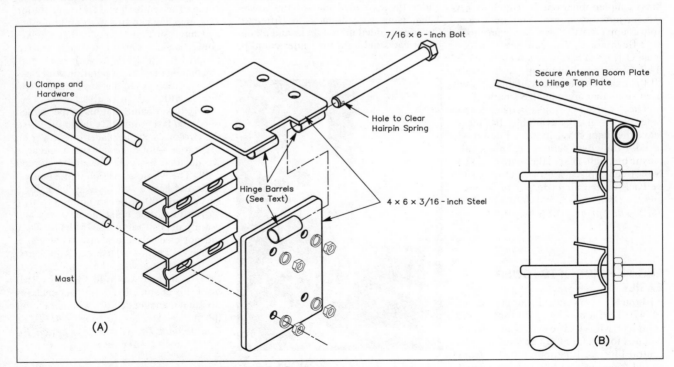

Figure 9.3—FD Antenna Flipper construction details. See text.

2—$3/16 \times 4 \times 6$-inch flat steel (Notch long side of one piece to clear center hinge barrel. See Figure 4.)
1—$7/16 \times 6$-inch bolt drilled to accept spring clip at threaded end
1—hairpin spring clip

1—6-inch long black gas pipe nipple, $1/2$-inch ID cut into three $1 1/2$-inch long parts
2—U-clamps to fit mast

steel and the hinge barrels are made of 1/2-inch ID black gas pipe cut to 1 1/2-inch lengths. The pipe pieces are deburred inside with a 1/2-inch drill to easily fit a 7/16-inch bolt. A notch on one plate gives clearance to the mating hinge. The pipe pieces are welded to the plates. Each flat piece is drilled to match the **U**-bolts on the mast and the antenna.[2] If your antenna is used only for Field Day, the parts can be left in place. The dimensions given here were used and tested with a TA-33 Jr tribander at 40 feet. Larger antennas call for more barrel sections and heavier-gauge plates.

The Cost

For less than $25, you can set up faster and put those stepladders and other shaky props away. Let gravity do the work for you. Start the new millennium safely and make Field Day 2000 the best one ever. —*Ken Secora, N9KS, W333 S4222 Connemara Dr, Dousman, WI 53118-9798;* **ksecora@ticon.net**

STEALTH ANTENNA SUPPORTS

◊ My stealth 80-meter full-wave horizontal loop is supported by those gold painted masts from RadioShack. After receiving glares from my neighbors and noticing several curious people drive by, I came up with an idea: camouflage. I painted the bottom of the poles to match the buildings and trees nearby. The top portion is painted flat black. For the most part, the poles are difficult to see unless you are looking for them.—*Lawrence E. Mergen, KØWVL, 209 S Morrison Rd, Raymore, MO 64083.*

PL-259 ASSEMBLY USING TUBING CUTTERS

◊ Here's another method of connector-cable assembly. I realize that it's common for more than one person to come up with similar ideas, but I have never seen this idea before.[3] I have been using it for more than 10 years, and it certainly simplifies connector assembly.

Please refer to **Figure 9.4**. I use small clamp-style tubing cutters to cut through the jacket—and later, the tinned braid. After first removing the cable jacket, tin the braid to make it smooth and solid.

[2]Templates for the author's version are available from the ARRL Web site. You can download this package from **www.arrl.org/files/qex/**. Look for 0003N9KS.zip.

[3]How true! A similar hint by Ralph Hirsh, K1RH, appeared in the Aug 1988 column on p 48. This method bears repeating, but be careful not to melt the dielectric when tinning the braid.—*Ed.*

Use the tubing cutter again to cut through the tinned braid. Use a hacksaw to cut (at an angle) through the waste side of the tinned braid to make it easier to remove. Remove the dielectric and prepare the center lead. Fit the cable into the body of the connector and solder the body to the tinned braid. The tinned braid makes this step easy and ensures a solid connection. Finally, solder the center conductor to the pin.—*Kevin Dean, VE7CFS, #207 15140 29A Ave, South Surrey, BC V4P 1H1, Canada*

AN ANTENNA THRUST BACKUP

◊ If the bolt in a bolt-secured thrust bearing becomes loose, the mast can drop, placing its full weight on the rotator. As a safety backup, install a heavy washer just above the thrust bearing with a heavy shear pin or bolt above the washer as shown in **Figure 9.5**. If the thrust bearing fails, the mast is still supported by the washer and pin.—*Richard Mollentine, WAØKKC, 7139 Hardy St, Overland, KS 66704-1710*

MORE ON AN ANTENNA THRUST BACKUP

◊ An astute fellow on the Tower Talk reflector (**towertalk@contesting.com**) observes that the location of the hole for the bolt or shear pin is near the worst possible point on the mast. He is correct. Wind force on the antennas is resisted at the point of the bearing, and there the

bending stress will be greatest. The hole for the bolt is near by and it does weaken the mast. If the mast loads and wind are such that the mast is stressed near failure, it will fail sooner because of the hole. (The basics of bending in antenna masts are presented on pages 22-20 and 22-21 of *The ARRL Antenna Book*, 19th edition.)

If the array wind load (area) perpendicular to the boom is substantially less

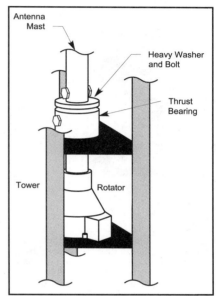

Figure 9.5—WAØKKC adds a washer and pin to insure against thrust bearing failure.

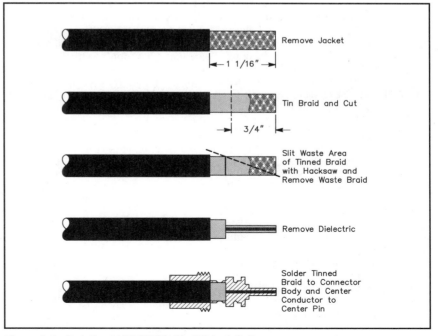

Figure 9.4—Details of VE7CFS's PL-259 installation.

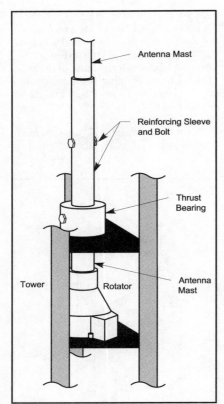

Figure 9.6—A sleeve arrangement permits moving the bolt away from the mast's area of greatest bending stress. This leaves the mast stronger than the washer hint presented by WA0KKC in the January column.

than it is in line with the boom, we can reduce the likelihood of failure by orienting the bolt axis perpendicular to the antenna boom(s). That way, the hole is positioned on the mast centerline with respect to the direction of greatest bending load—but maybe there's another way.

The bolt and washer could be replaced by a bolt and sleeve (see **Figure 9.6**). The sleeve prevents the mast from slipping as well as the washer did, but it allows the bolt (and hole) to be placed farther up the mast, well away from the area of maximum moment (bending stress). If the sleeve fits closely around the mast, it may also serve to strengthen it slightly by making it more difficult for the mast to fold at the bearing.

Those who want to study the stresses on masts and towers more closely should read "Tower and Antenna Wind Loading as a Function of Height," by Frank Travanty, W9JCC (*QEX*, Jul/Aug 2001, pp 23-33). In that article, Frank uses an *Excel* spreadsheet and some basic structural engineering to examine the stresses on a mast and free-standing tower. —*KU7G*

STAINLESS-STEEL FASTENER SOURCE

◊ Every Amateur Radio operator who installs outdoor antennas or towers, needs stainless-steel fasteners at one time or another. While some larger hardware stores carry a limited supply of stainless-steel bolts, nuts and washers, most don't or they're priced beyond what might seem reasonable to most of us. Boating and marine-supply stores are another potential source for stainless steel fasteners, but they may not be located anywhere near the vicinity for those hams who are land-locked.

One interesting source for such items recently came to my attention in the form of a catalog from Champion Trailers.[4] They supply finished boat and utility trailers along with a wide variety of trailer parts, including a nice selection of stainless steel **U** bolts, hex-head bolts, threaded rods, sheet-metal screws, wood screws, carriage bolts, lag screws, machine screws, washers and self-locking (nylon insert) nuts. Their prices seem reasonable (a bag of 10 #8-32×$\frac{1}{2}$-inch machine screws for $0.99) and their mail-order catalog is free for the asking. They're just the ticket for Amateur Radio antenna buffs.

Remember, although stainless-steel fasteners aren't supposed to rust, they can seize under certain environmental conditions, so use an anti-seize thread lubricant such as Bostik's Never Seez[5] on all fittings that will be exposed to the elements.—*Dave Miller, NZ9E, 7462 Lawler Ave, Niles, IL 60714*

SILENCE THAT WHISTLING ANTENNA!

◊ Does your ham radio antenna whistle while you drive? A few years ago, I read that new GM cars were equipped with antennas that don't whistle. A look around a parking lot produced what I thought was the fix—a normal antenna wrapped with wire and then covered with something like heat-shrink tubing. That sounds simple enough, and if it didn't work, I wouldn't lose much money.

Wrap something nonconductive, say $\frac{1}{16}$ to $\frac{1}{8}$ inch string or grass-trimmer line (not wire—it will affect your SWR), around the antenna in a neat, evenly spaced spiral. One turn per inch

[4]Champion Trailer Parts Supply, 56705 I-10 Service Rd, Slidell, LA 70458; tel 800-229-6690, fax 504-781-7701; **www.championtrailers.com**.

[5]Bostik, 211 Boston St, Middleton, MA 01949-2128; tel 978-777-0100, fax 978-750-7293; **www.bostik.com**. Check out their Never Seez selector sheet at **www.bostik.com/pdf/distribution/N23p1.pdf**.

is too tight. Use tape to anchor the string. Once the string is wrapped around the antenna, slide heat-shrink tubing on and heat it. The tubing is tough enough to survive repeated encounters with parking ramp overhangs, signs and trees.

My hunch was correct. The string-wrapped antenna no longer whistles. How? I think it has something to do with breaking up the antenna's surface area.—*Bob Morrow, N7PTM, 5254 Brindisi Ct #5, Middleton, WI 53562;* **bobmor@chorus.net**

STEALTHY LADDERLINE

◊ Like many hams, I discovered the advantages of using open-wire line, "window line" as some variants are called. While I was totally pleased with its performance, my XYL was less than amused by its appearance.

When working with camouflage, one of the goals is to mimic nature rather than man-made objects. I followed some camouflage principles and devised a way to significantly reduce the visual signature of window line, particularly when it has a background of trees, as in my installation.

My first step was to buy a pair of "nail-slot-hole pliers" as sold in hardware stores and elsewhere for punching oblong holes in aluminum and vinyl siding. With these pliers, you can remove extra material from the rectangles of solid plastic in the window line (see **Figure 9.7**). Neatness and uniformity are discouraged

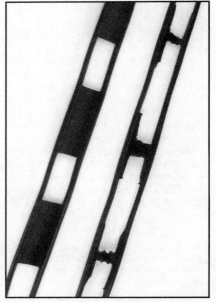

Figure 9.7—Pieces of window line before and after K9SQG modified the "windows" to maximize the camouflage ability of the line.

because the result then looks "man-made." A line with some rough edges actually looks more natural.

Second, I used some spray paint to break up the uniform color of the plastic insulation. Even without the paint, however, the reduction in visual signature is dramatic. If you elect to use spray paint, try to pick colors that resemble foliage in your area for the longest season, or the sunniest season, as appropriate. Avoid certain paints, however. For example, some "ultra flat black" paints use carbon black for pigmentation. While not a perfect conductor, carbon black can result in losses and disrupt the impedance, depending on the amount used.

While the modified window line can still be seen from the house, it is far less noticeable. From the street, it's easy to miss unless you are looking for it.—*Evan Rolek, K9SQG, 1295 Oakleaf Dr, Beavercreek, OH 45434-8002;* **k9sqg@aol.com**

RAISE YOUR PUSH-UP MAST SAFELY

◊ We hams tend to use the TV push-up masts for various antenna supports. I use a 40-foot TV push-up mast for part of my 160-meter vertical. The most dangerous part of the installation is erecting or lowering the mast. Because the sections of the mast telescope into each other, locking pliers are generally used to secure each mast section until the proper cotter pin or bolt is inserted to hold the section in place. Have you ever had the pliers suddenly lose their grip and let the mast section come down? I have, and this can be a very dangerous situation.

To alleviate this recurring problem, I laid out the mast on the ground and extended it as it would be in the vertical position. I left a one-foot overlap at each joint. Generally, the manufacturer drills a hole one foot below from the top of each mast section so a cotter pin can be inserted to hold the telescoping mast section in place. If a hole is not present, drill one. I drilled my holes large enough for a ¼-inch bolt. I then drilled a hole of the same size into the mast that is telescoped in the larger section. This hole is drilled just above the top of the larger section. While raising the antenna, place a Phillips screwdriver through the hole to temporarily prevent the mast from falling if the pliers suddenly lose their grip. You can then safely install the bolt and nut to secure this section of the mast.

For greater safety, I painted a red stripe around the hole drilled in the smaller mast. One foot above it, I painted a blue stripe around the mast. When the blue stripe appears, I know I have one

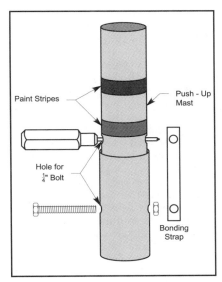

Figure 9.8—K6BX's scheme to ease erection of push-up masts. Two painted stripes signal when the joint fastening is near. The new hole in the inner section accepts a screwdriver shaft to prevent accidental slippage while installing the main fastener. Bolts through both holes hold a jumper strap that provides electrical continuity across the joint.

more foot to raise the mast before the hole appears. I also use the two holes for a bonding strap at the junction (see **Figure 9.8**). After securing the bonding strip, I raise the mast to the next section, and so on until the erection process is completed.—*John J. Roessler, K6BX, 392 N Westwind Dr, El Cajon, CA 92020;* **k6bx@arrl.net**

LONG LIFE FOR PERMANENT PUSH-UP MASTS

◊ If you use a push-up mast on a permanent basis, add a cap to the top and use silicone caulk to seal each joint against the weather (see **Figure 9.9**). This keeps the rain out and prevents internal rust. Without sealing, water inside the mast could freeze in winter and split the mast tubing. If there is any chance of internal water—no seal remains perfect forever—drill a couple of small "weep" holes at the bottom of the mast.—*Richard Mollentine, WA0KKC, 7139 Hardy St, Overland, KS 66704-1710*

WEATHER CAPS FOR CONNECTORS

◊ The rubber caps sold to protect floors from chairs and canes work nicely as protective end caps for coaxial connectors. The ⅝-inch size is just right for SO-239s. The ¾-inch ones fit over N connectors with a bit of a squeeze. They are great for keeping dirt and moisture

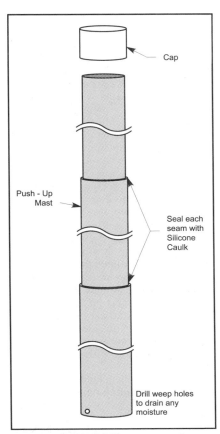

Figure 9.9—WA0KKC recommends sealing push-up masts against the weather.

out when storing or transporting equipment, say for Field Day or mountain-top operation. They are available in most hardware stores. Where I bought them, they sold both white and black.—*Emil Pocock, W3EP, Box 100, Lebanon, CT 06249;* **w3ep@arrl.org**

STEALTHY ANTENNA WIRE

◊ Premier Fence Systems[6] sells "GreenCote HT Smooth Wire," stock #301210 at $34 for a 2100-ft roll. This is #12 AWG electric fence wire, and it may have some use for stealth antennas. I got the Premier catalog after attending the Maryland Sheep and Wool Festival.—*Bill Riley, N3SNU, 12215 Malta Ln, Bowie, MD 20715-1811;* **n3snu@arrl.net** [From Premier's Web site, this appears to be high strength galvanized steel wire that has been painted green. It is meant to resist rust, and the greenish color may make the wire less visible than are many other conductors in outdoor settings. Remember that it is steel wire and has relatively high resistance compared to copper.—*KU7G*]

[6]Premier1Supplies, 2031 300th St, Washington, IA 52353; tel 800-282-6631, fax 800-346-7992; **info@premier1supplies.com; www.premier1supplies.com.**

USE A DRIP LOOP TO KEEP WATER OUT

◊ I have another approach to the Doctor's solution for Martin Feigert, AC8CW (*QST*, Apr 2002, p 56). Martin's mag-mount antenna and coax caused water to leak into his car. I have never had this problem with my many mag-mount antennas, that is, until recently using a mag-mount antenna in a friend's station wagon. The problem surprised me because the coax was very thin. I didn't have sealer and it wasn't my car, so it was either fix the problem, live with the dripping water or remove the antenna until it stopped raining.

During past roofing problems, I remember being told by a good roofer, "If you let water sit, it will find a way in. The object is to provide the water with a downhill path away from where it is on the roof." The basic idea is this: Route cables so water must go up hill and up wind to get into your car or house and it won't enter. Using this idea and a simple loop or bend we can keep water out of the car with no cost and without sealing the window shut.

I fixed the problem with a drip loop in the coax. Water follows the path of least resistance downhill. So, all I did was to provide a "downhill" path from where the coax enters the top of the door, then loop the coax back upward to the antenna. The coax entering the car now presents an up-hill and up-wind path, so the water drips off at the bottom of the loop and does not enter the car.

The bend in the coax need not go very far below the top of the door (see **Figure 9.10**). I had extra coax and looped it down about two or three inches so I could watch the water drip off as we drove in the rain.

It is a simple, no-cost way to solve the water problem.

This idea works for coax entering a house as well. I use it for all coax entries into my house and have no leakage problems. I even routed the TV cable into the house the same way. Although the TV installation was sealed, it never hurts to have gravity help the seal.

Larger coax must bend with a larger radius, but even if you can't bend the coax (for example, hardline), you can orient it so that it slopes gently upward to the entry point. We can use something wrapped around the coax to divert the flow away from it. Then, gravity will take the water down the wrap to drip off the end. This can be done with electrical tape, a piece of wire or a wire tie (see **Figure 9.11**). Just be sure the wrap you use contacts the cable nearly all of the way around. Tape sure wouldn't help much if used to seal a path into the house, but if it's wrapped around the cable with a hanging tail, water will follow it downhill. If the coax slopes too steeply, however, the wrap can't divert all of the water.

These ideas work everywhere, even in emergency installations, where we may find ourselves without sealer or might not be allowed to use it.

One more thing while I have your "ear": good engineering practice uses the laws of physics and nature to our advantage. A drip loop works because water relentlessly seeks its lowest level.

The Doctor's answer tries to stop nature from taking its course. It will work for some period, but it may eventually fail because it overcomes the natural character of water with brute force. When that force weakens, water will prevail. On the other hand, as the Doctor stated, "Of course, it follows that there is a 'Family Law': that window must never be opened. If the kids forget, just reseal it." What a short-sighted and painfully temporary solution that is!—*Phil Karras, KE3FL, AEC Carroll County Maryland, ORS, OES, Life Member, 3305 Hampton Ct, Mount Airy, MD 21771-7201;* **ke3fl@arrl.net**

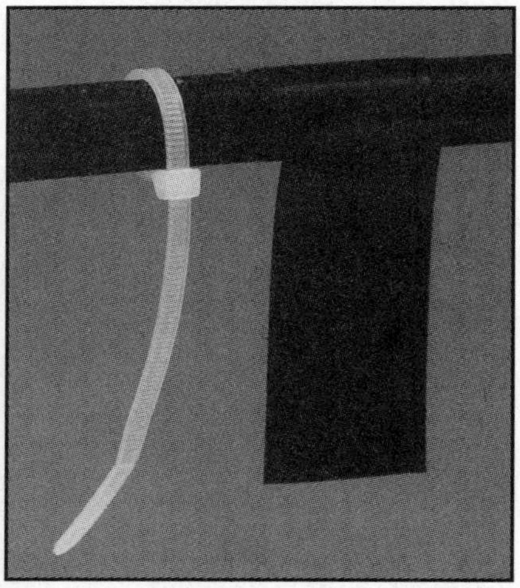

USE PVC PIPE TO EASE INSTALLATION OF ATTIC ANTENNAS

◊ I have been working recently on installing a 40-meter dipole (using two end-loading wires) in a small attic space of my rented townhouse. The antenna must be trimmed to resonance at four points, all of which are right along the edge of theattic under the eaves. Access is tight and normally requires a belly crawl along the narrow edges of ceiling joists through loose fiberglass insulation with roofing-nail points just inches overhead.

While contemplating the prospect of several trips out to the four endpoints of the antenna to trim it, I came up with a better way. I purchased four 10-ft sections of $^1/_2$-inch Schedule 40 PVC pipe and attached one end of each pipe to each end of the loading wires with cable ties.

I first drilled a small hole through one side of the PVC pipe about $^3/_8$ inch from one end. I slipped a cable tie through this hole and out the end of the pipe and created a loose loop. I fed a second cable tie through this loose loop and then tightened the second cable tie securely around the antenna wire several inches from its end. This holds the wire firmly enough to manipulate it, but allows the wire to slide enough to pull more wire through for trimming to resonance. (See **Figure 9.12**.)

Now I can work on the antenna from the more spacious interior of the attic by simply picking up the PVC pipes and bringing the wire ends back to my position, then extending them back into their tight working quarters when I'm done. The pipes are heavy enough to hold the wire stretched into working configuration. You could also use thicker-walled Schedule 80 PVC or $^3/_4$-inch diameter pipe if you need a heavier or stiffer pipe. If you need additional tension on the wire, use pipe straps or **J** hooks to secure the pipes, and therefore the antenna ends more firmly in place. You might also be able to use the PVC pipe and straps to hold the antenna off the attic floor if your design requires this.

If you have a longer wire that is difficult to reach but needs more careful

Figure 9.10—A simple drip loop keeps water from entering this vehicle. The front of the vehicle is to the right. The loop is oriented so that gravity and wind naturally move water away from the window opening.

Figure 9.11—"Wraps" such as electrical tape or a tie-wrap can help divert water away from a nearly horizontal cable or pipe entering a building or vehicle. Either wrap should work alone, we simply used a single photo to show both. (Note: A white tie-wrap is shown, but black ones are better for outdoor use.)

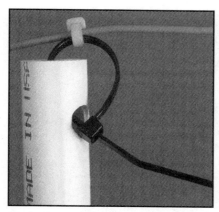

Figure 9.12—KB8WEV suggests PVC pipes as permanent handles to place antennas in cramped attic spaces.

placement, fashion an open hook or a **Y** that attaches to one end of a PVC pipe. Hold the wire a few inches above the ceiling joists with the hook or push it away from you with the **Y** as you lay it in the desired position.

Of course, a wooden dowel, closet rod or small rectangular stock could also serve these functions if you have them on hand. The PVC has good reach and is cheaper than wood if you're buying for the purpose. The PVC also has no sharp corners or grain and will not snag, tear or move attic insulation around as much as wood.

I find this method more appealing than a steady diet of fiberglass and dust or finding bits of my scalp hanging from the business end of a roofing nail.—*Lee W. Lumpkin, KB8WEV, 51 Glenhurst Dr, Oberlin, OH 44074;* **kb8wev@arrl.net**

WHIP ANTENNA STORAGE FOR YOUR MOBILE

◊ When I sold my station wagon and moved the mobile rig and antenna into a new sedan, I lost a convenient storage place for my 6-foot whip, just above the headliner. I could only stick an antenna through an opening in the back seat from the trunk. If you want to carry passengers, this is inconvenient and antennas can get filthy in the wind outside the car. I didn't want to get the seats or passengers dirty.

What I needed was a readily available place under the car. One evening I was looking at my great-grandfather's Civil War sword on the wall when an idea came to me. Why not make a sheath for my antenna?

My antenna sheath is made of CPVC pipe. This material is used for both hot and cold plumbing in house construction. It is a little different from PVC pipe. It has a yellowish tint, thinner walls and smaller connectors. The antenna sheath consists of six pieces of CPVC. Starting at the "business end" there is a $^3/_4$-inch threaded screw cap and a $^3/_4$ threaded male to $^3/_4$ slip-joint adapter. Next, there's a short (about three inches) piece of $^3/_4$ pipe, a $^3/_4$ to $^1/_2$ coupler, then a 6-foot piece of $^1/_2$-inch pipe and finally a $^1/_2$ cap. All of these parts—except the $^3/_4$ cap—are bonded together with CPVC glue. (See **Figures 9.13 and 9.14**.)

The short piece of $^3/_4$ pipe accommodates the antenna connector. The connector bottoms against the $^3/_4$:$^1/_2$ adapter so that the connector sticks out of the sheath about $^1/_4$ inch. This allows you to grip it with your thumb and forefinger when the $^3/_4$ cap is unscrewed and withdraw the whip. Adjust the length of the $^3/_4$ pipe to suit your antenna.

I mounted the sheath under the car with the screw-cap end at the bumper. Cable ties secure the sheath to the car every so often, starting at the rear bumper and going toward the front of the car. The last cable tie is at the $^1/_2$-inch cap end, about midway along the length of the car.

The CPVC pipe need not follow a straight path. If the $^1/_2$ pipe is bowed a little, the whip stores just fine. Just make sure that the assembly does not interfere with the vehicle suspension and is well clear of the exhaust system. The exhaust system could melt the CPVC pipe and possibly cause a fire if it's too close.

I have found this a very convenient arrangement for quick access to the antenna. After the picture was taken, I thought it would be nice to paint the whole sheath flat black. You can hardly see it under my car now.—*Raymond J. Schneider, W6JXW, PO Box 550, Big Stone Gap, VA 24219-0550;* **w6jxw@ arrl.net**

Figure 9.14— The sheath in place on the author's car. Stay clear of the exhaust and suspension systems, and watch out for big rocks!

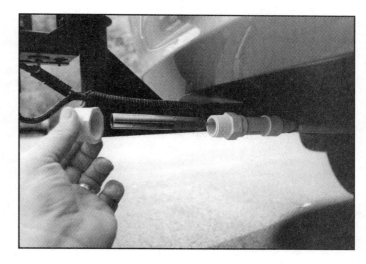

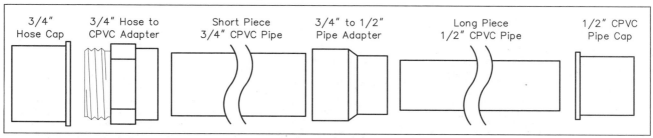

Figure 9.13—Parts of the under-chassis antenna sheath. Size the parts to suit your antenna.

SIMPLE PVC CENTER INSULATORS

◊ I have recently discovered two accessories can be used with PVC plumbing pipe to simplify making dipole center insulators and balun enclosures.

The first is a reducing bushing. It is designed to fit inside a pipe coupling or an end cap and accept a smaller size pipe than the cap does. A 1×¹/₂-inch bushing fits over ¹/₂-inch pipe and into a 1-inch cap. By a stroke of good luck, an SO-239 coax chassis connector will fit over the hole for ¹/₂-inch pipe and can be mounted there with #4 screws. **Figure 9.15** shows one of these bushings and a 1-inch cap, as they may be purchased at Home Depot or plumbing-supply stores. A completed center insulator is also shown; the eyebolts are mounted by nuts both inside and outside the cap. The opposing eyebolts are for the dipole wires. The eyebolt at the top is for supporting an inverted-**V** antenna when the center insulator will be the highest point of the antenna. Separate wires connect the center terminal of the coax connector to one half of the dipole and one of the SO-239 mounting screws to the other half of the dipole. The bushing and cap are glued together with PVC cement.

If you want a larger center insulator, a second reducing bushing can be used between the one shown, which mounts a coax connector, and a 1¹/₄- or 1¹/₂-inch pipe cap.

The second "discovery" is of PVC plugs, or inner caps, that fit inside ordinary PVC pipe. These make a nice enclosure when used to seal off the ends of a pipe. For example, when combining a center insulator with a balun, the enclosure can be lengthened with a piece of pipe that fits into the cap, and the coax connector can be mounted to one of these inner caps. They are available from United States Plastics Corporation.[7] Figure 9.15 shows 1¹/₄-inch pipe with a regular cap at one end and an inner cap with SO-239 ready to be inserted at the other end.

Notice that the reducing bushings fit into pipe connectors, not the pipe itself, but the inner caps do fit into the regular Schedule 40 pipe. They present some new options in making PVC enclosures.—*Robert Johns, W3JIP, Box 662, Bryn Athyn, PA 19009;* **ksjohns@ mindspring.com**

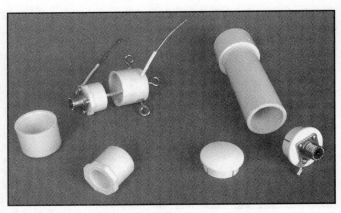

Figure 9.15— PVC internal caps and reducing bushings can be very helpful when fabricating center insulators for dipole antennas.

INSTALLING A HY-GAIN TAILTWISTER ROTATOR IN ROHN 25

◊ A hy-gain TX rotator *will* fit inside Rohn 25 tower sections, but it *cannot* be installed from the side. (The crossbars are too close for it to pass through them.) The rotator can be inserted from the ends of each tower section, as shown in **Figure 9.16.**—*Richard Mollentine, WA0KKC, 7139 Hardy St, Overland, KS 66704-1710*

PROTECTING COAX CONNECTIONS

◊ Over the years I have used various methods to protect exposed coax conductors at their attachment to the antenna. When a coax connector is used, one can protect from the weather with coax sealer, however when the center conductor and the braid are directly connected to the antenna, this does not work very well.

While getting some boating equipment last fall at a West Marine (marine supplies) store, I ran across a product called Liquid Electrical Tape.[8] I have used this on my coax with good results. It comes in a small can with an applicator brush attached to the cap. When it is applied to the braid of the coax it soaks in and makes a good seal. It is flexible also. I use it on the center conductor and dielectric and on the soldered connections. Since it fills the spaces in the braid and between the braid and the insulation, it prevents water from infiltrating and causing the coax to deteriorate.

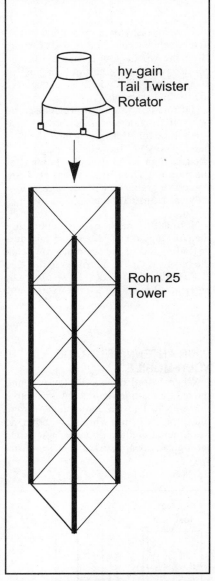

hy-gain
Tail Twister
Rotator

Rohn 25
Tower

Figure 9.16—WA0KKC points out that TailTwister rotators can be used in Rohn 25 towers. Simply remember to insert the rotator from the end of a tower section.

[7]United States Plastics Corp, 1390 Neubrecht Rd, Lima, OH 45801-3196; tel 800-537-9724. They take telephone orders with Visa or MasterCard and usually ship the same day. You will also receive a catalog that every builder should have. The order numbers for the inner caps are: 1-inch #28207, 1¹/₄-inch #28208 and 1¹/₂-inch #28209.

[8]The maker is PDI Inc (Plastic Dip International), 3760 Flowerfield Rd, PO Box 130, Circle Pines, MN 55014-0130; tel 763-785-2156, 800-969-5432, fax 763-785-2058; **www.plastidip.com/liqtape.html**. They make Liquid Electrical Tape in red, green, black and white. PDI products are sold at many home-improvement and hardware stores.

This material could also be used to apply to coax connectors.

Liquid Electrical Tape comes in black and in white. I have used the black. I use a generous amount and when it hardens, I apply a second coat. After it dries it is not sticky or messy.—*Hugh Inness-Brown, W2IB, 5351 State Hwy 37, Ogdensburg, NY 13669;* **w2ib@sric.com**

TECHNIQUES FOR WEATHERPROOFING CONNECTORS

◊ I have spent considerable time with professional antenna riggers (especially in the Northeast) and learned their recommended procedures to weatherproof connectors.

Radio amateurs (we are called "amateurs" but many of us attempt to do our hobby very professionally) experiment with various aspects of "ham radio." Some design and improve on their designs of antennae, power amplifiers, preamplifiers and so on. However, in some very important areas there are serious shortcomings.

For example, when an antenna system is installed and the transmission lines are connected and run to the shack, the connections are invariably taped to keep out moisture, whether the connections involve PL-259s, N or other connectors.

When an antenna system is installed, one doesn't want to climb a tower every few months to open a connection, dry out and retape it, especially in damper climates where the possibility of this occurrence is more frequent.

Here is a time-proven method:

1. Apply a small portion of silicon grease to the threads of the connection. *Do not* apply grease to the center pin!

2. Fasten the connectors and tape the connection about two to three inches along the transmission line beyond the connector.

3. Apply Mastic Seal[9] over the length of the tape and slightly past the tape ends.

4. Using Scotch 33 or 88 tape, cover the Mastic Seal starting from the lower end of the connection and tape upward (this is important). When you get to the opposite end of the connection *do not* cut the tape but *reverse* the wrapping direction back downward again. Repeat this process a total of *five* times—three upward and two downward. Now, this is *important: Do not* pull or stretch the tape

---

[9]Weatherproofing kits may be obtained from Site Advantage Inc, 206 Christopher St, Ronkonkoma, NY 11779; tel 631-467-2080, fax 631-467-0123, toll free 1-888-SITE-ADV (888-748-3238) for about $14 + s/h. There is enough in each kit to do several connections.

to break it, but cut it with scissors or a razor knife. The reason for this is that stretched tape has a tendency to "relax" to its original shape, thus lifting off the lower overlap. This could lead to unwrapping. I suggest that you install a black tie-wrap at each end of the tape.

5. Finally, coat the entire taped area with acrylic paint extending the coat past the tape on both ends.

Does this sound like overkill? It is—but it works!

Another suggestion: Color-code transmission lines at both ends, especially where you have more than two or three. It makes for easy identification.—*John Diefenbach, K1TLV, 231 Meeting House Hill Rd, Mason, NH 03048-4118;* **k1tlv@arrl.net**

◊ It is common to hear hams commenting over the air that they have experienced water in their antenna connectors. After spending 32 years preparing ocean-going data buoys for sea I can recommend a simple solution to the problem without spending much money. The 3M company markets a product called #23 Rubber Splicing Tape. It is available at most electrical supply stores that sell to electricians. All one need do is follow the

taping tips on the back of the box to achieve success.

The nice part is, if you have to replace the cable or connection you can use a razor blade to slit the wrap along its axis and peal the tape away like a banana. If the connection is to see a great deal of water and you want to protect it further, 3M makes another product called Scotchkote. It is a liquid in a can with a brush applicator to coat the entire surface of the splicing tape and more positively seal the connection. If necessary, it can be removed by the same method, but it will require a little more work.

Ocean data buoys must live at sea for upwards of a year or more and antenna cables, solar-panel wiring and such must survive constant soaking. 3M #23 works very well in all climates.—*Ed Denton, W1VAK, 14 Holland St, Falmouth, MA 02540;* **edenton@cape.com**

◊ There are many products available to protect coaxial connections from water contamination. However, the first line of defense is always to prevent direct exposure of the connection to rain and snow. After having one of my outside connections literally torn apart by freeze/thaw cycles in a Maine winter despite silicone-

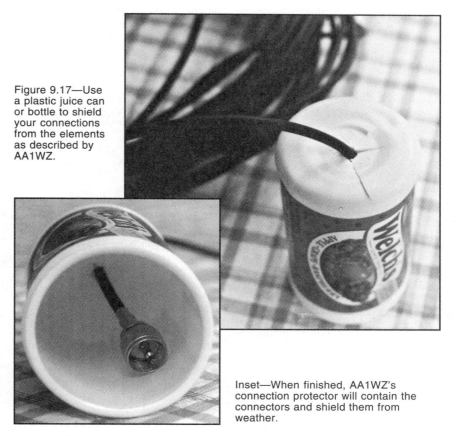

Figure 9.17—Use a plastic juice can or bottle to shield your connections from the elements as described by AA1WZ.

Inset—When finished, AA1WZ's connection protector will contain the connectors and shield them from weather.

tape waterproofing, I devised this almost-free means of protecting above-ground connections.

The technique involves using a plastic juice can or shampoo bottle. I used a juice concentrate can in **Figure 9.17**. If you use a shampoo bottle, cut off the end with the screw top. Make a hole just a tiny bit smaller than the diameter of your coax in the bottom of the container, so that its friction holds the coax. Attach the can to the upper side of the connection. If you have not attached the PL-259 yet, just slide the can out of the way up the cable and attach the connector. If you are working with a cable that already has a connector attached, cut a V as in the picture and push the cable and connector through. You will need to adjust the flap so that the bottom of the can is pretty much even, as in the photo. Make the connection and waterproof as usual. This trick *does not* take the place of silicone tape, coax seal, your favorite goop or whatever over the connection; you still need protection from condensation, humidity and such.

When the connection is finished, slide the can down over the connection. Put a small amount of silicone sealant around the coax (and V flap, if you had to make one) to seal and hold the can in place. I spray painted my can flat black before I hauled it up into position so my wife, who is politely tolerant of my antennas, would not be pushed over the edge by a midair Welch's can.

This addition takes about five minutes, weighs almost nothing (until it's covered in ice—*Ed.*) so there's no increase in cable stress, and the only cost is the silicone sealant.—*Ed Ringel, AA1WZ, 119 Highland Dr, Oakland, ME 04963; **aa1wz@arrl.net***

ELIMINATE PL-259 HASSLE

◊ I recommend taping the PL-259 coupler sleeves to the coax when installing UHF connectors at both ends of a piece of cable. This reduces the possibility of one of them falling off during installation.—*Zack Lau, W1VT, ARRL Lab Engineer;* **zlau@arrl.org**

MONEL WIRE FOR A CORROSION-FREE ANTENNA

◊ Will you be the first in your neighborhood to have a new long wire almost totally resistant to corrosion? It is something about which many of us who use wire antennas have long dreamed. It is now possible and within the budget of serious hobbyists.

When I was first licensed in 1947, my station, W2VMX, was located on one of New Jersey's barrier islands, only about a block from the ocean. My station was there for many years, and was at Ocean City for an additional 13 years of struggle

with the effects of salt spray. There were also nine years in Linden, a heavy-industry area with much pollution. I spent many hours trying to correct problems caused by these environments and was no stranger to brownish oxidation, greenish corrosion and general deterioration. Half a century after that original license was issued I found a solution.

The solution is wire made of an alloy known as *Monel* metal. The original patent was issued to Ambrose Monell in 1906, and a patent for a modified version went to the International Nickel Company in 1921. Monel is not new: During WW2, when we needed corrosion-resistant materials aboard ships and for use in the tropics, it was a precious and wonderful substitute for the elusive stainless steel. The propellers of the *USS Florida* and *USS North Dakota* were once made of Monel metal. The alloy is a mix of nickel, copper, iron and manganese. "Monel" has come to be an umbrella term for a group of similar alloys: some contain, for example, cobalt, silicon or titanium.

Recently, Monel wire has become readily available. It has a very high tensile strength and is almost totally resistant to corrosion. Stainless-steel wire is also available and less expensive, but it is considerably more difficult to handle. Monel wire is kink-resistant, which is an added benefit for many of us. It is normally sold in rolls of either 300 or 1000 feet, although longer or shorter lengths can be supplied by some sources. You may find that large fishing-tackle distributors are convenient retail outlets.

For fishing purposes, Monel is sold as "trolling wire." It is rated in pounds, an indicator of the load that the wire will hold without breaking. Depending on how your antenna is supported, you might opt for wire rated anywhere from 15 to 200 pounds. The label typically specifies the diameter of the wire in inches: from 0.016 for 15-pound test to 0.050 for 200-pound-test material. Wire gauges are not used: the nearest wire gauge number for 0.016-inch is #26 AWG, and for 0.050 it is #16.

My experience is with 25-pound wire (0.018 inches ≈ #25 AWG) and 60-pound wire (0.028 inches ≈ #21). I inquired locally about soldering the wire, and the responses conflicted: Two electronic shops thought only high-heat silver solder would suffice, and two metalworking places told me that welding or brazing would be required. Not so! I tried a 100/150-W soldering gun with some rosin-core tin/lead solder, and it works fine.

Some practice was necessary to achieve close windings, for example, in connecting a down lead to the main antenna wire. The Monel has more spring than typical copper wire, so winding it tightly with fingers is difficult. The solu-

tion is quite easy: Just reach for your long nose pliers. Rotate the pliers in the direction you want to wrap, closing them gently but firmly as you turn. The result can be a true work of art. If you want to solder a stainless connection, it can now be done. Because Monel is hard, it can be a bit inflexible. Handle it with care! I found that the 60-pound wire could easily puncture a finger.

Monel wire is more expensive than copper. A typical 300-foot roll of the 60-pound variety runs about $22 plus shipping and handling. A 1000-foot roll sells for about $65. On a cents-per-foot basis, it is no more costly than many varieties of wire at your local hardware store. Yes, there is one more catch. Some outlets have a minimum order around $75 or even $100. That may put it out of the range of an individual, but certainly, nothing prevents club members from pooling their needs for a single order. Some places will sell a single $15 roll. The handling charges may seem high, but you can get the quantity you want.

I obtained my rolls from Midland Tackle Company, a mail-order fishing-gear supplier.[10] Midland stocks the Mason Company's Monel wire as Silver-Lus Trolling Wire.[11] The owner-operator at Midland was patient with my inquiries and extremely prompt in shipping items ordered.

The telephone spokesperson for Mason gave me the name of the sales representative for my state. If you cannot locate such products locally, perhaps this is a good approach. It is also possible that a local sporting goods store would be willing to special order what you need.

On the Internet, I came across a page for the CBC Metal Supply Company.[12] These folks handle Monel wire in sizes from approximately AWG #30 up to AWG #8. There is a minimum order, but they welcome a pooled order from your local Amateur Radio club.

Okay, now you have the information. Hopefully, you're moved to join those of us with stainless skyhooks!—*Charles L. Wood, W2VMX, 1910 Glendale Ave, Durham, NC 27701-1326*

[Monel metal has much greater loss than copper. Comparing 20-meter λ/2 dipoles of #12 copper and 0.028" Monel at 30 feet, Monel has about 0.6 dB more loss. (I used 0.5 μΩ/meter for Monel and 0.0178 μΩ/meter for copper and compared peak gains as calculated by *EZNEC*.)— *Zack Lau, W1VT, ARRL Lab Engineer*]

[10]Midland Tackle Company, 66 Orange Tpke, Sloatsburg, NY 10974-2399; tel 800-521-0146 (orders only), 914-753-5440.

[11]Mason Tackle Company, PO Box 56, 11273 Center St, Otisville, MI 48463.

[12]CBC Metal Supply Company, 2-8 Central Ave, East Orange, NJ 07018; tel 973-672-0500.

A SOURCE OF MONEL WIRE

◊ There was an article about antennas made from Monel wire in the September 2001 Hints and Kinks column. Monel wire is used in the aircraft industry for safety wiring nuts, bolts and electrical connector lock rings. It is available in a variety of sizes at aircraft supply houses, and I think that an aircraft mechanic at any local airport might be willing to sell enough for an antenna. He buys it by the spool, but uses it by the inch. Special safety-wire pliers are available that lock shut on the wire ends and have a spinner mechanism (ala the Yankee screwdriver) for quickly and neatly twisting the wire. Safety wires are excellent insurance on tower hardware, and the author is right, it can be soft-soldered easily. The spool that I have here was manufactured by Brookfield Wire Co Inc of Brookfield, Massachusetts. Because of its loses, I do not use Monel wire for antennas, but I guess if one lives near the ocean its resistance to corrosion may make the loss acceptable.—*Jerry McCarthy, WA2DKG, 12 Indiana St, Hicksville, NY 11801-2527;* **WA2DKG@juno.com**

ROTATOR GEAR PROTECTION

◊ Every time your rotator starts or stops, a shock is imparted to the gear train. **Figure 9.18** shows a mechanical assembly that absorbs some of the shock and protects the rotator. To make the assembly, use new parts from an automotive shock absorber and longer bolts as required by the parts you use.—*Richard Mollentine, WA0KKC, 7139 Hardy St, Overland, KS 66704-1710*

[Other suitable parts sources include polymer cushions from bicycle shock absorbers and rebuild kits for automotive anti-roll bars.—*Ed.*]

WINTER ANTENNA HINT

◊ I find that outdoor soldering of wire antennas in the winter is much easier inside a cardboard box. Winter winds in Ohio make repairs very difficult, even with a high-powered iron. I take a box big enough to work in and cut slots down two opposite sides. Secure the wire ends together and slip the antenna into the box, centering the splice in middle. Now, solder away. The box keeps out the wind, rain and ice and protects your work. —*Jeff Rahmel, KA8ZAW, 923 W Washington St, Napoleon, OH 43545;* **rahmel @henry-net.com**

AN INEXPENSIVE COAXIAL CABLE SOURCE

◊ Here on the West Coast, we have an ethic that says "Reduce-Reuse-Recycle." As a Network Administrator, I

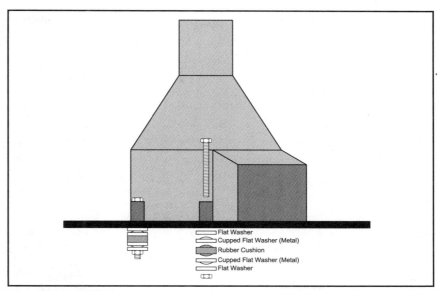

Figure 9.18—WA0KKC uses automotive shock-absorber parts to provide some cushioning against rotator drive-train shock.

have removed and recycled many yards of plenum-grade RG-58 computer networking cable, while converting to CAT-5 systems. Rather than add to our landfill problems, I have reused the cable for Amateur Radio. With Teflon-foam insulation, non-contaminating jacket and full-coverage foil-and-braid shield, it is premium-grade cable for RG-58 use. Ask computer network folks in your IT department at work or neighborhood if they remove some of this, and you may be surprised at the amount of quality coax you acquire. To make up standard compression connectors, just pull the braid back over the foil and trim the foil back even with the jacket with a sharp knife. [It's too small for RG-58 crimp connectors.—*Ed.*] Proceed to install the connector as usual. If you are using the bayonet type with a crimp ring, trim the foil back to at least $^1/_8$ inch behind the center conductor and install the connector as usual.—*Bob Kempter, WA7WJA, 12480 SW 129th Ave, Tigard, OR 97223-1881;* **wa7wja@arrl.net**

GUY WIRE SAFETY

◊ Plain guy wires are slender and dull in color. This makes them difficult to see, and an unseen guy wire can be hazardous. We can protect others and ourselves by making guy wires more visible. One way to do so is to place a brightly colored sheath on the wire. We can make inexpensive sheaths from $^3/_4$-inch PVC pipe and color them with brightly colored spray paint. On new tower installations, we can simply slip the pipes over the guy wires as they are secured to their anchors. For existing towers, we can slit the pipes,

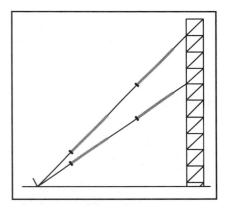

Figure 9.19—KB2UBO makes guy wires more visible with fluorescent-orange segments of PVC pipes.

lengthwise, on a table saw and slip them over the guy wires. I cut the pipes into segments and space them on the guy wires with cable clamps as shown in **Figure 9.19**.—*David Malara, Jr, KB2UBO, 5827 Bartlett Rd, Rome, NY 13440;* **mustang5@borg.com**

A FOLD-DOWN MOBILE-ANTENNA MOUNT

◊ Here is a description and photos of a unique mobile antenna mounting system. The system uses a three-position boat-trailer jack that has been modified to provide a three-position locking swivel mount for an antenna. The antenna shown is a heavy screwdriver style, the

BB-3 manufactured by the T J Antenna company.[13]

After removing the crank and screw from the jack, you are left with a very strong pipe collar and mounting plate with a swivel connection between them and a heavy-duty locking pin. Let's call this assembly the jack swivel. I welded a $3/8 \times 2 \times 4$-inch steel plate across the top of the collar (see **Figure 9.20**) to accept the antenna bolt. Drill a $3/8$-inch hole in the plate adjacent to the collar to receive the antenna stud.

A heavy ($3/8$-inch) welded steel **T** secures the jack swivel to the pickup bed. Size and drill the cap of the T to fit the mounting plate and bolt pattern of your jack swivel. **Figure 9.21** shows the **T**, with its leg bolted to the pickup bed rear post.

Figure 9.22 shows the installed jack swivel with the antenna in place. The assembly is locked in the forward-down position. I stow the antenna in this position when it's not in use. With the whip removed, the antenna lies within the

Figure 9.21—To use the mount in my pickup truck, I secured a $3/8$-inch thick plate to the pickup bed rear post. The swivel jack bolts to the plate.

[13]T J Antennas is part of nott ltd, 4001 La Plata Hwy, Farmington, NM 87401; tel 505-327-5646, orders only 1-800-443-0966, fax 505-325-1142; **k5ynr@tjantenna.com**; **www. tjantenna.com/**

Figure 9.20—A modified boat-trailer swivel jack with its crank and wheel-elevating screw removed. A $3/8 \times 2 \times 4$-inch steel plate is welded to the top of the jack, with a $3/8$-inch hole to mount the antenna. The braided strap is used to ground the antenna and mount to the vehicle.

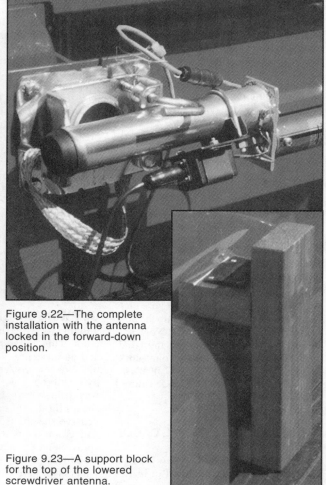

Figure 9.22—The complete installation with the antenna locked in the forward-down position.

Figure 9.23—A support block for the top of the lowered screwdriver antenna.

Figure 9.24—The antenna in the rear-down position with the whip installed.

pickup bed. My screwdriver antenna is very heavy, so I fashioned a wooden support post for its upper end. The post is secured to the fender well with adhesive-backed Velcro (see **Figure 9.23**).

To prepare for operation, I swivel the antenna to the rear-down position and lock it in place to install the 60-inch whip (see **Figure 9.24**). The whip is stored beneath the pickup bed mat when not in use.

With the whip in place, I lock the antenna in the vertical position for use. The total height with the antenna extended for 75 meters is 13 feet 6 inches. The mount is very sturdy, easily supporting the large screwdriver antenna at 70

mph.—*Joe W. Williamson, KB5YA, 1509 Conder St, Killeen, TX 76541;* **kb5ya@ juno.com**

STRENGTHEN YOUR CUSHCRAFT D40 ROTATABLE DIPOLE

◊ My Cushcraft D40 has been a very effective antenna in terms of performance, but I prefer that it be mechanically stronger than it came from the factory. I was concerned about the physical strength of the antenna from the time I first purchased it. After I assembled the antenna, I measured its sag. The ends of the antenna hung $2\frac{1}{2}$ feet below the center! I recommend purchasing a D40, but I would reinforce it as described here before installing it.

In truth, the D40 served well for nine years before I finally decided to do something about it. A windstorm bent one side of the antenna where the aluminum tubing connects to the center mounting plate (see **Figure 9.25**). Even more ominous was the extreme distortion where the tubing attaches to the mounting plate (see **Figure 9.26**). Over nine years, the sag had now reached an incredible four feet from the center to the ends! Here's the fix.

The Elements

The tubing used in this antenna has a $\frac{1}{16}$-inch-thick wall, and it is sold in

$\frac{1}{8}$-inch OD increments. This very common tubing should be easy to find. (Tubing with 0.058-inch walls is also available. It makes for an easier telescopic fit.—*Ed.*)

The center element sections must withstand the greatest bending moment, so I strengthen them by doubling the thickness of the first two sections (from the center out). I used an antioxidant paste[14] to lubricate the tubing and had no problem sliding smaller tubes into the larger ones. To do this, you will need two pieces of $1\frac{1}{8}$-inch-OD tubing 68 inches long and two pieces of 1-inch-OD tubing 48 inches long.

The first center section is a $1\frac{1}{4}$-inch-OD tube 72 inches long. The second section overlaps the first by four inches, which leaves 68 inches open inside the first section. I inserted a $1\frac{1}{8} \times 68$-inch length of aluminum tubing inside the $1\frac{1}{4}$-inch section.

The second section is $1\frac{1}{8} \times 48$ inches. Since the third (1-inch diameter) section overlaps the second by four inches, I used 1×48-inch reinforcing tube that extends four inches toward the center from the splice made by the two $1\frac{1}{8}$ OD pieces. This ties everything together and makes a strong joint. When the stainless-steel hose clamps that hold the sections together are tightened, the inserts do not move from their assembled locations.

Shortly after I erected my first antenna, the screws that hold the aluminum rods forming the X-shaped loading elements worked loose and fell off. To save yourself a lot of grief, use jam nuts and seal the nuts with glue to prevent them from working loose.

The Center Mounting Plate

The original center mounting plate is $\frac{1}{4} \times 4 \times 10$-inch aluminum. It has four plastic "clamps" to attach the elements to the plate, two on each side. These plastic

[14]Ox-Gard by GB Electrical. This is available at electrical supply houses. Any similar product would work as well.

Figure 9.26—This extreme distortion where the tubing attaches to the mounting plate is ominous.

Figure 9.25—This bent tubing at the center mounting plate resulted from a windstorm.

Figure 9.27—Broken plastic parts were evident when I took my antenna apart.

Figure 9.28—The strengthened antenna mounted on my improved mounting assembly.

clamps had become severely distorted. I replaced the original mounting plate with a larger one measuring $1/4 \times 4 \times 24$ inches and purchased four more clamps, for a total of four on *each side*.

I discovered that the plastic clamps are manufactured by Stauff Company and are used for pipe clamps in industrial applications. My local distributor sells them for much less than Cushcraft does. They will sell them by mail order and send them out by UPS.[15] The part number for the plastic clamps is 5320-PA. That is the part number for polyamide plastic, profiled inside, with tension clearance, for $1^{1}/_{4}$-inch OD tubing. The part number for the stainless steel cover plates is DP-5/SS. For four clamps, order eight 5320-PA and four DP-5/SS. Order them *without* weld plates and bolts, because the clamps will be bolted to the mounting plate with nuts on the back side of the plate. This application is different from the typical fastening method used with this product. You will need to purchase stainless steel bolts and nuts separately. They should be available in most hardware stores.

When I took my antenna apart, I discovered that some of the plastic pieces were actually broken (see **Figure 9.27**). The new clamps were of a slightly different height than the originals, but I compensated for the difference with stainless-steel washers between the clamps and the mounting plate.

The new mounting plate can be seen in **Figure 9.28**. The four larger clamps are the new ones. Notice that I also added a $1/4 \times 20$ screw at the center of the plate, which extends into a matching hole, drilled in the wall of the mast. This prevents the antenna from turning in the wind. The plate is threaded to accept the screw. After tightening, the screw is held in place with a jam nut.

After my antenna had been up for a number of years, I had a problem with

[15]Carrier-Oehler Company,16965 Vincennes, PO Box 40, South Holland, IL 60473-0040; tel 708-339-8200.

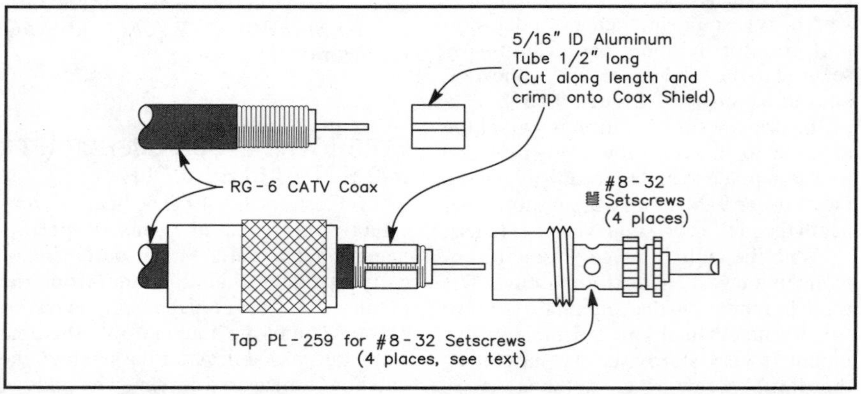

the coax connections loosening at the antenna. The problem was caused by birds sitting on the coax. My cure is to use jam nuts on the antenna terminal and tape a brace from the mast to the coax that supports the birds. The birds love to sit on my antennas! Before you put your antenna up, make sure that the terminal screws you got from Cushcraft are long enough for jam nuts. Mine were not and had to be replaced.

The Finished Product

When the modifications were complete, the sag at the antenna ends was slightly under one foot! This appears to be a very worthwhile and cost-effective way to improve the strength of a very good antenna. I am very pleased with the results that I've gotten with my D40 in the last nine years and I would buy another one, but I would strengthen it before erecting it.—*George Zurbuchen, K9CC, 10515 Hillcrest Dr, Palos Park, IL 60464;* **George.Zurbuchen@cognis-us.com**

AN IMPROVED CONNECTION TO RG-6 CATV COAX

◊ During the construction of a G5RV, I found an interesting method of connecting some RG6 CATV coax to a PL-259.

Figure 9.29—Details of AF4JX's mechanical connection of a PL-259 to RG-6 CATV coax, that has aluminum braid and foil shield.

Most connection approaches remove the messenger, taper the jacket a little and twist the PL-259 on—letting friction make the electrical connection to the braid. Many hams can attest that trying to solder to the braid on this stuff is thwarted by the aluminum and the anti-oxidant. When I did that, my connections would work loose about every 10 days. Sitting at my bench looking at a PL-259 and seeing a box of taps, I decided to try a mechanical approach. Here's how:

It turns out that a #8-32 tap will nicely tap the braid solder holes of a PL-259. Tap all four holes. If you're careful, you can tap the hole on the opposite side by continuing the tap through, but you must be lined up square on the first hole. (See **Figure 9.29**.)

Next, make four very short setscrews. Use a hobby grinder with a thin cutoff wheel to cut a screwdriver slot in the end of a #8-32 screw, then cut off the slotted piece so that it's about 3 or 4 threads long. (The screws must be short to clear the connector sleeve.)

If tightened directly onto the shield, the screws dig into the insulation around the center conductor. They need something to distribute their pressure. I found some thin, seamed aluminum spacers, opened them slightly and slipped them over the braid. (Slit $5/_{16}$-inch ID aluminum tubing or rolled aluminum flashing should work too. Use anti-corrosion compound at all of the aluminum joints —*Ed.*) I used a crimping tool with a spark-plug die to set the spacer on the shield. Slip the coax into the connector, solder the center conductor and tighten the screws. So far, my connection is doing well after four months, and it's easy to disassemble.—*Joe Semer, AF4JX, 324 Academy St, Johnston, SC 29832;* **joesemer@pbtcomm.net**

MORE ON AN IMPROVED CONNECTION TO RG-6 CATV COAX

◊ In his April 2001 hint, AF4JX recommends that we use four setscrews to secure a PL-259 to the shield of RG-6 CATV coax.[16] I'd like to suggest that using four setscrews is actually worse than using one. I learned this when I had my first job at MRC Corporation, where I helped design LASER bar-code readers. I put two setscrews on opposite sides of an optical mount and the thing kept falling apart after a bit of vibration. Removing one of the setscrews made the thing much more secure.

If you use setscrews in pairs opposite one another, you have only two (or four) points of contact (for two or four setscrews) because the parts ride on the points of the screws. If you use only one setscrew or two in adjacent holes, the force securely clamps the part against the side opposite the screw(s), where there are numerous points of contact.

My suggestion is to lose two of those setscrews! Ask any mechanical engineer who's dealt with them on a regular basis.—*Phil Karras, KE3FL, 3305 Hampton Ct, Mt Airy, MD 21771-7201;* **ke3fl@arrl.net**

MORE HARDLINE CONNECTORS

◊ The aftermath of "Ice Storm 98" has left the North Country with an abundance of 75 Ω hardline that may be used by hams as a good low-loss antenna feed line. The problem is: "How do we put a PL-259 fitting on it?"

This technique has worked well for me. (Please refer to **Figure 9.30**.) Go to your local hardware store and purchase a 1/2×1/2 compression union normally used on copper tubing. Inside the union is a concentric shoulder that positions it on the tubes to be joined. Remove the nuts and ferrules from both ends, clamp union body in a vise and drill a 1/2-inch hole through the shoulder inside the body to clear a 1/2-inch path all the way through

[16]J. Sever, AF4JX, "An Improved Connection to RG-6 Coax," *QST*, Apr 2001, p 74.

the union. Place one nut and a ferrule onto the rear of a PL-259 (*with* the barrel *on* the connector). Assemble the connector, ferrule and nut onto one end of the union and tighten the nut leaving just enough space so the connector barrel can wiggle a bit. Then solder just a bit of the connector body to the union for a good electrical connection.

Use a tubing cutter to cut through the aluminum jacket of the hardline in two places: 3/4-inch from the end and 7/8-inch back from that cut. Then cut a lengthwise slit through the jacket of these two pieces. (I used a Dremel tool with a cut-off wheel for this operation.) Pry the slit open slightly with a screwdriver and remove the two pieces of aluminum jacket. Next, carefully cut through the foam dielectric at the 3/4-inch cut and remove that piece of foam, being careful not to nick the center conductor.

Now, remove the barrel from a PL-259 connector and screw the connector onto the foam dielectric until it touches the aluminum jacket (it is difficult), then remove it by reversing the process. This essentially threads the foam to make sure the finished fitting will go all the way onto the hardline.

Now, put the remaining nut and ferrule on the hardline, then screw the fitting with the union attached onto the hardline until it is tight against the jacket. Slide the ferrule into place, slide the nut up and tighten it until the union securely grips the hardline. (You may want to put

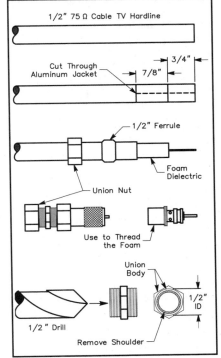

Figure 9.30—Details of KA2GHO's hardline/PL-259 connector.

on a bit of co-al jelly for dissimilar metals to prevent corrosion.) Connect hardline to fixed equipment through a short piece of coax for flexibility.

I have had 125 feet of this hardline running (buried) to my vertical antenna for nearly two years and it works great!— *Edwin N. Patience, KA2GHO, 24978 Ny St Rt 26, Redwood, NY 13679*

GREASING ANTENNA ROTATORS
New Synthetic Greases

◊ There are new low-temperature synthetic greases that will lubricate (flow) at lower ambient temperatures than older mineral-based greases, particularly below 0°F. If you have an older antenna rotator that needs service, remove the old grease from the rotator and bearing races and sparingly replace it with newer synthetic grease.—*Richard Mollentine, WAØKKC, 7139 Hardy St, Shawnee Mission, KS 66204-1710*

Grease Fittings

◊ Thrust bearings that lack zerk fittings can still be greased. Some kinds of grease are available in aerosol cans. Simply bend the applicator straw to reach into the bearing. For heavier greases, you may be able to get a grease needle from an auto-supply store or bicycle shop. —*Richard Mollentine, WAØKKC, 7139 Hardy St, Shawnee Mission, KS 66204-1710*

KLM KT-34XA ANTENNA BOOM/ MAST COUPLER FAILURE

◊ My KT-34XA antenna had been up for about 10 years here in north Texas. Sometime during the night of May 5, the 3/16-inch aluminum boom-to-mast coupler plate failed completely (See **Figures 9.31** and **9.32**). Saturday morning when I went out to go somewhere, I heard a strange noise from the direction of my antenna. I looked up—and gulped!! The

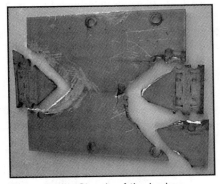

Figure 9.31—Shards of the broken boom-to-mast mounting plate.

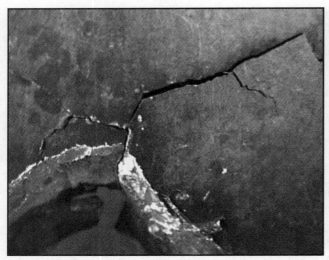

Figure 9.32—A close-up view of cracks in the failed mounting plate.

Figure 9.33—KC5UH's KT-34A hangs on its truss wires after the ancient mounting plate failed.

antenna was hanging by the boom-truss guys and had flipped on its side (**Figure 9.33**). It was also swinging wildly back and forth in the high winds we were having that day. I managed to remove the U-bolts and what was left of the plate from the mast and boom. Then I tied the boom to the mast with some rope and a heavy chain. I also stuck a piece of fence pipe through the tower next to the rotator, angled it upward and secured the boom to it with wire. This kept the antenna from swinging to self-destruction.

I am lucky that the antenna had a boom truss—only that kept it from crashing down into the trees and onto the roof of my house. KT-34 antennas don't have trusses because their booms are shorter, but I'm guessing that they use a similar mounting plate.

Hams who have KLM KT-34 or KT-34XA antennas should inspect their coupler plates—especially if they live in high-wind areas. Figures 9.31 through 9.33 show the broken coupler plate and the antenna hanging sideways.

Luckily, my employer does quite a bit of aluminum work, so I was able to get two pieces of 0.190-inch-thick T2024-T3 aluminum plate to make a new coupler (notice that I doubled the thickness). In addition, when I rotated the antenna back to horizontal, I found a one-inch hole worn through the bottom of the boom where it had been rubbing on the broken coupler.—*David Cash, KC5UH, 2405 Kingston St, Arlington, TX 76015; dncash@home.com*

[It is critically important to periodically inspect antennas and their hardware. Ten years is an acceptable life from a part such as this because aluminum is subject to failure from fatigue. I know of a bicycle mechanic who recommends retiring aluminum bicycles after five years, lest the frame fail.—Ed.]

A 2-METER SLEEVE-DIPOLE ANTENNA

◊ My car (a Geo Tracker) is a small SUV with a convertible top. The only place I could easily attach a standard mobile whip and have metal all around it was on the front hood, a position that had several disadvantages. I considered a cowl-mount antenna bracket, but that would put the antenna adjacent to passengers and require a hole in the car.

While preparing for a public-service event, N9REP showed me a 450-MHz ground-plane antenna he had made from welding rod for base operation. Inspiration struck and I made a similar ground plane antenna on a seven-foot mast strapped to the bicycle rack at the back of the car. The seven-foot mast was necessary to keep the ground radials above the heads of pedestrians but it also it gave me a 15-mile simplex range with my H-T.

While this antenna was good for work as a chase car at bicycle events, it had two disadvantages: I could not open the tailgate or enter a garage when this ungainly contraption was attached to the rear of the car. I pondered my options and studied the various spare parts lying around my garage. My solution is a sleeve dipole attached to the spare-tire mount on the rear of the car.

The sleeve dipole is simply a dipole antenna where one leg is a tube so that the feed line reaches the feed point through the tubular element, instead of at right angles to the elements. The antenna has been previously described as an easily transported portable antenna when

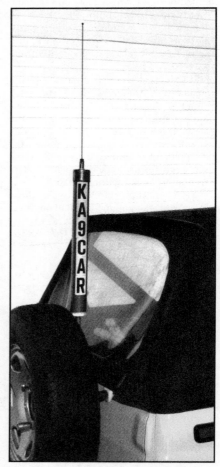

Figure 9.34—KA9CAR's sleeve dipole mounted on his vehicle.

made from a piece of coax cable. An amateur base-station version is the AEA Isopole antenna. My finished sleeve dipole is shown in **Figure 9.34**.

This sleeve dipole has several features: All parts were obtained at hamfests or a local hardware store. Only common hand tools were used for construction. It requires no vehicle ground plane. It can be easily scaled for other frequencies.

Design and Construction

The key to a sleeve dipole is the feed-point hardware. I used a RadioShack #21-961 feedthrough/adapter. (Let's call it the "feed point" for short.) It is essentially a bulkhead-mount SO-239 with the center conductor connected to a $3/8 \times 24$ stud as is common in whip-antenna hardware. The part comes with a lockwasher, a plastic shoulder washer and a $3/8 \times 24$ female coupler to secure it. Similar connectors are used with a metal flange to mount mobile antennas on vehicle drip rails, hood and trunk lips. Here, I used the connector to mount the whip and simultaneously connect to the antenna's other leg, a large copper sleeve. The feed point with its lock washer, shoulder washer and coupler are the parts near the end cap in Figure 9.35.

The ARRL Antenna Book[17] chart shows how much to shorten an antenna based on its slenderness. Considering that this is a whip of approximately $1/8$-inch diameter and a sleeve of approximately 2-inch diameter, I chose to use 96% as a compromise. For a frequency of 146 MHz, this yields an element length of 19.4 inches.

For the sleeve, I used a piece of 2-inch copper drain line and a matching copper end cap. Rough cut the sleeve several inches longer than needed for the antenna leg. Drill a $3/8$-inch hole in the end cap to fit the feed point (that's $3/8$-inch for the 21-961), then solder the end cap to the pipe.

Look closely at your feed point. Where does the path of the center and shield conductors diverge? That is the actual feed point of the antenna and the point from which the antenna-leg lengths are measured. Depending on the feed point you use, the point to measure from may be near the center of the cap, or could be an inch above that. The 21-961 makes the connection at the top surface of the copper pipe cap. Measure the sleeve length from the feed point, across the end cap, then along the length of the pipe to 19.4 inches and cut the sleeve to length. Drill a clearance hole for a sheet-metal screw (builder's choice; mine is #8×$1/2$-inch) about $1/4$-inch back from where the sleeve was just cut.

[17]Dean Straw, N6BV, Ed., *The ARRL Antenna Book* (Newington: ARRL, 2000) Order No 8047, $30. ARRL publications are available from your local ARRL dealer or directly from the ARRL. See the ARRL Publications ad elsewhere in this issue or check out the full ARRL publications line at **www.arrl.org/shop/**.

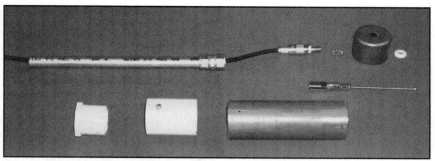

Figure 9.35—Sample parts used to construct a sleeve dipole.

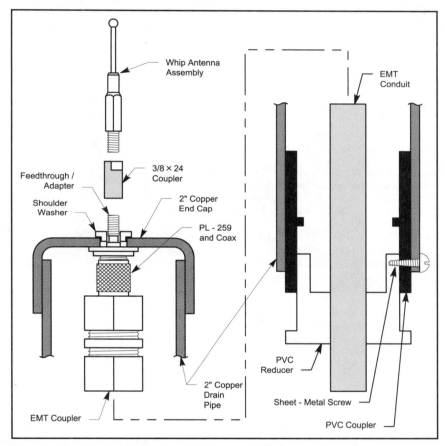

Figure 9.36—Construction details of the KA9CAR sleeve dipole.

A piece of $1/2$-inch EMT (electrical conduit) has approximately the same outside diameter as the sleeve of a PL-259 connector. In my case, the EMT serves as a mast, extending from the feed point to where I mounted the antenna on my vehicle's spare-tire carrier. The mast length varies among installations. An EMT coupler at the top of the mast holds the PL-259 that attaches to the feed point. Secure the coupling to the mast's upper end.

A bushing centers the copper sleeve on the mast; it also serves as an insulator between them. In the plastic-pipe section of the hardware store, I found a coupling for $1 1/4$-inch plastic pipe to be a good fit inside the 2-inch copper pipe. A plastic bushing (reducer) that adapts $1 1/4$ to $1/2$-inch threaded pipe fits over the mast after a little work with a rattail file. Temporarily slide the coupler-bushing assembly into the copper sleeve and drill a pilot hole for the sheet-metal screw.

Place the bushing on the mast, run the coax up the center of the mast, through the EMT coupler and then attach the PL-259. Secure the PL-259 to the feed point, then slip the PL-259 back inside the EMT coupler and tighten the coupler onto the connector sleeve. Now place the lock washer on the feed point, slip the copper sleeve over it, place the insulating washer and tighten down the nut. Be careful that the shoulder washer remains in place. Details of this assembly are shown in **Figure 9.36**.

Position the plastic parts in the copper sleeve to align the holes drilled previously and secure them with a small sheet-metal screw. Be sure that you don't short the sleeve to the mast with this screw.

Attach a whip to the feed point. Remember to measure and set the 19.4-inch whip length from the same point you measured the sleeve.

Matching

A dipole is a theoretically 72-Ω device. Most amateur transceivers are 50-Ω devices. I considered three ways to deal with this mismatch:

1. Use 75-Ω line for a good match to the antenna and tolerate a mismatch at the radio.

2. Use 50-Ω feed line cut to a length that a Smith chart shows should be a reasonable match.

3. Use a random length of 50-Ω feed line and see how well it matches.

I chose option three. Using a friend's VHF analyzer to check the match, I found the SWR to be 1.7:1 across the 2-meter band. This won't hurt the transmitter, and the feed-line length is short enough that additional losses resulting from the SWR are not important. You should use a method that you like.

Mounting to the Vehicle

On my SUV, there is enough room to attach the mast to the spare-tire mount between the tire and the tailgate. On some other vehicles, one might simply attach the mast to the spare-tire rack with hose clamps. On a car with a plastic body, one might devise a way to mount the mast to the frame or a trailer hitch. For fixed or portable operation, this antenna can be attached to a wood or metal balcony railing. Whether operating mobile or fixed, you should be sure that it is mounted so that it does not physically and electrically endanger people or risk contact with electric lines.

Results

Standing on the front porch with my H-T, communication through a repeater 12 miles away is marginal. When using this antenna held over my head, I received Q5 reports. Reports from the car using the mobile radio indicate that this antenna meets my needs well.—*John Dewey, KA9CAR, 37 Faringdon Dr, Crystal Lake, IL 60014-7811;* **ka9car@ arrl.net**

Figure 9.37—Two braces join the antenna to the van at the bottom of the upper coil. (The white fuzzy stuff is frost—*Ed.*)

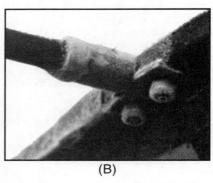

(B)

(A)

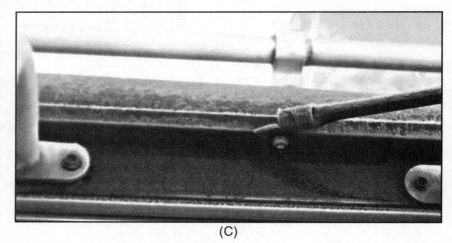

(C)

Figure 9.38—Details of the aluminum mounts for the braces: (A) at the antenna, (B) the short brace at the van and (C) the long brace at the van.

MODIFICATIONS FOR "A $20 HF MOBILE ANTENNA"[18]

◊ Having built this antenna, I thought others might be interested in seeing a small modification to the "stays" or antenna braces.

In the article, King uses braces made of ¹/₂-inch-diameter PVC pipe from the bottom of the upper coil assembly to the

[18]Frank King, KM4IE, "A $20 HF Mobile Antenna," *QST*, April 2000, pp 33-35.

vehicle roof. The large-diameter braces are a little too visible for my taste, so I went in search of something a bit less conspicuous. I finally arrived at a solution harking back a decade or so, to my sport-archery days: carbon-fiber arrow shafts.

The shafts are nonconductive, black in color and stronger, pound for pound, than steel. I chose a 31×0.347-inch OD unfletched shaft from my local archery supplier, and bought two (for a total of $5) in case I managed to destroy one in the process.

After measuring the length of the original PVC braces, I cut the carbon shafts to length with a Dremel tool and an abrasive disk. (The shafts shatter if sawn, so you must use a grinder to cut them.)

With the braces cut to length, I fashioned a pair of aluminum end pieces out of a strip of 0.047-inch-thick aluminum sheet purchased at the local hobby shop. The round portions were formed around the base of a $^{11}/_{32}$-inch drill bit. Once they were bent to shape, I forced the aluminum end pieces (they're a snug fit) on the carbon shafts and slathered the assembly

with clear epoxy, followed by a coat of flat-black enamel.

So far, the antenna has held up well, and the SWR didn't change when I exchanged the new carbon braces for the old ones made from PVC. I'll let you know how well they survive an Alaskan winter (grin). **Figures 9.37 and 9.38** show the installation better than I can explain it. Believe it or not, the van doors clear the braces by about $^5/_8$ of an inch.— *Greg Martin, KLØOM, 3127 Peterkin Ave, Apt 2, Anchorage, AK 99508-1049;* **gmartin@gci.net**

The Doctor is IN

Q Bob, VE3GND, asks, "I'm thinking about trying a Windom antenna in an inverted-V configuration. Are there any advantages to doing this?"

A There is only one antenna design that can be properly classified as a true Windom. The antenna was described in the September 1929 *QST* article written by Loren G. Windom, W8GZ, titled "Notes on Ethereal Adornments." It was a Marconi-type antenna, using a single-wire feeding into an off-center position of a long horizontal wire. With this design the whole antenna system radiated—there was no feed line used; the antenna was connected directly to the transmitter (see **Figure 9.39**). The resulting pattern is dependent upon the band of the transmission.

This antenna is not a good match to modern transmitters, but it worked quite well in its day, so a few modern antenna builders have capitalized on the famous name (much like the various "G5RV" antennas I have seen).

Commercial "Windoms" are generally not true Windom designs, but merely off-center fed (OCF) dipole antennas. Their chief advantage is that they resonate well on the frequencies that constitute a $^1/_4$-wavelength for each leg of the antenna (or an odd multiple thereof).

The advantages to an inverted-V configuration of an OCF dipole are pretty much the same as making a standard dipole into an inverted V. That is, you get more radiation off the ends for a tradeoff of broadside radiation, and you can install the antenna with a single support.

On the other hand, when an antenna is used in the inverted-V configuration on higher frequencies than where the

antenna is $^1/_2$ wavelength long, the pattern degrades considerably compared to the pattern produced by a flattop under similar conditions.

Q John, KF6EOJ, asks, "I just recently completed a modification of a RadioShack FM antenna for 2

meter use, but I am a little confused about the issue of vertical vs. horizontal polarization. Two members of my local club say that for FM use I should use the antenna vertically polarized, which means modifying the antenna mounting holes, which I have already done. Is this true? I only have a FM

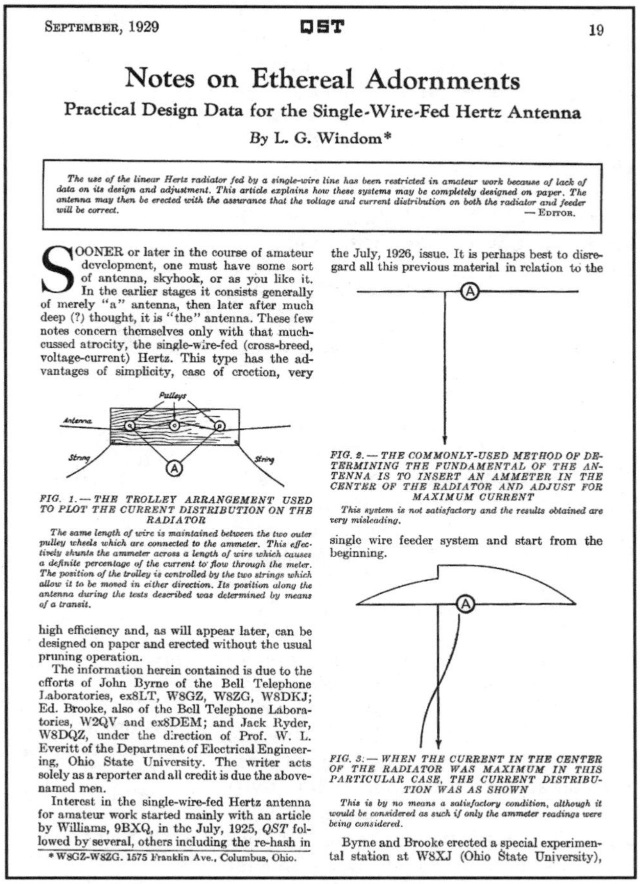

Figure 9.39—The true "Windom" antenna was described by W8GZ in his 1929 *QST* article.

SEPTEMBER, 1929   **QST**   19

Notes on Ethereal Adornments

Practical Design Data for the Single-Wire-Fed Hertz Antenna

By L. G. Windom*

> *The use of the linear Hertz radiator fed by a single-wire line has been restricted in amateur work because of lack of data on its design and adjustment. This article explains how these systems may be completely designed on paper. The antenna may then be erected with the assurance that the voltage and current distribution on both the radiator and feeder will be correct.—EDITOR.*

SOONER or later in the course of amateur development, one must have some sort of antenna, skyhook, or as you like it. In the earlier stages it consists generally of merely "a" antenna, then later after much deep (?) thought, it is "the" antenna. These few notes concern themselves only with that much-cussed atrocity, the single-wire-fed (cross-breed, voltage-current) Hertz. This type has the advantages of simplicity, ease of erection, very high efficiency and, as will appear later, can be designed on paper and erected without the usual pruning operation.

The information herein contained is due to the efforts of John Byrne of the Bell Telephone Laboratories, ex8LT, W8GZ, W8ZG, W8DKJ; Ed. Brooke, also of the Bell Telephone Laboratories, W2QV and ex8DEM; and Jack Ryder, W8DQZ, under the direction of Prof. W. L. Everitt of the Department of Electrical Engineering, Ohio State University. The writer acts solely as a reporter and all credit is due the above-named men.

Interest in the single-wire-fed Hertz antenna for amateur work started mainly with an article by Williams, 9BXQ, in the July, 1925, *QST* followed by several, others including the re-hash in

*W8GZ-W8ZG. 1575 Franklin Ave., Columbus, Ohio.

the July, 1926, issue. It is perhaps best to disregard all this previous material in relation to the

FIG. 1.—THE TROLLEY ARRANGEMENT USED TO PLOT THE CURRENT DISTRIBUTION ON THE RADIATOR

The same length of wire is maintained between the two outer pulley wheels which are connected to the ammeter. This effectively shunts the ammeter across a length of wire which causes a definite percentage of the current to flow through the meter. The position of the trolley is controlled by the two strings which allow it to be moved in either direction. Its position along the antenna during the tests described was determined by means of a transit.

FIG. 2.—THE COMMONLY-USED METHOD OF DETERMINING THE FUNDAMENTAL OF THE ANTENNA IS TO INSERT AN AMMETER IN THE CENTER OF THE RADIATOR AND ADJUST FOR MAXIMUM CURRENT

This system is not satisfactory and the results obtained are very misleading.

single wire feeder system and start from the beginning.

FIG. 3.—WHEN THE CURRENT IN THE CENTER OF THE RADIATOR WAS MAXIMUM IN THIS PARTICULAR CASE, THE CURRENT DISTRIBUTION WAS AS SHOWN

This is by no means a satisfactory condition, although it would be considered as such if only the ammeter readings were being considered.

Byrne and Brooke erected a special experimental station at W8XJ (Ohio State University),

H-T and I intend on using the antenna to increase my range.''

When amateur 2-meter FM repeaters came along in the 70s they were used primarily for mobile communication. Horizontal mobile antennas proved cumbersome (remember the Halo?) and so vertical whips were the favored. Repeaters followed suit, using vertically polarized antennas as well. The penalty for a polarization mismatch (using horizontal polarization when the other station is using vertical, or vice versa) is a substantial signal loss.

So, the established custom among FM operators is to use vertically polarized antennas. If you want to communicate with other FM stations, choose vertical polarization.

On the other hand, you should know that 2-meter SSB and CW operators use horizontal polarization—if you ever decide to give 2-meter DXing a try.

Q **Is it true that you can use a 40-meter dipole antenna on 15 meters as well?**

A In many cases, yes. Dipoles have harmonic resonances at odd multiples of their fundamental resonant frequencies. Because 21 MHz is the third harmonic of 7 MHz, 7-MHz dipoles are harmonically resonant in at least a portion of 15 meters. This is attractive because it allows you to install a 40-meter dipole, feed it with coax, and use it without an antenna tuner on both 40 and 15 meters.

There is a catch, though. This idea works if you cut the 40-meter dipole for use in the CW portion of the band, say around 7010 kHz. Such a dipole should also be resonant in the CW portion of 15 meters at about 21030 kHz (7010 × 3 = 21030). But what if the 40-meter dipole is cut for phone work at 7250 kHz?

7250 × 3 = 21,750

Oops! The 15-meter resonant frequency is out of the band.

The solution is to capacitively load the antenna. The simple loading wires known as *capacitive hats* shown in **Figure 9.40** lower the antenna's resonant frequency on 15 meters without substantially affecting resonance on 40 meters.

To put this loading scheme to work, first measure, cut and adjust the 40-meter dipole to resonance at your desired frequency. Then, cut two 2-foot long pieces of stiff wire (such as #12 or #14 house wiring) and solder the ends of each piece together to form two loops. Now twist the loops in the middle to create two figure 8s. Solder the twisted centers of your figure 8s to each leg of your 40-meter antenna at a point about a third of the way

out from the feed point (placement isn't critical). Adjust the loop shapes and take measurements on 15 meters until you reach an acceptable SWR on your chosen frequency. When you check the SWR on 40 meters you should only see a minor variation.

Q **Bill, WØLPQ, asks, "Is it true that an antenna tuner does not really 'tune' the antenna? And if an antenna is cut to resonance already, what good is a tuner?"**

A Yes, it's true—an antenna tuner doesn't really tune your antenna in the strict sense of the word. It does not, for example, adjust the lengths of your antenna elements, their heights above ground and so on. What an antenna tuner *does* do, however, is transform the impedance at the feed line input to a value that your transceiver can handle (typically 50 Ω—see **Figure 9.41**). Think of an antenna tuner as an adjustable impedance transformer and you'll better understand its function.

If the antenna is cut to resonance and is designed to match the impedance of the transceiver and feed line, an antenna tuner is not required. The transceiver is presented with a 50-Ω impedance (or something close to it) into which it can deliver its full output. However, the SWR bandwidths of many antenna designs are usually limited to only 200 or 300 kHz. If you cut a dipole, for example, to be resonant and provide a 1:1 SWR at 7100 kHz, you might find that the SWR climbs well above 2:1 when you attempt to use this

antenna at 7250 kHz. Most modern transceivers begin reducing output, or may shut down completely, at SWRs greater than 2:1. With an antenna tuner in the line you can transform the impedance to 50 Ω, reducing the SWR to 1:1. The transceiver delivers its full output once again and you'll be able to operate on 7250 kHz—minus some feed line attenuation between the tuner and the antenna. The attenuation is caused by the fact that the SWR on the feed line between the tuner and the antenna is not affected by the matching function of the tuner; it remains unchanged.

Q **I have a remote-controlled antenna tuner installed at the feed point of a vertical antenna in my back yard. Although the system works pretty well most of the time, the tuner will occasionally "open" (switch to a direct connection to the antenna) for no apparent reason. This seems to only happen on particular bands. Do you know of a cure?**

A Since the problem occurs only when you operate on certain bands, I suspect that RF is getting into the tuner control lines. If RF finds its way into the lines, it could easily wreak havoc with the tuner's microprocessor circuitry and cause it to exhibit strange behavior, such as switching to the direct-connect mode.

If you can obtain enough slack in the control lines where they enter the tuner, wrap them several times through an FT-43 or FT-77 ferrite core. This may sufficiently suppress the RF at the tuner.

Figure 9.40— Figure-8-shaped capacitance hats made and placed as described in the text and make your 40-meter dipole antenna resonate anywhere in the 15-meter band.

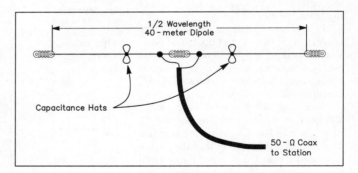

Figure 9.41— Think of an antenna tuner as an adjustable impedance transformer. Depending on the operational range of the tuner, it can match the antenna system impedance to 50 Ω for your transceiver.

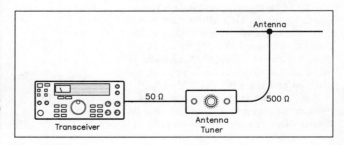

Update: Thanks Doc! I used an FT-43 core and that did the trick. I just wrapped about 10 turns through the core and now the tuner behaves itself.

Q Kaehu, WH6WW, asks, "I want to use one coax run for my VHF and UHF station, but I also want to have a vertical and a beam. I think a coax relay would provide the solution. Is this something I could fabricate from RadioShack components or should I buy one commercially?"

A When switching multiple feed lines, the impedance of the switching network is a prime consideration. The impedance of a feed line is a function of the conductor surface areas and the spacing between them. When you insert a standard type of relay in the line, you will have a point with a different impedance, with a resultant change in SWR. At HF, the SWR difference is not likely to be significant, but at VHF and UHF this is not the case. This doesn't make home-brewing impossible, but it does add a major complicating factor.

Remote coax relays are available for VHF and UHF, but they are costly (it may be cheaper to run multiple lengths of coax). If the cost is not a consideration, you can purchase a remote coax relay from these folks:

Electronic Switch Co
8491 Hospital Drive
Suite 328
Douglasville, GA 30134
tel: 770-920-1024
k4mzw@akorn.net

Q George, KD4KYM, asks, "I'm uncertain about how I should attach a 450-Ω ladder transmission line to my radio. I have SO-239 coax connectors on my Kenwood TS-520 transceiver. Can I assume that it is simply a matter of soldering one side of the ladder line to the center conductor of a PL-259 and the other to the outer conductor? I want to use the ladder line to feed a multiband 80-10 meter dipole antenna."

A Your TS-520 was designed for 50-Ω *unbalanced* coaxial cable. Your ladder line is 450-Ω *balanced*, so there is more to deal with than just the physical differences. If you were going to use the ladder line on just a couple of bands, you might be able to get away with feeding the ladder line to a *balun* (a balanced-to-unbalance feed line transformer) with an appropriate impedance ratio (4:1, for instance), then using coax between the balun and your radio. But since you're aiming for broad, multiband coverage, I'd recommend an antenna tuner.

Most antenna tuners are designed with built-in baluns to handle the impedance transformation. There are usually three posts in the back of a tuner—two for ladder-line and one for random wire antennas. There may be a jumper between the random wire post and one of the ladder-line posts. Make sure the jumper is removed—it is only used for a single random-length wire.

If your tuner does not have provisions for ladder-line, you can connect it as you say, by soldering the ladder line to a PL-259. It may work, but not as well as using a balun. Of course, you could always install an external balun in the line between the ladder-line and the antenna tuner (see **Figure 9.42**), although we don't recommend that you run high power with such a setup.

Q Hal Schaill, K4TTE, of Asheville, North Carolina, writes: I have a sloping delta loop antenna from high tree to house with a ladder-line feed to a large homebrew DPDT switch. The poles are on 5½ inch centers to ensure that the closest metal parts do not diminish the 390 Ω impedance of the #14 ladder line. The throw of the switch is 3⁵/₈ inches in each direction. It is protected from the weather on an outside basement windowsill, under a screened porch.

Closing the switch in one direction connects the antenna to the transceiver. Closing the switch in the other direction would connect the antenna by #4 copper wire to an 8-foot copper-plated ½ inch steel ground rod, separate from my station ground.

Now I am wondering if just opening the switch might be safer than grounding the antenna. By grounding, might I be creating a lightning attractor, with the possibility of the lightning charge jumping the 3⁵/₈ inch gap and entering the house and equipment?

A Any high object carries a risk of being struck by lightning. Trees make pretty good insulators, yet the tallest ones still get struck by lightning frequently. The reason is that they provide a shorter path to ground than the nearby surrounding air.

Your antenna, left ungrounded, would also provide a shorter path to ground. When the lightning energy reaches the open switch, however, it may not take the path to ground that you would desire. So I would indeed recommend closing the switch on the ground side when not in use.

Q Bob, W3GD, asks, "I recently bought several hundred feet of stranded #14 Teflon insulated wire to construct a double-extended Zepp antenna on 3.8 MHz. I plan to run the antenna through the trees in my yard. Is Teflon weatherproof and UV-resistant? I'm concerned about durability. My previous antenna was made from a single #18 copper-clad steel military surplus field-telephone wire and it broke after a year or two in the trees."

A Although not all Teflon cables are UV-resistant rated, the material is generally very good for antenna building. However, many folks have used inexpensive plastic-coated wire successfully as well, so I suspect the problem you had with your previous antenna was due chiefly to fatigue in the wire that developed after playing tug o' war with your trees. For runs of up to 150 feet or so, #14

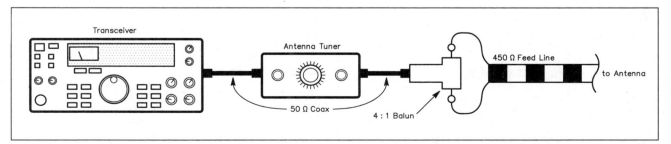

Figure 9.42—If you own an antenna tuner that does not include an internal balun, you can use an external balun. Just keep the coaxial connection between the balun and the tuner as short as possible.

is adequate (neglecting the "tree factor" for the moment. For longer runs, #14 may be usable, but I would recommend #12 or #10 preferably (twisting two lengths of #14 should also suffice). Two-conductor #18 zip-cord would probably fail in 5-6 years.

Q At a recent estate sale I picked up a Daiwa CNA-2002 automatic antenna tuner. Unfortunately, there was no documentation whatsoever. Can you tell me anything about this unit?

A Daiwa manufactured the CNA-2002 in the early '80s. It is the higher-powered cousin of the CNA-1001, which was reviewed in the November 1981 *QST*.

These units were among the first automatic HF antenna tuners designed for amateur use. The CNA-2002's tuning function was limited, though. You had to select the band manually, then apply 10 W or less while briefly pressing the **TUNE** button on the front panel. When the button was pressed, the control circuitry in the CNA-2002 would activate a dc motor and a system of gears to rotate two small variable capacitors. The SWR sensing circuits would trigger when the SWR dipped below about 2:1, abruptly stopping the motor. At that point you could accept settings the tuner "found" for you, or use the **FINE TUNING** control to reduce the SWR even further. The idea was to diminish the tedium of operating an antenna tuner.

The CNA-2002 was rated for 1.5 kW, but that was a PEP rating, not continuous power. The small, encapsulated variable capacitors had a tendency to arc at 100% duty cycle power levels greater than 500 W.

Q Gene, WA2FLN, asks, "For the last 20 years I've been feeding my antenna with a length of Belden RG-8U coax. If I place a dummy load at the antenna I still measure a 1:1 SWR in the shack, but I wonder whether I should replace the old feed line anyway. What do you think?"

A The conductors inside the cable have a tendency to oxidize over time and the dielectric may begin to absorb some moisture. All of this leads to increased loss, which will make your SWR look better than it actually is. I would consider 15-20 years to be the useful limit for coax, but it will vary quite a bit depending upon the environment and the materials used to make the coax.

If you really want to evaluate the condition of your coax, the best thing to do is to measure the RF power at the input of the cable, and at the dummy load on the other end. Subtract the input power from the power measured at the dummy load and you'll know how much RF you're losing in the cable. Compare the total loss to the specifications for your cable. This will tell you how much your 20-year-old coax has departed from its original pristine condition. For RG8U, the power loss in a 50-foot section at 14 MHz should be roughly 0.4 dB, which is about 9 W out of 100 W.

Q Tim, WD8OQX, asks, "I live in an apartment and I need to run a length of coax from my radio through a window to an outdoor antenna. The trick is that I need to do it without modifying or damaging the window. Do you have any ideas?"

A The Doctor was once faced with a similar problem while living in a condominium. My solution was the old open-the-window-slightly-and-place-a-board-there scheme.

See **Figure 9.43**. Cut a piece of 2×4 lumber so that it fits snugly into the lower sash. Drill a hole large enough to pass your coaxial cable. Pass the cable through the board and through the window. Close the window onto the board and use another length of board between the top of the window and the upper frame to prevent the window from being opened from the outside. Connect the coax to your antenna, but leave enough slack in the cable to form a drip loop just outside the window. Finally, buy some packing foam material and use it to block any drafty gaps created by your new installation. When it's time to move, the entire assembly can be torn down in minutes without damage to the window.

Q Mark Schoonover, KA6WKE, asks, "I'm just getting started in low-power (QRP) operating and I have two questions. How do you establish an RF ground while out in the field? In the Army we pounded in ground rods for field operations. Most of my QRP will involve hiking to various sites and the thought of dragging along a ground rod and hammer is not too exciting."

A Depending on the type of antenna system you use, grounding in the field may not be all that important. Many antennas, such as dipoles, Yagis, and so on, do not require ground connections for proper operation. Consider the space shuttle; it is nowhere near a ground, but it works just fine!

Other antennas *do* require grounds—end-fed wires, most verticals, etc. In those cases, you establish the best ground possible with a *counterpoise*, which can consist of one or more $1/4$-wavelength wires connected to the "ground" point such as a short ground rod. Counterpoise radials work best if they are a few inches above the soil.

RF notwithstanding, don't forget the role grounding plays in lightning protection. If you are truly in the field, however, you shouldn't be anywhere near the antenna if lightning is about.

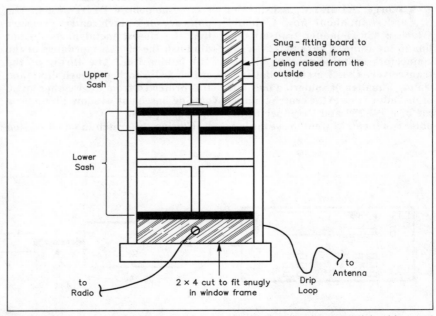

Figure 9.43—A narrow 2×4 with a properly drilled hole will pass a coaxial cable through a window without damaging or modifying the window itself.

Q I'd like to set up a 30-meter antenna in my back yard, but I'm really tight on space. I've been told that I can use a technique known as 'linear loading' to reduce the size of a dipole. Can you enlighten me?

A What you've heard is true—linear loading can significantly reduce the required lengths of resonant antennas. For example, it is easy to make a resonant antenna that is 30 to 40% shorter than an ordinary dipole for a given band. The shorter length comes from bending back some of the antenna wire. The increased self-coupling lowers the resonant frequency.

NNØF constructed a linear-loaded dipole using 25-feet of common 450-Ω ladder line and capacitive end hats (see **Figure 9.44**). The end hats are simply 6-foot lengths of stiff wire. Both conductors of the ladder line at each end are soldered to the hat wires. At the middle of the antenna (12 feet 6 inches from the ends) you cut through one of the ladder line conductors and attach your 50-Ω coaxial feed line. Cut through the other conductor as well, but leave it open. This antenna should provide a good match (no tuner required) and it fits easily within most back yards.

Q I'm familiar with Yagi antennas, but I also hear occasional references to antenna designs known as *quads*. What are these?

A Like a Yagi antenna, a quad is *directive*. That is, it focuses your RF power in a particular direction. In terms of how they are put together, quads are different animals. They consist of two or more loops of wire, each supported by a bamboo or Fiberglass cross-arm assembly. The loops are a quarter wavelength per side (one full wavelength overall). One loop is driven and the other serves as a parasitic element—usually a reflector. A variation on the quad is called the *delta loop*. The electrical properties of both antennas are the same. Both antennas are shown in **Figure 9.45**. They differ mainly in their physical properties, one being of plumber's delight construction, while the other uses insulating support members. One or more directors can be added to either antenna to obtain additional gain and directivity.

Q Woody, WD4NSB, asks, "I have a 45-foot pole in my front yard that has my 10-meter Yagi antenna mounted on it. All of my coaxial feed lines are routed to the pole through a PVC pipe buried under the ground. I have just put up a McCoy Dipole (nonresonant random length) and will be feeding it with 450-Ω ladder line from a tuner for operation on all bands (160-10 meters). Can I run the 450-Ω ladder line through the PVC pipe with no problems? If I can't run the 450-Ω ladder line directly in the pipe, can I make up a 100-Ω balanced line from two lengths of coax (using the center conductors as the feed line and grounding the braids)?"

A Running ladder-line underground through your PVC pipe is not a good idea. Other than very short lengths, or short points of contact, ladder line needs to be kept about 2 feet from any conductors. Running it through your pipe will place it just fractions of an inch away

from ground, not to mention the other feed lines in the pipe, for a considerable distance.

Making a balanced line from two pieces of coax is also counterproductive in your situation. The reason for using ladder line in the first place is because of its low loss—this advantage is negated when using the coax balanced line.

If the feed line *must* go through the pipe to your dipole, my advice would be to use parallel multiple dipoles fed together at a common feed point with good quality coax. You probably won't need to use an antenna tuner. See Figure 5 on page 7-3 of the 18th edition of the *ARRL Antenna Book*.

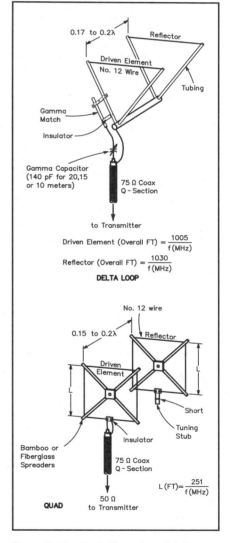

Figure 9.45—Typical quad and delta loop antenna designs. The ¼ wavelength of 75-Ω coax acts as a matching transformer between the 100-Ω feed point impedance and the 50-Ω impedance of the station coax.

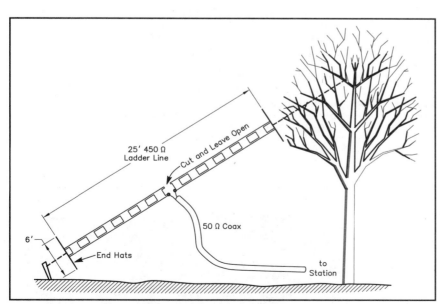

Figure 9.44—A two-wire linear-loaded antenna for 30 meters using 450-Ω ladder line.

Q Joe, NC4D, asks, "I'm curious about connecting two VHF antennas. Can you use a T connector to connect one feed line from a 6-meter beam, and another from a 2-meter beam, to a single piece of coax going back to the radio? Would this be any different than having multiple dipoles in parallel, all connected to the same feed line?"

A Parallel dipoles work as they do because the antennas that are nonresonant to the frequency of the transmitted signal provide a high impedance at the connection point while the antenna that *is* resonant provides a low (approximately 50 Ω) impedance.

A 6-meter beam may or may not offer sufficiently high impedance to 2-meter RF, and vice versa. Either way, you still have the issue of what happens in the coax. Coax that is terminated in its characteristic impedance will present the same impedance on the other end. Coax that is terminated in a high impedance will present a different impedance on the other end, dependent upon the length. Consider an open coax stub: the far end is about as high an impedance as you could want. If the coax is $1/2$ wavelength (or a multiple thereof), the near end will also be a high impedance. However, if the coax is a $1/4$ wavelength (or an odd multiple thereof), the near end will be a very low impedance. Lengths in between will give other impedance values.

So, to do what you describe, you would have to adjust the length of the coax going from the **T** to the 6-meter beam in such a way that it offers a high impedance to 2-meter RF. You'll need to meet the opposite condition with the coax that runs between the **T** and the 2-meter beam.

Perhaps an easier alternative would be to purchase a diplexer. These matching/coupling devices are primarily designed to allow multiband VHF/UHF transceivers with single feed line ports to operate on several bands without changing antennas. Feed lines from each antenna connect to the diplexer, then a single coax feed line runs between the diplexer and the radio.

ance to 50 Ω for your radio. The relationship between all of the elements is complex. The high impedance of the end-fed radiator is determined by its length and diameter and, to a smaller degree, the presence of nearby dielectric insulators.

The impedance of the matching section is determined by its conductor diameter and spacing. This is not very critical in most **J** pole designs. The transmission line transformer is usually cut to a quarter wavelength, shorted at one end. It is then tapped at the point that corresponds to an impedance of 50 Ω. Minor variations in the length of the radiating element and the transmission-line transformer can be compensated for by either changing the length of one or both elements slightly, or by changing the tap point on the transformer.

Most **J** poles are either designed by trial and error, or by modeling them on a computer. You can start with the half-quarter-wavelength dimensions (don't forget the approximately 0.97 velocity factor on the transmission line section), then adjust the tap point and length of the radiating element. If you have access to an impedance bridge, such as the MFJ-259B or Autek VHF Analyst, you can adjust the tap position for 50 Ω resistive and the length of the radiating element to get the reactance down to zero.

Of course, there is nothing magical about the half-/quarter-wavelength combination. I recently modeled a **J** pole whose dimensions are much shorter than the norm, and it, too, gives 50 Ω at the feed point.

Q Paul Brenner, W6RLF, asks, "I have a question concerning the MFJ Artificial Ground. I'm using a 100-foot long-wire antenna fed with an MFJ tuner. I have about 5 feet of tinned copper braid going to a six-foot copper rod ground just under the window where the tuner is located. The performance of the long wire on 40 meters seems just so-so, although it's a decent length ($3/4$ wavelength) on 40. If I add the MFJ Artificial Ground to

improve my RF grounding, will that help the performance of my antenna system?"

A It would seem unlikely to be of much help. The MFJ Artificial Ground (see **Figure 9.46**) does a fine job taming RF in the shack. It is also an excellent "counterpoise tuner" for hams who are using end-fed wire antennas in apartment situations without a short access path to an outdoor ground or radial system, but this isn't your problem.

Have you considered improving your antenna system? At $3/4$ wavelength on 40 meters, it is technically not a long wire but a random wire ("… the power gain of a long-wire antenna as compared to a half-wave dipole is not considerable until the antenna is really long [its length measured in wavelengths]"—*ARRL Antenna Book, 18th edition*). Try adding as much wire as possible to your antenna; it can run in just about any direction. Get your antenna as high in the air as possible. In addition, attach some 33-foot radial wires to your ground rod. Begin with 4 or 5 wires, either lying on top of the soil or buried underneath. My guess is that you'll see an improvement in your antenna performance.

Q John, KU4KZ, asks, "I have a Yaesu FT-990 transceiver that I use with a Carolina Windom antenna. Most of the time I use my antenna tuner, but the other day the tuner was accidentally in the bypass mode. I noticed that the tuner's SWR meter was moving as I talked. It seemed to kick up as high as 2:1. I was running about 100 W output. When I brought the antenna tuner into the line, the needle did not move when I transmitted. Can you explain this?"

A Yes, I believe I can. To answer your question, let's briefly discuss what an antenna tuner and an SWR meter do.

Part of the function of an SWR meter is to measure any power that is reflected back to your transceiver that's caused by an impedance mismatch in the antenna system. Most modern rigs are designed

Q Howard, KK7KL, asks, "Can you tell me how one figures the spacing for the matching section of a J antenna? Is there a rule of thumb? Any assistance you could pass along would be greatly appreciated."

A The **J** pole is an interesting antenna. It is essentially an endfed half-wavelength antenna, and the transmission line is used as a transmission-line transformer to transform the high feed-point imped-

Figure 9.46—The MFJ-934 Artificial Ground.

to accommodate antenna impedances of 50 Ω. If the impedance at the antenna system input is anything other than 50 Ω, power will be reflected back to the radio. The reflected power needle on your SWR meter will indicate this power. If it reads zero, there is no measurable reflected power.

The job of the antenna tuner is to match the antenna system impedance to that of the transceiver. Note that an antenna tuner doesn't "tune" anything—it matches two dissimilar impedances. The antenna tuner transforms whatever impedance exists at the end of your coax to 50 Ω for the radio. When impedances are matched there is no reflected power and, again, the reflected power needle will read zero.

So, when your antenna tuner was bypassed you were seeing the result of having your transceiver connected directly to the antenna system. The SWR meter indicated that reflected power was present as you spoke. (In SSB, power is generated only when you actually speak.) When you switched your tuner back in, the impedance mismatch was transformed to 50 Ω and the reflected power at the SWR meter dropped to zero.

By the way, don't worry too much about harming your FT-990 this way. Like most transceivers, the FT-990 includes a foldback circuit that senses when there is too much reflected power getting into the radio. The foldback automatically reduces the output to a safe level.

Q I live on the top floor of an apartment building. We have a small balcony, but I can't hang wire antennas for HF because they'll droop onto the balconies below. I also need an antenna that I can remove quickly. Can you help?

A You actually have more options available than you think. You could try a compact tuned loop antenna such as those sold by MFJ. Other extremely compact antennas such as the Bilal Isotrons (**www.rayfield.net/isotron**) may help. You might also try using a lightweight mobile antenna such as a Hamstick. You could mount the Ham-stick on the balcony railing, for example, and attach a counterpoise wire to the ground side of the antenna mount. (The counterpoise wire should be 1/4 wavelength for the desired band.) Just route the counterpoise wire along the floor of the balcony. Be sure to stay away from the ends of these counterpoise radials, where high RF voltages can exist even at modest transmitter power levels.

All of these antenna options are, of course, compromises. They sacrifice

efficiency to save space. Don't expect any of them to outperform even a full-sized dipole mounted high in the clear, but they *will* get you on the air and provide many enjoyable contacts.

Q Tom, KF6DRI, asks, "Direct TV has changed over from Primestar and left me the old 24-inch Primestar dish. Can these dishes be used on the amateur microwave bands?"

A Yes, your Primestar 24-inch dish should work just fine on 1296 MHz and higher microwave bands up to at least 10 GHz. In chapter 1 of the *UHF/Microwave Projects Manual*, Paul Wade, W1GHZ, describes how to design a feed for these types of offset dishes. Paul also has a microwave Web site at **www.w1ghz.cx**.

Q Dave, WD8DK, asks, "I am using a G5RV on 80-6 meters. How efficient is this antenna on 6 meters? I have been told that it is very inefficient on this band. In fact, I have been told that a 1/2 wavelength dipole is more efficient than the G5RV on 6 meters. Any comments?"

A On 20 meters, where the G5RV was designed to operate, it boasts a little gain over a conventional half-wave dipole. Given a reasonably efficient feed line (450-Ω line) and a good antenna tuner, there's no reason why the G5RV can't be at least as "efficient" as, say, a coax-fed dipole in the HF bands.

However, on 6 meters the G5RV acts as a long-wire antenna, with an azimuthal pattern with multiple, very narrow lobes. The narrow lobes are what give it gain, but also what make its performance compared with a regular garden-variety dipole inferior in directions other than the ones it favors. The *EZNEC* plot shown in **Figure 9.47** assumes that the antenna is mounted as a flat top at 50 feet above average ground. The G5RV has significantly more gain than the simple dipole, but it achieves this mainly in four, narrow-beamwidth directions. For the rest of the azimuths, its pattern has nulls that the dipole covers well.

Any multiband antenna is a compromise, but most of us can't have five or more dipoles hanging in our backyards. On 6 meters I would recommend a separate antenna designed for that band. There are a couple of inexpensive

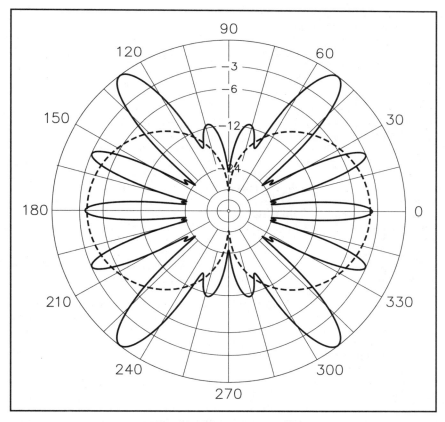

Figure 9.47—This is an EZNEC plot of a G5RV antenna on 6 meters compared to a dipole cut for 6 meters. The solid line represents the G5RV pattern while the dashed line represents the dipole. Notice that the G5RV is creating numerous narrow lobes of radiation.

6-meter wire antenna designs on the ARRL TIS Web site at **http://www.arrl.org/tis/**. Go there and click on "Antenna Projects," and then "Other VHF Antennas."

Q Gery, KD6FXW, is in stealth mode—keep it among yourselves—and needs some advice about antennas: I have a spool of 0.0035-inch tungsten wire that would be a real invisible antenna. Would the small size of the wire have to be longer than the magic $(468/f_{MHz})$ formula—what percent of length would have to be added? What would be the maximum power limit of such thin wire?

A While tungsten is very hard wire, it would not make a good choice for antennas. Such thin wire has a high resistance and you would be losing a lot of power as heat. Tungsten is quite brittle—if you actually succeeded in putting up a dipole with this wire, it probably wouldn't last a week. Besides, it isn't necessary to be that thin to achieve invisibility. A wire that is #26 AWG or smaller will be invisible to the naked eye at distances of more than 25 feet. The best bet for thin wire antennas is copper-clad steel (CCS). The drawback to this wire is that (for thin sizes), the copper can acquire small flaws that allow water to contact and rust the steel, and the wire will subsequently break. However, CCS is available in insulated form that greatly extends the useful life. Radioworks (**www.radioworks.com**) is one source for this wire.

Q Andy Strubbe, K8AND, of Akron, Ohio writes: I live on the top floor of an apartment building. I have a balcony with a metal railing about 4^1/$_2$ feet high. I've mounted a 10-foot long 2-meter vertical on three 5-foot sections of 1^1/$_4$-inch TV mast held to the railing with two hose clamps. Do you think I could raise the mast to 20 or 25 feet? Regular guying wouldn't be possible.

A There are a few things to consider. Will the railing be able to stand up to the wind loading of 20-25 feet of mast plus the 10 feet of antenna? If your balcony is made of wood, this is likely to cause the bolts holding the railing to work loose over time. If the railing and its mounts are sturdy enough, stacking five unguyed sections of TV mast won't be stable—the RadioShack 19 foot telescoping mast (15-5065, $39.99) is a better choice. Guying is going to be a problem for a permanent installation. Guying at two points 180 degrees apart is not enough. With a structure totaling some 30 feet, you need at least three guys, 120 degrees apart.

Q From Quebec, Stephan, VE2OWL, writes: I am mostly interested in HF antennas. I often see that there should be no current flowing on the outside of a coax to prevent the coax from radiating. If no current is flowing on the outside of the coax, but there's some on the center...where's the return path?

A The return path for the RF is the *inside* surface of the shield. A coaxial cable will only radiate if there is RF flowing on the *outside* of the shield. A current balun prevents this, while still allowing current to flow on the inside of the shield. Unlike dc or low frequency ac, the flow of current at RF is a "surface" phenomenon—that is to say, it flows through conductor on the surface, to a depth of a few thousandths of a millimeter. This is known as "skin effect." For a tubular conductor such as the shield of a coax, it can (and often does) have *different* magnitudes of current flowing on the inside and outside surfaces, and this current can even be in different directions between the two. Although you might think that in a braided shield the current would tend to follow the braid strands, this is not the case—to RF, a braided shield is just a tube with a rippled surface. So with a balun you can prevent current from flowing on the outside of the shield, while the return path on its inside surface is completely unaffected.

Q Todd Bruner, WB1HAI, of Annapolis, Maryland, asks: Our house is undergoing renovations. I am concerned that there will be no more cold water pipes that go to ground and I am concerned that my antenna cable path is not known.

So that I do not have to drill holes and pull cables after the new walls have been constructed, I am placing cable in the walls with convenient junction boxes for access. Having read *The ARRL Handbook* and *Antenna Book*, I think I have the ground issue down: size of wire, length of the run and tying them all together.

Can you make a recommendation with respect to coax? Should I run one set for HF and another set for higher frequencies. Can I use one coax type for all HF and VHF? The tables in both our books are great, especially in design of antenna, loss factors, capacitance, etc. But as for transmission lines I am looking for the quick pragmatic solution. My intention is run from the rig to these internal transmission lines to an antenna coupler, patch panel or junction box and then through a transmission line to the antenna.

What would you do with this opportunity to pre-install these transmission

lines (other than determining where the ham shack will be first)?

A The main advantage of new construction is that you can run the lines in places that you can't readily get to before the rooms are complete—lines can be run around walls horizontally, up or down a level vertically and even across a room in the floor or ceiling. Punching a hole through an outside wall is perhaps a bit easier when that wall is being built, but that can still be done afterward.

However, I strongly recommend that you try to get your wife to commit to a particular room for your shack. The key to a good installation is to keep the ground wire length to a minimum—if you have to run a wire 30 feet or more to an outside ground rod, you will have a poor ground on the higher bands.

The best transmission line to use depends on a number of factors, but key among them is the frequencies you will be using and the length of the lines. RG-213 is a good choice for HF and lengths under 150 feet. For VHF you might prefer a low loss line like a Belden 9913 type or even one of the lower loss types if the feed line run will be long. Although you can use VHF type coax at HF as well, it really is overkill and the expense can be significant (the last time I checked, 9913 was about 70 cents a foot with the lower loss lines at a buck or more per foot). For this reason, it would be helpful if you could determine where you are going to mount the antennas as well, so you can keep the feed line lengths as short as possible.

Q KT4SP asks, "I am using a Hustler 4-band trap antenna fed with coax. At the antenna the coax is attached not by a connector, but by the shield and center conductor to screws. I assume that this is proper, since the antenna does not have an SO-239 connector. The antenna is mounted about three inches above ground with no radials. I have been using this setup for a number of years, but my power output on phone is only about 45 W from a 100-W transceiver. Would the addition of a 1:1 balun to the system improve or degrade the output? Is this type of vertical considered a balanced or an unbalanced antenna?"

A While a vertically oriented half-wave dipole would be a balanced antenna, a quarter-wavelength vertical—with its "missing bottom half" made up using an image antenna reflected in the ground plane—is indeed an "unbalanced antenna."

However, just because this is an unbalanced antenna fed with an unbalanced (coax) feed line doesn't mean that everything is hunky-dory in the installation. The real clue to the nature of this problem is that your system doesn't have ground radials. Two concerns immediately arise: (1) power reduction in the radio due to common-mode currents and (2) poor radiation efficiency.

If the ground plane or radial system is inadequate under the vertical, then there's a really good chance that common-mode currents are being radiated onto the shield of the coax cable running on the ground under the vertical. Such common-mode currents can fool a transceiver's SWR sensor and cause it to reduce the output power. Putting a balun at the feed point may, or may not, reduce the level of common-mode currents, but this isn't really the proper approach—putting down radials is what is really required here!

Consider this: a quarter-wave vertical with a perfect ground system should show a feed-point impedance of about 36 Ω, and this is only a $^{50}/_{36} = 1.388:1$ SWR—not enough to cause an SWR shutdown unless common-mode currents are involved. Indeed, because of the lack of radials, the feed-point impedance due to losses might be even closer to 50 Ω, even if the radiation efficiency is poor. So, unless common-mode currents are involved, the SWR alone wouldn't cause a power reduction to protect the radio.

Adding ground radials would improve the radiation efficiency and increase your output power (by eliminating common-mode currents that are falsely activating your radio's SWR sensor).

Q Ray, AH6LT, asks, "I have an antenna mounted on my apartment balcony with a counterpoise wire laying on the floor. The RF safety regulations don't say anything about counterpoises, but I presume that they radiate. What is the safe distance one should be from a counterpoise?"

A You are correct—a counterpoise is a radiating part of the antenna, especially if it is located significantly above ground. There are several ways you can evaluate it.

If you had accurate field-strength measurement equipment, you could measure the fields. This is, however, usually beyond the scope of most amateurs.

Most evaluations will be done by calculation. You can use the rather straightforward calculation methods outlined at the RF Safety Calculator Web page at the University of Texas at: **http://n5xu. ae.utexas.edu/rfsafety/**. The calculator will help you estimate the distance people need to be from any part of your antenna system (including the counter-poise). This is generally a conservative estimate; fields are usually less than the calculation would indicate. You could also use one of the antenna modeling software packages to get a more accurate estimate.

See **http://www.arrl.org/news/ rfsafety** for ARRL info on the subject, plus links to the FCC.

Q I've been using a G5RV antenna for years. It was damaged in a windstorm recently. It broke where the ladder line connects to the dipole. Can this be easily repaired, or should I just break down and buy another antenna?

A This is a minor repair. Clean the areas to be reconnected using sandpaper, emery cloth or steel wool until the metal is shiny. Make a good mechanical connection depending on where the break is and how it connects. If there is an eye for the wire to go through, loop the wire and twist it tight. If you are connecting wire to wire, twist the wires together so that they make a strong connection. Solder the connection using rosin flux solder.

Soldering outdoors can be difficult because any cool breeze keeps the connection from getting hot enough to melt the solder. Either use a torch, or bring the antenna indoors for this repair.

Q I'm confused about the concept of "SWR bandwidth." Can you explain?

A "SWR bandwidth" is a term you'll often encounter when you're reading about antenna designs, or checking the specifications of commercial antennas. Basically, the SWR bandwidth is the frequency range after the antenna has been tuned at one frequency, over which the SWR is 2:1 or less. This is easier to explain visually, so take a glance at **Figure 9.48**. Let's say that we have a 40-meter dipole antenna that is tuned to resonance at 7100 kHz. If our dipole has an SWR bandwidth of 200 kHz, we'd expect the SWR to rise to 2:1 at 7000 kHz and 7200 kHz.

Some types of antennas such as compact tuned loops have extremely narrow SWR bandwidths when tuned to resonance. Trap dipole and vertical antennas will have varying SWR bandwidths for each band, usually becoming narrower on the lower bands. Be wary of an antenna that claims a 2:1 SWR bandwidth covering all of a wide band, such as 80 meters. This band covers 3.5 to 4.0 MHz, a percentage bandwidth of more than 13%. While a wide SWR bandwidth may seem ideal, it's often the hallmark of an inefficient design with high losses. After all, dummy loads have the "best" SWR bandwidths of all! Read all about broadband antennas in Chapter 9 of *The ARRL Antenna Book*.

Q Ray, K4YDI, asks, "I have just put up a used vertical antenna. I'm not getting the SWR I want (1.5:1 or less). Would an antenna tuner improve the match and make the antenna work better?"

A Unfortunately, you did not mention what SWR you are seeing now. An antenna tuner may bring your SWR down to 1:1, but if your SWR is already under 2:1, it is not necessary.

Remember that an antenna tuner doesn't tune the antenna—it only matches the impedance shown at the station end of the coax to that of the transceiver. Your transceiver is probably capable of delivering its full output at the 2:1 SWR, so a sufficient portion of your RF output is already reaching the antenna.

Whether your antenna radiates most of that power depends on the physical characteristics of the antenna and its associated ground system, not the impedance seen by the transmitter.

To improve the radiation of a vertical, make sure you have a good ground/radial system. Don't rely on a single ground rod driven into the soil. Try stringing out as many radial wires as you can by just laying the wires directly on the ground—the

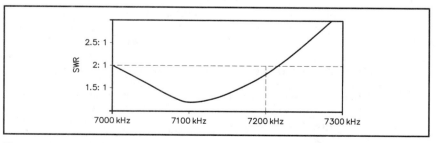

Figure 9.48—An SWR vs. frequency plot of a 40-meter dipole with a 2:1 SWR bandwidth of 200 kHz (see text).

more the better—and connecting them together at your antenna's ground point. Your SWR may not be reduced (it may even rise), but I'm willing to bet that your antenna will "play" better. If you find this to be the case, *then* you can worry about burying the wires to keep them out of harm's way.

Q I have a dipole cut for 20-meters fed with 45 feet of coax and I'm trying to use it on 40-meters with an antenna tuner. However, I need the full amount of tuner capacitance to get the SWR to 1:1. Does that mean that I am consuming a lot of power in the tuner?

A How much 40-meter power gets to your 20-meter dipole depends upon both the loss in the tuner and the loss in the feed line. According to the *EZNEC* antenna-modeling software, if your dipole is 35 feet above average ground, the feedpoint impedance at 7 MHz is about $13.6 - j1000\Omega$.

While that doesn't tell you what you get at the tuner end of the line, N6BV's *TL* and *TLW* programs (from the *ARRL Antenna Book* disk) will. If you are using RG-213 coax, the shack-end impedance will be $546 + j806\ \Omega$ (SWR 35:1). The same programs also give you the total feed line loss for a given SWR. In this case, the line loss is 16 dB. Clearly, the loss in the tuner is not all you need to worry about!

If you substitute 450-Ω ladderline instead, the shack-end impedance is $14 + j667\ \Omega$ (SWR 115:1), but the feed line loss drops to 3 dB. Why is it lower than the coax if the SWR is higher? The answer is that the additional loss due to the SWR is proportional to the line's characteristic loss, and ladderline has much less loss than coax. A 2.7-dB loss is half of your power, though. If you operate on 40 meters a lot you might want to consider a longer antenna (an 80-meter dipole on 40 meters gives a total feed line loss of less than 0.5 dB with 45 feet of ladderline).

Concerning the loss in the tuner, every tuner design will have a certain amount of loss. Some tuners are more lossy than others.

Q John Mosley, N6MZN, writes: I am building my first HF station. Can you use a piece of angle iron for a ground rod or does it have to be copper? There are no cold-water pipes near my station. How do I ground the equipment?

A While inexpensive steel can be used for grounding material indoors, it is absolutely not suitable for use outdoors because it will very quickly rust and lose its effectiveness. Copper does oxidize fairly quickly, but it does not corrode like plain steel does. Copper piping is a reasonably priced alternative to conventional ground rods.

Your station equipment should have a connection to an outdoor ground rod, connected to the equipment by a heavy wire run as short a distance as possible. A safety ground is required by electrical codes. A good article on grounding, both safety and RF, is available on the ARRL's Technical Information Service Web site at **www. arrl.org/tis/info/grounding.html**.

Q I want to build a trap dipole antenna for 20 and 30 meters using manufactured traps, but I don't know their inductance. The plan was to cut the dipole to 20 meters and install the 30 meter traps on each end. If the inductance can be determined, what length of wire should be added after the trap?

A A common trap to fall into! Traps act as a high impedance at the trap frequency and as an inductance at lower frequencies. The trap isolates a short section of a longer antenna so that it can be resonant on the higher frequency band. The inductance then is added to the natural inductance of the entire antenna, which then resonates on a lower frequency band. 30-meter traps would only be useful for building an antenna for 30 meters plus a lower frequency band like 40 or 80 meters, not a higher frequency band such as 20 meters. To build a trap dipole for 20 and 30, you would need traps for 20 meters instead.

Q I'd like to try microwave operating from home, but I can't put up antennas outdoors. Is it possible to at least receive microwave signals with an attic antenna? Will the signals make it through a standard shingled roof? I'm thinking specifically of receiving satellite microwave downlinks.
Bob Bruninga, WB4APR, answered this question with an interesting experiment:

A "Since I have a Direct-TV 1-meter dish on a tripod that I use for demonstrations, I decided to check its performance through various materials. The unit has a bargraph signal-strength meter for use during alignment. The meter scale goes from 0 to 100. Here are the results:
Outdoors in the clear: 92
1/4-inch plywood covering: 80
7/16-inch plywood covering: 77

3/4-inch plywood: 60
3/4-inch Masonite: 70
3/4-inch stack of paper: 60
1.5 inches of plywood: 43
(Note that the signal drops out completely at 35.)
"I have no idea if the scale is at all linear or logarithmic, and my arm was too short to both hold the wood and see the monitor well. So, your mileage may vary.

"With digital the picture is always perfect. You don't lose any quality until it drops out completely. Of course, most of this margin is needed in case of rain. But it looks to me like it should be possible to receive microwave downlinks through a simple 3/4-inch roof and shingles, as long as rain, ice or snow are not involved."

Q Glenn Becklund, NØHBK, asks, "I am putting up a tower this spring and it will be approximately 100 feet from my shack. I don't know if I should bury the coax, bury PVC or string a wire from the house to the tower and hang the cable from it."

A Most hams run coax above ground to dipoles and towers. Although this makes the coax more visible, it is also the easiest installation and it lends itself to quick repair if necessary. For relatively short spans, the coax can be run without any additional support. Longer runs should be supported with rope or wire, as you suggest. Always be sure to include a "drip loop" at the shack end to keep water from entering the connectors. Also, the connectors at the antenna end should also be sealed to be watertight.

Practically speaking, coax can be buried by itself only if it is specifically rated as "direct bury." Ordinary coax can be buried for short-term installations, but I wouldn't expect it to last for an extended period of time.

Although coax can be buried in PVC, proper drainage has to be provided so that the PVC does not fill up with water. This can be accomplished by installing the PVC on a slope and providing a place for the water to drain out. You should also seal the upper end of the pipe and screen the lower end of the pipe to keep out dirt and burrowing critters.

Q Frank Giambrone, KA2VTI, writes, "I presently have a 700-foot dipole fed with ladder line and running pretty much N-S at approximately 30 feet average height. I rarely chase DX and focus on a 75-meter net that encompasses Florida to Maine and as far west as Minnesota. It does not perform nearly as well as a

half-wave dipole running E-W. Would a curtain or some other design do better?"

A A 700-foot dipole is going to show a pretty complex pattern. In some directions, the antenna will have quite a bit of gain, even on 75 meters, but in most other directions, it will actually perform less well than a half-wave dipole. As a dipole's length exceeds one half-wave, the pattern begins to break up into lobes at lower angles along the wire's axis. For good regional coverage on 75 meters, you need to radiate most of your energy nearly vertically (see "The NVIS—A Low Antenna for Regional Communications" in June 2002 *QST*). If you have the real estate, perhaps you could run two half-wave 75-meter dipoles at right angles to each other. That way, at least one of the antennas would work well for any particular path. Try to raise the antenna as high as possible.

Q When it comes to HF antennas, how important is the elevation angle?

A Presuming that you are interested in working worldwide DX on the HF bands, the vertical (elevation) angle of maximum radiation is of considerable importance. An elevation angle of 5° is very shallow, while 90° is straight up (not a good angle for long-distance communication!). You want your radiation pattern to be at a low elevation angle so that the signal energy will be refracted by the ionosphere in such a way that it propagates as far as possible (see Figure 9.49).

Tables 9.1, 9.2 and 9.3 from *The ARRL Handbook* (see next page) show optimum elevation angles from locations in the continental US. These figures are based on statistical averages over all portions of the solar sunspot cycle.

Since low angles usually are most effective, this generally means that horizontal antennas should be high—higher is usually better.

Q Lou, KB6JLI, asks, "While reading an advertisement for a vertical antenna, I noticed the ad mentioned that no radials are needed, but it also says that you need to use an 80-foot counterpoise. Please clarify for me the difference between a radial and counterpoise. Aren't they basically the same?"

A The difference between the terms "radial" and "counterpoise" is subtle, but significant. Radials usually consist of multiple bare wires either buried in, or laid upon, the ground and are not tuned to a specific frequency. Such wires don't really show a resonance because they are coupled so heavily to

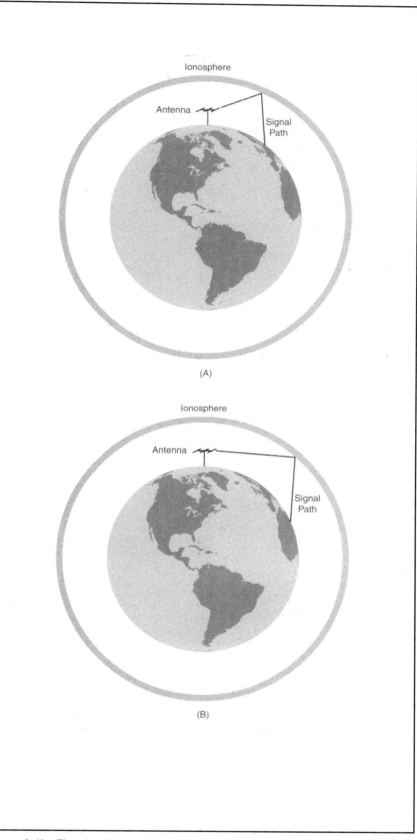

Figure 9.49—The elevation angle advantage. If your signal takes off at a high elevation angle (A), it won't propagate very far. Lower the angle (B), and the increase in distance can be considerable. A wavelength of height at a particular frequency results in a peak elevation angle of about 15°.

Table 9.1
Optimum Elevation Angles to Europe

Band	Northeast	Southeast	Upper Midwest	Lower Midwest	West Coast
10 m	5°	3°	3°	7°	3°
12 m	5°	6°	4°	6°	5°
15 m	5°	7°	8°	5°	6°
17 m	4°	8°	7°	5°	5°
20 m	11°	9°	8°	5°	6°
30 m	11°	11°	11°	9°	8°
40 m	15°	15°	14°	14°	12°
75 m	20°	15°	15°	11°	11°

Table 9.2
Optimum Elevation Angles to Far East

Band	Northeast	Southeast	Upper Midwest	Lower Midwest	West Coast
10 m	4°	5°	5°	5°	6°
12 m	4°	8°	5°	12°	6°
15 m	7°	10°	10°	10°	8°
17 m	7°	10°	9°	10°	5°
20 m	4°	10°	9°	10°	9°
30 m	7°	13°	11°	12°	9°
40 m	11°	12°	12°	12°	13°
75 m	12°	14°	14°	12°	15°

Table 9.3
Optimum Elevation Angles to South America

Band	Northeast	Southeast	Upper Midwest	Lower Midwest	West Coast
10 m	5°	4°	4°	4°	7°
12 m	5°	5°	6°	3°	8°
15 m	5°	5°	7°	4°	8°
17 m	4°	5°	5°	3°	7°
20 m	8°	8°	8°	6°	8°
30 m	8°	11°	9°	9°	9°
40 m	10°	11°	9°	9°	10°
75 m	15°	15°	13°	14°	14°

the lossy Earth. Their purpose is solely to reduce ground losses (very good information on this topic can be found in the 19th edition of *The ARRL Antenna Book*, starting on page 6-24).

A counterpoise is a wire or group of wires mounted close to ground, but insulated from ground, to form a low-impedance, high-capacitance path to ground. The purpose of a counterpoise is to provide an RF ground for the antenna.

Q George Fletcher, AD5CQ, asks, "I have a VHF/UHF transceiver. The center conductor on the SMA antenna connector has receded inside the connector and does not make contact with the center conductor of the screw-on antenna. Is this a common problem with SMA type antenna connectors? Is there a fix available other than replacing the whole connector?"

A I'm afraid that you will indeed have to replace the connector. To avoid this problem in the future, replace it with special "captivated" contact connectors. These exist not just for SMAs, but also for N and other connectors in which the normal design may allow for movement of the center conductor.

SMAs are rated at only 500 mating/unmating cycles, which is rather low compared to other connector types. The lifetime can be reduced even further by twisting the connector on and off, so that the center conductor rubs horizontally. It is preferable to hold the body of the connector fixed and just rotate the hex nut to tighten the connector.

Q Lamont Matin, N3ROR, of Baltimore, Maryland writes: Is it practical to use a tuner with a bug catcher type antenna to receive some gain in 10 meter mobile operation? That is, using a 40 meter coil (bug catcher type) tuned via mobile tuner?

A It is possible, but not efficient—you will receive no additional gain; in fact, possibly quite the reverse. On 10 meters, the tuner will see the 40-meter mobile system as a lossy antenna that is electrically longer than a quarter-wave antenna (sort of like a random wire). If the tuner is not placed at the base of the antenna, the SWR on the feed line between the tuner and the antenna will be very high, adding to the losses. What you suggest might work for convenience sake if you can get the SWR down to a reasonable level—2:1, but I would not use this as a permanent antenna.

Q Is it true that an antenna must be resonant to radiate RF?

A Some hams steadfastly cling to the confusing notion that somehow "resonance" is necessary in an antenna system in order for radiation to occur. (In this sense I am using the term "antenna system" to include the antenna, the transmission line, the antenna tuner—and the environment in which all these are placed, including the ground, nearby conductors, etc.)

Resonance is by no means necessary for radiation to occur! If the impedance at the shack for an antenna, its feed line and its environment happens to end up at, say, $120 - j\,400\ \Omega$, and if the transmitter is designed to work into exactly this impedance directly—or even more interestingly, if the transmitter consisted of a voltage source and a lossy resistive attenuator pad—no antenna tuner at all would be required. In this case, the transmitter wouldn't be very efficient, admittedly, but it also wouldn't care what the load impedance is at all. Where would resonance come into the act in such a situation? It wouldn't.

However, most transmitters are indeed designed to work into a 50-Ω nonreactive load, so the function of an antenna tuner in this case would be to transform $120 - j\,400\ \Omega$ into $50 + j\,0\ \Omega$. Is there "resonance" in this system with such an antenna tuner as an impedance transformer? Let me submit that the answer most antenna engineers would give is "Why are you asking this question?"

They'd simply state that the antenna tuner provides a 50-Ω load to the transmitter. The SWR on the line between the antenna and the tuner isn't changed by the presence of an antenna tuner. The "additional SWR" due to the mismatch between the characteristic impedance of the line and the antenna load adds extra loss beyond the matched-line loss for that length of line at that frequency. But where does "resonance" come into play?

It doesn't.

It is quite possible to look mathematically at the way the impedance changes along the physical length of the line, using the hyperbolic transmission line equation—and the impedance as it varies along the length of the line has absolutely nothing to do with the source impedance of whatever appears at the input of the line. The impedance at any point along a transmission line depends solely on:

1. The complex characteristic impedance of the line itself
2. The physical length of the line
3. The velocity factor of the line
4. The matched-line loss of the line
5. The impedance at the load end of the line (the antenna in this case)

Q Ray, WA3CLD, asks, "I have an old Swan TB-3HA tribander beam antenna. How can I check and recondition the traps? It has 4 driven-element traps, 2 director traps and no reflector traps. Can I adapt one of the driven element pairs of traps for the reflector?"

A The biggest problem with old traps is corrosion, both external and internal. To "recondition" them, you'll have to take them apart and thoroughly clean the inside. You can check a trap for internal corrosion without taking it apart by putting an ohmmeter across it—the resistance should be a relatively low value. If it is over 100 Ω, you probably have a corrosion problem.

Traps are designed to present a high impedance at the "trapped" frequency and to act as a loading coil at lower frequencies, so you should indeed be able to use driven element traps for the reflector by adjusting the tubing lengths slightly.

If you have an antenna analyzer or a dip meter, you can check the resonance of just the reflector (it should be about 5% lower than the driven) by assembling it as a unit. You may need to get it at least 10 feet up in the air, however, because the effect of the nearby ground detunes a low antenna, changing the resonant point from where it will be when the antenna is installed later.

Q George, VE3LTU, asks, "When a beam antenna such as a Yagi or quad produces a major radiation lobe at, say, 35°, would the radiation angle be improved by tilting the boom 20° toward the Earth? Would the radiation angle with respect to the Earth now be 15°, resulting in improved DX performance?"

A The short answer is "no."

An array as you describe has its major lobe aimed directly along the boom (0° elevation) when it is in free space. When ground is considered, it increases the elevation of the lobe. Therefore, it is the relation of the antenna to ground (height) that determines take-off angle.

We can look at it another way. The radiation pattern of an antenna is a summation of the radiation each of many antenna segments as they interact with each other and the ground below the antenna. We can visualize the result by imagining a mirror image of the antenna below the ground surface by a depth equal to the antenna's height above the ground. Thus, as we tip the antenna boom downward, the imaginary boom tips upward to counter it—we achieve nothing.

Q George, AD5CQ, asks, "I have two low pass filters. If I put them both in series with my transmission line, will I get more reduction of harmonics or would the input losses be excessive?"

A The answers are "yes" and "maybe" respectively.

The amount of loss would be double that of a single filter, but depending upon the filter design, it may be acceptable. I have seen filters with insertion losses as low as 0.25 dB and a 0.5-dB total loss would be quite acceptable to most folks.

The best way to check is to put a power meter in line after the filter. A 1-dB loss is about 21 Ω out of 100. If you don't have an external power meter, you can check the difference in receive signal strength. Find a strong steady signal like WWV or W1AW and try switching the filters in and out of line to see how much the S-meter changes. A 1-dB change would be just about noticeable in terms of meter movement (it's about 1/6 of an S-unit by the old Collins standard—not that any modern rigs follow the standard, but it should be in the ballpark).

Q John, N9QC, asks, "I am currently running a Yaesu FT-901 transceiver with a Cushcraft triband Yagi antenna. I'm considering adding a long-wire antenna for 80 and 160 meters and upgrading to a more modern transceiver. Do you think the automatic antenna tuners included with many of today's rigs would work for both antennas?"

A Most of the auto tuners incorporated into new rigs have limited tuning ranges. They'll only deal with SWRs up to about 3:1. That may be sufficient to

extend your ability to use your tribander beyond its 2:1 SWR bandwidth on each band. Don't count on the built-in tuner having enough range to handle the long-wire, though. You will need a separate, wide-range tuner to load your long-wire.

Q I have a question about the new/old antenna you are using at HQ—I believe you called it a "cage" antenna. Okay—now you have piqued my interest. What the heck is a cage antenna? Is it suitable for multi-band operation?

A The bandwidth of an antenna is affected by the diameter of the conductor. Hams who use a conventional single-wire dipole or inverted V for 80 meters usually find that it works in the CW band or the phone band, but not in both without a tuner.

The cage antenna is a classic design from the early days of radio that uses multiple conductors instead of a single one.

What the cage antenna does is "fool" the RF into thinking that it is seeing a very "thick" conductor. Therefore, you can operate over a very broad range of frequencies on the band for which the antenna is designed without the need of an antenna tuner—the "fatter" the cage, and the more conductors used, the broader-banded the antenna.

Since W1AW transmits bulletins in at the low (CW) portion of the 80-meter band and also at the upper (SSB) end, this is an ideal 80-meter antenna.

The cage antenna is not intended as a multiband antenna. On bands other than that for which the antenna is constructed, a tuner would have to be used and the performance would be comparable to that of any other random wire antenna.

Q I have a Cushcraft AR-270 Dual Band (2-meter/70-cm) Ringo antenna mounted on the side of my house. I changed its location the other day and checked the SWR after installing coax. It now reads 5:1. I changed coax, checked it again and the SWR is still 5:1. I have checked all connections and everything seems in good shape. What's next?

A By any chance, when you relocated the antenna, did you mount it near (within 6 feet or so) anything metal of a significant size? If so, the Ringo is probably "coupling" to this and changing the antenna's resonance as a result. If not, there may have been something internal to the antenna that broke when you moved it.

Q Every time you double your antennas, say, going from a single VHF/UHF Yagi to a stacked pair of Yagis, you realize an increase in gain, but you also lose a certain amount of power through the power divider or phasing harness. How do you manage to come out ahead?

A It is true that stacking antennas produces additional directivity and gain. You can stack antennas vertically (**Figure 9.50**) or horizontally, although vertical stacking is most common.

The "secret" is in the fact that gain can only come from taking power that would otherwise be radiated in other direction(s) and concentrating that power into the main, desired lobe(s).

The most easily understood physical demonstration is one that I've used for years at radio club meetings (see **Figure 9.51**). I take a balloon, blow it up so that it is roughly circular in shape and then declare that this is a radiation pattern from an isotropic radiator. Next, I blow up another balloon to the same size and shape and tell the audience that this will be my "reference" antenna.

Then I squeeze the first balloon in the middle to form a sort of figure-8 shape and declare that I've now created a dipole and compare the maximum size to that of my reference "antenna." The dipole can be seen to have some "gain" over the reference isotropic. Next, I squeeze the end of the first balloon to come up with a sausage-like shape to demonstrate the sort of pattern a beam antenna would have, again comparing the gain to the reference isotropic antenna, er, balloon.

By combining antennas in a stack, you can accentuate this gain and directivity even further. In the end, you have created much more total gain in the antenna system than would be lost in the power dividers or phasing harnesses. Stacking isn't easy or inexpensive, but the performance gain can be substantial.

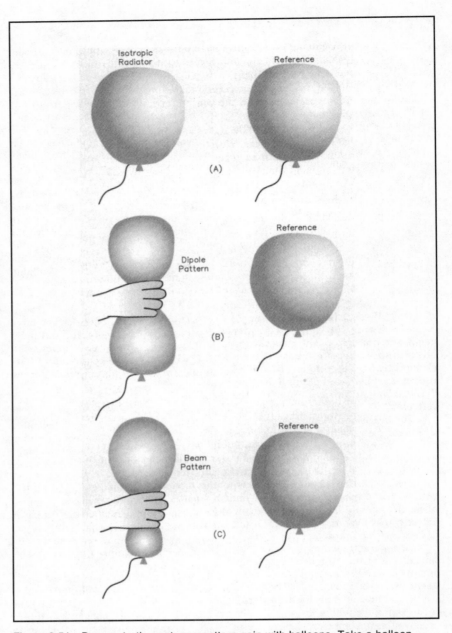

Figure 9.51—Demonstrating antenna pattern gain with balloons. Take a balloon, blow it up so that it is roughly circular in shape and then declare that this is a radiation pattern from an isotropic radiator. Next, blow up another balloon to the same size and shape and tell the audience that this will be the "reference" antenna (A). Then, squeeze the first balloon in the middle to form a sort of figure-8 shape and declare that this is a dipole and compare the maximum size to that of the reference "antenna" (B). The dipole can be seen to have some "gain" over the reference isotropic. Next, squeeze the end of the first balloon to come up with a sausage-like shape to demonstrate the sort of pattern a beam antenna creates (C).

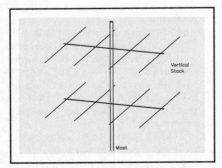

Figure 9.50—An example of vertical antenna stacking.

Q Jerry, KC8OTH, asks, "What does the 'dBi' mean when used to rate an antenna?"

A I will presume that you are somewhat familiar with the decibel. If not, at least a few numbers will put it into perspective. Decibel is a term that can compare two powers or voltage levels. The formulas are:

$dB = 10_{log} (P1/P2)$ where P1 and P2 are two power levels.

It can also compare voltages, if the voltages are at the same impedance. The formula is:

$dB = 20_{log} (V1/V2)$ where V1 and V2 are the two voltage levels.

(For "extra credit," if the resistances are not equal, you can use the formula

$$dB = 10_{log} ((V1^2/R1)/(V2^2/R2)).$$

Now, in antenna gain, there are two common references. The first is an imaginary antenna called an "isotropic" radiator. This is an antenna that radiates equally in all directions. An isotropic radiator placed at the center of a sphere would illuminate the sphere equally. No such antenna exists in real life. A practical example of what is nearly an isotropic radiator is a light bulb.

When gain is expressed in dBi, it indicates how much louder a signal from that antenna will be *in the main beam of the antenna* than it would be if the same amount of power were applied to an isotropic radiator in free space. The thing to remember about gain is that an antenna develops gain by concentrating energy in one direction and not radiating energy in other directions. Two examples of gain are flashlights, and the technique of cupping your hands when you shout to make the sound louder in the desired direction.

A directional antenna such as a Yagi can have considerable gain. Typical HF Yagi beams can have 8 dBi gain or more; a large VHF or UHF beam can have 20 dBi gain, or even more.

Some easy numbers to remember are:
1 dB = 1.25 × power
2 dB = 1.6 × power
3 dB = 2 × power
10 dB = 10 × power

A 20-dBi-gain antenna would have 10 × 10 or 100 times the power gain of an isotropic radiator. One watt fed into a 20-dBi-gain antenna would be as loud as 100 Ω fed into an isotropic source, *but only in the direction the antenna is beaming.*

Decibels also work in the other direction, too. An antenna with –3 dBi "gain" actually has a loss of 3 dB—it will lose half of the power applied to it. An antenna that is –10 dBi is radiating $^1/_{10}$ the signal of one with 0 dBi gain; one that is –20 dBi is radiating $^1/_{100}$ the signal and so on. A –20 dBi gain antenna with 1 W fed to it would sound as loud as an isotropic antenna being fed with 10 mW.

Most H-Ts have antennas that are not very efficient. A gain of –10 dBi would be about typical. This can work very well if you are near a repeater, but if you are right at the edge of a repeater's range, or operating simplex over a few miles, this will not give a very good signal; it will sound "scratchy" on the receiving end.

Another reference point is dBd, or referring the gain to a half-wave dipole in free space. The half-wave dipole in free space has a gain of 2.15 dBi, so gain expressed in dBd is always 2.15 dB less than gain expressed in dBi. Don't worry, the gain of the antenna is the same in both cases, only the reference has changed. If you want to compare an antenna whose gain is in dBd to one whose gain is in dBi, add 2.15 to the gain of the antenna in dBd.

I don't want to make it too complicated, but I will add that most antenna gain figures tell you what the antenna would be if it were in free space—infinitely far away from the Earth. In the real world, the ground affects the antenna performance by reflecting signals upward. This actually adds up to about 5 dB to the gain of an antenna. So, a half-wavelength dipole over ground can actually have about 5 dBd of gain! Slick, eh? The half-wavelength dipole over ground has 5-dB gain over a half-wave dipole in free space.

Q I think I have just enough room in my backyard to put up a wire dipole antenna for 17 meters, my favorite band. Can you give me some installation and tuning tips? And what if I can't string the dipole in a straight line? Is that a problem?

A Let's start with the basics. A classic dipole antenna is $^1/_2$ wavelength long and fed at the center. The feed-point impedance is low at the resonant frequency, f_0, and odd harmonics thereof. The impedance is high near even harmonics. When fed with coax, a classic dipole provides a reasonably low SWR at f_0 and its odd harmonics.

When fed with ladder line (see **Figure 9.52**) and an antenna tuner with a balanced output, the classic dipole should be usable near f_0 and all harmonic frequencies. (With a wide-range tuner, it may work on all frequencies.) If there are problems (such as extremely high SWR or evidence of RF on objects at the operating position), change the feed line length by adding or subtracting $^1/_8$-wavelength at the problem frequency. A few such adjustments should yield a workable solution. Such a system is sometimes called a "center-fed Zepp."

Most dipoles require a little pruning to reach the desired resonant frequency. Here's a technique to speed the adjustment. When assembling the antenna, cut the wire 2 to 3% longer than the calculated length and record the length. When the antenna is complete, raise it to the working height and check the SWR at several frequencies. Multiply the frequency of the SWR minimum by the antenna length and divide the result by the desired f_0. The result is the finished length; trim both ends equally to reach that length and you're done.

Here's another trick, if you use nonconductive end support lines. When assembling the antenna, mount the end insulators in about 5% from the ends. Raise the antenna and let the ends hang free. Figure how much to prune and cut it from the hanging ends. If the pruned ends are very long, wrap them around the insulated line for support.

Dipole antennas need not be installed in a horizontal straight line. They are generally tolerant of bending, sloping or drooping as required by the antenna site. Remember, however, that dipole antennas are RF conductors. For safety's sake, mount all antennas away from conductors (especially power lines), combustibles and well beyond the reach of passersby.

A *sloping dipole* is often used to favor one direction (the "forward direction" in the figure). With a nonconducting support and poor earth, signals off the back are weaker than those off the front. With a nonconducting mast and good earth, the response is omnidirectional. There is no gain in any direction with a nonconducting mast.

A conductive support such as a tower acts as a parasitic element. (So does the coax shield, unless it is routed at 90° from the antenna.) The parasitic effects vary with earth quality, support height and other conductors on the support (such as

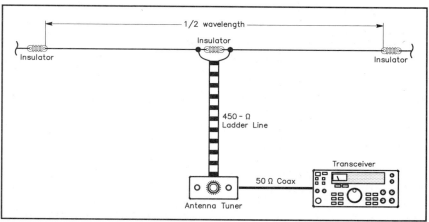

Figure 9.52—The classic flattop dipole antenna. This version is fed using an antenna tuner and 450-Ω ladder line for multiband operation.

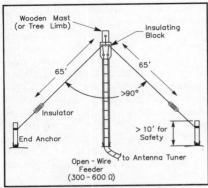

Figure 9.53—The Inverted V takes its name from its shape.

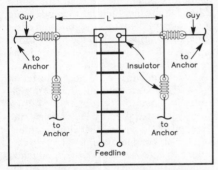

Figure 9.54—Dipole antennas can be bent a number of ways to fit in the available space.

a beam at the top). With such variables, performance is very difficult to predict.

Losses increase as the antenna ends approach the support or the ground. To prevent feed-line radiation, route the coax away from the feed point at 90° from the antenna, and continue on that line as far as possible.

An *Inverted V* antenna appears in **Figure 9.53**. While "V" accurately describes the shape of this antenna, this antenna should not be confused with long-wire **V** antennas, which are highly directive. The radiation pattern and dipole impedance depend on the apex angle, and it is very important that the ends do not come too close to lossy ground.

Bent dipoles may be used where antenna space is at a premium. **Figure 9.54** shows several possibilities; there are many more. Bending distorts the radiation pattern somewhat and may affect the impedance as well, but compromises are acceptable when the situation demands them. When an antenna bends back on itself, some of the signal is canceled; avoid this if possible.

Remember that current produces the radiated signal, and current is maximum at the dipole center. Therefore, performance is best when the central area of the antenna is straight, high and clear of nearby objects.

Q Jim Jolly, W6RWI, writes: Is there a device available to enable two transceivers to use a single antenna and one will be protected while the other is transmitting?

A It depends on exactly what you are looking to do. If you merely want to switch back and forth between two radios using a single antenna, but would only be using one radio at a time, then a very basic coax type antenna switch will suffice. These typically provide more than 60 dB of isolation from one port to another and at power levels up to 100 W, this would be a level of 100 microwatts (–10 dBm) or less into the transceiver that is not being used.

If you want to use both transceivers at the same time, then that is another matter altogether. You did not mention what frequencies would be involved, so I will outline the different possibilities. First, I would note that, with one particular exception, the transceivers would either have to be on different bands or on fixed frequencies within the same band.

The solution for the former would be to install bandpass filters on the output of both transceivers. If the transceivers under discussion are both multiband HF rigs, note that switchable bandpass filters are available from a couple of sources. For VHF/UHF, the solution is known as a diplexer (although some manufacturers call it a duplexer).

For two transceivers on the same band, a very large amount of rejection is needed with a very narrow filter spacing. Such rejection can be achieved only with tuned cavities (as in a duplexer) and these are not readily adjustable. Because of this, the frequencies used would have to be fixed. Duplexers are of reasonable size at VHF and UHF, but then to be impractically large (and expensive) at HF.

The exception mentioned above is, when you have two transceivers but they will only be confined to separate parts of the same band (such as having one on SSB and one on CW during Field Day), very narrow bandpass filters can be made to isolate one from the other. These are not available commercially, however—you would have to build your own. Plans for an 80 meter version appeared in the September 1998 issue of our experimenter's magazine, *QEX*. The 40 meter version appeared in November 1998 *QEX*.

Q I recently purchased an A3S triband beam. The instruction manual suggests a coil of 8 turns, 6 inches in diameter, be constructed of RG-8 feed line next to the feed point of said antenna. This is referred to as an RF choke. Why would one want an RF choke inserted into one's feed line?

A What they are referring to is fully named a choke balun. What it does is choke off RF that would otherwise flow down the outside of the shield of the coax. Now, as you know, the shield of the coax provides the return path for the RF flowing through the center conductor. Well, RF is a "surface phenomenon," so it flows along the surface or wire and braid and you can have different RF currents flowing on the outside and inside of a hollow conductor like braid.

Ideally, the braid that makes up the coax shield shouldn't have any RF current flowing on the outside. If it did, it would radiate and therefore wouldn't be a shield anymore. The "choke" formed by coiling coax suppresses current flow on the outside of the shield, but does not have any effect on the RF on the inside. Why is that? Because in order to act like a choke, adjacent conductor windings have to be magnetically coupled. While adjacent turns of the outside of the shield form a coil, the shield keeps the inside of the coax from coupling between adjacent turns.

Q Kwame E. Davis, K2RMC, writes: From my home location in northern New Jersey, I am having a very hard time breaking through the QRM/QRN on CW contacts. I also have difficulty breaking through pileups. Would it be advisable to incorporate a 600-watt HF amp to my setup?

I don't want to go higher than that for fear of interfering with the neighbors' televisions and radios. What type amp would function best with the Kenwood TS-850S and a Butternut HF9V vertical antenna?

A An amplifier may well help overcome QRM and QRN, although sometimes when propagation is not there or when there are a lot of "big gun" stations in a pileup, that amplifier may not solve all of your problems. And you are right—adding more power can cause more RFI problems.

First, analyze how much the amplifier will do to help. If I assume you are running 100 watts RF output right now, by going to a 600-watt amplifier, you will add 7.8 dB to your signal. If an S unit is 6 dB (the old Collins standard), then using a 600-watt amplifier would add just over an S unit to your signal strength. In bad conditions or heavy QRM, this can make a difference.

You can also add about the same amount of signal by improving your antenna system. Unless you are in an area with excellent ground, a vertical antenna can operate at a significant disadvantage compared to a horizontal antenna up a

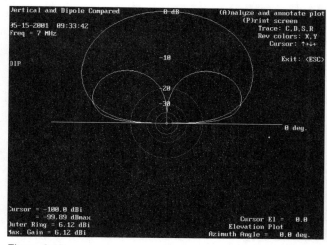

Figure 9.55

Figure 9.56

reasonable height. For an example comparing a vertical antenna and horizontal antenna on 7 MHz, see **Figure 9.55**.

This figure shows the vertical elevation pattern of a vertical with a modest ground system and a horizontal dipole up 30 feet on 7 MHz. As can be seen, at the very lowest angles (i.e., DX), the vertical and dipole are about the same, but at somewhat higher angles (i.e., up to about 500 miles on 40 meters), the dipole shows a distinct advantage.

Changing to a Yagi antenna will give you even more "gain." Here is the pattern of the same vertical antenna compared to a Yagi up 40 feet on 14 MHz. See **Figure 9.56**.

As you can see, going to the Yagi antenna gives you more than the 7.8 dB that the amplifier will give you. It has an additional advantage that the gain you get is on both transmit and receive and the additional advantage that the front-to-rear ratio of the gain antenna reduces QRM coming from other directions. The final advantage is that it is only an increased RFI potential in the direction it is pointing.

All things considered, the antenna may represent a better bang for the buck.

Q Dennis, KB9SDS, asks, "Recently a storm passed over and I put the radio end of my coax into a glass jar. Every time a bolt of lightning was about to flash, I could hear popping sounds coming from the connector. After a flash, the sounds would cease. Does the noise mean that static electricity in the atmosphere is discharging?"

A You bet it does! That was an interesting experiment, but like Benjamin Franklin's kite flying, a bit dangerous. If there had been a direct

hit on your antenna you may well have had shards of glass flying about. I strongly recommend that you *not* repeat this experiment!

However, disconnecting the antenna coax from the station is a very prudent thing to do. Although lightning arrestors and such will protect your station from the ground surge caused by a near hit, nothing can protect your station from a direct hit to the antenna system other than separating the system from the station completely. If possible, you should, as the Doctor does, keep your coax, or ladder line, disconnected and well away from the station whenever it is not in use—this will keep a storm from sneaking up on you while you are away from home.

The ideal, although not practical, would be to disconnect the coax and toss it out the window onto the ground. But a good grounding system on the coax, and the connector lying well away from the station, is the next best thing.

A practical solution is to have your coax from the antenna connected to a bulkhead at the window or other entry point using feed-through connectors, and then connect your equipment to the feed-through when in use. It is then very convenient to connect and disconnect the system.

Q Bob, W6XS, writes: Can Yagi antenna elements be made of wooden dowel rods covered with aluminum kitchen foil? I've never seen anything published on this subject. A recent article in *QST* (July 2001, p 38) may be relevant. Elements of a 20-meter Yagi are made of fiberglass fishing poles paralleled with #14 copper wire. This seems reasonable. Yet the author recommends lightweight carbon-fiber composite sections as a

substitute. Carbon-fiber is a lossy material, even more so than wood. Can you sort this out?

A Certainly elements can be made out of wood and either covered with foil or strung with wire. Of course, they would be far heavier than the carbon fiber poles, and nowhere near as strong.

As to loss, almost all insulating materials have some loss. Air is just a bit worse than a vacuum and steatite (a specialized form of ceramic often used in roller inductors) is probably next best. However, steatite is not particularly suited to portable Yagi applications for obvious reasons.

There are several forms of plastic that are fairly low loss, but these are either very brittle (like Lexan) or very heavy (like Micarta). Fiberglas is a good compromise between loss and strength, but basic "mixes" of fiberglas (the white, yellow and greenish ones) are rather heavy in the sizes needed for decent stiffness.

Carbon fiber is a very stiff material indeed. In its original form, it is also quite brittle and is actually unsuitable for use in making things. Everything you see that is labeled "carbon fiber" is not pure carbon fiber, but is actually a kind of fiberglas made with carbon fiber strands (incidentally, there is a really good series of articles on this topic in recent issues of *Sports Car* magazine, which I receive for being a member of the Sports Car Club of America).

Anyway, the carbon fiber strands in finished products are isolated from each other by the binder material as well as (depending upon the "mix") strands of other materials. This isolation prevents circulation of RF current, therefore limiting the loss.

Generally speaking, "carbon fiber" poles are only slightly more lossy than "standard" fiberglas ones (which are not widely available anymore due to the structural advantages of carbon fiber based material).

For what it's worth, the fellow who evaluated the antenna prior to its publication in *QST* also did an "extreme case" RF loss test—he placed a sample of the material in a microwave oven, whereupon it was irradiated with 1500 W continuous of RF for two minutes. The result was moderate warming, indicating some amount of loss, but not a great deal. As a best guess to what the actual antenna material loss would be, the Lab's estimate is something less than 1 dB.

Q Larry, K6DEF, writes: How do you measure resonance of an antenna? Some articles say something like "make it too long and prune it for lowest SWR." This *only* tunes the entire system for lowest SWR and includes the feed line. Years ago we used to measure resonance with a grid dipper but recall that somewhere somebody said this was a very poor way. There surely must be a good simple way other than "cut to freq and forget it" or "put it up, work 'em, and shut up."

A "Resonance" is the condition in which the feed-point impedance of the antenna is entirely resistive. From a purely technical point of view, an antenna does *not* have to be resonant to radiate efficiently. For example, many hams use a 135-foot long dipole, fed with low-loss open-wire transmission line, on all amateur bands from 80 to 10 meters. Down in the shack they use a balanced antenna tuner to tune the system so that their transmitter sees a 50-Ω load at each frequency. Here, the dipole itself is definitely not resonant in most of the bands. In fact, the feed-point impedance varies all over the place, meaning that the SWR on the open-wire line also varies all over the place. What keeps things perking is that open-wire line has low losses, despite relatively high levels of SWR.

Coaxial transmission line is another matter. Let's look at another typical situation, where you use the same 135-foot long dipole on 80 meters, but now you feed it with high-quality RG-213 coaxial cable. Here, you want your dipole to be at least close to resonance. Why is this so? While coax is convenient to use, it is also far more lossy than open-wire line, and coax losses increase when the antenna's feed-point impedance departs from 50 Ω.

Since the exact feed-point impedance of an antenna varies with its height over ground and with influences from nearby conductors (power lines, other antennas,

guy wires, support wires, etc), you must usually prune the length for the lowest SWR when you use a coax-fed antenna. A simple rule-of-thumb is to keep the SWR below about 5:1 in the lower HF bands to keep cable losses within reasonable limits. This is the kind of SWR range you'll see across the 3.5-4.0 MHz band for a simple dipole. You will still need an antenna tuner down in the shack to present your transmitter with a load into which it can properly operate.

And yes, trying to use a grid dip meter to indicate resonance in an antenna/feed-line system can be a frustrating exercise. This is because the transmission line itself acts as an impedance transformer and can thus mask the actual frequency of the antenna itself. Pruning for a low SWR is far more reliable.

Q George Trujillo, KØEZX (k0ezx@juno.com), of Jefferson, Colorado, writes: I have purchased a G5RV antenna, and I am trying to figure out an optimum installation. I have been told by fellow hams that best performance is an install of an inverted V, but I am not aware of how many degrees to form the inverted V. Also, does a flattop install better than a "V," and how about height above ground level?

A The original G5RV designed by Lou Varney is the flat-top dipole configuration. The optimum (flat-top or inverted V) would depend on the effect you are trying to achieve. There's a discussion of this subject on pages 7-3 to 7-5 of *The ARRL Antenna Book*, 19th Edition.

Height above ground also depends. If you intend to use it as a 20 meter antenna (its original purpose), then 33 feet would be good. If you intend to use it as a multiband antenna (as most people do), then 60+ feet to accommodate 40 meters would be nice.

Q Scott McNutt, N3ADP (smcnutt@monmouth.com), of Perrineville, New Jersey, writes: I have two different antennas for AO-27 and OSCAR 14: one for the 2-meter uplink and one for the 70-cm downlink. I'd like to use these with my new transceiver that has only a single antenna jack. What's the best way to accomplish this?

A What you need is a 2-meter/440 MHz diplexer—a little box with one connector on one side and two on the other, and some filters inside. They are made by Diamond and several other antenna manufacturers, are sold at most ham radio stores such as AES and sell for $35-$50 depending on the brand and retailer.

Q Maury, WB6RLP/Ø, writes: I have a 134 foot dipole feed with a ladder line. On the farm I have trees and buildings for support. The end result is that the south end is at a height of 27 feet and the north end is at a height of 16 feet. The feed point is at a height of 18 feet. When I model this antenna on EZNEC 3.0 it shows greater gain on the lobes in the northeast and northwest direction in comparison to the lobes in the southeast and southwest direction. According to my EZNEC manual, +Y is at the top of the AZ antenna plots. The runs were made with a real earth and an elevation angle of 20 degrees. My actual antenna has a bend on the south end that I included in the model. To verify this behavior I modeled the same antenna without any bends and got the same result, more gain in the lobes on the low end. Is this a characteristic of sloping dipole antennas? And is the gain greater in the direction of the lower end or is my reference off by 180 degrees?

A Yes, in a sloping dipole over "real" ground, the directivity is indeed slightly higher toward the lower end. This is due to the fact that real earth has both loss and capacitance and the amount of phase shift that occurs from the reflections off real earth varies at different angles from the antenna. The result is that the pattern shows directivity—more signal is transmitted in one direction than another. Try it again with "perfect" ground and note the difference!

I would not use the term "gain" though, because the losses in the ground reflections that show this pattern actually subtract a few dB from the pattern one would get with a horizontal antenna. Try modeling a horizontal half-wave dipole in free space and note the gain. Then, put the antenna up about a half wavelength over "average" real ground and notice the gain that is added by the ground reflection. Then, try it again over perfect ground. The term dBd is often used in describing antenna gain. It is a reference to a half-wave dipole in free space. Over perfect ground, a half-wave dipole has 6 dBd of gain—6 dB more than a half-wave dipole—because of the ground reflection.

Q Duane, AA6EE, writes: Which of your antenna books would have info on Bazooka antennas?

A Chapter 9 of the 19th Edition of *The ARRL Antenna Book* gives a high-level review of the controversial Bazooka antenna. Here's a short history of the term "bazooka." Because it resembles the shoulder-held rocket launcher used by foot soldiers against

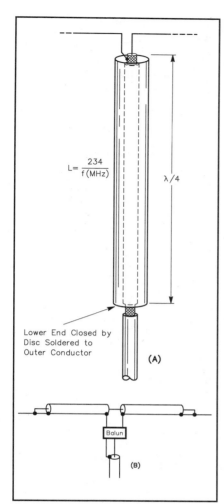

$$L = \frac{234}{f(MHz)}$$

λ/4

Lower End Closed by Disc Soldered to Outer Conductor

(A)

Balun

(B)

Figure 9.57—At A, a quarter-wave sleeve or "bazooka" balun. At B, a "Double Bazooka" coax-dipole antenna.

tanks, the quarter-wave detuning sleeve shown in **Figure 9.57A** has been called a "bazooka balun." It is also known as a "sleeve balun."

The so-called "Double Bazooka" antenna was developed as a means to broadband the frequency response of a dipole. See **Figure 9.57B**. The need is to cover a wide amateur band, such as the 80-meter band from 3.5 to 4.0 MHz. This antenna is also known as a "coax dipole" and does achieve a moderate amount of broadbanding. As Frank Witt, AI1H, wrote in Chapter 9 of *The ARRL Antenna Book*: "The antenna offers a 2:1-SWR bandwidth frequency range that is only 1.14 times that of a simple dipole with the same feeder. And the bandwidth enhancement is partially due to the 'fat' antenna wires composed mostly of the coax shield. No improvement in antenna gain or pattern over a thin-wire dipole can be expected from this antenna."

With the moderate amount of broadbanding comes disadvantages of cost and weight of the coax, not to men-

tion the loss in the cable. Chapter 9 of *The ARRL Antenna Book* provides a number of other alternatives, including the TLR (transmission-line resonator), developed by AI1H.

Q Joe Nehm, W1JN, writes: My 80 meter dipole is installed as a horizontal "L" (fed at the corner). What are the trade-offs compared to installing the dipole in a straight line? I know I should be able to answer this question myself with antenna modeling software, but I am not set up yet. Thanks for your help.

A Your horizontal L, or more commonly called the horizontal V, will radiate slightly more in the direction that the open arms of the V are facing.

On 80 meters, you will find the difference very slight unless you have your antenna at 1/2 wavelength above ground-over 60 feet. Most hams do not have their dipoles this high and so in your case the ground effect of a low mounted antenna is causing your antenna to radiate, rather than out toward the horizon, somewhat up toward the sky and scatter back down in all directions. This is affectionately called a "cloud warmer" antenna. But on 80 meters for mostly local communications (several hundred miles out at night) this is just fine.

Q Chuck, KD7MDA, of Tucson, Arizona, writes: I have just purchased a G5RV dipole antenna and am going to attach the center of it to my tower for an inverted V. How far away should the center be from metal tower for the standoff? Or does it really matter?

A It is probably a good idea to keep the antenna wire itself at least a few inches from the tower. While *EZNEC* doesn't predict much interaction between a horizontal wire and a vertical tower, you don't want to risk any arcing or sparking between the antenna and the tower. You should ideally keep the ladder-line at least 2 to 3 times the line spacing from the tower (about 6 inches for common window ladder-line). So in your case, keep the center of the G5RV about 6 to 8 inches away from the tower, or at least run the ladder line directly away from the tower, then down the tower with the required spacing.

You can compromise a bit with smaller spacing, but the fields near the ladder line are pretty high and you might couple some of the energy into the tower. If the feed line is not symmetrical with respect to any nearby conductor, one of the two conductors may couple into that nearby conductor, causing the currents

on both wires to be unequal. This would result in a bit of radiation from the feed line. One trick to minimize this effect is to put a few twists into the feed line, minimizing the effect of that imbalance on the feed line currents.

The coaxial cable used with a G5RV antenna can be any distance from the tower—even electrically connected to it.

Q Ray Collins, WX3A, of Sterling, Pennsylvania, writes: Our club recently received a used HF beam that may have spent its earlier life near salty air. What is an effective method of removing significant salty residue?

A If the beam has traps and you are pretty sure that salt water or salt air has not gotten into them, be careful not to get any moisture inside the traps. Clean them sparingly with a detergent such as 409 or Fantastic—then dry thoroughly. If you suspect that salt *has* penetrated the traps, open them and flush them with water, then dry all parts thoroughly.

The antenna should first be cleaned with a mild detergent (dishwashing liquid) and copious amounts of water to remove any crystalline salt that may remain (again being careful not to get any traps wet). The remaining discoloration is due to severe oxidation. This will have to be removed with fine-grained emery cloth or sand paper. When as much as possible has been removed, the aluminum can be polished to a high luster using Nevr-Dull. This product can be purchased in most hardware and home improvement stores—a can should last many years. See **www.nevrdull.com/How.htm**. Replace any rusted hardware and use a corrosion inhibitor such as Penetrox inside the telescoping tube sections.

Q What is the correct method for mating coax connectors?

A Before joining connectors, inspect mating surfaces for dirt, dust, debris and bent or broken contacts. When mating connectors, always turn the coupling nut rather than the body. Many connectors are destroyed by over-torquing the coupling nut. In general, the tighter you make the coupling mechanism, the better the performance. Paired connectors tend to be inductive due to gaps of various types. While tightening down on the coupling nut will close many of these gaps, it also permanently modifies the shape of the connector components.

Connectors with knurled nuts are designed to be finger tightened. A torque wrench is quite useful when mating connectors with wrench flats, like SMA and TNC connectors.

Q Mark Horowitz, WA2YMX, of Plantation, Florida writes: I was wondering if you could help me identify a 3-element Yagi. I picked it up from a widow of a ham. It's probably over 15 years old. The dimensions are: Boom—18 ft. Elements—23 feet 9 inches, 25 feet 1½ inches, and 25 feet 2½ inches. I'm fairly sure it's a tribander for 10-15-20 meters. Each element has one trap on each end.

A Sorry, but it is virtually impossible to identify an antenna from such a description—unless you by chance happen to talk to someone who owns the same antenna, and even then it's not a sure thing. Antennas obey the laws of physics and two antennas from two different manufacturers could well have identical dimensions (the differences being in the subtleties in the manufacture of the traps or the hardware).

In addition, such detailed dimensions are not usually given in ads (if you could somehow remember all the ads you've seen) and you would have to search through the instruction sheets of all beam antennas to find a match (if you had access to such a collection).

A special case is when the antenna is intact on a tower and the coaxial feed is still functional. Assuming the ham gear in no longer connected to the antenna (the easiest way to determine which bands the antenna supports), you can use a dip meter to determine the resonant frequencies of the antenna. If you know ahead of time that there is an antenna for sale, borrow a dip meter, such as the Alfa Electronics DM-4061A or an MFJ SWR Analyzer. The MFJ unit is much easier to use than a dip meter; simply plug in the coax and find the SWR of the antenna on any frequency in the 10-160 meter range.

In the end, we do not recommend purchasing an "unknown" antenna at hamfests or estate sales without the original instruction sheet. What you may well have here is a good source of aluminum and possibly traps (if you can backward engineer them) with which to design and build another antenna.

Q What is the definition of microvolts per meter? Is this related to distance from the source or the size of the antenna?

A This is a measure of electric field strength in an electromagnetic wave and specifies how much electrical potential exists between two points 1 meter apart. It is usually designated with the letter E. A magnetic field is also developed in an electromagnetic wave. Its magnitude is expressed in A/m. It is usually designated with the letter H. E and H are usually used in conjunction with power flow or density.

In the far-field of an antenna, the electric and magnetic field will be related to each other such that E / H = 377 ohms. 377 ohms is the impedance of free space. In the far field, power density, the amount of power that flows through a given unit area, is found by the formulas $E \times H$, $E^2/377$ or $H^2 \times 377$, giving the power density in W/m^2.

Q James Crawford, AE6BO/ VK8JAC, writes: My ham shack is located on the 2nd story of a townhome style complex. If I want to keep my wife happy, and I do, moving the shack to the ground floor is not an option. I rent the place as well, so making any modifications to the property is not authorized. There is not a single water pipe accessible upstairs. The only way I can get a ground is to run a line out the ham shack window to the ground into a grounding stake. This makes the run 15 to 20 feet in length approximately, maybe a little bit more. I believe this is too long of a run and may radiate at certain frequencies.

Is there any other way to safely get a ground for my rig from a second floor ham shack?

A Yes. Safety ground can be accomplished by connecting to the ground in your house wiring. A way to do this is to check with an ohmmeter (with the circuit breaker off) that the little screw that holds your wall plug plate is grounded to the ground hole in the socket (the third D shaped hole). If it is, you can connect all your station equipment together with a ground strap (one made from the braid of discarded coax is fine) and then connect this to the little screw. That takes care of the safety ground.

Now you must provide an RF ground. This can be accomplished in two different ways. The MFJ-931 Artificial RF Ground (www.mfjenterprises.com/) can do the job. Or, you may choose to you lay a counterpoise (wires) along the floor, possibly one for each band used. One place that works well is out of sight along the baseboards.

Q John Mientus, KG4GRZ, of Charlotte, North Carolina writes: I have a dual band (2 meter/70 cm) base station antenna in my attic. I also have a base rig with separate VHF and UHF antenna connectors. Will a duplexer/ diplexer allow me to transmit on 2 meters and simultaneously receive on 440 or vice/versa? My rig is capable of this. A brief explanation of how the duplexer accomplishes this would also help.

A Yes—a diplexer would allow simultaneous operation on two bands. A diplexer is a pair of filters. One routes 2-meter energy between the 2-meter port and the antenna, but not the 70-cm port. The other routes the 70-cm energy between the antenna and 70-cm port but not the 2-meter port.

A duplexer is also composed of filters, but it normally operates on a single band, such as 2 meters. Duplexers are commonly used with repeaters, since they allow a transmitter and receiver to share a single antenna simultaneously.

Q Jim Houser, WA8JIM, of New Concord, Ohio writes: I have a RadioShack ¼-wave magnetic mount antenna and a ½-wave collinear triple magnet-mount base on my car (1985 Olds). I am about to purchase a new car. Is there anything I can use to protect the paint job on my brand new car?

A You can use a small piece of plastic sheet cut to size between the antenna and the car roof. Anything from a sandwich baggie to a parts bag will do, as long as it's thin and pliable. The effect on antenna efficiency will probably be negligible. Be prepared to replace the plastic frequently, since accumulated dirt will scratch the paint.

Q Jim, K4UHL (k4uhl@aol.com), of N Augusta, South Carolina, writes: I am just getting together a station for AO-40 and have been interested in what I could find about building a dish antenna to receive the 1.2 GHz downlink. In my part of the country, there are many 10-foot satellite dish systems that can be had simply by taking it off the owner's hands. Can they be used for 1.2 GHz and do you recommend them? What modification would be necessary and where could I find info about converting them to ham use?

A Sorry, but there is no 1.2 GHz down link, as there is no allocation for the satellite to transmit on 1.2 GHz. There is a 1.2 GHz uplink—you can transmit to the satellite on 1.2 GHz.

We don't recommend a 10 foot dish for AO-40—the beamwidth is just 5 degrees. However, if you can figure a cheap and easy way of tracking the satellite with such a big antenna, I'm sure many *QST* readers would like to see an article.

One possibility is to just use the central portion of the dish. This has the

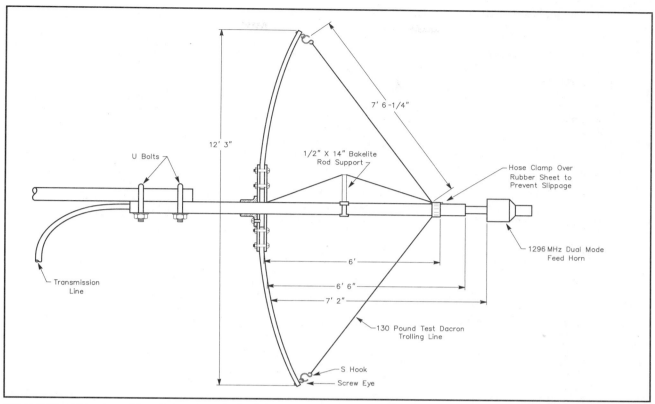

Figure 9.58—Side view of the stressed parabolic dish designed by Dick Knadle, K2RIW. A full description appears in Chapter 19 of *The ARRL Antenna Book*, 19th Edition.

Labels in figure:
U Bolts
Transmission Line
12' 3"
7' 6-1/4"
1/2" X 14" Bakelite Rod Support
Hose Clamp Over Rubber Sheet to Prevent Slippage
1296 MHz Dual Mode Feed Horn
6'
6' 6"
7' 2"
130 Pound Test Dacron Trolling Line
S Hook
Screw Eye

advantage of increasing the focal point distance to dish diameter so that simpler feed systems work reasonably well. However, you can run into problems with the dish not being accurate—some dishes are only accurate at the outer surfaces, which provide most of the gain. *The ARRL Antenna Book* is a very good reference on antennas—particularly the information written by Dick Knadle, K2RIW. See **Figure 9.58**.

Q **James Curran, KB4ET, of Paxton, Florida writes: I have now heard from two reliable sources that triband antennas do not like CATV 75 Ω coax. They further state that a monobander has no problem with CATV 75-Ω feed line. Do you agree with this and if so, why?**

A As far as the feed line is concerned, a 50-Ω load is a 50-Ω load is a 50-Ω load. The 75-Ω line should work okay, giving a 2:1 SWR or better to the rig. If the 75-Ω line is a half-wavelength long connected to a 50-Ω load, the input impedance will be 50 Ω looking into the line, since a characteristic of a half-wavelength long line is that whatever impedance it is connected to is seen at the

input end, too.

Most ham Yagi antennas are designed to have a 50-Ω feed-point impedance when the antenna is mounted at "typical" heights. The actual feed-point impedance of an antenna is a function of the exact height above ground, the presence of nearby conductors, and the conductivity of the ground. That 50-Ω impedance really is nominal.

If you connect a 75-Ω transmission line to a 50-Ω resistive impedance, you will have a 1.5:1 standing wave ratio on the line. For any reasonable line length, the additional loss caused by the mismatch will be a fraction of a dB. From a practical point of view, the line can be used on a "50-Ω" nominal antenna with little loss. The 75-Ω line will operate with a standing voltage and current wave on it, so the impedance seen looking into that line will vary along its length. If it is connected to a 50-Ω resistive load, if the line were a quarter-wavelength long, the impedance looking line will be about 110 Ω resistive. A transmitter operated into that load would see about a 2:1 SWR. In most cases, this would be an acceptable load for the transmitter. However, the SWR protection circuitry in some rigs may kick in and reduce the power somewhat.

Q **Michael J. Linden, N9BDF, writes: Conventional wisdom says that when you build a dipole, you cut each leg to the exact same length. Then, when in place, you tune it by trimming (or adding wire) the same length (always) from each side until you get the dipole to resonate where you want it to in the band.**

Is there ever a case where it would be advantageous to trim each side individually to decrease the minimum SWR? In my case, I'm working with a unique situation. My dipole is in the attic of my house and, although the antenna clearly shows a point of resonance, I'm having problems getting the minimum SWR below 2:1 (even with a feedpoint balun). It has occurred to me that this may be a result of interaction with metallic objects at the base of the attic (conduit, cable TV coax, etc) or on the roof (six or so aluminum roof vents). Is it possible that one leg of the dipole is interacting with something in the attic such that the length of this leg should be adjusted with respect to the other leg? I guess my assumption (which could certainly be wrong) is that the electrical length of one leg of the dipole may need to be adjusted due to "coupling" with something while the other leg's electrical length is fine because it is not interacting with anything nearby. Is this possible?

I should mention that the antenna is a multiband trap dipole that covers 10/15/20/40. I'm having the SWR problem (minimum is 2:1) on 10/15/20 m, while 40 m seems okay.

I've asked Santa to bring me a copy of *The ARRL Antenna Book* for Christmas, but in the meantime, I'd appreciate any input you have on this matter.

A The feed-point impedance of a center fed dipole varies with height above ground, so the 2:1 SWR might not be related to assymetry in the antenna system.

Here is the *EZNEC*-predicted feed-point impedance of an 80-meter antenna at different heights above ground:

Height	Feed-point-impedance (ohms)	SWR
10'	4.8–j33.4	15.0:1
20'	12.7–j14.9	4.3:1
30'	25.7–j0.0	1.95:1
40'	41.6+j9.8	1.3:1
50'	58.2+j12.9	1.3:1
60'	73.2+j10.0	1.5:1
90'	93.7–j19.0	2.0:1
120'	78.0–j40.8	2.2:1

The antenna was adjusted to be resonant at a height of 30 feet above ground, but at that height, the SWR is 2:1, because the feed-point impedance is about 25 ohms. As the antenna is lowered or raised, its feed-point impedance changes with height above ground. Although the SWR could be improved a bit by adjusting the length of the antenna, if the resistive part of that feed-point impedance is not 50 ohms, the SWR will never get to 1:1.

In practice, a 2:1 SWR on your feed line is really not all that bad on HF. If the feed line were 100 feet of RG-213, the loss if the line were matched (ie, 1:1 SWR) would be 0.36 dB. If the SWR were 2:1, the additional loss caused by the mismatch would result in a total of 0.42 dB of feed line loss. This loss is insignificant. The only problem you might encounter is that some transmitters' SWR protection circuitry may reduce power if the SWR exceeds 1.5:1 or so. In that case, you could use an antenna tuner to ensure that the transmitter operates into a 50-ohm load.

The feed-point impedance shown above is for the antenna fed exactly in the center. If the feed point is moved closer to one end, the feed-point impedance will go up. For example, if the antenna shown above at 30 feet above the ground is fed at a point 25% from one end, the *feed-point imp*edance increases to 50 ohms re-

sistive. However, this off-center feed comes with a price—the feed line is not seeing a balanced load, so there can be problems with common-mode currents on the feed line. The most common manifestation of this is going to be problems with RF in the shack. It might be possible to tame this with a common-mode choke or balun at the transmitter end of the feed line. For more on this subject, see Zack Lau, "Making Off-Center Dipoles Work," *QEX*, Apr/May 2001.

If I were to speculate about the cause of your 2:1 SWR, I would guess that the antenna height is relatively low, causing the feed-point impedance to be less than 50 ohms. Coupling into nearby objects can also lower the feed-point impedance, so perhaps the best approach is to consider the use of an antenna tuner.

Q Paul R. Lovell, AG4LQ, of Roanoke, Virginia writes: I have to install coax without an RF choke (8 turns of RG-8/U, 6-inch diameter) due to length problems. Will a commercially made 1:1 current balun do the same thing without degrading performance?

A Yes, a well-made 1:1 "current" type balun will be a good substitute for the coiled coax. You may not be able to find one rated for a kW in a continuous carrier mode, but unless you like to operate RTTY contests with an amp, that shouldn't be a problem.

Q Willie, AG4HY, of Adrian, Georgia, writes: What is wrong with traps, as in a dipole? I received two new catalogs and there is a discussion of traps, but I'm still not clear about them. One of the catalogs says that "traps have a narrow bandwidth, and it doesn't make sense to use only part of the wire length." Saw some other discussion on this and the party answering said "If you don't mind slightly less bandwidth and a shorter antenna, then there's nothing wrong with traps." One of the catalogs is for the "Carolina windom."

A I agree; traps can be a reasonable choice in antenna design. Of course, traps can be somewhat lossy, and antenna manufacturers that don't use them in their designs have every right to tout their wares. If you want a somewhat shorter antenna and don't want to use an antenna tuner, however, you can easily use a trap design.

In fact, there are sometimes good reasons *not* to want to use all of the wire in an antenna. If, for example, you use an

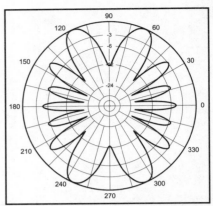

Figure 9.59—If you use an 80-meter wire antenna on 10 meters, the antenna pattern will look something like this.

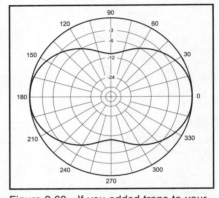

Figure 9.60—If you added traps to your 80-meter antenna, the pattern would look like this on 10 meters.

80-meter half-wave antenna on 10 meters, either a center-fed dipole with ladder line and a tuner, or an off-center-fed design such as the windom variant you mention, you will get a pattern on 10 meters like the one shown in **Figure 9.59**. If you used traps, the effective radiating part of the antenna on 10 meters would be shorter, so you would get a typical dipole pattern, such as the one shown in **Figure 9.60**. On 10 meters, only the inner part of the antenna would radiate. On the lower band, the entire antenna would be active.

While the more complex pattern does have gain on 10 meters, the gain may or may not be in the direction you want to communicate. It is also possible that your favorite direction may be in one of the nulls. This is not necessarily bad, just something you want to consider as you select your antenna.

Q William Riley, N3SNU, needs the formulas for the dimensions of a J-pole antenna: I already have an MFJ pocket roll-up J-pole for 2-meters, but I'd like to assemble others for other bands, including Marine VHF and the General Mobile Radio Service, to add to my "go kit."

A The J-pole antenna is a ½-wave radiator fed with a ¼-wave matching stub. See **Figure 9.61**. The length of the ½-wave portion is calculated using the standard 468/f (MHz) formula (same as a dipole) and the length of the ¼-wave section is calculated using the free-space wavelength (246/f), multiplied by the velocity factor of the section used as a transmission line. For twin-lead J-poles, this is about 0.85; for copper pipe, about 0.95. The attachment point on the ¼-wave section is adjusted for the best SWR, but starts roughly 0.015 wavelengths from the shorted end of the ¼-wave stub.

Feeding the balanced stub of the J-pole with unbalanced coaxial cable requires a balun. Use a split ferrite bead (Palomar Engineers FSB-1/4 using Type 43 material is a good choice for VHF) and place it around the coax about 13 inches from the antenna's feed point (this is a high current point on the coax). You can use electrical tape to hold it in place. Ferrite beads can be purchased directly from Palomar, Box 462222, Escondido, CA 92046; tel 760-747-3343; fax 760-747-3346; **info@Palomar-Engineers. com**; **www.Palomar-Engineers.com**.

Q Ron Ziegler, W1RZ, writes: I want to make a 4:1 balun using a ferrite toroid (FT-240-61) that requires bifilar windings. I have conflicting information about how many turns to wind on this type of toroid for this design.

A The Doctor suggests going with the design dimensions suggested by Jerry Sevick, W2FMI, in his excellent book *Building and Using Baluns and Ununs*.[19] For a 4:1 ratio with bifilar windings on a core with a permeability of 125, use 14 turns of #14 tinned copper (bare), covered in number 13 Teflon tubing (wall thickness of 20 mils). The windings should be equally spaced around the whole core so that the ends of the windings are close to each other. Be sure to label each end of the windings.

Connect the input coax center conductor to the first end of "winding 1" and the shield to the first end of "winding 2." Connect the second end of winding 1 to

[19] Available from the ARRL Bookstore (order no. 7644); tel 888-277-5289; **www.arrl.org/ shop/**.

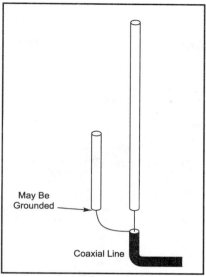

Figure 9.61—Two versions of the J antenna, used in mobile applications or in vertical arrays where parasitic elements are rotated around a fixed radiator.

May Be Grounded

Coaxial Line

the first end of winding 2 (same connection as the coax shield). Connect the balanced output across the first end of winding 1 (same point as the coax center) and the second end of winding 2 (which isn't connected to anything else).

Q Bryan Chick, K5KFL/KP2, writes: I have been inactive for many years, but now I wish to get on the air again. If I make an 80-meter ½-wavelength dipole, can I then use an antenna tuner to operate on the higher bands, or must I make a multiband antenna? I live on St Thomas and do not want to erect a beam and tower due to our hurricanes.

A Yes, you can erect a dipole of any reasonable size and use an antenna tuner to operate on different bands. In that sense, any dipole is effectively a "multiband" antenna.

There are some points to consider. First, the larger the antenna the better and an 80-meter dipole is a good size to use. Depending on many factors, such as orientation, height, obstacles, length of feed line, design of the tuner, etc, you may not be able to get a good match on each and every band. Regardless, you will still be able to make contacts on some bands. Be prepared to experiment with the length of the feed line and tuner settings.

Because you'll be using the antenna on bands where SWR at the antenna may be high, try using windowed "ladder-line." You'll have *much* less loss under

high-SWR conditions than if you fed the dipole with coax. However, this means that you'll also need to purchase an antenna tuner with a built-in balun. That usually isn't a problem because most good-quality antenna tuners on the market today include these baluns.

One last tip: Try to find ladder line with *stranded* conductors. This type of line tends to hold up better in breezy conditions. Twist the feed line once every 18 inches or so to reduce the wind surface area.

Q Bob Rice, W7HAP, of Wheatland, Wyoming, writes: I am constructing a 600 foot horizontal loop and it has to be fed with 450 Ω ladder line. My problem is that I cannot attach 450 Ω ladder line to my equipment; it must be fed with 50 Ω coax. I need to construct a 9:1 balun. I have not been able to figure out what toroid core to use to wind the balun on and what wire to use or number of windings. My power will be no more than 500 W.

A Unless your loop has a 450-Ω impedance, a 9:1 balun isn't the ratio you want because the impedance will vary on the various HF bands on which you will use the antenna. Any time you have a feed line connected to something with an impedance that is different than the characteristic impedance of the feed line, the impedance at the other end of the line will vary according to the length of the line and several other factors. As a good example, recall a ¼ wavelength matching stub. If one end is shorted, the other end will be a very high impedance—regardless of whether the line is 50 Ω or 450 Ω. A ½ wave line will give you the same exact impedance at both ends (eg, 50 Ω at the antenna gives 50 Ω in the shack).

I assume that you will be using this antenna on multiple bands, so you will need to use an antenna tuner. You may be able to use the balanced output of the antenna tuner to feed the balanced line. The actual impedance looking in the line may range from a few ohms to a few thousand ohms, possibly with a lot of reactance. Baluns work well when they are used near their design impedance — for example, most amateur 4:1 baluns are designed to match 200 to 50 Ω. If you deviate significantly from that impedance, one of two things may happen — the balun may overheat or it may not function well to choke off the common-mode currents on the line. In many cases, especially at low power, the latter may not be very important — the result could be no worse than the slight radiation from the feed line filling in the nulls that may exist in your antenna pattern. If the balun in the tuner is not overheating, you can be comfortable that you can use it safely. The balun may be quite warm to the touch, but it should not be too hot to handle. If it is, you will either have to forgo operation on that band or try a different length of feed line. This will not change the SWR on the line, but will result in a different impedance at the tuner—hopefully one the tuner's balun can handle. Of course, you may solve the problem on one band and create a similar problem on another, so be prepared to experiment a bit. The 19th edition of *The ARRL Antenna Book* has some excellent information on feed lines and baluns.

QMartin Feigert, AC8CW, of Findlay, Ohio, writes: I have a rooftop mag mount antenna on top of a 2002 Ford Explorer Sport. It has RG-58 type coax and I can't seem to run it into the car without letting water in when it rains. I've tried every nook and cranny I can think of. I currently have it going into the car through the rear quarter window down along the rear part that opens up—the windows open by swinging outward about an inch with a latch that fastens and unfastens the window. This seemed to be the best choice as there is no wind noise so I thought I had finally found the best entrance point, because the cable was not being pinched and didn't seem to be

Figure 9.62—They don't make 'em like this anymore!

1972 Pinto

Figure 9.63—Windshield sealer can be used to waterproof the entry point for the coax into your home. It will also work for mobile installations.

crushing the weather seal around the window.

After the first rain there was water on the inside of the vehicle on the passenger armrest for the rear seat—just

enough to be a nuisance. I think the water is following the cable down inside. Is there something I can spray on the weather seal to help or can you suggest another entrance point for the cable? Should I put it all the way around the seal or just where the coax runs across it?

AAs it happens, I had a similar arrangement in my 1972 Pinto Wagon (**Figure 9.62**) and sealed it with "Windshield Sealer." It comes in a tube (about $5) and is sold in most auto supply stores or departments. Of course it follows that there is a "Family Law": that window must never be opened. If the kids forget, just reseal it. The soft rubber did a good job of keeping the water out the rest of the way. I opened the window, held the coax in place, blopped the goo on, pushed the window closed, went inside and closed the latch. As I recall, I just put it a couple of inches on either side of the coax. That did it, neat as a pin.

I also use the same stuff to seal my home antenna connections and entry point. See **Figure 9.63**.

QWhat is the thread size for an SO-239, and where can a tap in that size be found?

AAccording to the Amphenol catalog, the thread size is $5/8$-24. As to where to get a $5/8$-24 tap or die, try Enco, 400 Nevada Pacific Hwy, Fernley, NV 89408; tel 800-873-3626; fax: 800-965-5857; **sales@use-enco.com**; **www.use-enco.com**.

CHAPTER 10

Operating

FOR A CLEAN FIST, TRY CLEAN EARS

◊ "For a clean fist, try clean ears," says Mark Hansbarger, AA9MU. Display your vintage keys and keep dust off the contacts for little cost by using simple plastic dust covers, as AA9MU did, using an oversize cotton-swab package (see **Figure 10.1**).

Measure the height, width and depth of your key, then be on the lookout for a plastic cover available from many differently packaged products.

Custom fit the cover by placing the plastic over the key. Then mark positions for the finger grips, other protrusions and parts of the container to be trimmed off, with a nonpermanent felt tip marker. Finally, cut the cover to fit.

Instead of cutting off the pieces completely, AA9MU recommends folding them out of the way in case of an oversize cut, as shown in **Figure 10.2**. Thus, the flap can be folded back into place and secured with clear adhesive tape.

To make an adjustable cover, cut the plastic container from side to side to allow the long ends to neatly slip inside each other, then tape them in place. Cutting precisely and drilling a tight fit for the top arm pivot screw allows using the key while it's covered.—*Mark B. Hansbarger, AA9MU, 1000 Lane 440 Lake James, Angola, IN 46703;* **mark@hansbarger.com**

CW IS ALIVE AND ON THE MOVE!

◊ It's been a few years since I've operated HF mobile. In that time, it has been getting harder to mount radios in vehicles. Now, with a new wave of tiny, remotely mounted HF radios, the time had arrived to get my mobile station back on the air! This year at the Dayton Hamfest the prices on those rigs were too good to pass up, so I picked up an IC-706Mk2G. I found a convenient place to mount the control head where it's easily accessible and I need not take my eyes far off the road. Okay, so off I go making HF contacts—even working a fair amount of DX.

Nonetheless, something was missing. I guess I never really did get excited about HF phone operation. My heart is still in CW! If I want to talk, I can do that on VHF and UHF with my dual-band mobile.

So, where could I put the key so it wouldn't get in the way and would be easy to send while rolling down the road at 65 MPH—okay, maybe 30 MPH with the rush-hour traffic. Did I mention this is my commuter car and it has a stick? So where to put the key? My first thought was on the stick, but it just didn't feel right in all gears. I settled on the emergency-brake handle, but my Vibroplex is a little clunky and I really didn't want to take it out of my main shack. I saw a little iambic key at a hamfest for under $20, so I decided to try it.[1] It came prewired and ready to mount on almost anything. How would I attach it to the handle without damage and still have the key easily removable?

So I took a trip to see the helpful hardware man. After looking in the electrical, plumbing and garden departments, I finally found some great little clamps

[1]BullDog Classic Iambic Key, Attn: Lou Petkus, K9LU, General Busness Software, 2 S 872 Wagner Rd, Batavia IL 60510; **www.AmateurRadioProducts.com**; 630 406-1654.

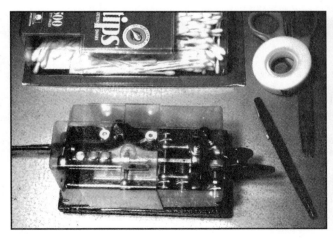

Figure 10.1—AA9MU makes key covers from clear-plastic packaging, such as those used for cotton swabs. Notice how the container was cut in half with the two ends telescoped together to match the key-base length.

Figure 10.2—Cables exit the AA9MU key cover.

meant for hanging brooms, etc, from walls. Two of those screwed to a little piece of scrap aluminum made a neat key mount that snaps on and off the emergency brake handle (see **Figures 10.3, 10.4 and 10.5**). It has a nice feel sending as I roll down the road. Now, where am I going to mount the computer for RTTY?—*Skip Allison, K9SA, 452 N Country Ridge Ct, Lake Zurich, IL 60047;* **Sallison@megsinet.net**

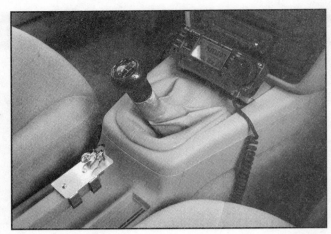

Figure 10.3—An HF shack on the roll.

Figure 10.4—An iambic key mounted on the emergency-brake handle.

Figure 10.5—A view of the broomstick-mounting clamps.

The Doctor is IN

Q I know that the ARRL Contest Branch is checking logs very carefully these days. My question, however, is what happens when I work someone in a contest and that person doesn't turn in a log? Will the log checkers throw out that contact?

A No. The contacts in your log are only matched against contacts in logs actually received. The Contest Branch is well aware of the fact that many hams participate in contests, yet do not turn in logs. For example, Sweepstakes is an excellent contest if you are hunting for new states to complete your Worked All States award. You could probably work all 50 states during Sweepstakes by just pouncing on the stations you need—and never turning in a log after the contest.

On the other hand, if your contest log contains a high number of contacts with stations that apparently did not turn in logs, it might raise a red flag. The Contest Branch may opt to "spot check" your log. This would involve contacting some of the stations to verify that they really worked you.

Q I've heard of ATV repeaters, but is there such a thing as a slow-scan TV (SSTV) repeater?

A SSTV repeaters do exist, although they are really simplex repeaters by definition, not duplex systems that transmit and receive at the same time. SSTV repeaters receive images, store them briefly, then retransmit—often on the same frequency.

Some SSTV repeaters are controlled through a tone-access system. You transmit a 1750-Hz tone to get the repeater's attention and, if the frequency is not already in use, the repeater will send a Morse "K" back to you. This means that you have about 10 seconds to begin transmitting your image. When you've completed the transmission, the repeater will retransmit the image in the same mode it was sent. In other words, if you used Martin 1, for example, the repeater will retransmit in Martin 1.

There are some SSTV repeaters that are open at all times and do not use a tone access system. They will accept and retransmit images whenever the fre-

quency is clear. Most SSTV repeaters also send ID beacons at regular intervals. You can learn more about SSTV repeaters on the Web at **www.mscan.com/mscan/repeaters.html**.

Q This may seem like a silly question, but what exactly is SSB?

A First of all, there is no such thing as a silly question. In Amateur Radio we often kick these acronyms around without bothering to define them. We just assume that everyone knows what we're talking about! SSB stands for "single sideband." It is basically a form of amplitude modulation (AM).

Modulation is a mixing process. When RF and audio signals are mixed together you wind up with a total of four signals: (1) the original RF signal, or carrier, (2) the original audio signal, and (3-4) two sidebands whose frequencies are the sum and difference of the original audio and RF signals, and whose amplitudes are proportional to the original audio signal. The sum is the upper sideband (USB) and the difference is the lower sideband (LSB).

All of the information is contained in the sidebands, but 2/3 of the RF power is in the carrier. The carrier serves only to demodulate the signal in the receiver. It is essential for AM reception, but for SSB we can simply generate a carrier signal in the receiver and use it to recover the information (the voice, for example). There is no need to send the carrier along with the sidebands.

There is also no need to send two identical sidebands when one will do. Depending on the mode you've chosen to operate, the upper or lower sideband is eliminated from the transmitted signal. The final result of all this "paring down" is a solitary *single sideband*—SSB—signal.

There are several advantages to using SSB. SSB transmitters are very efficient, requiring less bulky power supplies. SSB signals are also narrower than standard AM signals, meaning that you can fit more SSB signals into a given band. With the transmitted power concentrated in a narrower spectrum, the effective communication range can also be increased somewhat compared to AM or FM.

The main disadvantage of SSB is its relative lack of audio quality. You must tune your receiver precisely to achieve a natural-sounding voice. Even then, the frequency range of the audio is limited. A properly tuned SSB signal is perfectly readable, but it does not have the audio quality of AM or FM.

Q I live in western Montana and I was told that I could use the "Evergreen Intertie" to talk to hams all over the northwest with just my H-T. That sounds great, but what is the Evergreen Intertie?

A The Evergreen Intertie is a linked repeater system that covers much of the Pacific Northwest. The Intertie is composed of about 24 VHF and UHF repeaters. Each repeater is connected to a backbone made up of both radio and nonradio links. One backbone connects northwest Oregon to Seattle, while another connects Seattle to points east. The system configuration changes constantly as repeaters are added or removed. See **Figure 10.6**.

In a linked repeater network you can indeed use an H-T to span substantial distances. DTMF (TouchTone) codes are often used to access the system. That's how you go about linking your signal to distant points. These DTMF codes are usually provided by the clubs that maintain the various parts of the network, so it is a good idea to seek out a participating club and join. You'll find more information about the Evergreen Intertie on the Web at **www.lloydio.com/evergreen.html**.

Q Rick, WØPC, of O'Fallon, Missouri, writes: My question is about handling Doppler shift on satellites. I used to work satellites up through OSCAR 7. I'm trying to get back into it but find some things different. I notice that QSOs just let their Doppler shift go and don't make uplink changes to maintain the same downlink frequency. I thought you should always maintain the downlink so as not to drift into another QSO in progress.

A Actually, either tuning method can now be used. Given today's current crop of satellites, it's just as easy to maintain a standard uplink frequency, and adjust the downlink frequency accordingly. This method is used at W1AW for most birds.

While some may argue the point about tuning either uplink or downlink frequency, I personally feel it's now on a case-by-case basis. For example, a number of birds have downlinks in the 70 cm (and higher) range. Doppler shift is more critical here than, say, 2 meters. (And of course, Doppler shift "worsens" the higher in frequency you go.)

As for unintentionally QRMing another QSO: Although it happens, it doesn't appear to be too much of a problem. After all, Doppler is affecting everyone, at different levels. In other words— short of the satellite being directly overhead and stationary—every user is adjusting for Doppler.

On 2 meters, you may have to tune 4 kHz or so total during a good pass if you wish to maintain a stable uplink. However, you'll still find the downlink (70 cm, for example) shifts so much faster and greater in frequency that it would have been just as easy to tune the downlink. This is not too much of a problem if your radio has full Doppler correction (FDC) capabilities— but that is another subject!

Doppler shift is such a broad topic that I would be doing it an injustice if I tried to give a comprehensive answer here. If you're looking to get back into satellites, may I suggest our publication *The Radio Amateur's Satellite Handbook* (ARRL order no. 6583). It contains the latest information on satellite operations, including information on some of the newer equipment available.

Q Bill Kendrick, WA6TMT, asks, "Can you define a couple of acronyms for me? I often see mentions of DTMF, CTCSS and DCS in *QST*, but I'm not sure what they mean."

A DTMF: Dual-Tone Multi Frequency. Everyone in the country has encountered DTMF signaling, but they wouldn't recognize it by that acronym. DTMF is better known to the masses as *TouchTone*. In the DTMF system two audio tones are combined whenever you press a button on a telephone or radio keypad. Both tones must be decoded on the

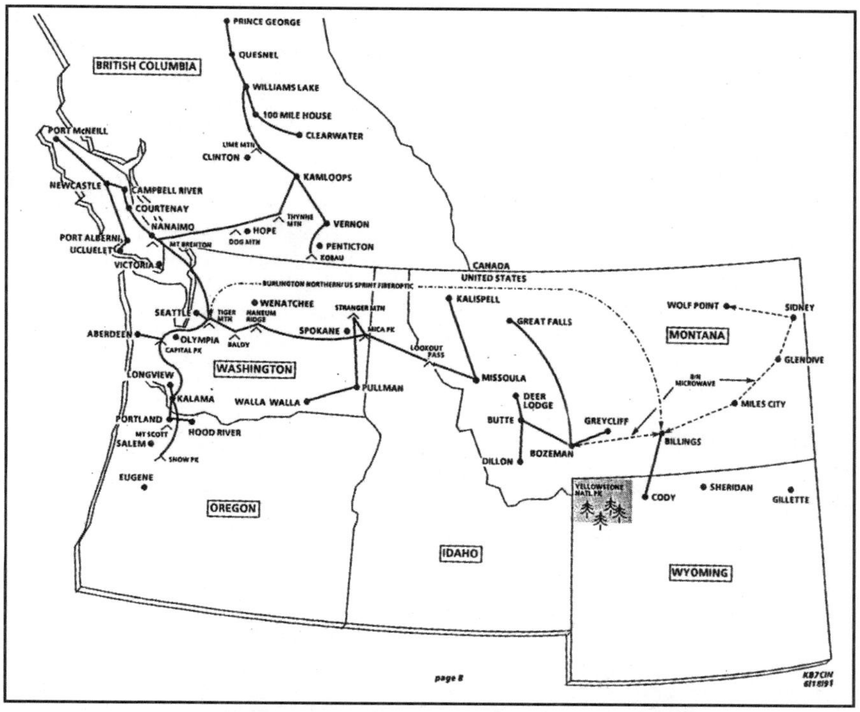

Figure 10.6—This is the Evergreen Intertie as it appeared a few years ago. Like most linked repeater systems, the routes change constantly so it's best to get an updated diagram from a local participating club.

receiving end for the signal to be "valid." This provides a certain measure of reliability. In amateur applications DTMF is commonly used for remote control.

CTCSS: Continuous Tone-Coded Squelch System. Many hams know this one by the Motorola trade names *Private Line*, or simply *PL*. CTCSS uses individual audio tones of very low frequency. The frequencies are so low, in fact, they are below the normal receiver audio passband. This means that the tones can be sent along with voice audio without causing interference. A receiver with CTCSS enabled will be silent unless it receives a transmission that includes the proper tone. Repeaters often use CTCSS to control access in situations where there is interference from other repeaters on the same input frequency.

DCS: Digital Coded Squelch. This popular method of signaling uses a burst of data tones. As with CTCSS, a DCS-equipped receiver will remain silent until it "hears" a data burst that it has been programmed to recognize.

Q N1AHT asks, "Whenever I send a QSL directly to a DX station I include an SASE and a dollar. Is this the correct procedure?"

A Including an SAE (Self-Addressed Envelope) is always a good idea, but not an SASE (Self-Addressed *Stamped* Envelope). A US stamp is of no use at all to a ham in another country. He has to put his country's stamp on the return envelope.

As for the dollar, opinions on this practice differ. Many US hams include "greenstamps" (US dollars) with their QSLs to pay for the return postage. One US dollar will pay for return airmail postage from most areas of the world. The exceptions appear to be France and Germany where $2 may be necessary, depending on the exchange rates at the time.

Sending US dollars is an expensive way to QSL, but the advantage is that you will probably have your coveted card much sooner. Going through the QSL bureau system is more cost effective, but

you could wait a year or longer to receive the card. It all boils down to how eager you are to have the confirmation in hand.

Be advised that receiving foreign currency is illegal in a few countries. In addition, the postal workers in some countries have become remarkably adept at spotting Amateur Radio correspondence. They know these envelopes could contain money and are not above stealing the contents.

The alternative to the greenstamp is the IRC—International Reply Coupon. By international agreement, these are each valued at one unit of air mail postage at the destination. You'll find IRCs at your local post office.

Q Kim, N6LP asks, "There's a contest on HF again this weekend. The stations are reporting 59 zero-three-four or something else. I'm not a contester, but I like giving them a point for my contact (and picking up new DXCC entities and states in the process). I've heard several different reporting methods. Sometimes it's your grid square (I know that one), and other times it's something else. Why are there so many different contest exchanges? How do I find out what they are looking for without having to waste their time and ask?"

A Contest exchanges depend on the sponsors of the event and generally are different in order to provide variety. Exchanges will range from grid squares (primarily in VHF/UHF contests) to serial numbers (in many contests) to names and states (North American QSO Parties, for example) to multiple pieces of information (ARRL November Sweepstakes). In contests sponsored by the League, you may find the exchange includes your ARRL/RAC section or state. In most contests sponsored by *CQ*, you will find that you exchange the *CQ* zone in which you reside (see **Figure 10.7**). Similarly, during the IARU HF World Championship in July you send your ITU zone (which is different from

your CQ zone. See **Figure 10.8**).

The easiest place to start to unravel the mystery of the contest exchanges is "Contest Corral" which is published monthly in *QST*. See what contests are taking place on a given weekend and listen to several of the stations sending their exchanges. Also, "Contest Corral" will often provide Web links for more extensive rules and other information.

Rules announcements for all ARRL sponsored contests are usually published in *QST* in the month preceding the contest (i.e. September VHF QSO party rules are found in the August issue of *QST*.) You can also find all of the current ARRL contest rules and forms at the ARRL Contest Branch Web page at: **www.arrl.org/contests/forms**.

Q Craig, KC8POE, asks, "I am a new ham and I am studying for my General license. When shopping for radios, I keep seeing the terms WARC and MARS. Can you elaborate? What are they, and do I use them when using my radios?"

A WARC stands for World Administrative Radio Conference. These are the folks (meeting in Geneva, Switzerland) who allocate radio frequencies. At the 1979 WARC they gave Amateur Radio three additional HF bands:

30 meters: 10,100-10,150 kHz
17 meters: 18,068-18,168 kHz
12 meters: 24,890-24,990 kHz

To this day, many hams call them the WARC bands.

Amateur radio gear made before 1979 was not capable of operating in these new bands. Almost all modern radios, however, offer these bands as standard features.

MARS stands for Military Affiliate Radio System. This is an organization that runs traffic nets on designated frequencies just above or below most Amateur Radio bands. MARS stations also run phone patches from troops overseas. This was very popular during the Viet

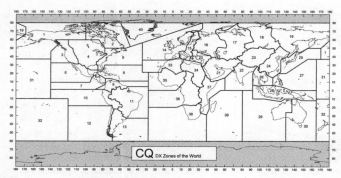

Figure 10.7—CQ Zones of the world.

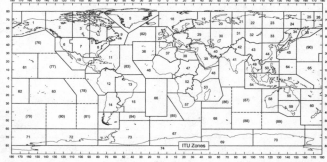

Figure 10.8—A map of ITU zones.

Nam and Gulf Wars. Most MARS members are volunteers that make their time and stations available, although there are some MARS stations on US military bases.

Most radios in the past were manufactured so that the tuning circuits would work slightly above and below the amateur bands, allowing them to run on MARS frequencies.

Today's solid state transceivers are capable of operating across the whole HF spectrum and are locked out by the microprocessor from operating outside the amateur bands. A procedure must be performed to "open up" the MARS frequencies. Military personnel at a military installation may operate using only the MARS license, but civilian volunteers must have an Amateur Radio license and a MARS authorization and special call sign for use on MARS frequencies.

Q Tim, KC4BBI, asks, "I am blind. As you might guess, I take a lot of taxis. I often call them from restaurants, malls, and other places where pay phones are hard to find. I do not have a cell phone. I would like to use the autopatch of our local repeater to call taxis. Does this violate the 'no commercial use' rule for Amateur Radio?"

A When the FCC liberalized the business rules they stated that amateurs may use Amateur Radio to conduct their personal communications, including ordering food over the air or making appointments.

Between 1972 and 1993, the FCC laid down stringent "no business" rules. Talk-ins to conventions and hamfests weren't legal, among many other things! Effective September 13, 1993, the "no business communications" language was replaced with a prohibition on communications for compensation on behalf of one's employer, or in which the amateur has a pecuniary interest [97.113(a)(2), (3)]. The current language is almost, but not quite, as relaxed as the pre-1972 rules. Now, instead of a flat prohibition on providing an alternative to other radio services, there is a less restrictive one against doing so on a regular basis [97.113(a)(5)].

These rules permit wider use of Amateur Radio to satisfy personal communications needs. To cite a classic example, as far as the FCC is concerned you may now use an autopatch to order a pizza. You may call your dentist's office to let them know you'll be late, or even to make an appointment. On your way home you may ask your spouse if you should pick up a loaf of bread on the autopatch without worrying about whether this will "facilitate the business affairs" of the

grocery store. Repeater owners or trustees may set tighter standards if they want, but it's no longer an FCC issue.

The Commission doesn't want to hear questions about whether such-and-such is permitted. The FCC Report and Order, which carries the weight of a regulation, said:

"We [the FCC] have decided to amend the amateur service rules substantially…to allow amateur operators more flexibility to provide communications for public service projects as well as to enhance the value of the amateur service in satisfying personal communications needs. Amendment of the rules as proposed by the League will allow licensee to use amateur service frequencies, for example, to facilitate such events as races and parades, to support educational activities, to provide personal communications such as making appointments and ordering food, to collect data for the National Weather Service, and to provide assistance voluntarily even where there are other authorized services available. We believe that this action will expand the benefits derived from the amateur service by the general public as well as amateur service licensees."

The Report and Order also said, in part, that ". . .any amateur-to-amateur communication is permitted unless specifically prohibited, or unless transmitted for compensation, or unless done for the pecuniary benefit of the station control operator or his or her employer" [PR Docket 92-136, Report and Order].

How can you tell if a particular communication is legal? A simple checklist may help you determine if a communication is permissible under 97.113:

1. Is it expressly prohibited in the rules (music, obscenity, etc) [97.113 (a)(1)]?

2. Is it transmitted for compensation [97.113(a)(2)]?

3. Does the control operator have a pecuniary interest? That is, could he or she benefit financially [97.113(a)(3)]?

4. Does the control operator's employer have a pecuniary interest [97.113(a)(3)]?

If you can answer "no" to all of these questions, the communication is okay as far as the FCC is concerned. In that regard, it is perfectly legal for you to use the autopatch to order a taxi.

Having said all that, you could face resistance from repeater owners. Some may not understand the new regulations, or they may simply not allow that type of use of their systems. Remember that repeaters are private property, although the frequencies on which they may operate are public. Some repeater owners may not permit the type of communications you are proposing, even though it isn't a

rule violation. Since the repeater is their private property, you must comply.

Q What is wrong with operating FM simplex between 145.8 and 146 MHz? I hardly ever hear signals in that part of the band.

A This touches on the issue of voluntary band planning, which was addressed in "Washington Mailbox" in the December 2000 QST. You might want to take a look at that column.

The problem with operating in the 145.8 to 146 MHz segment is that the amateur satellite community uses this portion of the spectrum. There are several FM repeater satellites that operate with *uplinks* in this segment. If you're chatting with a local friend on 145.85 MHz, for example, there is a chance that OSCAR 27 will hear you and relay your conversation over thousands of miles without you even realizing it! The FM satellites are crowded already, so they don't need "unintentional signals." Other SSB and digital satellites have uplinks here as well, and your signals could make it impossible for these birds to hear the signals intended for them.

SO-35 and AO-10 have *downlinks* in this portion of the band. These signals are often weak and your terrestrial FM QSOs will obliterate them.

Just because you can't hear the satellite signals, doesn't mean that they are not there. With the typical FM setup, you're not likely to hear satellites in this portion of 2 meters at all.

Voluntary band planning allows everyone to enjoy Amateur Radio in all of its various forms, but it only works if we all respect the plans. It isn't so much a legal issue as it is one of common courtesy.

Q Fred, W9MMZ, asks, "Our club's 2-meter repeater has recently become inhabited by a group who are using it as a party-line, often holding QSOs lasting one, two and sometimes three hours, often in the wee small hours of the night. You rarely hear call signs. When users of a repeater fail to follow the FCC rules for proper station identification, is the control operator liable?"

A If a person operates through a repeater in violation of FCC rules, it is up to the control operator (CO) to take control of the situation. In short, the CO must shut down the repeater as soon as he or she is aware that violations are occurring. If they are aware of the fact that illegal communication is taking place and do not disable the system, they can indeed be held liable.

Of course, most control operators are

not monitoring their repeaters in the middle of the night. Whatever takes place on a repeater operating under automatic control while the CO is unavailable is classified as "inadvertent" activity. In this situation, the CO is not liable. According to Part 97:

§97.205 Repeater station.

(g) The control operator of a repeater that retransmits inadvertently communications that violate the rules in this Part is not accountable for the violative communications.

Q John, K2CF, asks, "Sometimes on 10 or 15 meters I can make contact with stations that are 300 to 400 miles away. We can communicate, although we both report weak signals. The distance seems to be too great for so-called 'ground wave' propagation, and these stations are definitely in the skip zone, which would seem to preclude normal ionospheric propagation. Is there another mechanism involved?"

A The most likely explanation is that you are working them on what is known as "backscatter." Within the skip zone a small amount of RF is scattered off the ionosphere itself, or from irregular ground at an intermediate reflection point within the zone. The levels are usually such that 100-W stations can just hear each other. Occasionally, you may also encounter situations where a sporadic-E cloud of intense ionization is located somewhere between you and another station within the skip zone. This cloud can reflect signals, creating what is known in amateur circles as "short skip."

Q Bruce, KC7ENB, asks, "What are the frequencies of the Citizen Band channels?"

A See **Table 10.1**.

Q Frank Caputo, WA2AAW, asks, "What is an iambic keyer or iambic keying?"

A An iambic keyer is an electronic keyer that can be operated by a set of two paddles. By convention, for a right-handed person, the right paddle (index finger) produces continuous dits when depressed and the left paddle (the thumb) produces continuous dahs. The iambic part comes into play when the paddles are squeezed together (both thumb and index finger). This causes the iambic keyer to produce an alternating dit-dah-dit-dah.

From Webster's dictionary: **i·amb** (ì'àmb´, ì'àm´) *noun*

A metrical foot consisting of an unstressed syllable followed by a stressed syllable or a short syllable followed by a long syllable, as in *delay*.

Q I have always worked CW, until I went mobile. Because I drive a stick shift, it is hard to do CW while driving the hills of Pennsylvania (although it can be done). I thought that I would give SSB a chance, but I am having trouble tuning the signals for clarity. I think I am not tuning properly because I have difficulty getting a signal that I can understand, and when I do, I turn out to be way off their receive frequency. Can you give me some pointers?

A The best tuning of an SSB signal is accomplished by tuning from the high pitch to the low. I'll explain.

As you know, on 160, 80, and 40 meters, lower sideband is used and on the higher bands, upper sideband is the norm. Let's use 20 meters as an example.

Set your rig for 20-meters and upper sideband. Tune down to the lower end of the 20-meter phone band (14.150 MHz) and slowly tune up in frequency. You will soon hear a high-pitched squeaky voice.

Keep tuning slowly and you will hear the pitch become lower and lower. Soon it will become intelligible, but still too high. Keep on tuning up and the voice will eventually sound natural. There, you've done it!

If you continue tuning up, the voice will become lower and lower until it sounds like a 45 RPM record played at 33 RPM, then it will become unintelligible again.

On the bands that use lower sideband, the process is reversed. You start at the *upper* portion of the band and tune *down* slowly. The voices will go from the squeaky down to intelligible speech.

Q Steve, N6PHX, asks, "What are the rules governing the use of a ham transceiver outside the amateur bands? Can one use an amateur transceiver on CB, for example?"

A You can only use radios that have been FCC certified for use in the service for which they are intended. That makes it illegal to use a ham transceiver on CB, for example, because a ham rig is not FCC certified for use as a CB radio.

Q Trey, WL7BG, asks, "What kind of simplex range would an average 2-meter mobile enjoy in a mountainous area like south central Alaska?"

A That is a difficult question to answer because it depends on the nature of the terrain, which can change from moment to moment as you drive. Keep in mind that 2 meters is, for FM applications, a line-of-sight band. Barring atmospheric conditions, or reflections, if you are in a deep valley surrounded on mountains, you'll be limited to communicating within the immediate area of the valley—period. If you are in a long, straight valley you could realize a range of 10 to 20 miles depending on the antenna location of the other station. Of course, if you're on top of a ridge or mountain, you could enjoy distances up to a hundred miles or more.

Q Jean-Pierre, VE2GDA, asks, "I log all of my contact times using UTC, but the question of which *date* to use is not always clear. Suppose I log a contact that was made at a 2230 local time on June 4. The UTC time will be local time plus four hours, so I log it at 0230 UTC. But does the date become June 5, or does it remain June 4?"

A Many hams are often confused about this point. The simple answer is that

Table 10.1—Citizen Band Channel Frequencies

Channel	Frequency (MHz)	Channel	Frequency (MHz)	Channel	Frequency (MHz)
1	26.965	15	27.135	28	27.285
2	26.975	16	27.155	29	27.295
3	26.985	17	27.165	30	27.305
4	27.005	18	27.175	31	27.315
5	27.015	19	27.185	32	27.325
6	27.025	20	27.205	33	27.335
7	27.035	21	27.215	34	27.345
8	27.055	22	27.225	35	27.355
9	27.065	23	27.255	36	27.365
10	27.075	24	27.235	37	27.375
11	27.085	25	27.245	38	27.385
12	27.105	26	27.265	39	27.395
13	27.115	27	27.275	40	27.405
14	27.125				

the date must match the time. In your example, the "UTC date" would be June 5. It may have indeed been June 4 according to your *local time*, but for UTC it is after midnight and, henceforth, the next day (June 5).

Q Is there a site on the Web where I can obtain pass predictions for Amateur Radio satellites?

A There is indeed. Point your browser to **www.heavens-above.com**. This fascinating site is primarily devoted to observing objects in the night sky, but it tracks all kinds of satellites, too. It can provide a 24-hour listing of passes for various Amateur Radio satellites.

Q Mike, AA9RH, asks, " I travel often on business and I am considering the idea of operating HF QRP from the various hotels where I stay. However, most of my trips take me to large urban or suburban hotels which offer great height (say 20-30 stories), but definitely confine one to indoor operating. Is it possible to enjoy success from inside one of these large, sealed-up hotels?"

A The answer depends on how you define "success." Doc has been able to make a few QRP contacts from hotel rooms using indoor antennas, but the antennas usually didn't load well. In addition, they tended to pick up a lot of noise from hotel computers, TVs, hair dryers and so on.

Some hotel windows are not completely sealed; they can be opened slightly. If this is the case, you could discreetly drop a long, thin wire. With a good antenna tuner, and a $1/4$-wavelength counterpoise wire on the floor, you may be able to load your "stealth antenna" and make some contacts.

If you are fortunate to have a room with a balcony, you might be able to put up a mobile whip and counterpoise. These are not the most efficient antennas, but they may do the job in a temporary hotel-room application.

Q Bernard, K8LIX, asks, "The Dovetron stealth antenna uses house wiring as part of the radiating system. I live in a condo with neighbors on both sides. If I use it with my 150-W transmitter, what kind of measurements will I have to make in order to satisfy the FCC RF safety requirements?"

A You can make the same calculations for this as for any antenna. Unless you and your neighbors are on the same circuit, you can probably safely assume

that all of the wiring in your unit could be radiating. These types of antennas are *not* very efficient, so a calculation assuming 0-dBi gain is probably reasonable.

At 150 W, with a 40% duty factor and 67% on/off operating times, you have 40 W of average power for the purposes of the safety calculation. Your neighbors would need to be the following distances from any part of your residential electrical wiring:

28 MHz: 6.2 feet
14 MHz: 3.1 feet
7 MHz: 1.5 feet

Assuming the same conditions and 100% on/off time (in 6 minutes), you and your family would have to be:

28 MHz: 3.4 feet
14 MHz: 1.7 feet
7 MHz: 0.8 feet

Q I was licensed as a Technician in 1989 and I passed the code test, of course, at that time. I'm confused about where I stand in the restructured license system. I mean, if somebody hears me operating on HF and looks me up in the database, how do they know if I passed a code test?

A They don't.
In the restructuring proceeding of 1998, the Commission elected to no longer distinguish between the Technician and Technician Plus classes, effective April 15, 2000. The Technician Plus class is being phased out by issuing Tech Plus licensees new licenses that are stamped "Technician." The ARRL believes this is an error, and has petitioned for reconsideration, but since the Commission works very slowly, there is no reason to believe that relief is imminent.

You do not lose privileges in this situation, but if you want to upgrade someday, the onus to prove that you passed a code test is yours. The easiest way to do this is to retain your Technician class license document issued before February 14, 1991. Another way is to retrieve your license record from **QRZ.com**. When I looked up your call sign, it indeed showed a Technician license issued in 1989, which means you passed a code test.

You can obtain a 24-hour list of Amateur Radio satellite passes for your location on the Web at Heavens Above at: **www. heavens-above.com/**.

Welcome to Heavens-Above

If you're interested in satellites or astronomy, you've come to the right place! Our aim is to provide you with all the information you need to observe;

- **satellites**
- **Mir and the International Space Station**
- **the Space Shuttle**
- **the dazzlingly bright flares from Iridium satellites**

as well as a wealth of other spaceflight and astronomical information. Many people don't even realize that satellites can easily be seen with the naked eye. We not only provide the times of visibility, but also detailed star charts showing the satellite's track through the heavens. All our pages, including the graphics, are **generated in real-time** and **customized** for your location and time zone.

Heavens-Above GmbH is a private company which was founded to further the development of the pages which were so successful when operated by the German Space Operations Center. We continue to draw on the support of GSOC, where the pages are still hosted.

Q John, KD5JUP, asks, "I'm a new ham and I was wondering if you could suggest some active HF bands that I might monitor to get a sense of what goes on there. I presently hold a Technician license, but I can listen with my TS-430S transceiver. Can you suggest a few HF 'hot spots'?"

A A frequency chart is a good tool for new hams. One is available for download and printing from the *ARRLWeb* at **www.arrl.org/field/regulations/ bands.html**. Or, you may request one by sending an SASE to:

ARRL
Field and Education Services
225 Main St
Newington, CT 06111
…and ask for the US Amateur Band Chart.

The key to capturing hams on the air is knowing which bands are open, and therefore in use, at what times of the day and year.

For the most part, 20 meters (14.000-14.350 MHz) is open from early morning to late evening all year around and is a "round-the-world" band—the best place to hear DX (foreign) stations. You should be able to turn your radio on and tune between 14.000 and 14.060 MHz and hear CW; and 14.150 and 14.350 and hear SSB just about any time from 8 AM to 8 PM Local, almost 365 days a year.

Eighty meters is a "local" band and is populated in the early morning (before folks go to work) and early to late evening, but the band is more active in the winter than in the summer. Summer produces electrical storms that emit static that can be heard for hundreds of miles. The upper portion of the phone sub-band (3.850-4.000 MHz) is densely populated with conversations on all sorts of topics. A plus is that on this band you can almost always hear both sides of the conversation.

Forty meters is a 24-hour-a-day band. It is good out to about 300 miles during the day and worldwide at night. CW is fun all the time on this band, but foreign broadcast stations start to creep into the phone portion in late afternoon and into wee hours of the morning.

Fifteen meters often has activity in the daytime, but it tends to fall off in the evening. The same is true of 17 meters.

Ten meters is a different animal. It is greatly affected by the solar cycle. A good place to look for activity is in the phone portion between 28.400 and 28.500 MHz. Since we're presently at the peak of a solar cycle, 10 meters will open almost every day from early morning to evening. At the bottom of the cycle (probably around the year 2005), 10-meter band openings will not be as common.

Q Last night I heard a strange CW signal on 6 meters. It was hissing and buzzing, but I was still able to copy. To my astonishment, I learned that the station was 500 miles away from me. Was this sporadic E propagation?

A My guess is that you heard auroral propagation. The clue is your description of the signal as having a hissing or buzzing characteristic.

Those of us who reside at the higher latitudes are occasionally treated to the visual spectacle of the aurora borealis, better known as the "northern lights." (Yes, there are "southern lights" as well, visible occasionally in South America and Africa.) The aurora is caused when the Earth intercepts a stream of charged particles ejected from the Sun, resulting in a "geomagnetic storm." These fast-moving particles funnel into the polar regions of the Earth thanks to our magnetic field. As the particles interact with the upper atmosphere, the air glows, which we see as an aurora. The shimmering, ghostly curtain of light is not only a treat for the eyes, it can reflect radio signals like a giant mirror (see **Figure 10.9**).

Like sporadic E, you'll encounter auroral propagation more often on 6 meters than on 2 meters. Nevertheless, 2-meter aurora is far more common than 2-meter sporadic E. You can also work distant stations using auroral propagation on 222 and 432 MHz.

As you've discovered, auroral DX signals are very distorted. That's why CW is the most commonly used mode, although you'll hear SSB from time to time. Auroral CW signals have the raspy, buzzing quality you heard. (It sounds like the other guy is operating an ancient spark-gap transmitter!) Just listen carefully and you'll be able to decode the signals.

You do not need directional antennas and high power to work aurora on 6 meters. The Doctor has done it with dipoles and 100 W. Many hams have even enjoyed success with 6-meter aurora from mobile stations!

Q Joe, WT7V, asks, "Over the past two years or so, I have received dozens of QSL cards from DX stations that I've never worked. In fact, many of these QSLs confirm contacts supposedly made when my rig was completely off the air for weeks at a time. Do you think someone could be bootlegging my call sign?"

A Bootlegging is always a possibility, but it is rare. If the cards seem to arrive in spurts, there is a more likely explanation.

It is not at all unusual for a call to be consistently misrecorded in contests. For example, KØNS gets several cards per year intended for KØDI, a very active CW contest operator. If you sound out the suffixes of both call signs in Morse, you can understand how someone could blur the two together. Early this year, NT1A inquired about some cards that were apparently meant for our own Dave Patton, NT1N, here at Headquarters. In the heat of a contest, missing or transposing the individual letters is easy to do.

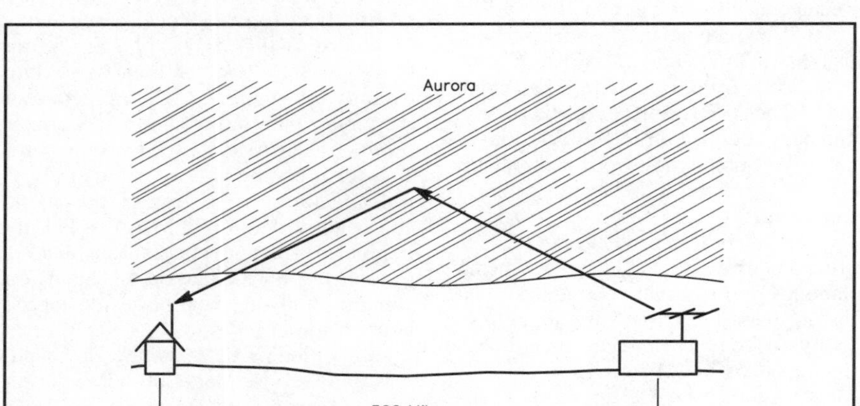

Q John Tencza, W1ECI, from South Windsor, Connecticut, writes: I have two radios, an ICOM 746 and a Yaesu 901. Both units exhibit the same strange problem when working split: when I hear someone come back to me they are much weaker than before I set up the split operation. Do the receiver manufacturers intentionally desensitize receivers when they are placed in split mode?

A The receivers are being desensed by the hordes of stations still calling the DX station. When you established the split operation, you had an opportunity to listen to the DX station when few competing stations were calling. However, when a DX station first responds to your call, other station operators haven't yet realized that the DX station is in a QSO. It takes a little while for the pileup—and the desensing—to dissipate.

Q Can strong solar activity have an influence on 2.4 GHz terrestrial data links?

A Good question! I don't know how one could completely rule out possible effects. There may be propagation mechanisms not described in the current literature that could be well known a few decades from now. This is one of the benefits of having an Amateur Radio Service—it is an ideal medium for experimentation.

However, conventional theory today does not indicate any obvious direct links between 2.4 GHz propagation and solar activity. Atmospheric refractivity is the primary influence with such links. It could be argued that solar activity affects the weather, which influences propagation, but convincing proof is still unavailable.

Q I've been fascinated by what I've read in *QST* about hams who are into moonbouncing. Can you tell me a little more about it? Do you need a monster station to do it?

A EME (Earth-Moon-Earth) communication, also known as "moonbounce," is based on a simple concept: use the moon as a passive reflector for VHF and UHF signals. With a total path length of about 500,000 miles, EME is the ultimate DX!

Amateur involvement in moonbounce grew out of experiments by the military after World War II. While the first amateur signals reflected from the moon were received in 1953, it took until 1960 for the first two-way amateur EME contacts to take place. Using surplus parabolic dish antennas and high-power klystron amplifiers, the Eimac Radio Club, W6HB, and the Rhododendron Swamp

Figure 10.9—The auroral "curtain" can function like a giant mirror in the sky, reflecting radio signals over substantial distances.

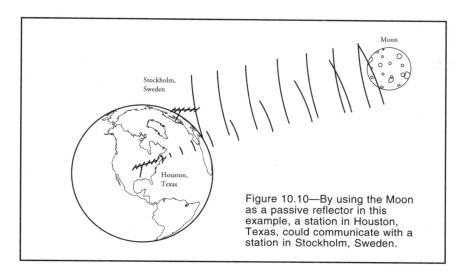

Figure 10.10—By using the Moon as a passive reflector in this example, a station in Houston, Texas, could communicate with a station in Stockholm, Sweden.

VHF Society, W1BU, achieved the first EME QSO in July 1960 on 1296 MHz. Since then, EME activity has proliferated onto most VHF and higher amateur bands. (See **Figure 10.10**.)

EME is primarily a CW mode. However, improvements in equipment now allow the best-equipped stations to make SSB contacts under the right conditions. Regardless of the transmission mode, successful EME operating requires:

• Power output as close to the legal limit as possible.

• A good-sized antenna array. Arrays of 8, 16 or more Yagis are common on the VHF, while large parabolic dish antennas are common on UHF and microwave frequencies.

• Accurate azimuth and elevation.

• Minimal transmission line losses.

• The best possible receiving equipment, generally a receiver with a low system noise figure and a low-noise preamplifier mounted at the antenna.

What I've just described is probably what you'd call a "monster station." I'm talking about the type of station that would assure you of success most of the time. However, it's possible to get a taste of moonbounce with just a single Yagi antenna and a 2-meter all-mode radio. The trick is to listen during the ARRL International EME Competition this fall. That contest brings all of the big-gun moonbouncers out of the woodwork. Assuming your radio is sufficiently sensitive (or assuming you're using a receive preamplifier), you should be able to hear the big-gun signals as they reflect off the Moon. It is an experience you're not likely to forget.

You'll find an excellent source of EME information on the ARRLWeb at **www.arrl.org/tis/info/moon.html**.

Q Brad, W1AMC, asks, "I noticed that both W1AMC and KB1FZZ are listed as my call signs in the FCC database. KB1FZZ was assigned to me when I received my license. I later requested and received W1AMC as a vanity call. Is it legal to use both calls when this happens?"

A Searching for your name on the FCC's ULS Web site (**www.fcc. gov/etb/uls**) does, indeed, give two call signs. However, if you click on KB1FZZ in the search results, you will find a cancellation date listed—the same date on which W1AMC was granted.

Any amateur who has changed his call since ULS was implemented will find all previous call signs when searching under his name. Only the most recently issued call is valid.

Q Thomas, WB2LEB, writes: I am interested in 2-meter SSB from my location in New Jersey. I would like to know if there are set rules and a limit of frequencies available for SSB. I have heard about the calling frequency of 144.200 MHz. Could you explain how this works?

A Yes, you do not want to operate below 144.100—144.000 to 144.100 is CW only. The way the calling frequency works is that you use it to locate other stations—you call or listen for CQs on this frequency. Then, when you have located another station, you move off frequency, preferably by more than 10 kHz. This allows other stations to use this frequency to locate stations. It is quite rude to monopolize this frequency, unless you happen to be a rare DX station. In this case, many people wish to contact the rare DX station, so it is often desirable for the DX to sit on 144.200 and work everyone. If the DX station moved off 144.200, many people might miss an unusual band opening.

For example, I worked a station in West Virginia, on the microwave liaison calling frequency of 144.260 MHz. Nor-

mally, I'd move off to 144.270 or 144.250, but he was 400 miles away. It was also the first time I'd heard WV in several days of listening. By staying on 144.260, I was able to give K1TEO an excellent chance of working K4EFD/8 on 10 GHz; immediately I worked K4EFD/8 on 10 GHz. However, if you aren't sure whether it is a good idea to stay on the calling frequency, you should probably move off. In this case, I wanted to inform other stations of the band opening.

Using just one frequency for CQing simplifies operating with a highly directional beam. Otherwise, the chances of having both the frequency and direction right are significantly reduced—contacts are much harder.

Q Can you offer some tips on chasing radioteletype (RTTY) DX?
A Glad to!
Like any other form of DXing, the quest for RTTY DX demands patience and skill. When a DXpedition is on the air with RTTY from a rare DXCC entity, your signal will be in competition with thousands of other HF digital operators who want to work the station as badly as you do. Sometimes pure luck is the winning factor, but there are a couple of tricks you can use to tweak the odds in your favor.

Let's say that you're tuning through the HF digital subbands one day and you stumble across a screaming mass of RTTY signals. On your computer screen you see that everyone seems to be frantically calling a DX station. Oh, boy! It's a pileup!

You can't actually hear the DX station that has everyone so excited, but what the heck, you'll activate your transceiver and throw your call sign into the fray, right? *Wrong!*

Never transmit even a microwatt of RF until you can copy the DX station. Tossing your call sign in blindly is pointless and will only add to the pandemonium. Instead, take a deep breath and wait. When the calls subside, can you see text from the DX station on your screen? If not, the station is probably too weak for you to work (don't even bother), or he may be working "split." More about that in a moment.

If you can copy the DX station, watch the exchange carefully. Is he calling for certain stations only? In other words, is he sending instructions such as "North America only"? Calling in direct violation of the DX station's instructions is a good way to get yourself blacklisted in his log. (No QSL card for you—ever!) Does he just want signal reports, or is he in the mood for brief chats? Most DX stations simply want "599" and possibly your location—period. Don't give them more than they are asking for. (A DX RTTY station on a rare island doesn't care what kind of weather you are experiencing at the moment.)

When DX RTTY pileups threaten to spin out of control, many DX operators will resort to working split. In this case, "split" means split frequency. The DX station will transmit on one frequency while listening for calls on another frequency (or range of frequencies).

A good DX operator will announce the fact that he is working split with almost every exchange. That's why it is so important to listen to a pileup before you throw yourself into the middle. If you tune into a pileup and cannot hear the DX station, tune below the pileup and see if you copy him there. If his signal is strong enough, he shouldn't be hard to find if he is working split. His signal will seem to be by itself, answering calls that you cannot hear. This is a major clue that a split operation is taking place.

Finally, don't neglect the other modes if you're hunting digital DX. An increasing number of DX stations are now using PSK31, so make sure you add that to your list of operating modes.

Q I plan to vacation in Europe this fall and I'd like to try some 2-meter FM repeater operating. I'm a little confused, though, about using 1750-Hz access tones vs. subaudible CTCSS access. Which of these systems do the European repeaters use?

A They may use both. It's standard practice in Europe to transmit a 1750-Hz tone to access a repeater. Virtually all European repeater systems are configured in this way. Many, however, include CTCSS access as well. This means that you must send the required 1750-Hz access tone and then include the necessary CTCSS tone during your transmission. Fortunately, most modern FM transceivers include the ability to transmit the 1750-Hz burst *and* CTCSS tones.

Q Rod Vlach, NNØTT, writes: When operating split on the same band, is there any advantage to "split mode" versus "XIT" (Transmit Incremental Tuning)? My rig has XIT of ±10 kHz, and I use it almost exclusively in pileups. It is quicker and easier than initiating split mode. The only advantage I can see in split mode is if I would need more range (more than 10 kHz).

A Well, on many radios, XIT/RIT and split operation can be used to accomplish the same thing, so it really depends on your radio's features and your operating preferences. I often use XIT if the pileup is small and the DX station is listening up a few kilohertz. If he's listening over a wide range, and I want to find

the stations he is working, I often find split operation more convenient. In either case, be sure you understand exactly where you are transmitting so you don't interfere with the DX station or other users of the band.

Q Denny Bowman, W7SNH, of Edmonds, Washington, writes: One of the newer hams I was helping to get into this hobby just passed his General and was putting up a new tower and beam antenna. His question: The maps/charts put out by the ARRL showing headings for DX entities: Are these headings referenced to *Magnetic* Headings (without Declination) or *True* (Geographic) headings (with Declination added for your particular location)?

A The ARRL maps are calibrated in True degrees, referred to True North ("straight up" on the maps). Magnetic headings are calculated by taking the True headings and adding the Magnetic Declination (also called the Magnetic Variation in nautical applications). For example, if the map shows a variation (declination) of 12° east, this means that Magnetic North is 12° east of "straight up." So, a heading of 45° True is equivalent to a magnetic heading of 45° + 12° east = 57° magnetic. For a westerly variation (for example 6° west), subtract the value for variation. Thus, 45° True – 6° west = 39° magnetic.

The magnetic north pole is presently located in northwestern Canada, near 78° N, 104° W. It shifts in location a small amount each year. If the magnetic pole were actually located at the true north pole, it would be at 90° north latitude, and the longitude wouldn't matter.

Q John asks, "I've just started studying for my Technician license and I have a question about the term 'meter' as it relates to the various labels used for amateur bands. Does the 'meter' of a given band correspond to the wavelength of the frequency of that band?"

A Not necessarily. When you're discussing Amateur Radio frequency bands, consider their metric labels in broad terms only. This will be easier to understand once you know the historical background. However, let's start by defining a "meter" in terms of wavelength.

To convert wavelength to frequency, the speed of light is used, as it is also the speed of radio waves. In metric, this is 300 million meters per second. So the conversion formula is:

F(MHz) = 300/wavelength
   conversely,
  wavelength = 300/F(MHz)

So, 6 meters is really 50 MHz; 2 meters is actually 150 MHz and 70 centimeters (0.7 meters) is 428 MHz. Notice that the frequency that corresponds to 2 meters is well above what hams consider to be "2 meters."

While some folks would like to have the bands named more accurately (2 meters would be 2.1 meters, for example), tradition runs deep in this hobby and the majority feel this tradition should be preserved.

In this day of computer-controlled rigs, it is easy to forget that radio technology was once crude indeed. Before the advent of vacuum tubes, there was no such thing as an amplifying oscillator with feedback to control it. Radio signals were generated via a spark gap.

Anyone who has listened to an AM broadcast radio when a thunderstorm is approaching knows that sparks generate wideband RF. The lightning discharges will create bursts of RF that cover the entire AM band. Thus it was in the early days of radio—transmissions were made by spark and the best one could do to limit the output bandwidth was to use an output filter made of a couple of inductors and capacitors along with a narrow-bandwidth antenna. This determined what "band" you were on and you could hear everyone else on the same band at the same time.

Yes, it was bedlam after a fashion, but the range you could work was quite short (a couple hundred miles was "DX") and there were far fewer operators then. The label for a particular band was broadly interpreted because the signals themselves were broad—and that legacy remains today. That's why we have a "20-meter band" at 14 MHz even though the true frequency equivalent of 20 meters is 15 MHz!

Q What is the precise ratio of frequency (in hertz) to bandwidth (in meters)? I have seen a six-digit figure floating around, but that may not be very exact. It's likely that the ratio number could go on forever in precision, but can you give it to me in as many digits as possible?

A Is this sufficiently precise? 1 Hz = 299,792,458 meters
You'll find a terrific page on the Web for looking up constants at: **physics.nist.gov/cuu/Constants/index.html**.

Q Bob, KC2DT, asks, "I have recently returned to the air after a long absence. I notice that the readability report on CW is sometimes followed by NN. For example, RST 5NN. What does NN mean?"

A "NN" is simply shorthand for "99." So, 5NN is actually 599. You'll often hear this used during contest and DX exchanges because it is easier (and faster) to send.

CHAPTER 11

Around the Shack

DON'T THROW AWAY THOSE OLD HEADSETS

◊ Headphones need not be scrapped just because metal-on-nylon cords are difficult to solder. Repair using readily available junk-box materials without soldering is simple. Clean off the insulation carefully leaving the metal-on-nylon conductor intact. Form a "crimpable" ferrule by removing the ring from a small (#18 AWG) crimp lug/termination. Slide some heat-shrink tubing over the headphone cord and move it well away from the joint area. Insert the clean conductor-on-nylon into the ferrule. If the joint is at the plug end of the cord, insert a short length of flexible bare stranded wire into the ferrule at the opposite end. Crimp the joint. (I prefer the type of crimping tool that dimples rather than squashes the ferrule.) Slide the heat-shrink tube over the ferrule and shrink it. You can now solder the bare stranded wire to a phone plug without fear of damaging the fragile nylon core. If the break is somewhere in the middle of the headphone cord, omit the bare flexible wire and slide the other broken end of the metal-on-nylon into the ferrule and crimp as before. Sometimes it helps to tightly fill the ferrule with short lengths of bare stranded wire. Either way you have a good electrical connector that will survive many years of use.

This same technique is excellent for installing ring terminations on telephone extension cords, a requirement for connecting many models of telephone patch equipment to the telephone service line.—*Bruce McCaffrey, N7OJ, PO Box 153, Poulsbo, WA 98370;* **bim@tscnet.com**

A SOLID-STATE FLASHLIGHT

◊ I wanted to experiment with the new white LEDs and see if they would work in a flashlight application. Lo and behold, they do. I found an old beat up mini-Maglight flashlight for the purpose. I determined that two AA cells driving the LED do not need a dropping resistor because 3 V only drives the LED to 6 mA. So, I just clipped off the leads of the LED

to match the lengths of the old Maglight bulb leads.

Then, I drilled out the back of the plastic reflector to match the larger diameter of the LED. Drilling the reflector can be tricky. I used several drill bits of different sizes so that each cut only a little from the reflector. I was very careful and took my time.

Finally, I plugged the LED into the Maglight—observing the polarity—and Voilá! A Maglight flash light that will probably last forever. It's not as bright as with the stock lamp, but it's useable nonetheless and a good experiment.—*Jeff Montgomery, WB4WXD, 104 Rosewood, Palestine, TX 75801;* **jmonty@flash.net**

AN "ARM HOLSTER" FOR YOUR H-T

◊ What a treat to see all the tiny H-Ts on the market. The problem with these little gems is where to carry them. While they easily fit in a shirt pocket, the display is not visible there and the antenna is often against your body. Because they're so light, it's possible to carry them right on your arm in my "arm holster."

What's an arm holster? It's the best thing to hold your lightweight H-T: a simple elastic strap that snugly fits your biceps. (See **Figure 11.1**.) A friction buckle lets one strap adjust to fit many arm sizes. With the strap in place, slide the radio belt clip over it. The radio is held safely with the display near eye level and the antenna at shoulder height. With the antenna so high and clear, reception is much better than with the radio on your belt or in a pocket. It is so nice to see the display, and be able to change frequencies without removing the radio from my belt.

Some radios—such as the Alinco D series—have no belt clip. To accommodate them, sew a two-inch strip of hook-and-loop fastener (hook side) onto the strap and install a similar loop-side self-stick strip on the radio.

For larger radios, increase the width

Figure 11.1—W7VEW's "arm holster" for small H-Ts.

of the elastic strap. A two-inch wide strap works great for the larger units.—*Steve Kimber, W7VEW, 180 N 1100 E #12, Washington, UT 84780;* **ckimber@infowest.com**

DX ON A BABY MONITOR

◊ When out of the shack in another part of the house, I used to wonder what good DX I was missing. Now, I can hear the DX spots I need over DXTelnet and I'm still able to get other things done throughout the house or yard. After logging on to DXTelnet and activating the voice spell feature, I place the transmitter unit of a baby monitor close to my computer speakers. Next I clip the battery powered receiver unit to my belt or put it in my shirt pocket. Baby monitors are relatively inexpensive and are available at most toy stores. Now I don't have to miss that rare DX spot because I'm not in the shack. —*Dr. Charles C. Doggett, WA3EEE, 3723 Marriottsville Rd, Randallstown, MD 21133;* **CDoggett@prodigy.net**

GOO REMOVERS

◊ Often at hamfests, you may come across a nice piece of equipment, but perhaps it has a price sticker left on it that just won't come off. Or, maybe it was a surplus unit and has some other stickers or tape that you can't remove.

Telephone companies have used a citrus based cable cleaner for years to remove the waterproof gel from cables when resplicing phone lines. Such cleaner is made by 3M and others, but is hard to find, especially in small quantities.

However, something similar is available almost anywhere, for a few bucks. The best thing I have found to remove sticky goo residue is available at Walmart and other home and automotive stores. It's MEDO[1] brand Ultra Citrus Air Freshener, in a 6-ounce pump spray bottle. You can find the air freshener in the automotive section of the store. It's 100% natural, according to the label, and comes in many "flavors or scents." I've only tried the orange scent, however. The citrus in it will remove almost any sticky goo residue, and it will also loosen those stubborn labels left on equipment. When I get the equipment home, I just spray some on the label or tape and let it soak for a minute or two. The label usually slides right off.

One word of caution: The Ultra Citrus will attack some plastics, so always test it on the material to be cleaned in an inconspicuous place before spraying.—*E. Kirk Ellis, KI4RK, 203 Edgebrook Dr, Pikeville, NC 27863;* **kirke@ goldsboro.net**

◊ Several other products also work well for this purpose:
 • Goo Gone (Magic American Corporation)
 • Goof Off, Goof Off2, Goo Remover (Lilly Industries)
 • Krud Kutter (Supreme Chemicals of Georgia)
These products are available at many department stores, hardware stores and supermarkets.—*Bob Schetgen, KU7G, ARRL Staff*

YOUR GPS UNIT MAY DISPLAY GRID SQUARES

◊ Many VHF/UHF contesters and other hams make use of the Maidenhead system of grid squares. The grid squares are one degree of latitude tall by two degrees of longitude wide. They were agreed upon at a conference held in Maidenhead, England. Many of the populated

[1]MEDO Industries Inc, 660 White Plains Rd, Tarrytown, NY 10591; tel 914-332-4343, outside New York state 800-431-1358, fax 914-332-8686; **info@medo.com**.

areas of the world exist in the middle latitudes where the lines of longitude have converged to about half of the separation they have at the equator. This makes the grid squares look approximately square in the middle latitudes.

Over a year ago, I moved to Friendship, Maryland, so I am designing a new QSL card reflecting the new station location. In order to find my grid square for the new card, I took my latitude and longitude readings from a Garmin GPS-12 handheld GPS unit. Then I went out on the Web and found one of the many grid-square lookup pages. The lookup page wanted the latitude and longitude coordinates in degrees, minutes and seconds. The GPS was displaying degrees, minutes and decimal fractions of minutes. Well, it is easy enough to do the math and convert to seconds, but I chose to look in the GPS setup menu and have it display seconds. As I scrolled through the many display formats, I was surprised to find a choice labeled "Maidenhead." What a great deal! Just standing there in my backyard with a GPS and presto! I find that I am in Grid Square FM18QR.

Actually FM18 is the 1°×2° square. The fifth and sixth characters "QR" refine the location to 2.5′ of latitude by 5′ of longitude. For more information go to **www.arrl.org/locate/gridinfo.html**.

—*Ric Creager, KK4GV, 24 Scrivner Dr, Friendship, MD 20758-9778;* **creager@ erols.com**

A HOMEBREW PTT HAND SWITCH

◊ I made this handheld PTT switch (**Figure 11.2**) for less than $5 with scraps from around the shack, a switch and a 1/4-inch monoaural phone plug. I use a Heil GM-4 Goldline mic on its stand and want freedom from needing to key the mic on its stand or using the foot switch. The HH PPT allows me to be farther away from the radio to key the desktop mic, and I can interchange it with the foot switch on my Kenwood TS2000. (See **Table 11.1** for a complete parts list.)

Drill a hole in the copper end cap to accommodate your switch (**Figure 11.3**). Insert the switch and lock it in place with the nut, from the inside (**Figure 11.4**). Attach and solder the wires to the switch, thread the wire through the PVC pipe and fit the switch snugly in the end of the PVC. (Some filler may be needed.—*Ed.*) You may need to file the inside of the PVC a little for the end cap to fit. Wire the phone plug to the other end of the cable and you are talking!—*James R. Kinney, KB9LUK, E3078 70th Ave, Eau Galle, WI 54737;* **kb9luk@wwt.net**

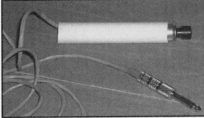

Figure 11.2—KB9LUK's completed homebrew PTT switch.

Table 11.1—Parts List
3/4×5-inch PVC pipe
5/8-inch ID copper end cap (as for 1/2-inch copper pipe—*Ed.*)
1/4-inch monaural phone plug
1 normally open momentary push-button switch
2-conductor stranded cable #20 AWG wire or better, of any length

Figure 11.3—The end cap drilled to accept the switch parts.

Figure 11.4—The switch mounted in the end cap.

A DX-BEACON CLOCK

◊ This homebrew beacon clock enables one to track the 18 NCDXF beacon transmissions.[2,3] Driven by a 1/3-RPM clock motor,[4] it presents a realistic view of what's going on with each of the 18 NCDXF beacons on all five HF DX bands. It takes 180 seconds to complete one full rotation of the clock face.

I have seen computer programs that are intended to serve this same purpose, but the screen characters were too small to read unless I wanted to sit in front of the monitor all day long! The clock described here is large enough to be viewed from anywhere in the room!

Figure 11.5 shows the 8-inch clock face.[5] Each of the 18 segments spans 10 seconds. My friends and I find this far easier to follow than the mini-spreadsheets often used for this purpose. The clock is useful when CW beacon signals are fluttery or otherwise too distorted to be discerned. While I have no trouble copying the beacons' CW IDs, those who do also find it a fascinating appliance to have around the shack. Nonham visitors to the shack seem to enjoy it, as well. It is an excellent advertisement for ham radio and might even be a good club project.

The clock can also be helpful when a beacon is *not* coming through. When a particular time slot passes the band of interest and nothing is heard, one can be reasonably certain that propagation on that band is poor to nonexistent. Either that or the beacon is inoperative!

Construction

The largest component of the beacon clock is its "face plate." Mine is a 12×12×0.048-inch double-sided printed-circuit board. Almost any other thin, rigid material would do as well. A 1 1/8-inch

diameter hole in the exact center of the board accommodates the dial drive coupler. Any hole size that will pass the drive coupling would be acceptable.

The rotating dial is eight inches in diameter and made from PC-board material. Secure the dial and faceplate escutcheons onto their respective surfaces with glue or another method of your choice.

A 120-V SPST ON-OFF switch was installed on the faceplate to facilitate synchronization of the clock with WWV. An optional 100-Ω, 5-W resistor was connected in series with the motor to reduce motor heating. The resistor reduces the motor-terminal voltage to 115 V.

Orient the motor on the rear of the faceplate and align it with the center hole (see **Figure 11.6**). Mark the two motor-mount holes. Using a #33 bit, drill two holes. Assemble the motor to the faceplate using two #4-40×1-inch screws, spacers and hex nuts.

The coupler axle I used is made from 1/4-inch-diameter phenolic rod. Brass is a suitable substitute. The motor shaft fits into the coupler's hole, where a setscrew secures it. (Commercially manufactured 1/8-to-1/4-inch-diameter shaft adapters are

occasionally available at larger hardware stores. If you can find one, use it!)

The dial hub was salvaged from a discarded volume-control bushing for a 1/4-inch-diameter shaft. After drilling a suitable mounting hole, the bushing was secured to the dial with the hex nut taken from the same control. The phenolic rod was slightly larger than 1/4-inch—just

[2]J. G. Troster, W6ISQ, and R. S. Fabry, N6EK, "The NCDXF/IARU International Beacon Project," *QST*, Sep 1997, p 48.

[3]For a history of the NCDXF beacons, visit **www.ncdxf.org**.

[4] 1/3-RPM synchronous clock motors are available from McMaster Carr, PO Box 4355, Chicago, IL 60680-4355, Sales, tel 630-833-0300, fax 630-834-9427; e-mail **chi.sales@ mcmaster.com**; **www. mcmaster.com/**. Order #6502k999 pear-shaped synchronous ac gear motor, standard torque, 115 V ac, 1/3 rpm, 9 in/lb torque, counterclockwise rotation, flatted shaft. Delivery on this item is 35 business days. You may refer to quote number 27974 when placing your order. They were $41.95 each at the time of publication. You can visit the manufacturer's Web site at **www.crouzet.com**.

[5]If you want to build the clock, take Figure 11.5 to a copy center and have them make an enlarged color copy to fit your clock face. You can also download this image from ARRLWeb **www.arrl.org/files/qst-binaries/**. Look for 02HK04Fig1.zip.

Table 11.2—Parts List

Crouzet 1/3-RPM synchronous motor (see Note 3)
12×12×0.048-inch PC board.
8-inch-diameter PC board
Phenolic or brass rod, 1/4-inch diam 1-inch long
Dial escutcheon
Dial hub, salvage hardware from a potentiometer
Faceplate escutcheon
two #4-40 screws, 1-inch long
two #4-40 hex nuts
two 1/2-inch-long motor standoff spacers
one #4-40 setscrew
SPST mini switch
120-V line cord
one 100-W 5-W ceramic resistor (optional)

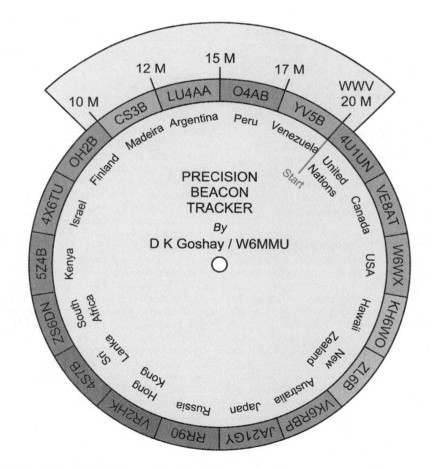

Figure 11.5—The DX Beacon clock face (see Note 5).

enough to fit snugly into the hub. Had this not fit so conveniently, the bushing could have been secured with cyanoacrylate (CA) adhesive.

I fashioned a pair of wooden feet to support the clock in an upright position on the operating table. You may prefer to mount yours in a picture frame and hang it on the wall. (See **Table 11.2** for a complete parts list.)

Operation

Plug the line cord into a 120-V, 60-Hz outlet. With the SPDT switch set ON, allow the red START line on the dial to rotate to the WWV mark on the faceplate. Then switch the motor off. Tune in WWV or WWVH at 5, 10 or 15 MHz. Wait for a minute that is evenly divisible by three: 0, 3, 6, 9, 12, etc. At the sound of the beep, switch the motor ON. I prefer to start the motor slightly prior to the beep, then observe synchronization on successive minutes. If the clock appears to be slightly ahead of WWV, switch the motor off and on quickly, thereby introducing a time-lag increment to bring the clock into precise synchrony.

All electric power grids lag behind during heavy load periods and catch up during light load periods. Thus, it is normal for any ac-powered clock to gain and lose up to five seconds on a given day. When this happens, the power grid nearly always corrects itself within several hours. If one can't live with that, the clock must be occasionally reset. Even if it is never reset, the clock will remain within about plus-minus five seconds indefinitely. I have rarely seen the power grid off by as much as one-half of a 10-second beacon period.

My thanks to Ken Bates, KF5WD, who took the Figure 11.5 photo and gave valuable assistance in designing and producing the dial face.—*Don Goshay PE, W6MMU, Rte 1 Box 1107, Golden, MO 65658;* **w6mmu@mo-net.com**

A POOR MAN'S ANEMOMETER

◊ When I started this project, I already had a Davis weather station, but wanted to design and build one as cheaply as possible for a friend of mine. I wanted to be able to use parts that were readily available to 95% of most hams and do it in such a way that everyone could build one without a college degree. I want to thank Jack Demaree, WB9OTX, for his input. Jack told me how he built them with small toy dc motors and Leggs egg-style panty-hose containers. I took his information, converted it to another style, added a visual weather vane and here it is in **Figure 11.7**.

I used an AOL CD for the rotor, a small dc motor—this one was out of a handheld fan that used two AAA batteries. The meter in this case reads 150 mA

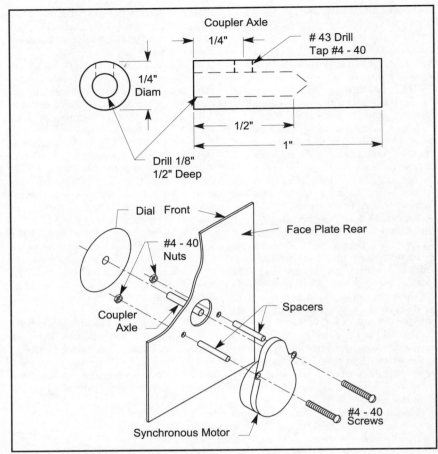

Figure 11.6—Mechanical details of the DX Beacon clock.

at full scale. It was loaned to me by John Charlton, W9DIH. The structure is made from PVC pipe, but this is not the permanent mount. Use the smallest tubing that will accept your motor.

The only part of this that is not from my junk box is a blade adapter (see **Figure 11.8**), which came from a hobby shop. This adapter mates a propeller from a model airplane gas-engine drive shaft (about 1/4 inch diameter) to fit an electric motor shaft. I used some heat-shrink tubing on the motor shaft to help secure it in the blade adapter. The blade adapter comes with a compression washer: When this is turned upside down, it not only helps to secure your disk, but also centers it!

Check Tower Hobbies[6] or your favorite hobby shop, or make your own, but make sure to use aluminum or lightweight material. (The center hole of a CD is about 1/2 inch. Any adapter that mates the motor shaft to the CD or to a flat plate secured to the CD will work.—*Ed.*)

[6]Tower Hobbies, PO Box 9078, Champaign, IL 61826-9078; tel 800-637-6050; **www. towerhobbies.com/**.

The cups to catch the wind are from pill bottles, the ones I used are 2 1/8-inch in diameter and seem to work well with the diameter of the disk. The holes are equally spaced around the disk. You can lay out three equally spaced radials by measuring 104 mm straight between the points where the radials cross the disk circumference. (Or, you could draw an equilateral triangle with 104-mm sides and lay it on the disk.—*Ed.*) Secure the cups to the disk with some very small screws and a little silicone caulk to help keep them in place.

The circuit is simple: A wire pair connects the motor leads to the meter. Almost any wire will do; I used telephone wire on one and wire from an old Motorola Motrac radio on the second. Solder the wires to the motor but not to the meter—yet. First, route the wires through the PVC assembly and mount the motor.

The motor is held within the PVC tubing by a friction fit. I achieved this with a piece of rubber cut from a bicycle inner tube (see **Figure 11.9**). Any pliable rubber should work. (You could also do this by wrapping the motor with electrical

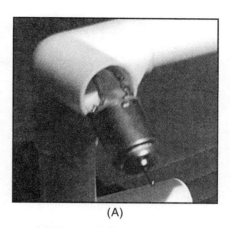

(A)

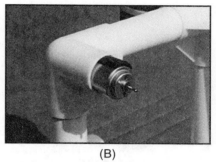

(B)

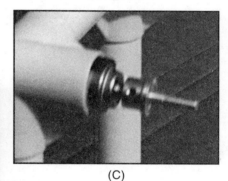

(C)

Figure 11.7—N9PUG's junk-box anemometer for stingy meteorologists. The horizontal CD (at left below center) is the anemometer. The horizontal pipe and CD at the top form a weather vane for visual observation. (Perhaps readers could adapt rotator direction sensors for remote reading or develop new techniques for the task. Send in the hints!—*Ed.*) The wind-speed meter is cleverly mounted to the pipe at center, but it would normally be located conveniently indoors. Although Greg made this complex PVC arrangement to stand on its own, one made for roof or tower installation could be much simpler, as fewer legs and bends are needed.

Figure 11.9—The dc motor mounts in the pipe structure by means of a friction fit facilitated by a builder-fitted rubber shim. At (A), the motor hangs free before fitting. (B) shows the rubber shim at the top and right side of the motor. (C) shows the shaft adapter in place on the motor.

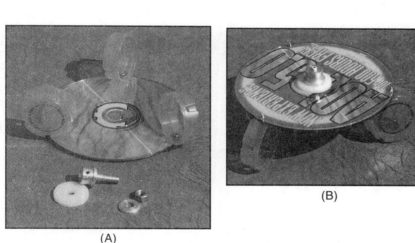

(B)

(A)

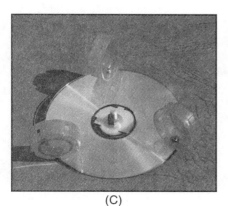

(C)

Figure 11.8—The anemometer CD assembly. (A) shows the CD with pill-bottle tops attached. The hardware in front is for the shaft-adapter assembly. Notice the setscrew hole in the side of the shaft adapter. (B) is a top view with the shaft adapter installed. (C) is a bottom view. The small hole in the center of the shaft adapter accepts the electric motor shaft, which is secured with a setscrew.

tape for a snug fit—*Ed.*)

Now, connect the wires to your meter, but don't solder them yet. First, give the motor a spin to check the polarity for the meter. (That is, the meter needle will deflect upward when the CD spins.—*Ed.*) If it works, permanently connect the meter leads; if not, reverse them first.

Once the system is installed and working, use silicone caulk to seal the motor mount against the effects of weather. The PVC pipe ends can be sealed with caps made for that purpose or many alternatives: plain rubber sheeting,

Figure 11.10—The meter is mounted to the pipe by a tie-wrap and adhesive mounting pad: a handy technique!

plastic caps from pill bottles, rubber chair-leg tips or whatever you can dream up, also attached with silicone.

The weathervane was made from a length of PVC about a foot long. I attached a disk on one end, found the balance point of the weathervane and installed a ball bearing to support it. The ball bearing makes this vane spin very easily. Make sure your ball bearing is a snug fit. To make sure it will keep spinning easily for a long time with no upkeep, I used a nylon washer underneath the vane and a stainless-steel screw.

Now, here comes the work: How do you calibrate it? There are several ways. Since I already had a calibrated anemometer, I mounted this one within two feet of it, and with a good steady wind, was able to mark the meter and label it with 5 mph, 10 mph and so on. Alternatively, you could mount it to a car, then have a

helper drive at steady speeds as you mark the dial. Don't try this alone! (Be sure that you choose a calm day and mount the instrument well clear of the car body for accurate readings.—*Ed.*)

Most panel meters can be disassembled and repainted or marked as needed. In addition, a variable resistor can be put in line to help with calibration if needed. Well, that's about it. A project that's simple, fun and pretty darn accurate. Best of all, you will probably have less than five bucks in it. Don't forget to seal up all holes or the bugs and bees will have a new home.[7]—*Gregory Tatlock, N9PUG, 637 East 15th St, Seymour, IN 47274-1138;* **n9pug@hotmail.com**

[7]Actually, it's a good idea to leave one very small opening unsealed, so that pressure and moisture are not trapped inside.—*Ed.*

The Doctor is IN

Q **How old does a radio have to be before it is considered "collectible?" Can an FM transceiver from the '70s be considered "vintage?"**

A The answer depends on who you ask. Some radio collectors strictly adhere to the 50-year rule. That is, a radio must be at least 50 years old to be considered an antique. Others are more generous. For example, many collectors covet Ten-Tec Power Mite QRP transceivers from the early '70s. The Heathkit HW-series QRP transceivers from the same period are often in high demand. Among the FM rigs, Drake TR-22s are often considered collectible as are the early Clegg and Regency transceivers. As always, "collectible" is in the eye of the beholder.

Q **I use a station clock that has large, red LEDs. I've noticed that if I am chewing on something (a mid-contest snack!) and happen to glance at the clock, the numbers seem to be jumping or flickering. Assuming that this isn't the symptom of some dreaded disease, what really causes the flickering?**

A If you're chewing on something hard (crunchy potato chips, candy, etc) you set up vibrations in your jaw that propagate to your eyes, shifting their positions ever so slightly. The LED segments are "refreshing" themselves at a high rate of speed and, because of the movement of your eyes, the bright "moving" segments are in different places from where the vi-

sual centers of your brain expect them to be. You may see the same effect while watching your computer monitor.

This phenomenon involves something called the *critical fusion frequency*, which

The Clegg FM-27B was among the first synthesized 2-meter FM amateur transceivers and is now considered collectible by some hams. This advertisement appeared in the February 1974 *QST*.

is the point where we begin to perceive things that are flickering as if they are solid. Different factors influence that frequency, including the size of the object, its brightness, and which part of the retina it is seen by. The brighter the background, for example, the greater the flicker. The action of chewing jars the visual axis and changes your line of sight relative to the particular point you are focused on, moving it far enough off the central retina to change your ability to perceive a flickering image as a stable one.

Q **How fast do electrons flow in copper wire?**

A It turns out that the electrons in copper travel quite slowly even though electricity travels at almost the speed of light. That's because there are so many mobile electrons in copper (and other conductors) that even if those electrons move only an inch per second, they comprise a large electric current.

The fact that electricity itself travels at almost the speed of light just means that when you start the electrons moving at one end of a long wire, the electrons at the other end of the wire also begin moving almost immediately. But that doesn't mean that an electron from your end of the wire actually reaches the far end any time soon. Instead, the electrons behave like water in a long hose. When you start the water moving at one end, it pushes on water in front of it, which pushes on water in front of it, and so on so that water at the far end begins to leave the hose. In a wire, the motion proceeds forward at the speed of light in the wire (actually the speed at which electromagnetic waves propagate along the wire), which is only slightly less than the speed of light in vacuum.

Q Forrest Wilson writes: Is there some kind of lockable power strip that could be used to "tamper proof" radio gear? Our club shack is in a classroom, and at times the students have access to it. If the power could be locked off, it would prevent tampering. We already lock up the microphones.

A The best thing to do is have the electrician install a separate circuit breaker box next to the station console. Use one that has a locking handle to open the cover. A combination or key lock can be use to disallow access to unauthorized personnel. When the station is in operation, this approach also makes a dandy safety "kill" switch.

Q How do lightning trackers work? Is this something that a ham could do at home?

A A single-site lightning tracker detects the low frequency radio signals produced by lightning's electrical discharge. These signals are the cracklings you hear on AM radios when thunderstorms are nearby. Lightning signals travel for hundreds of miles and can be detected by directional low-frequency antennas. Specialized software plots the approximate direction of each strike and analyzes the signal strength to calculate the distance. The results are typically plotted on a map display. More sophisticated systems combine strike data from several receiver sites to create more accurate position plots.

Yes, you can set up a lightning tracker at home. The Boltek Corporation, among others, makes a lightning tracking system based on a receiver board that plugs into your PC. (See **Figure 11.11**.) The directional LF antenna can be installed

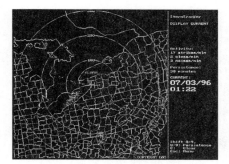

Figure 11.11—The Boltek lightning tracker in action.

outdoors or in your attic. The entire system costs about $500. Contact the Boltek Corporation, 2316 Delaware Ave, Buffalo, NY 14216; tel 905-734-8045; **www.boltek.com**.

Q Larry, KØLWV, asks, "While tuning around 1600 kHz I heard a very weak AM signal that appeared to be repeating an announcement about a house for sale nearby. Is this kind of thing legal?"

A So-called "Talking House" transmitters generate the signals you are hearing, and they are becoming popular among realtors.

When a house comes on the market, the seller's real estate agent may install one of these transmitters to continuously broadcast a sales pitch about the home. The sign on the front lawn invites drivers to tune to a particular frequency to hear the broadcast. Talking House transmitters are FCC Part 15 devices that do not require licenses to own and operate. (They are in the same class as AM and FM "wireless microphones.") The Talking House units typically operate above 1600 kHz and have an output of 100 mW or less. Their range is limited to about 1500 feet. Believe it or not, some hardcore broadcast-band DXers attempt to receive these signals at much greater distances, although their success varies!

Q Anthony Manser, AF7J, of Centerville, Utah, writes: I would like to know how to evaluate my antenna system for RF radiation in the QTH, etc (health concerns).

I'm using two R7 verticals in phase at 60 ft spacing. Height above ground is 10 ft at the base where the radials are. The verticals are positioned at each end of my QTH, so I'm right in the middle of the system and approximately 10 ft below the bases.

Also, is my maximum field at the center of the verticals, like a simple vertical dipole antenna?

A This is one evaluation that is really not well covered by "the book." You can use the RF-safety calculator at the University of Texas to estimate the worst-case exposure from your station. Fed in phase like that, the two verticals would have a gain of as much as about 5 dBi. If you run this through the calculator, assuming 28 MHz (your worst-case HF frequency) and assume 100 W of continuous power, this gives you a required separation distance of 7.8 feet for controlled exposure (you and your household, if they are aware of RF energy) and 17.4 feet for your neighbors.

If you and your family are 7.8 feet

below the antenna, your evaluation using the simple methods was sufficient.

I ran EZNEC (**www.eznec.com**) to calculate the near field under your antenna, at a height 10 feet below the antenna whose bottom was 20 feet in the air, starting below one antenna and going toward the other. The exposure level does go up and down along the line extending to below one antenna to below the other, but the minimum exposure is below either antenna and the maximum exposure is toward the area midway between the two antennas.

For more information, including links to the University of Texas site, see **www.arrl.org/rfsafety/**.

Q Steve, N8UBR, asks, "I put up a 10-meter quarter-wave-length ground plane antenna on my property in my subdivision. When doing an RF safety evaluation for this system, is the distance measured from the main vertical radiator or the ground plane radials? (I plan to use 100 W.) The radials are currently above the ground, but will be buried in the spring when the ground thaws."

A If I were doing your evaluation, I would consider radials that were within a few inches of the ground to be grounded and would do my calculations from the main antenna itself. If I had a ground-plane antenna with elevated radials, I would, to be conservative, consider them as an active part of the antenna system. The simple evaluation methods, such as the one found on the University of Texas Web page (see "The Doctor is IN," February 2000), works very well for ground-mounted verticals. You can assume about 1 dBi of antenna gain and do use the ground-reflection factor.

Start with your 100 W output and adjust it for the operating mode and typical duty cycles.

100 W CW = 40 W

100 W SSB = 20 to 40 W, depending on speech processing, use 30 W for average speech processing

100 W FM, RTTY, other digital = 100 W

Then, adjust it by the amount of time you *might* be transmitting continuously during the averaging time of 6 minutes for controlled exposure or 30 minutes of uncontrolled exposure. For "conversational" operating, you can use 100% for controlled exposure and about 67% for uncontrolled. If you wish, you can also make further adjustments for feed-line loss, but I will refer you to *RF Exposure and You* for more info on that.

For a 1-dBi-gain antenna on 28 MHz, this typically works out to:

Mode	Controlled Distance (feet)	Uncontrolled Distance (feet)
SSB	2.7	4.9
CW	3.1	5.8
FM	4.9	9.0

This all assumes 100 W, 1 dBi, 28 MHz, 10 minutes on, 10 minutes off, 10 minutes on and moderate speech processing for SSB. If you and your family are greater than 4.9 feet from the antenna and your neighbors are greater than 9 feet from the antenna, you can run 100W continuous duty (carrier) for an indefinite period.

The required distances are from your antenna to any point where people could actually be exposed. Most hams choose to control exposure in their backyard by instructing their families not to linger closer than the controlled distance to their antennas when they are on the air. You should also take some steps to ensure that no one can accidentally contact your antenna. Hams generally use their property line as the criterion for the uncontrolled distance because they have no way of knowing whether their neighbor might be spending time near the property line. With the above assumptions, if you operate SSB on 10 meters with 100 W and your antenna is located 4.9 feet from the property line, you are in compliance.

Q When I was working as a broadcast engineer I once had the misfortune to touch a high voltage terminal in a transmitter power supply. Thank goodness I wasn't killed outright, but the shock threw me across the room, seriously injuring my back when I slammed against the wall. To this day, I've wondered how the electricity was able to propel me through the air in such a fashion. Do you have the answer?

A Prepare yourself for another shock: the electricity didn't propel you anywhere—your own muscles did!

When a large electrical current runs through your body, your muscles are stimulated to contract powerfully—often much harder than they can be made to contract voluntarily. Normally the body sets limits on the proportion of muscle fibers that can voluntarily contract at once. Extreme stress can cause the body to raise these limits, allowing greater exertion at the cost of possible injury. This is the basis of the "hysterical strength" effect that allows mothers to lift cars if their child is trapped underneath, or allows psychotics the strength to overcome several nursing attendants.

When an electric current stimulates muscles, these built-in limits don't ap-ply, so the contractions can be violent. The electric current typically flows into one arm, through the abdomen, and out of one or both legs, which can cause most of the muscles in the body to contract at once. The results are unpredictable, but given the strength of the leg and back muscles can often send the victims flying across the room with no voluntary action on their part. Combined with the unexpected shock of an electrocution this feels as if you are flung, rather than flinging yourself.

A common side effect of being thrown across the room by an electric shock, apart from bruising and other injuries, is muscle sprain caused by the extreme muscle contractions. This can also damage joint and connective tissue.

Q I am new to HF and purchased the ARRL Amateur Radio Map of the World so I can have an idea of where to point my beam antenna for different places I want to contact. I would like to know exactly how to use it and the 0-360 degree part. I live in Homestead, Florida, about 25 miles south of Miami.

A The world map you have is centered on the geographical center of the US—Kansas. The numbers around the perimeter of the map can be used to point a beam. Your rotator control should have a compass-heading indicator of some sort. Just point the antenna at the number that appears on the map. For example, placing one finger at the center of the map and another on France, you will see that you are heading in a direction of 45 degrees. Rotate your antenna in this direction using the device on your controller.

Since you are not in Kansas, it is not perfectly accurate, but it will work well enough.

If you want the best accuracy, you need a beam-heading map centered on your location. You can print such a map at the following Web site: www. wm7d.net/azproj.shtml.

Q Harry, W2HML, asks, "I'm a fairly new ham, and would like some help regarding my transceiver. I have an old Yaesu FT-102, coupled to an MFJ-949E antenna tuner and a multiband dipole antenna.

"The instructions for tuning the transmitter indicate that the LOAD, DRIVE and PLATE controls should be tuned for a reading of 300 mA on the meter. At that point the instructions state that I should dip the meter reading with the PLATE control. This will tune the transmitter for 100 W output.

I have had no problem following the instructions for tuning, and I'm reading 100 W when tuning into the antenna tuner's dummy load. However, the tuner instructions say that I can only use a maximum of 30 W output when initially adjusting the tuner when it is connected to the antenna. Am I supposed to somehow 'detune' the transceiver to reduce its output after peaking it into the dummy load?"

A The answer to your problem is the transceiver DRIVE control. Tune your radio into the antenna tuner's dummy load as you describe. Now, adjust the DRIVE control counterclockwise until the antenna tuner meter reads 30 W. Stop transmitting, switch from the tuner dummy load to the antenna, start transmitting again and adjust your tuner. When you reach the lowest SWR, crank the DRIVE control back up to full output. During all these procedures, remember not to hold the key down for more that 10 seconds at a time—this may damage the finals. Do your tuning in short spurts.

Q I know that VOX is voice-operated switching, but what is "MOX"? I see this popping up in transceiver feature lists from time to time.

A MOX is manually operated switching. It is a front panel button that places the rig in the transmit mode. MOX is handy when you need to transmit, for antenna tuning purposes, for example, but don't have a mic or key connected to the transceiver.

Q I'm studying to upgrade my license and I am having difficulty with some of the terminology that keeps popping up. In particular, the abbreviation "IF." Can you help?

A In a *superheterodyne* receiver, the radio frequency (RF) signal picked up at the antenna must be converted to a lower frequency prior to demodulation. This conversion takes place in the mixer stage of the receiver when the RF signal is mixed with another signal generated by the local oscillator (LO). This mixing process produces sum and difference signal frequencies. The difference frequency is amplified and becomes the Intermediate Frequency, or IF (see **Figure 11.12**). The IF is usually high enough to still be considered RF, but it may be substantially lower than the signal at the antenna. For example, FM receivers commonly convert to an IF of 10.7 MHz. AM broadcast receivers often use an IF of 455 kHz. The exceptions are so-called "up conversion" receivers that use IFs that are *higher* than the highest received

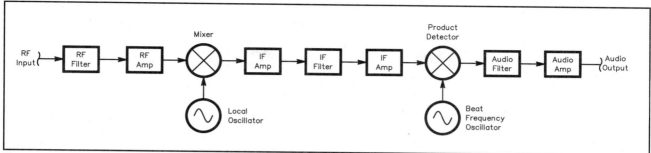

Figure 11.12—A basic block diagram of a superheterodyne receiver.

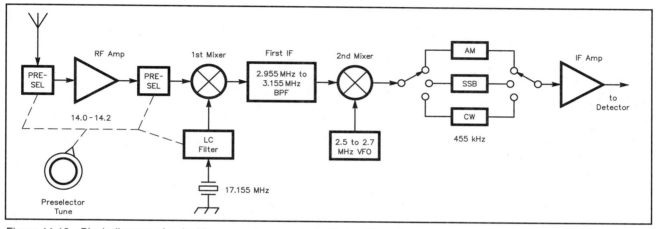

Figure 11.13—Block diagram of a double-conversion superhet with two IF sections.

signal frequency. To complicate matters further, superhet designs may also include more than one mixer/IF section (**Figure 11.13**).

It's interesting to note that in a *direct conversion* receiver the RF conversion takes place in one huge step—mixing the signal from the antenna with a local oscillator signal at nearly the same frequency. This puts the difference frequency in the audio range for immediate demodulation.

Q Doug Rambo, KA3KHZ, of Dover, Delaware, writes: Have there been any articles that you know of that look at RF Safety and EME stations? I am working on building a 144 MHz EME station (4 Yagis) and I can't find any "clear" information regarding general steps to follow for EME... i.e., antenna height with respect to neighboring residences (1-2 story). Any references you might be able to supply would be helpful.

A The requirements for an EME station are really no different than for any other station. Any of the methods used, ie "worst-case" analysis, use of antenna pattern, antenna modeling or field-strength measurement, for examples, can be used.

The problem is that the "worst-case" analysis gives some pretty dismal results. If I use the "University of Texas" Web-page calculator (one of the links from the ARRL site at **www.arrl.org/rfsafety**) and assume 1500 W CW at a 50% on/off operating time, over a 30 minute time period, this results in 300 W of average power. If I assume 20 dBi antenna gain, about what one would get from a 4-Yagi array using 17-element Yagi antennas, this would require 181.4 feet of distance between your antenna and any human exposure in the direction the antenna is pointed. This may work for some EME stations, but others might find some difficulty if they are pointed at a neighbor's house. (The FCC does permit amateurs to control their station operation, however, so if a ham determines that his or her operation exceeds the limits in a neighbor's house, not pointing the antenna at a neighbor's house if the neighbor is home is a possible solution.)

Fortunately, the University of Texas site gives a true "worst-case" analysis that assumes one is in the main beam of the antenna. This does not apply to all

EME stations, however, because the main beam of the antenna is not always pointed at the horizon—to the contrary, the antenna is pointed skyward more often than not.

The *EZNEC* (**www.eznec.com**) calculated free-space pattern of a 4×17-element Yagi array is shown in **Figure 11.14** (also available on *ARRLWeb*, **www. arrl.org/tis/info/2m4x17.jpg**). This pattern can be used to estimate the amount of power actually radiated toward any given point.

There are two factors that you may be able to consider. First, if the antenna is located high in the air, the downward angle of the radiated energy toward a neighbor's house is not in the main beam of the antenna. You would have to use a little trigonometry to calculate the angle for any given height and distance, or draw it all out and use a protractor to measure the angle. As a real simple example, if the antenna is 70 feet in the air and it is 60 feet from a neighbor's one-story house with a first floor 10 feet above the ground, the angle downward is 45 degrees. If you look at the pattern, the pattern is way down at that angle, into the sidelobes. Because we are really in the near-field region, let's be conservative

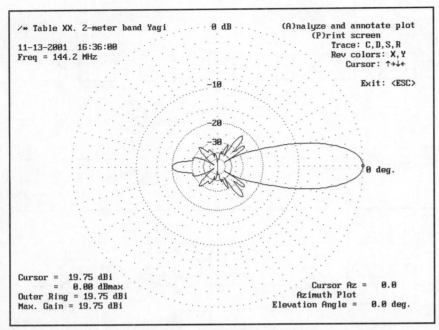

```
/* Table XX. 2-meter band Yagi      0 dB        (A)nalyze and annotate plot
                                                 (P)rint screen
   11-13-2001  16:36:00                           Trace: C,D,S,R
   Freq = 144.2 MHz                             Rev colors: X,Y
                                                    Cursor: ↑→↓←

                                                    Exit: <ESC>




                                                            0 deg.




   Cursor =  19.75 dBi
          =   0.00 dBmax                       Cursor Az =    0.0
   Outer Ring = 19.75 dBi                      Azimuth Plot
   Max. Gain = 19.75 dBi                Elevation Angle =    0.0 deg.
```

Figure 11.14—Free-space pattern of a 4×17-element Yagi array, as calculated by *EZNEC*.

and assume that no sidelobe will be down more than 20 dB from the main beam of the antenna. In this case, if the antenna is pointed right at the horizon, right at your neighbor's house, the gain at the downward angle of 45 degrees is 0 dBi (or less). If we then run that through the RF calculator, the estimate is that the exposure needs to be 18.1 feet away from the antenna, diagonally. The antenna is 60 feet in the air, so the EME station evaluation for this hypothetical station is over.

Unfortunately, as the antenna is lower than 60 feet, the angle decreases, so the amount of energy directed downward goes up. The method still applies, but if the antenna is 25 feet in the air, 60 feet from a neighbor's one story house, the angle becomes −12.25 degrees, and the antenna gain at that angle is still a respectable 15 dBi. This requires a "worst-case" calculated diagonal distance to the antenna of 100 feet, not quite a "pass" if this hypothetical antenna is pointed at the horizon.

Even in that case, though, you can consider the amount of time that the antenna is actually pointed at the horizon. If you transmit for 15 minutes, then increase the elevation angle of this 35-foot high antenna to 10 degrees above the horizon to track the moon, the antenna gain for the next 15 minutes is back at 0 dBi (using the pattern and the protractor). The average power really is now just over 150 W (300 W average power, for 15 minutes, then about 30 W EIRP for the next 15 minutes). The required dis-

tance is now a diagonal distance of 72 feet—enough to "pass" for the antenna 25 feet in the air.

In the near-field of an antenna, the fields are almost always less than the far-field formula used to make the above calculation. You can take advantage of this by using the near-field analysis of *EZNEC*, if you model your antenna accurately. I used the model I put at **www.arrl.org/tis/info/2m4x17.zip** and used *EZNEC* to do a near-field calculation. *EZNEC* gives the good news—if the antenna is 35 feet in the air, pointed at the horizon, and a neighbor's house is 10 feet above the ground, the transmitter is 1500 W EME CW (300 W average power), in the direction the antenna is pointed, the electric and magnetic fields never exceed the permitted exposure levels at any point below the antenna, 10 feet or less above ground.

Now, there are a lot of variables here, and my sample calculation is intended only as an example (although if it applies to your station, and you "pass," your evaluation is over.

As I have said in many of my talks about RF exposure, the present rules really are not a major burden for Amateur Radio. It took me about an hour to run through all of the various calculations for the two hypothetical EME stations I posed here, and even with 1500 W EME pointed right at a neighbor's house, the 35- and 60-foot high antenna/station combinations were below the required exposure limits. For most hams, the simple "worst-case" calculations suffice, but for the high-power, high-gain EME station, the more accurate *EZNEC* calculation is probably a better choice.

Q As a new ham I am a little confused about the concept of "phase." Can you enlighten me?

A When tracing a sine-wave curve of an ac voltage or current, the horizontal axis represents time. We call this the *time domain* of the sine wave. Events to the right take place later; events to the left occur earlier. Although time is measurable in parts of a second, it is more convenient to treat each cycle as a complete time unit that we divide into 360°. The conventional starting point for counting degrees is the zero point as the voltage or current begins the positive half cycle. The essential elements of an ac cycle appear in Figure 11.15.

The advantage of treating the ac cycle in this way is that many calculations and measurements can be taken and recorded in a manner that is independent of frequency. The positive peak voltage or current occurs at 90° along the cycle. Relative to the starting point, 90° is the *phase* of the ac at that point. Thus, a complete description of an ac voltage or current involves reference to three properties: frequency, amplitude and phase.

Phase relationships also permit the

Figure 11.15—An ac cycle is divided into 360° to measure phase.

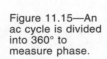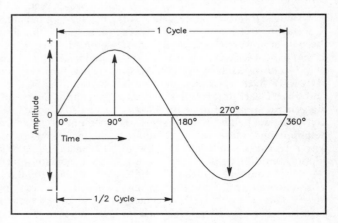

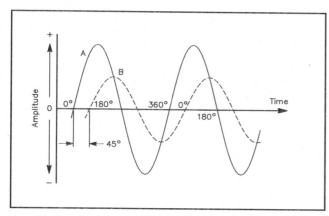

Figure 11.16— When two waves of the same frequency start their cycles at slightly different times, the time difference or phase difference is measured in degrees. In this drawing, wave B starts 45° (one-eighth cycle) later than wave A, and so lags 45° behind A.

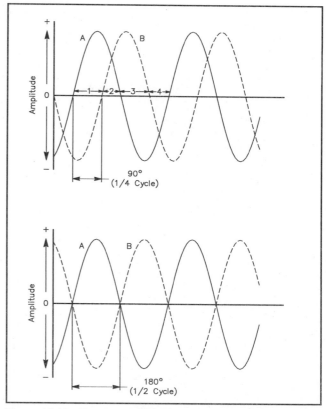

Figure 11.17—Two important special cases of phase difference: In the upper drawing, the phase difference between A and B is 90°; in the lower drawing, the phase difference is 180°.

comparison of two ac voltages or currents at the same frequency, as **Figure 11.16** demonstrates. Since B crosses the zero point in the positive direction after A has already done so, there is a *phase difference* between the two waves. In the example, B *lags* A by 45°, or A *leads* B by 45°. If A and B occur in the same circuit, their composite waveform will also be a sine wave at an intermediate phase angle relative to each. Adding any number of sine waves of the same frequency always results in a sine wave at that frequency.

Figure 11.16 might equally apply to a voltage and a current measured in the same ac circuit. Either A or B might represent the voltage; that is, in some instances voltage will lead the current and in others voltage will lag the current.

Two important special cases appear in **Figure 11.17**. In Part A, line B lags 90° behind line A. Its cycle begins exactly one quarter cycle later than the A cycle. When one wave is passing through zero, the other just reaches its maximum value.

In Part B, lines A and B are 180° *out of phase*. In this case, it does not matter which one is considered to lead or lag. Line B is always positive while line A is negative, and vice versa. By properly adjusting the amplitudes of two signals 180° out of phase and combining them, they can be made to cancel each other out completely.

CHAPTER 12

Interference (RFI/EMI)

A COMPUTER INTERFERENCE CURE

◊ Those small EMI filters with telephone connectors (**Figure 12.1**) are intended to keep interference from getting into telephones, but they have another use! They are excellent for keeping computer interference from getting into the ham shack. I discovered that the majority of interference from my computer was being radiated from the telephone line attached to the modem. I placed one of the filters on the phone line where it plugs into the modem, and presto, ham shack interference from the computer was virtually eliminated.—*Dick Wheelock, AA7NI, 177 Brook Dr, Chehalis, WA 98532;* **aa7ni@i-link-2.net**

Figure 12.1—A telephone common-mode RFI filter can protect a telephone from RF, but it can also block computer RFI that would radiate from the telephone line connected to a modem. Modular filters are convenient, but homebrew common-mode chokes work too.

AUDIO RFI AND THE TS-850

◊ After upgrading to the Kenwood TS-850, I began to experience RF feedback in my microphone audio. Several hours of trial and elimination indicated the problem was in the Heil Pro headset. A quick call to Heil Sound had Donna talking me through the "usual" fixes for the problem. After the "usual" fixes were unsuccessful, Bob Heil came on the line. Bob related a problem with a floating ground that appears in many TS-450 and TS-850 radios. Since the problem did not happen with another desk mic that has a **HI/LO** impedance switch, I decided to try isolating the Heil Pro microphone from the rig input with a 1:1 audio transformer (RadioShack 273-1374 or equivalent, see **Figure 12.2**).

To avoid cutting the headset cables, I used 3.5-mm mono jack and plug set to insert the transformer in the line. The worst part was trying to decide how to package the unit. While looking around my shack, I noticed an old 35-mm film container. The shielded cables enter the container through holes drilled in each end. Inside, they are soldered the leads to the 1:1 transformer (see **Figure 12.3**). Hoping for the best, I fired up the rig and amplifier, then called "CQ." I listened to

the monitor with an amazed look on my face (at least that's what my wife called it!). The audio is clear, with no trace of RF. If you experience a similar problem, give this a try!—*Tom Branch, K4NR, 8559 Athenian, Universal City, TX 71848;* **k4nr@arrl.net.**

Figure 12.2—A 1:1 audio transformer cures audio RFI in a TS-850. See text for details.

Figure 12.3—K4NR housed the isolation transformer in a film can with the connections made through two-conductor plugs and jacks on "pigtails."

The Doctor is IN

Q Erik Iddings, KF4KRK, asks, "I'm having problems with RFI to my neighbor's (and my own) telephone. One neighbor picked me up on a 900-MHz cordless phone. She said she could not understand anything but could tell I was on the air. My mother has picked me up on a corded telephone, again nothing legible. And my other neighbor picks me up on his 49-MHz cordless.

"I operate 6-meter SSB using an ICOM IC-706 MkII with 100 W PEP. My radio and tuner are properly grounded. I even made up a coax balun at the shack entry point hoping that would solve the problem. The interference is still there.

"One of my fellow ARES members is an engineer with the telephone company. I called her the other day and told her about the problem. She had the customer service manager and a line technician come out and install an RF suppresser on one neighbor's incoming line. That didn't work.

"I'm about to go out of my mind trying to figure this out. Unless I can get this RFI problem resolved, it looks like I'm going to have to give up operating on 6 meters unless all the neighbors are at work!"

A Start with the premise that the FCC rules require that spurious emissions (signals outside the ham bands) not cause interference with other radio services. This is your sole regulatory responsibility.

Now, those 900 MHz and 49 MHz cordless phones are regulated by Part 15. Part 15 says that these devices must not cause harmful interference and are *not* protected from interference from licensed users. The FCC's material on interference also adds that non-radio devices (telephones, alarm systems, etc) that experience interference are "improperly functioning" as radio receivers. Although you may want to help your neighbors resolve these problems, the rules may help you put that into perspective. For RFI that is not caused by a rules violation, your help is simply neighborly and you should see yourself as a *locator* of solutions, not a provider of solutions.

For general info about RFI, info for your neighbor, info on telephone interference, info on Part 15, see **www.arrl.org/tis/** and follow the TISPAGES and RFI links.

I will add that you can sometimes correct problems with cordless phones by filtering the base unit. Get a RadioShack telephone interference filter for the line and a Palomar F-140-43 ferrite core for the power supply lead (wind about 5 turns or so). If this doesn't work, it is the RF end of the phone being overloaded. For the 49 MHz phone, it is rare that base-unit filtering works to suppress interference from a 6-meter signal. The wireless phones or their owner's manuals should have a label that indicates that they are not protected from interference.

Q Michael, KD5BBC, asks, "I live in a second-floor apartment, so attaching a ground wire to a ground rod is out of the question. Since I can't connect to a ground rod, should I still connect the grounds of all of my equipment together? I don't seem to have a problem with RF feedback in the shack, and transmitting on 40 through 10 meters with 100 W doesn't seem to affect either my computer on the other side of the room or my TV in the next room. I have what appears to be an active ground on the 3-plug electrical line (according to the tester I bought at RadioShack). Should I try to ground to that, or would that also be asking for problems?"

A Yes, absolutely connect all the equipment in the shack together and then to the ground on the wall socket. A good way to accomplish this is to check that the screw holding the cover in place is grounded. You can do this by first turning off the circuit breaker to the plug and measuring between the screw and the ground plug with an ohmmeter. Then strip the braid off some old coax to make a nice flexible ground strap between your station and the screw. That takes care of the safety ground. You'll still need an RF ground, which often takes the form of a counterpoise wire.

Also, check out "Antennas and Grounds for Apartments" on the TIS Web page at: **www.arrl.org/tis/** under **Antennas/Grounding**.

Q Ron, N9RC, asks, "I have a 1994 RCA 35-inch console TV fed by cable. Twice this year I have been transmitting at the full legal limit and my TV set has 'popped off.' According to my TV repairman, the horizontal circuit has 'shorted.' (Apparently the horizontal transformer failed.) He says he has seen this happen in another case when a ham was transmitting at the house.

"This costs $400 per incident! I never had the problem until this year, but we have added a few VCR cables that I have now belatedly removed. I'll be adding common mode chokes to these cables and elsewhere. I can't afford for this to keep happening! Is there a fix?"

A Ouch! This sort of problem is rare, but it can happen. RF energy is usually picked up on any wiring connected to the TV (TV sets do not make good antennas, but wires do), then gets conducted onto the chassis of the TV, into its power supply and into its circuitry. In this case, it looks like the horizontal circuitry is particularly sensitive. There are a few things I'd suggest, although to find out if they work does entail some degree of risk.

First, the greater the separation between your transmit antenna and the TV *and* any wires connected to it (ie, ac, cable, antenna, speaker, etc.), the lower the RF energy will be. So, raising the height of your antenna or locating it farther away from the house could be helpful. In this case, do not use end-fed wires—only antennas fed with coaxial cable. If you have any problems with RF in the shack, correct the underlying transmit antenna problem.

Adding common-mode chokes to all of the wires connected to the TV may also help keep the RF energy from getting into the set. You can make a common-mode choke with an F-240-43 ferrite core, wrapping about 10 turns of wire (coax, speaker, etc.) onto the core, just where it enters the TV set. For smaller wires, you can use an F-140-43 size core. You will have to treat the cable or antenna lead, the ac wiring and anything else connected to the TV. You may also want to add an ac line filter to the TV.

Some companies have developed service bulletins to deal with RFI problems, although this is generally the exception. Contact RCA and see if they have any info for you.

Q Les, KL7J, asks, "Do you have any suggestions for an inexpensive AM receiver I could use to locate power line noise sources?"

A For close-in tracking (*DFing*) of a wideband noise source, you need a receiver that is fairly high in frequency. The AM aircraft band at 120 MHz works well and inexpensive receivers can be found that cover it. Many of the H-Ts on the market today also include AM reception in that frequency range, so if you know someone who has bought an H-T in the last couple of years, ask them if it has AM aircraft and if they would be willing to help you track down the problem.

Quite a few portable shortwave receivers also have AM airband reception. Another alternative is a couple of portable receivers from Radio Shack that feature AM aircraft reception. Model 12-456 retails at $35 and model 12-615 (handheld) sells for $25. Although these receivers do not have coax connections, you can still use them by connecting the center conductor of the coax from your DFing antenna to the existing antenna with a clip lead. Connect the shield of the coax to a case screw. The mismatch will give you some attenuation, but it will be a useful setup nonetheless.

You can find more information on hunting down power line RFI on the ARRL Web site at: **www.arrl.org/tis/ info/rfi-elec.html**. Also, check out "A Line Noise 'Sniffer' That Works" by William Leavitt, W3AZ, in the September 1992 *QST*. If you don't have the issue you can get a photocopy of the article for $3 ($5 for nonmembers) by contacting the ARRL Technical Secretary at 860-594-0278; **reprints@arrl.org**.

Q Colin, VE1CSM, asks, "I've built a computer interface for use with my Kenwood transceiver. The interface works, but it seems to be generating interference. Can you help?"

A Computer interfaces and their connecting cables are all potential sources of interference, both in terms of RF radiated from the cable and in terms of RF feedback into the devices the cables are connected to.

The fix for both involves two parts: proper shielding and common-mode noise suppression via the use of ferrites. If you haven't put the interface into a metal box, that's the first thing you want to do. Second is that you would want to use a cable where all the signal-carrying conductors are enclosed in a foil (preferably) or high-density braid shield. A stranded braid wound around the outside of the other wires is not sufficient.

Even with all that, you may still have problems. The next step is the judicious application of Type 43 ferrite cores. To suppress *common-mode* signals (where the interfering signal is being picked up by the whole cable), you would take a suitable-size ferrite and wrap a number of turns of the cable around it. Donut-shaped (toroid) cores are best in that they couple the energy back into the core, whereas rods tend to "leak" a little at the ends. As far as the number of turns goes, more is generally better, but there is a limit. If you wrap three turns around the

ferrite and it helps, that's great, but if it doesn't, it usually means you need more turns. However, if you get a dozen turns around the ferrite and it doesn't help, chances are two dozen turns won't be any better.

Q Arnold, AA3HO, asks, "I have a problem when I transmit on HF. When my wife is on the Web my transmissions apparently garble the incoming and outgoing data, preventing her from reaching her desired sites. The computer does *not* lock up, and the dial-up connection isn't lost. What tips can you give me to locate and fix the problem?"

A There is a whole chapter in the *ARRL RFI Book* (**www.arrl.org/catalog/ 6834/**) on computers—I can't reproduce it all for you here. It covers interference both ways—to and from computers.

Here is a plan of action. The book points out that many of the same fixes for RFI *to* computers are those for RFI *from* computers. These may be found in an article on the TIS Web site: **www.arrl. org/tis/**. Click on RFI/EMI in the menu, then choose "Computer Interference." Try those fixes.

Also, from personal experience, make sure *everything* is grounded. All of your ham equipment should be grounded together. Ground your computer; a strap made from discarded coax cable shield running from a screw on the computer's metal case to ground works nicely. A good ground point for the computer is the little screw on the cover plate of your wall power socket. Test this by shutting off the circuit breaker to that plug and use an ohmmeter between the screw and the ground wire hole. At the very least, make sure your PC is attached to your *station* ground.

Incidentally, the problem may not be the computer at all and may be your external modem, if that's what you use. Use the same techniques on it if possible.

Finally, make sure you have no RF coming back into the shack from the antenna. If, per chance, you are using an end fed random or long wire antenna, you may have to try another type. For balanced antennas, such as dipoles, consider adding a 1:1 balun at the feed point.

Q Brent, AB5UM, asks, "In my Jeep Cherokee I have my ICOM IC-706 transceiver in the back and my remote control head up front at the driver's seat. I was getting RFI on almost all bands, which caused my digital display on the remote head to go crazy. Installing the entire radio up front is not an option. I wrapped the

separation cable in aluminum foil and grounded it. That cured the problem except for the 10-meter band. Can you suggest anything else?"

A The aluminum foil shield may not be as effective on 10 meters as it is on other bands. Perhaps you could obtain some 1-inch copper braid. Most copper braid is actually hollow, so if you separate it, you may be able to slip the cable through it. Experiment with grounding it at either end, or both.

I also suggest you try a ferrite toroid. Use an FT-240-43 and get three turns of the cable onto the core. This should be enough to help on 10 meters.

Other than that, you may need to do a bit of sniffing around the vehicle to find the specific source of noise. A 1-inch loop at the end of a piece of coax, connected to your radio, may help. Do not get the loop anywhere near the ignition wiring; a high-voltage spike can be induced into the loop, possibly causing damage to your radio. Once you find the hot spots, the above hints, coupled with keeping the control cable away from the hot spots, may help.

Q Bob, K4RFK, asks, "I live in Cape Coral, Florida. The local radio station, WINK-WNOG, transmitting on 1200 kHz AM, can be heard on my transceiver on several HF bands. I called the station and informed them of the situation and they said it was my problem. Can you help?"

A The type of interference you describe can come from several possible sources. The first could be the broadcast transmitter. Their transmitter could be transmitting some signals other than the one they are licensed to use. These signals are usually exact multiples (2.4 MHz, 3.6 MHz, etc.) of the transmitting frequency, but modern transmitters can also transmit other signals due to the internal mixing processes. These unwanted signals are collectively called *spurious emissions*, or simply *spurs*.

Much like the regulations that govern the Amateur Radio Service, there are stringent FCC regs governing the levels of broadcast spurs. Even if the spurs are below the FCC limits, however, the regulations require that radiated signals not cause harmful interference. The FCC, however, has stated that simple *reception* of a spurious emission does not constitute harmful interference. The signal is only considered "harmful" if it causes repeated disruptions of communication.

It is also possible that the problem is in your station receiver. A very strong signal can overload a receiver, resulting in spurious responses. These can range from image responses, to receiver responses, to various internal spurious signals in your receiver's local oscillator or phase-lock-loop circuitry. There are a few things you can try to diagnose whether this may be occurring. The easiest is to try an entirely different receiver. Its internal design will be different than the receiver on which you are hearing signals, so it will have a different set of spurious responses. It is best to use a receiver built by a different manufacturer for this test. If the interfering signals disappear, then you clearly have a problem.

If you are unable to use a different receiver, there are some tests you can try that may help diagnose the problem. Switch in your receiver's attenuator. If you select a 10-dB attenuator and the unwanted signal drops by significantly more than 10 dB, it is a clear indication that the signal is an unwanted receiver spurious response. Also, note how the receiver tunes in the unwanted signals when in the CW or SSB mode. If the tuning seems "fast," meaning that the beat note of the carrier seems to be changing in pitch at a faster rate than normal as you tune across it, this also is a clear indication that a receiver spurious response is the cause of the interfering signals.

Not all receiver responses will necessarily be found with the above tests. In that case, you may want to try a filter on the receiver to eliminate the broadcast spurs. You can use the search engine at **www.arrl.org/tis/tisfind.html** to search the database for companies that sell broadcast band filters.

Q Ron, WB4GWA, asks, "I have what seems to be an incurable noise problem in my Chevy Blazer. My HF mobile antenna mount is bolted and grounded into the frame. I run all power cables as suggested in the *ARRL RFI Book*. I have tapped the dc power at the battery. Despite all this, I still get a huge amount of noise. When the ignition switch is off, my transceiver S meter is at zero and when the switch is on I still enjoy clear reception. When I start the Blazer, however, I get so much ignition noise that the blanker will not take it out. When I look at the S-meter it reads S9. Can you help?"

A You have the negative power wire going to the battery, right? Assuming so, when you turn the ignition switch to **RUN** without starting the car, do you hear the noise for a few seconds with the ignition in the **RUN** position, but with the engine not running? If you hear noise for the first few seconds, it is probably coming from the fuel pump and you should focus your suppression effort there.

But if you do not hear the noise at all

until the engine is actually started, we need to follow a different path. If you remove the antenna mast from the mobile mount, does all the noise go away? If it does, no noise is being coupled through the power wiring—it is being radiated directly to the antenna. Look under the hood with the engine running at night, or in a darkened garage. Do you see any sparking from the ignition system? Sparking would indicate a poor connection that's generating the noise. If you don't see sparks, it's likely that the noise is ignition radiation.

Try a new set of plugs and wires, but not the factory type. Take a portable volt-ohm meter (VOM) to the auto parts store and find plugs and wires that measure at 5 kW or more each. Measure the wires from one end to the other, the plugs from the top post to the center electrode.

By the way, if you can look at your transceiver's receive audio with a scope, you may pick up a few more clues. In general, computer noise may appear as an overmodulated carrier; ignition noise looks like individual pulse bursts (37 Hz for a 6-cylinder engine at idle); motor noise appears as overlapping pulses.

Q I recently received an "Atomic Clock with Wireless Temperature," a WWVB receiver clock purchased at Wal-Mart. The wireless temperature sensing unit sends its signal at 433 MHz. While I haven't yet heard it, my son, N1TUI, has picked it up on his ham equipment. The manual states that it has a maximum transmitting range of 82 feet. The box is marked: "Distributed by SWC, Bentonville AR 72716. Made in China"

While this unit is pretty low powered it seems as though the Chinese have taken to the ham bands for yet another product. I paid attention to this as I am just starting in on satellite work.

I don't know if "flea" power gets an exemption to FCC Registration but there is no mention of it in the manual.

A ARRL has received a number of reports about devices that operate near 433-434 MHz. This is a common frequency internationally for unlicensed devices. In the US, such devices can be authorized under Part 15 of the FCC rules. Most are authorized as "periodic emitters" under Section 15.231. This rule permits field strengths that are generally useful for up to about 300 feet, but limits the transmissions to short bursts, with longer quiet periods in between.

To be legal in the US, the device needs to be Certificated under FCC rules. If so, the manufacturer is required to put an FCC ID number somewhere on the unit,

or in the operator's manual. If the device has been certificated, it can be marketed in the United States.

In addition to the manufacturer's meeting the radiated emissions limits and certification requirements, the operators of unlicensed devices are required to operate them in such a way that they do not cause harmful interference to other radio services. Much the way Amateur Radio is secondary to commercial users on 30 meters and to government operation on 70 centimeters, Part 15 devices are secondary to Amateur Radio, subject to the requirement that they not cause harmful interference.

Although your son may very well be able to hear the signal in the 70 cm band, merely hearing a Part 15 device in "our" bands is not harmful interference. In this case, the rules define harmful interference as the repeated interruption of a radiocommunications service. It is much like our use of 30 meters. The commercial operators sometimes hear amateur stations in "their" bands, but unless our operation causes them interference, it is okay for us to be there. We certainly wouldn't think it fair if they said that we had to get out of their bands because they sometimes hear us on channels they are not using.

Under the rules, Part 15 devices can, if certificated, legally use nearly any frequency. The real issue then becomes one of harmful interference. For more information about Part 15 and Amateur Radio, see: **www.arrl.org/tis/info/part15.html.**

Q Jon Maguire, W1MNK, writes: I've got a question regarding the 15.25 kHz TV horizontal sync pulses. I can receive them (I think that's what I'm hearing) on many frequencies and with multiple receivers (Yaesu FT-847, ICOM IC-756PRO, Ten-Tec Jupiter and Kachina 505DSP. My antenna is a Cushcraft R5 vertical, mounted at about 6 feet above ground on a steel mast. The signals have the characteristic raspy sounds of H sync. The nearest TV in my home is about 15 feet away, but I can hear the pulses with all the TVs and computers shut down (which means they are probably coming from the neighbors' houses, which are 30 feet away on either side). I was wondering if you have any ideas.

A If you are hearing buzzy signals every 15.75 kHz on HF, you are listening to the harmonics of the horizontal circuitry in TV sets. This is usually radiated by the TV's antenna/cable system or its connection to the ac line.

If it is an antenna-connected TV, try a high-pass filter on the antenna lead. This will prevent the HF signals from getting to the TV antenna, where they can be radiated. You should also try a common-mode choke on the TV's feed line. Wrap about 10 turns of the line onto a Palomar F-240-43 ferrite core. You need a number of turns onto a suitable ferrite material to expect any common-mode suppression at HF. Try a similar choke on the TV's ac line cord. In extreme cases, you may need a "brute-force" type ac line filter, similar to the RadioShack catalog #15-1111. Note that this is *not* the same as a surge filter.

Q Craig Stadler, KG4EOM, writes: My new Ford F150 is producing so much static in my Yaesu FT-100 it makes it unusable. I used it in a Dodge diesel with no problems. Is there any way to stop the problem?

A Unfortunately, there are a number of different problems that can create what most hams call "ignition noise." There are a number of reasons for this: modern vehicles need to meet all sorts of regulatory objectives with respect to pollution, fuel economy and vehicle safety. One way that manufacturers have met those guidelines is to make improvements to the ignition systems of vehicles. They have done things such as increasing the voltage to the spark plugs and decreasing the rise time of the ignition pulses. You guessed it—both of those "improvements" increase ignition noise. In today's vehicles, the old coil-distributor are gone, with the vehicle's electronic control module (ECM) sending signals to high-voltage modules at each plug. The backyard mechanic of yore would scarcely recognize some of today's vehicles.

And, of course, the problem could extend past "ignition noise." Some fuel injectors, also controlled by the ECM, can make the same pop-pop sound at low speeds, changing to a whine at higher speeds, that is characteristic of ignition noise. Today's alternators often have to deliver much higher current than older models, increasing their noise-generating potential.

Ed Hare, W1RFI, recently visited the EMC laboratories at Chrysler, General Motors and Ford in Detroit. At one of the Labs, he was shown a test fixture that contained the vehicle wiring and electronics, all laid out on a large table. In that vehicle, there were over 30 electronic modules, and the EMC engineer giving him the tour told him that some vehicles have over 60 such modules—some of them containing several ICs. There is simply no way that such a vehicle can be as quiet as Ed's 1978 GMC pickup (nicknamed the Deathmobile by *QST* QRP columnist Rich Arland, K7SZ).

Add to the mix some of the traditional noise sources, such as the numerous electric motors in today's vehicles, and you have an interference potential that is much higher that even a few years ago.

You didn't mention what the noise sounds like. One "classic" problem in today's vehicles comes from the in-tank fuel pump used in many cars today. Ford has recognized this problem and has published a Technical Service Bulletin to describe how to install a filter in the tank.

ARRL has created or identified a number of Web pages that may help you. Start with *RFI—Automotive*: **www.arrl.org/tis/info/rficar.html**. This is where you'll find the automotive RFI "home page."

Other pages that may help are:
Automotive Electric Motor and Fuel Pump Noise: **www.arrl.org/tis/info/fuel.html**. How to diagnose and cure noise from fuel pumps and other electric motors. This includes a reprint of the information in the Ford TSB on the subject.
Automotive Interference Problems: What the Manufacturers Say—**www.arrl.org/tis/info/carproblems.html**. This page gives the RFI policy statements of vehicle manufacturers.
Lab Notes—Mobile Installations and Electromagnetic Compatibility—**www.arrl.org/tis/info/pdf/39574.pdf**. Some general guidelines on various automotive RFI problems.
Off-site Web links:
NOISE and How to KILL It—**www.primenet.com/~nx7u/mobile/noise.html**. More information on Ford fuel pump noise solutions.
Engine Noises—**www.arrl.org/tis/**. This section is devoted to helping you diagnose engine and ambient noises.
HF Mobile's Home On the Web—**www.mindspring.com/~nx7u/mobile/noise.htm**. General information on automotive noise.
Ford Explorer Radio Frequency Interference—**www.4x4central.com/tips.htm#rfi**. Still more information on Ford fuel pump noise solutions.
Radio Interference to/from two-way radio receivers.—**dodgeram.com/technical/tsb96/08_30_96.HTM**. Models: Dodge 1995-1997 BR Ram Truck.
Radio Telephone / Mobile Radio Installation Guidelines—**service.gm.com/techlineinfo/radio.html**. GMNA Engineering Centers General Motors Corporation installation guidelines.

Q Bill Wilson, W5IKB, asks, "Recently I have been bothered with HF interference that appears to be coming from a new satellite dish that my neighbor has just installed on his chimney. It was on a small slab on the ground originally and gave no trouble. The dish is now about 20 feet in the air and about 30 feet from the end of my 40-meter dipole and 60 feet from my beam. The resulting interference is especially intense between 1 and 11 MHz. Any ideas?"

A My guess is that the dish's downconverter is using a switch-mode power supply and that it is generating the usual switch-mode interference. This is often somewhat tunable, perhaps with broadband noise that varies regularly across the band, every 25 kHz or so, to a very uniform broadband noise that tapers off slowly in frequency.

The diagnostic, if your neighbor would allow it, would be to unplug the downconverter and see if the noise goes away.

If it is the downconverter, you may be able to filter it. First, try a common-mode choke on the power connection and on the coax going in and out of the unit. You usually need to use an F-240-43 core. To suppress HF, you usually need about 10 turns of wire, so those little clamp-on beads won't work. In some cases, you may need to use a "brute-force" type ac-line filter. The RadioShack catalog #15-1111 filter will work. Do keep in mind that surge suppressors are not filters, so make sure you use a suitable filter.

FCC Part 15 rules put the burden of cleaning up the problem on the operator of the device. This would either be your neighbor, if he owns the equipment, or the satellite company, if it is rented. Unfortunately, it is sometimes very difficult to persuade a neighbor, or even the satellite provider, that a satellite receiving system is being operated in violation of federal law.

Q Ken Pendarvis, AD6KA, has an RFI gremlin. "I want to increase the audio output of a homebrew 20-meter QRP SSB rig. I built a 7-W amplifier, which works great on receive, but when I try to transmit, I get distorted transmit audio in the speaker. This is only a 3-W transmitter and I can't figure out how to cure the problem. Would shielded cables like RG-174 coax help? What about "bypass" capacitors? I'd like to have both pieces of equipment in a single enclosure."

A What you probably have is RF pickup in the audio amplifier kit on either the power supply leads or the audio input leads. The first step is to shield both the audio amplifier and the transceiver if they're not already shielded. To prevent RF pickup, RG-174 will also work fine for both power and audio cables. Bypass caps are just disk ceramic capacitors of a value of 0.01 to 0.1 µF. They are typically connected at the affected equipment between the power supply lead and the chassis so as to "bypass" the RF energy to ground. Do not use bypass capacitors on the amplifier output as that can cause instability—use ferrite beads or cores instead. If you do place both pieces of equipment in a single enclosure, make sure the audio amplifier is not located near the RF output section of the transceiver. If you can, place a metal shield between the two assemblies.

Q John Gregson, KL1AS, is having trouble with a TV: I just had to have my TV repaired and I was told by the repair facility the problems were caused when I transmitted. I live in a condo and my antenna is on the balcony just outside the living room where the television is located. How far should my antennas be from the TV? Can filters eliminate the risks of damaging other electronic equipment when transmitting?

A Unfortunately, there is no definite answer about antenna placement. It is most unusual, but not impossible, to cause physical damage to the circuitry in the TV unless maybe you are running a legal-limit amplifier. Did you notice any interference effects prior to the TV failure? RF overload to consumer electronics equipment is normally a result of the wires associated with the device acting as antennas. It gets worse if the length of the wire approaches that of a resonant antenna. There is really no way you can filter the output of your transmitter if it is getting directly into the device, since the device is acting improperly as a receiver of those frequencies.

The best approach to reducing unwanted RF pickup is to install some common-mode chokes on ALL the wires connected to the device you are concerned with. This includes power cords, speaker leads, interface cables and antenna cables. They will usually significantly reduce the amount of RF received. For some more information on common-mode chokes, take a look at **www.arrl. org/tis/info/HTML/catvi/index.html**.

Q Fill Nutter, W8FIL, writes: I'm planning to move to a house within 1 mile of the Charleston, West Virginia NOAA Doppler radar station. The radome overlooks the area where I will be installing antennas for HF, VHF and UHF. Will my proximity to the radar cause any problems with my ham operations?

A It is possible for radar to cause interference to Amateur Radio, particularly to broadband receivers that offer little immunity from out-of-band signals. The NOAA sites are distributed throughout the country and since many of our allocations are shared, there is no guarantee that radar signals will even be out of band—and in-band interference can be tough to deal with.

It may be worthwhile to inquire about what frequencies are in use—keeping in mind they may change as technology improves. Putting narrow-band filters in front of VHF, UHF and microwave receivers significantly improves performance at locations with strong transmitters. One source for these filters is DCI Digital Communications Inc, Box 293, Hummingbird Bay, White City, SK S0G 5B0, Canada, 306-781-4451, **dci@ dci.ca**, **www.dci.ca/**. You may need to homebrew suitable filters. One possibility is a helical filter. A good article to read is "A Low-Cost 222-MHz Helical Band-Pass Filter" by W1VT in the May 2001 issue of *QEX*.

Q Frank Connelly, W7ND, of Seattle, Washington writes: last night I was on 20 meters running pretty high power. My neighbors called me and told me their TV set went "extra nuts." The picture blacked out from the interference, but after a couple of minutes the screen started shrinking as if the vertical/horizontal outputs were decreasing. Eventually the set turned off and now won't turn back on. In section 6 of the *ARRL RFI Book* "over voltage sense circuitry" is discussed that will trip if the TV power supply voltages exceed a set limit. Does this sound to you like what happened?

A It sounds like you may be experiencing the relatively rare nightmare of having had a neighbor's piece of equipment fail in the presence of strong RF. What you describe could be caused by two factors: RF getting into the set's power supply, changing a voltage inside the TV, or RF getting into the CRT's high-voltage regulator, causing the picture-tube high voltage to go up. Either of these could have the effect of making the picture appear smaller on the screen. Unfortunately, this may have caused permanent damage to the TV if it won't return to normal when you are not transmitting. This is a case of plain old fundamental overload and the FCC would not expect you to fix the neighbor's TV. Your neighbor will probably see it differently, though.

The problem you describe is not caused by RF getting into the tuner, so a high-pass filter probably won't help. The Doctor suggests common-mode chokes on the TV feed line and ac line cord, and especially if the power supply is involved, a brute-force ac-line filter. Generally, an F-240-43 ferrite core is best. The little "clamp-on" ferrites don't usually have enough inductance to function well as chokes on HF. See **www.arrl. org/tis/tisfind.html** to look up ferrite and ac-filter suppliers.

Q Rich Myers, KC0MFR, of Lakewood, Colorado, also has RFI troubles. "I have a dipole mounted on top of my house—about 10 feet above the ridge—for the 20 and 40 meter bands. The dipole is about 18 feet from a small parabolic dish for my wife's

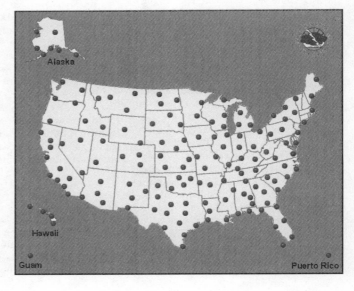

A map of NOAA weather radar sites throughout the US.

TV satellite system. When using CW on the 40 meter band, the TV picture completely disappears. Installing high-pass filters on the video cables or between the dish and the TV also causes the picture to disappear. Installing a low-pass filter on my rig's output or winding my cables on toroids have had no effect. Any advice would be appreciated."

A In fact, those filters may be working just the way they were designed. The problem is most likely a case of simply overloading the receiver because the signal is being picked up improperly. All the cables associated with the affected device can act as antennas and when that happens, the RF is picked up and conducted into the device, where it is detected and causes all sorts of mischief. Tuning the antenna, adding filters, and so on, really won't help to cure it. The best way is to make sure the RF doesn't have a way to blast its way into the affected device. This is true for smoke alarms, stereos, satellite TV receivers or any other type of consumer electronic device. To cure the problem in most cases, install "common-mode" chokes on any and all wires and cables connected to the device. This includes antenna cables, power cables and audio lines—they are all possible culprits. The chokes are constructed by winding the wire you are trying to protect around a ferrite core. F-240-43 cores work well since they have large openings and allow large wires to be coiled around them. Split-bead cores also allow several turns to be made and then the core snapped back together. One caution: Using more than about 8 turns may allow the RF to bleed past the choke. For more information about common-mode chokes, see the ARRL Technical Information Service Web page at **www.arrl.org/tis/info/ HTML/catvi/index.html.** While this page deals with Cable TV issues, the common-mode choke information is the same for any sort of problem involving receiver overload.

Q Frank Long, N3ZOC, of Glen Burnie, Maryland writes: I have a Kidde Nighthawk carbon monoxide alarm. It uses a wall wart power source. When I transmit, the Nighthawk gives me false alarms. This happens with CW transmissions generally on 40 or 15 meters, and it's driving my wife crazy. Apparently the carbon monoxide alarm thinks it is a radio receiver.

A Almost certainly, you are experiencing what we call "Fundamental Overload," which results when the wires attached to the affected device act like long-wire antennas. This serves to bring large levels of RF into devices that are not designed, as they should be, to reject such signals.

Your only practical option is to contact the manufacturer for assistance, which is, based on our experience, unlikely to be provided. Or, you can attempt to add some RF protection to the alarm. This is best done by installing some common-mode chokes on all wires connected to the alarm. Assuming that your CO_2 detector is a standalone device, the only wire you need to be concerned with is the power cord from the wall wart. Even though it is specifically concerned with cable TV problems, the page you can find at **www.arrl.org/tis/info/HTML/ index.html** discusses common-mode chokes, and even shows some photos. Also, the main EMI/RFI page, found at **www.arrl.org/tis/info/rfigen.html**, will give sources of the toroid cores you need to make the common-mode chokes.

Q Jack Shirley, N8DX, of Middletown, Ohio, writes: I wonder if you could help with a possible Part 15 nonintentional radiator problem that I am experiencing. About a month ago, I purchased an ozone generator for our spa and found that it was causing interference on 18/21/24 MHz amateur bands. The device generates ozone using an HV coronal discharge. It seems to peak in RF energy at 21.400 MHz.

I contacted the manufacturer, Watkins Manufacturing (Hot Springs Spas), and they were aware of the problem and said it should have been fixed with the model revision that I have. In talking to a competitor who manufactures one using UV rather than corona discharge, I found out that early models had enough RF output to cause the GFI circuit breakers to trip at times.

In the installation instructions, the manufacturer specifically warns not to have any of the wires from the ozone generator close to the main controller board or you may have problems. In addition, there is no FCC number on the unit.

A Under the FCC Part 15 rules, a device like that is an incidental emitter, meaning that it doesn't intentionally generate any RF signals inside itself, but just happens to do so as an incidental part of its operation. Other examples of inci-

dental emitters include motors and power lines. Incidental emitters don't need an FCC ID number, and the rules have no specific emissions limits, just a very general requirement that they use good engineering practice. That is the sole responsibility of the manufacturer. Part 15 also has a requirement that the *operator* of a Part 15 device not cause harmful interference. Unfortunately, in this case, the operator is you, so, under the rules, you are the one responsible for mitigating the interference.

I don't know how much time has elapsed since you first contacted them. Sometimes, these things take a while to trickle up and down the chain of command. Although the manufacturer has no regulatory responsibility, it is somewhat encouraging that they responded at all. If you think it would be helpful, ARRL could write them a letter, asking that they share any information they have.

As a practical matter, you may be able to add an external ac-line filter as close as possible to the ozone generator. Filters made by Industrial Communications Engineers (**www.arrl.org/tis/ tisfind.html**) should be suitable.

Q Phil Finkle, K6EID, of Marietta, Georgia, is concerned about an impending power line installation. "Our utility is planning to install new 230 kVA transmission lines less than a quarter mile from my house. They have published an Environmental Assessment (EA) that says the lines will have no impact on radio reception. Is there a study that would show the effect of these lines on noise impacting ham radio reception?"

A While these lines may be big and ugly, they are not normally the source of significant EMI from arcing. Unless you live almost directly under the lines where you might be affected by corona noise, it should not be a problem. There are several reasons for this. First, the poles are usually made of steel, and hence they do not swell and shrink over time as environmental conditions change. Most power-line noise comes not from HV transmission lines, but from distribution lines mounted on wood poles that are frequently quite old. If you have ever passed under a large transmission line while listening to the AM band in your car, you may have noticed a loud hum. This is a characteristic of corona noise and it is usually centered on lower frequencies than is noise due to arcing. Because the corona currents are minuscule, little noise is propagated.

Abbreviations List

A

a—atto (prefix for 10^{-18})

A—ampere (unit of electrical current)

ac—alternating current

ACC—Affiliated Club Coordinator

ACSSB—amplitude-compandored single sideband

A/D—analog-to-digital

ADC—analog-to-digital converter

AF—audio frequency

AFC—automatic frequency control

AFSK—audio frequency-shift keying

AGC—automatic gain control

A/h—ampere hour

ALC—automatic level control

AM—amplitude modulation

AMRAD—Amateur Radio Research and Development Corp

AMSAT—Radio Amateur Satellite Corp

AMTOR—Amateur Teleprinting Over Radio

ANT—antenna

ARA—Amateur Radio Association

ARC—Amateur Radio Club

ARES—Amateur Radio Emergency Service

ARQ—Automatic repeat request

ARRL—American Radio Relay League

ARS—Amateur Radio Society (station)

ASCII—American National Standard Code for Information Interchange

ATV—amateur television

AVC—automatic volume control

AWG—American wire gauge

az-el—azimuth-elevation

B

B—bel; blower; susceptance; flux density, (inductors)

balun—balanced to unbalanced (transformer)

BC—broadcast

BCD—binary coded decimal

BCI—broadcast interference

Bd—baud (bids in single-channel binary data transmission)

BER—bit error rate

BFO—beat-frequency oscillator

bit—binary digit

bit/s—bits per second

BM—Bulletin Manager

BPF—band-pass filter

BPL—Brass Pounders League

BT—battery

BW—bandwidth

C

c—centi (prefix for 10^{-2})

C—coulomb (quantity of electric charge); capacitor

CAC—Contest Advisory Committee

CATVI—cable television interference

CB—Citizens Band (radio)

CBBS—computer bulletin-board service

CBMS—computer-based message system

CCITT—International Telegraph and Telephone Consultative Committee

CCTV—closed-circuit television

CCW—coherent CW

ccw—counterclockwise

CD—civil defense

cm—centimeter

CMOS—complimentary-symmetry metal-oxide semiconductor

coax—coaxial cable

COR—carrier-operated relay

CP—code proficiency (award)

CPU—central processing unit

CRT—cathode ray tube

CT—center tap

CTCSS—continuous tone-coded squelch system

cw—clockwise

CW—continuous wave

D

d—deci (prefix for 10^{-1})

D—diode

da—deca (prefix for 10)

D/A—digital-to-analog

DAC—digital-to-analog converter

dB—decibel (0.1 bel)

dBi—decibels above (or below) isotropic antenna

dBm—decibels above (or below) 1 milliwatt

DBM—doubly balanced mixer

dBV—decibels above/below 1 V (in video, relative to 1 V P-P)

dBW—decibels above/below 1 W

dc—direct current

D-C—direct conversion

DDS—direct digital synthesis

DEC—District Emergency Coordinator

deg—degree

DET—detector

DF—direction finding; direction finder

DIP—dual in-line package

DMM—digital multimeter

DPDT—double-pole double-throw (switch)

DPSK—differential phase-shift keying

DPST—double-pole single-throw (switch)

DS—direct sequence (spread spectrum); display

DSB—double sideband

DSP—digital signal processing

DTMF—dual-tone multifrequency

DVM—digital voltmeter

DX—long distance; duplex

DXAC—DX Advisory Committee

DXCC—DX Century Club

E

e—base of natural logarithms (2.71828)

E—voltage

EA—ARRL Educational Advisor

EC—Emergency Coordinator

ECL—emitter-coupled logic

EHF—extremely high frequency (30-300 GHz)

EIA—Electronic Industries Alliance

EIRP—effective isotropic radiated power

ELF—extremely low frequency

ELT—emergency locator transmitter

EMC—electromagnetic compatibility

EME—earth-moon-earth (moonbounce)

EMF—electromotive force

EMI—electromagnetic interference

EMP—electromagnetic pulse

EOC—emergency operations center

EPROM—erasable programmable read only memory

F

f—femto (prefix for 10^{-5}); frequency

F—farad (capacitance unit); fuse

fax—facsimile

FCC—Federal Communications Commission

FD—Field Day

FEMA—Federal Emergency Management Agency

FET—field-effect transistor

FFT—fast Fourier transform

FL—filter

FM—frequency modulation

FMTV—frequency-modulated television

FSK—frequency-shift keying

FSTV—fast-scan (real-time) television

ft—foot (unit of length)

G

g—gram (unit of mass)

G—giga (prefix for 10^9); conductance

GaAs—gallium arsenide

GDO—grid- or gate-dip oscillator

GHz—gigahertz (10^9 Hz)

GND—ground

H

h—hecto (prefix for 10^2)

H—henry (unit of inductance)

HF—high frequency (3-30 MHz)

HFO—high-frequency oscillator; heterodyne frequency oscillator

HPF—highest probable frequency; high-pass filter

Hz—hertz (unit of frequency, 1 cycle/s)

I

I—current, indicating lamp

IARU—International Amateur Radio Union

IC—integrated circuit

ID—identification; inside diameter

IEEE—Institute of Electrical and Electronics Engineers

IF—intermediate frequency

IMD—intermodulation distortion

in.—inch (unit of length)

in./s—inch per second (unit of velocity)

I/O—input/output

IRC—international reply coupon

ISB—independent sideband

ITU—International Telecommunication Union

J

j—operator for complex notation, as for reactive component of an impedance ($+j$ inductive; $-j$ capacitive)

J—joule (kg m^2/s^2) (energy or work unit); jack

JFET—junction field-effect transistor

K

k—kilo (prefix for 10^3); Boltzmann's constant ($1.38\infty10^{-23}$ J/K)

K—kelvin (used without degree symbol) absolute temperature scale; relay

kBd—1000 bauds

kbit—1024 bits

kbit/s—1024 bits per second

kbyte—1024 bytes

kg—kilogram

kHz—kilohertz

km—kilometer

kV—kilovolt

kW—kilowatt

ký—kilohm

L

l—liter (liquid volume)

L—lambert; inductor

lb—pound (force unit)

LC—inductance-capacitance

LCD—liquid crystal display

LED—light-emitting diode

LF—low frequency (30-300 kHz)

LHC—left-hand circular (polarization)

LO—local oscillator; Leadership Official

LP—log periodic

LS—loudspeaker

lsb—least significant bit

LSB—lower sideband

LSI—large-scale integration

LUF—lowest usable frequency

M

m—meter (length); milli (prefix for 10^{-3})

M—mega (prefix for 10^6); meter (instrument)

mA—milliampere

mAh—milliampere hour

MCP—multimode communications processor

MDS—Multipoint Distribution Service; minimum discernible (or detectable) signal

MF—medium frequency (300-3000 kHz)

mH—millihenry

MHz—megahertz

mi—mile, statute (unit of length)

mi/h—mile per hour

mi/s—mile per second

mic—microphone

min—minute (time)

MIX—mixer

mm—millimeter

MOD—modulator

modem—modulator/demodulator

MOS—metal-oxide semiconductor

MOSFET—metal-oxide semiconductor field-effect transistor

MS—meteor scatter

ms—millisecond

m/s—meters per second

msb—most-significant bit

MSI—medium-scale integration

MSK—minimum-shift keying

MSO—message storage operation

MUF—maximum usable frequency

mV—millivolt

mW—milliwatt

Mý—megohm

N

n—nano (prefix for 10^{-9}); number of turns (inductors)

NBFM—narrow-band frequency modulation

NC—no connection; normally closed

NCS—net-control station; National Communications System

nF—nanofarad

NF—noise figure

nH—nanohenry

NiCd—nickel cadmium

NM—Net Manager

NMOS—N-channel metal-oxide silicon

NO—normally open

NPN—negative-positive-negative (transistor)

NPRM—Notice of Proposed Rule Making (FCC)

ns—nanosecond

NTIA—National Telecommunications and Information Administration

NTS—National Traffic System

O

OBS—Official Bulletin Station

OD—outside diameter

OES—Official Emergency Station

OO—Official Observer

op amp—operational amplifier

ORS—Official Relay Station

OSC—oscillator

OSCAR—Orbiting Satellite Carrying Amateur Radio

OTC—Old Timer's Club

oz—ounce (force unit, $^1/_{16}$ pound)

P

p—pico (prefix for 10^{-12})

P—power; plug

PA—power amplifier

PACTOR—digital mode combining aspects of packet and AMTOR

PAM—pulse-amplitude modulation

PBS—packet bulletin-board system

PC—printed circuit

P_D—power dissipation

PEP—peak envelope power

PEV—peak envelope voltage

pF—picofarad

pH—picohenry

PIC—Public Information Coordinator

PIN—positive-intrinsic-negative (semiconductor)

PIO—Public Information Officer

PIV—peak inverse voltage

PLL—phase-locked loop

PM—phase modulation

PMOS—P-channel (metal-oxide semiconductor)

PNP—positive negative positive (transistor)

pot—potentiometer

P-P—peak to peak

ppd—postpaid

PROM—programmable read-only memory

PSAC—Public Service Advisory Committee

PSHR—Public Service Honor Roll

PTO—permeability-tuned oscillator

PTT—push to talk

Q-R

Q—figure of merit (tuned circuit); transistor

QRP—low power (less than 5-W output)

R—resistor

RACES—Radio Amateur Civil Emergency Service

RAM—random-access memory

RC—resistance-capacitance

R/C—radio control

RCC—Rag Chewer's Club

RDF—radio direction finding

RF—radio frequency

RFC—radio-frequency choke
RFI—radio-frequency interference
RHC—right-hand circular (polarization)
RIT—receiver incremental tuning
RLC—resistance-inductance-capacitance
RM—rule making (number assigned to petition)
r/min—revolutions per minute
RMS—root mean square
ROM—read-only memory
r/s—revolutions per second
RS—Radio Sputnik, Russian ham satellites
RST—readability-strength-tone (CW signal report)
RTTY—radioteletype
RX—receiver, receiving

S

s—second (time)
S—siemens (unit of conductance); switch
SASE—self-addressed stamped envelope
SCF—switched capacitor filter
SCR—silicon controlled rectifier
SEC—Section Emergency Coordinator
SET—Simulated Emergency Test
SGL—State Government Liaison
SHF—super-high frequency (3-30 GHz)
SM—Section Manager; silver mica (capacitor)
S/N—signal-to-noise ratio
SPDT—single pole double-throw (switch)
SPST—single-pole single-throw (switch)
SS—Sweepstakes; spread spectrum
SSB—single sideband
SSC—Special Service Club
SSI—small-scale integration
SSTV—slow-scan television
STM—Section Traffic Manager
SX—simplex
sync—synchronous, synchronizing
SWL—shortwave listener
SWR—standing-wave ratio

T

T—tera (prefix for 10^{12}); transformer
TA—ARRL Technical Advisor
TC—Technical Coordinator
TCC—Transcontinental Corps (NTS)
TCP/IP—Transmission Control Protocol/ Internet Protocol
tfc—traffic
TNC—terminal node controller (packet radio)
TR—transmit/receive
TS—ARRL Technical Specialist
TTL—transistor-transistor logic
TTY—teletypewriter
TU—terminal unit
TV—television

TVI—television interference
TX—transmitter, transmitting

U

U—integrated circuit
UHF—ultra-high frequency (300 MHz to 3 GHz)
USB—upper sideband
UTC—Coordinated Universal Time (also abbreviated Z)
UV—ultraviolet

V

V—volt; vacuum tube
VCO—voltage-controlled oscillator
VCR—video cassette recorder
VDT—video-display terminal
VE—Volunteer Examiner
VEC—Volunteer Examiner Coordinator
VFO—variable-frequency oscillator
VHF—very-high frequency (30-300 MHz)
VLF—very-low frequency (3-30 kHz)
VLSI—very-large-scale integration
VMOS—V-topology metal-oxide semiconductor
VOM—volt-ohmmeter
VOX—voice-operated switch
VR—voltage regulator
VSWR—voltage standing-wave ratio
VTVM—vacuum-tube voltmeter
VUCC—VHF/UHF Century Club
VXO—variable-frequency crystal oscillator

W

W—watt (kg m^2s^{-3}), unit of power
WAC—Worked All Continents
WAS—Worked All States
WBFM—wide-band frequency modulation
WEFAX—weather facsimile
Wh—watthour
WPM—words per minute
WRC—World Radio Conference
WVDC—working voltage, direct current

X

X—reactance
XCVR—transceiver
XFMR—transformer
XIT—transmitter incremental tuning
XO—crystal oscillator
XTAL—crystal
XVTR—transverter

Y-Z

Y—crystal; admittance
YIG—yttrium iron garnet
Z—impedance; also see UTC

Numbers/Symbols

5BDXCC—Five-Band DXCC
5BWAC—Five-Band WAC
5BWAS—Five-Band WAS
6BWAC—Six-Band WAC
°—degree (plane angle)
°C—degree Celsius (temperature)
°F—degree Fahrenheit (temperature)
α—(alpha) angles; coefficients, attenuation constant, absorption factor, area, common-base forward current-transfer ratio of a bipolar transistor
β—(beta) angles; coefficients, phase constant current gain of common-emitter transistor amplifiers
γ—(gamma) specific gravity, angles, electrical conductivity, propagation constant
°—(gamma) complex propagation constant
δ—(delta) increment or decrement; density; angles
Δ—(delta) increment or decrement determinant, permittivity
ϵ—(epsilon) dielectric constant; permittivity; electric intensity
ζ—(zeta) coordinates; coefficients
η—(eta) intrinsic impedance; efficiency; surface charge density; hysteresis; coordinate
θ—(theta) angular phase displacement; time constant; reluctance; angles
ι—(iota) unit vector
κ—(kappa) susceptibility; coupling coefficient
λ—(lambda) wavelength; attenuation constant
Λ—(lambda) permeance
μ—(mu) permeability; amplification factor; micro (prefix for 10^{-6})
μF—microfarad
μH—microhenry
μP—microprocessor
ξ—(xi) coordinates
π—(pi) 3.14159
ρ—(rho) resistivity; volume charge density; coordinates; reflection coefficient
σ—(sigma) surface charge density; complex propagation constant; electrical conductivity; leakage coefficient; deviation
Σ—(sigma) summation
τ—(tau) time constant; volume resistivity; time-phase displacement; transmission factor; density
ϕ—(phi) magnetic flux angles
Φ—(phi) summation
χ—(chi) electric susceptibility; angles
Ψ—(psi) dielectric flux; phase difference; coordinates; angles
ω—(omega) angular velocity $2\pi f$
Ω—(omega) resistance in ohms; solid angle

Supplier List

These companies or individuals are cited in this edition of Hints and Kinks. Updated contact information can often be obtained by doing a TIS database search on the *ARRLWeb*: **www.arrl.org/tis/tisfind.html**.

A & A Engineering
2521 West La Palma, Unit K
Anaheim, CA 92801
714-952-2114
fax 714-952-3280
e-mail w6ucm@aol.com

Absolute Value Systems
John Langner, WB2OSZ
115 Stedman St
Chelmsford, MA 01824-1823
978-256-6907
e-mail JohnL@world.std.com
web www.ultranet.com/~sstv/
index.html

AEA
1487 Poinsettia Ave, Suite 127
Vista CA 92083
760-798-9687
800-258-7805
fax 760-798-9689
web www.AEA-wireless.com

Aero/Marine Beacon Guide
Ken Stryker
2856-G West Touhy Ave
Chicago, IL 60645

Alexander Aeroplane Co
(sold to Aircraft Spruce and
Specialty in 1995)
Aircraft Spruce East
900 S. Pine Hill Road
Griffin, GA 30223
770-228-3901
fax 770-229-2329
web www.aircraftspruce.com

Alinco Electronics
438 Amapola Ave, #130
Torrance, CA 90501
web www.alinco.com

All Electronics Corp
PO Box 567
Van Nuys, CA 91408-0567
888-826-5432 Orders
818-904-0524 Customer Service
fax 818-781-2653
e-mail allcorp@callcorp.com
web www.allcorp.com

Allied Electronics
7410 Pebble Dr
Fort Worth, TX 76118
800-433-5700
web www.alliedelec.com

Allstar Magnetics
6205 NE 63rd St.
Vancouver, WA 98661
360-693-0213
fax 360-693-0639
web www.allstarmagnetics.com

Alpha-Delta Communications
PO Box 620
Manchester KY 40962
606-598-2029
fax 606-598-4413
web www.alphadeltacom.com

Alpha Power
Crosslink, Inc.
6185 Arapahoe Ave.
Boulder, CO 80303
303-473-9232
fax 303-473-9660
web www.alpha-amps.com

Aluma Tower Company, Inc
PO Box 2806
Vero Beach, FL 32961-2806
561-567-3423
fax 561-567-3432
e-mail atc@alumatower.com
web www.alumatower.com

AM Press/Exchange
Don Chester, K4KYV, Editor &
Publisher
2116 Old Dover Rd
Woodlawn, TN 37191
web www.amfone.net/AMPX/
ampx.htm

Amateur Television Quarterly
(ATVQ)
Harlan Technologies
5931 Alma Dr
Rockford, IL 61108-2409
815-398-2683
fax 815-398-2688
e-mail atvq@hampubs.com
web www.hampubs.com/
atvq.htm

AMECO Corporation
224 E 2nd St
Mineola, NY 11501
516-741-5030
fax 516-741-5031
e-mail sales@amecocorp.com
web www.amecocorp.com

American Design Components,
Inc.
6 Pearl Court
Allendale, NJ 07041
800-803-5857
web www.adc-ast.com

American National Standards
Institute (ANSI)
1819 L Street, NW
Washington, DC 20036
202-293-8020
fax 202-293-9287
web www.ansi.org

American Power Conversion
132 Fairgrounds Road
West Kingston, RI 02892
800-788-2208
web www.apcc.com

Ameritron
116 Willow Rd
Starkville, MS 39759
662-323-8211
fax 662-323-6551
e-mail amertron@ameritron.com
web www.ameritron.com

Amidon Inc.
Amidon Inductive Components
240 Briggs Ave.
Costa Mesa, CA 92626
800-898-1883
fax 714-850-1163
web www.amidon-inductive.com

AMRAD
Drawer 6148
McLean, VA 22106-6148
web www.amrad.org

AMSAT-NA (Radio Amateur
Satellite Corp.)
850 Sligo Ave., Suite 600
Silver Spring, MD 20910-4703
301-589-6062
fax 301-608-3410
e-mail martha@amsat.org
web www.amsat.org

ANARC (Association of North
American Radio Clubs)
Mark W. Meece, Chairman
529 Sandy Lane
Franklin, OH 45005-2065
e-mail radioscan@siscom.net
web www.anarc.org

Anchor Electronics
2040 Walsh Ave
Santa Clara, CA 95050
408-727-3693
fax 408-727-4424
web www.demoboard.com/
anchorstore.htm

Angle Linear
PO Box 35
Lomita, CA 90717-0035
310-539-5395
fax 310-539-8738
e-mail chip@anglelinear.com
web www.anglelinear.com

AntenneX Magazine
P. O. Box 271229
Corpus Christi, TX 78427-1229
361-855-0250
888-855-9098
fax 361-855-0190
web www.antennex.com

Antique Electronic Supply
6221 South Maple Ave
PO Box 27468
Tempe AZ 85285-7468
480-820-5411
fax 480-820-4643
web www.tubesandmore.com

Antique Radio Classified
PO Box 2-V75
Carlisle, MA 01741
978-371-0512
fax 978-371-7129
web www.antiqueradio.com

Ar² Communication Products
Box 1242
Burlington, CT 06013
860-485-0310
fax 860-485-0311
web www.advancedreceiver.
com

Array Solutions
350 Gloria Rd
Sunnyvale, TX 75182
972-203-2008
fax 972-203-8811
e-mail
wx0b@arraysolutions.com
web www.arraysolutions.com

Arrow Electronics
25 Hub Dr
Melville, NY 11747
631-391-1300

ARRL—The national association
for Amateur Radio
225 Main St
Newington, CT 06111-1494
860-594-0200
fax 860-594-0259
e-mail tis@arrl.org
web www.arrl.org

ARS Electronics
7110 De Celis Pl
PO Box 7323
Van Nuys, CA 91409
818-997-6200
800-422-4250
fax 818-997-6158

ATCI Consultants
11720 Chairman Dr, #108
Dallas, TX 75243
214-343-0600
fax 214-343-0716
e-mail atci@dallas.net
web www.dallas.net/~atci

Atlantic Surplus Sales
3730 Nautilus Ave
Brooklyn, NY 11224
718-372-0349

ATV Research, Inc
1301 Broadway
PO Box 620
Dakota City, NE 68731-0620
402-987-3771
800-392-3922 (orders)
fax 402-987-3709
e-mail sales@atvresearch.com
web www.atvresearch.com

Avantek
3175 Bowers Ave
Santa Clara, CA 95054-3292
408-727-0700

Barker and Williamson Corp
(B&W)
603 Cidco Rd
Cocoa, FL 32926
321-639-1510
fax 321-639-2545
e-mail
custsrvc@bwantennas.com
web www.bwantennas.com

B.G. Micro
555 N 5th St, Ste 125
Garland, TX 75040
800-276-2206
fax 972-205-9417
e-mail bgmicro@bgmicro.com
web www.bgmicro.com

Brian Beezley, K6STI
3532 Linda Vista
San Marcos, CA 92069
760-599-8662 (product support)
e-mail k6sti@n2.net

Bencher, Inc
831 N Central Ave
Wood Dale, IL 60191
630-238-1183
fax 630-238-1186
e-mail bencher@bencher.com
web www.bencher.com

Bird Electronic Corporation
30303 Aurora Rd
Cleveland, OH 44139
440-248-1200
web www.bird-electronic.com

British Amateur Television Club
Grenehurst, Pinewood Rd
High Wycombe
Bucks HP12 4DD
United Kingdom
+44-01494-528899
e-mail memsec@batc.org.uk
web www.batc.org.uk/index.htm

Buckeye Shapeform
555 Marion Rd.
Columbus, OH 43207
800-728-0776
614-445-8433
fax 614-445-8224
e-mail
info@buckeyeshapeform.com
web
    www.buckeyeshapeform.com

Buckmaster Publishing
6196 Jefferson Highway
Mineral, VA 23117
800-282-5628 (orders)
540-894-5777
fax 540-894-9141
e-mail info@buck.com
web www.buck.com

C3i Antennas
7197 N Starcrest Dr
Warrenton, VA 20187-3579
540-349-8833
800-445-7747
web www.c3iusa.com

Caddock Electronics
1717 Chicago Ave
Riverside, CA 92507-2364
909-788-1700
fax 909-369-1151
web www.caddock.com

Calogic, LLC
237 Whitney Pl
Fremont, CA 94539
510-656-2900
fax 510-651-1076

Jim Cates, WA6GER
3241 Eastwood Rd
Sacramento, CA 95821
916-487-3580

(Cetron power tube distributor)
Richardson Electronics, Ltd.
P. O. Box 393
La Fox, IL 60147
630-208-2200
fax 630-208-2550
web www.rell.com

Circuit Specialists Inc.
220 S Country Club Dr, Bldg #2
Mesa, AZ 85210
480-464-2485
800-528-1417
fax 480-464-5824

Coilcraft
1102 Silver Lake Rd
Cary, IL 60013
847-639-6400
fax 847-639-1469
e-mail info@coilcraft.com
web www.coilcraft.com

Communication Concepts, Inc
    (CCI)
508 Millstone Dr
Beavercreek, OH 45434-5840
937-426-8600
fax 937-429-3811
e-mail ccidayton@pobox.com

Communications and Power
    Industries
Eimac Division
301 Industrial Way
San Carlos, CA 94070-2682
800-414-TUBE (414-8823)
fax 650-592-9988
web www.eimac.com

Communications Quarterly
(see CQ Communications)

Communications Specialists Inc
426 West Taft Ave
Orange, CA 92865-4296
714-998-3021
800-854-0547
fax 714-974-3420 or 800-850-
    0547
web www.com-spec.com

Condenser Products Corp
2131 Broad St
Brooksville, FL 34609
352-796-3561
888-598-0957
fax 352-799-0221

Contact East, Inc
335 Willow St
North Andover, MA 01845-5995
978-682-9844
fax 800-743-8141
e-mail sales@contacteast.com
web www.contacteast.com

Courage HANDI-HAM System
3915 Golden Valley Rd
Golden Valley, MN 55422
763-520-0512
866-426-3442 (toll free)
763-520-0245 (TTY)
fax 763-520-0577
e-mail handiham@courage.org
web www.mtn.org/handiham

CQ Communications
25 Newbridge Rd
Hicksville, NY 11801
516-681-2922 (business office)
fax 516-681-2926
e-mail cq@cq-amateur-
    radio.com
web www.cq-amateur-radio.com

Dave Curry Longwave Products
PO Box 1884
Burbank, CA 91507
818-846-0617
web www.fix.net/~jparker/
    currycom.htm

Cushcraft Corp
48 Perimeter Road
Manchester, NH 03103
603-627-7877
fax 603-627-1764
e-mail hamsales@cushcraft.com
web www.cushcraft.com

Custom Computer Services, Inc
PO Box 2452
Brookfield, WI 53008
262-797-0455
fax 262-797-0459
web www.ccsinfo.com

Jacques d'Avignon, VE3VIA
1215 Whiterock Street
Gloucester, ON K1J 1A7
Canada
613-745-6522
e-mail monitor@rac.ca

Peter W. Dahl Co., Inc.
5896 Waycross Ave.
El Paso, TX 79924
915-751-2300
fax 915-751-0768
e-mail pwdco@pwdahl.com
web www.pwdahl.com

Dallas Remote Imaging Group
4209 Meadowdale Dr.
Carrollton, TX 75010
972-898-3563
e-mail consulting@drig.com
web www.drig.com

Dan's Small Parts and Kits
Box 3634
Missoula, MT 59806-3634
406-258-2782 (voice and fax)
web www.fix.net/dans.html

Davis RF Co, Div of Davis
    Associates, Inc.
PO Box 730
Carlisle, MA 01741
800-328-4773 (orders)
978-369-1738 (technical info)
fax 978-369-3484
e-mail davisRFinc@aol.com
web www.davisRF.com

DC Electronics
PO Box 3203
2200 N Scottsdale Rd
Scottsdale, AZ 85271-3203
800-467-7736
fax 480-994-1707
e-mail clifton@dckits.com
web www.dckits.com/index.htm

DCI Inc
20 South Plains Road
Emerald Park, SK S4L 1B7
Canada
306-781-4451
800-563-5351
fax 306-781-2008
e-mail dci@dci.ca
web www.dci.ca

Digi-Key Corp
701 Brooks Ave S
Thief River Falls, MN 56701-0677
218-681-6674
800-344-4539 (800-DIGI-KEY)
fax 218-681-3380
web www.digikey.com

Digital Vision, Inc
270 Bridge St
Dedham, MA 02026
617-329-5400
617-329-8387 (BBS)

Dover Research
321 W 4th St
Jordan, MN 55352-1313
612-492-3913

Down East Microwave
954 Rte 519
Frenchtown, NJ 08825
908-996-3584
fax 908-996-3072
web
    www.downeastmicrowave.com/

East Coast Amateur Radio, Inc
314 Schenck St
N Tonawanda, NY 14120
716-695-3929
fax 716-695-0000
web www.eastcoastradio.com

EDI, Inc
1260 Karl Ct
Wauconda, IL 60084
708-487-3347

Edlie Electronics, Inc
2700 Hempstead Tpk
Levittown, NY 11756-1443
orders 800-647-4722
516-735-3330
fax 516-731-5125
e-mail Elieblinng@aol.com
web www.edlieelectronics.com

Eimac
(see Communications and Power
    Industries)

Electric Radio Magazine
14643 County Rd G
Cortez, CO 81321-9575
970-564-9185 (voice and **fax**)
e-mail er@frontier.net

Electro Sonic, Inc
100 Gordon Baker Rd
Toronto, ON M2H 3B3
Canada
416-494-1666 (outside of
    Canada)
416-494-1555 (sales)
fax 416-496-3030

Electronic Emporium
3621-29 E Weir Ave
Phoenix, AZ 85040
602-437-8633
fax 602-437-8835

Electronic Industries Alliance
    (EIA)
2500 Wilson Blvd
Arlington, VA 22201-3834
703-907-7500
web www.eia.org/

Electronic Precepts of Florida
11651 87th St
Largo, FL 34643-4917
800-367-4649
fax 727-393-1177
web www.theepgd.com/books/
    east/dist/365.htm

Electronic Rainbow, Inc
6227 Coffman Rd
Indianapolis, IN 46268
317-291-7262
fax 317-291-7269
web www.rainbowkits.com

Electronics Now
500-B Bi-County Blvd
Farmingdale, NY 11735
516-293-3000

Elktronics
12536 T.77
Findlay, OH 45840
419-422-8206

Elna Magnetics
234 Tinker St
PO Box 395
Woodstock, NY 12498
800-553-2870
845-679-2497
fax 845-679-7010
web http://elna-ferrite.com

Embedded Research
PO Box 92492
Rochester, NY 14692
e-mail sales@embres.com
web www.embres.com

EMI Filter Company
9075-C 130th Ave N
Largo, FL 33773-1405
800-323-7990
727-585-7990
fax 727-586-5138
web www.emifiltercompany.com

Encomm, Inc.
1506 Capitol Ave
Plano, TX 75074
214-423-0024

Engineering Consulting
583 Candlewood St
Brea, CA 92821
714-671-2009
fax 714-255-9984

ESF Copy Service
4011 Clearview Dr
Cedar Falls, IA 50613-6111
319-266-7040

ETO, Inc
(see Alpha Power)

Fair Radio Sales Co, Inc
2395 St. Johns Road
PO Box 1105
Lima, OH 45802-1105
419-227-6573
419-223-2196
fax 419-227-1313
e-mail fairradio@fairradio.com
web www.fairradio.com/

Fair-Rite Products Corp
PO Box J, 1 Commercial Row
Wallkill, NY 12589
845-895-2055
888-324-7748
fax 845-895-2629
fax 888-337-7483
e-mail ferrites@fair-rite.com
web fair-rite.com/

Fala Electronics
PO Box 1376
Milwaukee, WI 53201-1376

FAR Circuits
18N640 Field Court
Dundee, IL 60118-9269
847-836-9148 (voice and **fax**)
email farcir@ais.net
web www.farcircuits.net/

Federal Emergency Management Agency (FEMA)
500 C Street SW
Washington, DC 20472
202-566-1600
web www.fema.gov

Gateway Electronics
8123 Page Blvd
St. Louis, MO 63130
800-669-5810
314-427-6116
fax 314-427-3147
e-mail gateway@mvp.net
web www.gatewayelex.com/

Glen Martin Engineering
13620 Old Hwy 40
Boonville, MO 65233
800-486-1223
660-882-2734
fax 660-882-7200
e-mail info@glenmartin.com
web www.glenmartin.com/

Grove Enterprises Inc
PO Box 98
Brasstown, NC 28902
800-438-8155 (orders)
828-837-9200
fax 828-837-2216
e-mail nada@grove-ent.com
web www.grove-ent.com/

HAL Communications Corp
1201 W Kenyon Rd
Urbana, IL 61801-0365
217-367-7373
fax 217-367-1701
e-mail
  halcomm@halcomm.com
web www.halcomm.com/

Hammond Mfg Co, Inc
256 Sonwil Dr.
Cheektowaga, NY 14225-2466
716-651-0086
fax 716-651-0726
e-mail rsc@hammondmfg.com
web www.hammondmfg.com/

Hammond Mfg, Ltd
394 Edinburgh Rd, N
Guelph, ON N1H 1E5
Canada
519-822-2960
fax 519-822-0715
e-mail rsc@hammondmfg.com
web www.hammondmfg.com/

Hamtronics, Inc
65-Q Moul Rd
Hilton, NY 14468
585-392-9430
fax 585-392-9420
e-mail jv@hamtronics.com
web www.hamtronics.com/

Heathkit Educational Systems
455 Riverview Drive, Building 2
Benton Harbor, MI 49022
800-253-0570
616 925-6000
fax 616-925-2898
e-mail info@heathkit.com
web www.heathkit.com/

Henry Radio
2050 South Bundy Dr
Los Angeles, CA 90025
310-820-1234
800-877-7979 (Orders)
fax 310-826-7790
e-mail henryradio@earthlink.net
web www.henryradio.com/

Herbach and Rademan
  (H & R Co)
353 Crider Avenue
Moorestown, NJ 08057
800-848-8001 (Orders only)
856-802-0422
fax 856-802-0465
e-mail sales@herbach.com
web www.herbach.com/

HERD Electronics
220 S 2nd St
Dillsburg, PA 17019-9601
717-432-3248
fax 717-432-7850

Heritage Transformer Co, Inc
13483 Litchfield Rd
Eastview, KY 42732
270-862-9877
e-mail Ed-Heri-Tran@
  KVNet.org

Hi-Manuals
(see Surplus Sales of Nebraska)

HI-Tech Software, LLC
6600 Silacci Way
Gilroy, CA 95020
800-735-5715
fax 866 898 8329
e-mail hitech@htsoft.com
web www.htsoft.com/

Hosfelt Electronics
2700 Sunset Blvd
Steubenville, OH 43952
800-524-6464
fax 800-524-5414
e-mail order@hosfelt.com
web www.hosfelt.com/

Howard W. Sams and Company
5436 W. 78th St.
Indianapolis, IN 46268-3910
800-428-7267 (428-SAMS)
317-298-5565
fax 800.552.3910
e-mail
web www.samswebsite.com/
  index.html

ICOM America, Inc
2380 116th Ave NE
PO Box C-90029
Bellevue, WA 98004
425-454-8155
425-450-6088 (literature)
fax 425-454-1509
e-mail
  amateur@icomamerica.com
web www.icomamerica.com/

Idiom Press
PO Box 1025
Geyserville, CA 95441-1025
707-431-1286
E-Mail Sales@IdiomPress.com
web www.idiompress.com/

IEEE (Corporate Offices)
3 Park Avenue, 17th Floor
New York, NY 10016-5997
212-419-7900
fax 212-752-4929
web www.ieee.org/

IEEE Operations Center
445 Hoes Ln
PO Box 1331
Piscataway, NJ 08854-1331
732-981-0060
fax 732-981-1721
web www.ieee.org/

Industrial Communications Engineers (ICE)
PO Box 18495
3318 N Gale St
Indianapolis, IN 46218-0495
317-545-5412
800-423-2666
fax 317-545-9645

Industrial Safety Co
1390 Neubrecht Rd
Lima, OH 45801
877-521-9893
800-809-4805
fax 419-228-5034
fax 800-854-5498
web http://www.indlsafety.com/

International Components Corp
175 Marcus Blvd
Hauppauge, NY 11788
877-791-9477
631-952-9595 (NY)
fax 631-952-9597
e-mail oemsales@icc107.com
web www.icc107.com/

International Crystal Mfg Co
10 North Lee
PO Box 26330
Oklahoma City, OK 73126-0330
800-725-1426
405-236-3741
fax 800-322-9426
e-mail
  customerservice@icmfg.com
web www.icmfg.com/

International Radio
13620 Tyee Rd
Umpqua, OR 97486
541-459-5623
fax 541-459-5632
e-mail inrad@rosenet.net
web www.qth.com/inrad/

International Telecommunication Union (ITU)
Place des Nations
1211 Geneva 20, Switzerland
+41-22-733-7256
e-mail itumail@itu.int
web www.itu.int/

International Visual Communications Association (IVCA)
James Gaither, Jr, W4CR
PO Box 140336
Nashville, TN 37214
web http://www.mindspring.com/
  ~sstv

Intuitive Circuits
2275 Brinston Ave
Troy, MI 48083
248-524-1918
fax 248-524-3808
e-mail sales@icircuits.com
web www.icircuits.com

IPS Radio and Space Services
PO Box 1386
Haymarket NSW 1240
Australia
+61-2-9213-8000
fax +61-2-9213-8060
e-mail office@ips.gov.au
web www2.ips.gov.au

Jameco Electronics
1355 Shoreway Rd
Belmont, CA 94002
800-831-4242
fax 800-237-6948
e-mail info@jameco.com
web www.jameco.com/

James Millen Electronics
PO Box 4215BV
Andover, MA 01810- 0814
978-975-2711
fax 978-474-8949
e-mail info@jamesmillenco.com
web www.jamesmillenco.com

JAN Crystals
2341 Crystal Dr
PO Box 60017
Fort Myers, FL 33906-6017
800-526-9825 (JAN-XTAL)
941-936-2397
fax 941-936-3750
e-mail sales@jancrystals.com
web www.jancrystals.com/

JDR Microdevices
1850 South 10th St
San Jose, CA 95122-4108
800-538-5000 (Orders)
408-494-1400
fax 800-538-5005
e-mail sales@jdr.com
web www.jdr.com/

Jolida Inc. (Tube Factory)
10820 Guilford Rd
Suite 209
Annapolis Junction, MD 20701
301-953-2014
fax 301-498-0554
e-mail
  Jolidacorp@email.msn.com
web www.jolida.com/

K-Com
PO Box 82
Randolph OH 44265
877-242-4540
330-325-2110
fax 330-325-2525
e-mail K-ComInfo@
  K-ComFilters.com
web www.k-comfilters.com/

Kanga US
3521 Spring Lake Dr
Findlay, OH 45840
419-423-4604
e-mail kanga@bright.net
web www.bright.net/~kanga/
kanga/

Kangaroo Tabor Software
1203 County Road 5
Farwell, TX 79325-9430
fax 806-225-4006
e-mail ku5s@wtrt.net
web www.taborsoft.com/

Kantronics
1202 East 23rd St
Lawrence, KS 66046-5099
785-842-7745
fax 785-842-2031
e-mail sales@kantronics.com
web www.kantronics.com/

Kenwood Communications Corp
2201 East Dominguez St
PO Box 22745
Long Beach, CA 90801-5745
310-639-4200 (customer
support)
800-950-5005
fax 310-537-8235
web www.kenwood.net

Kepro Circuit Systems, Inc
3640 Scarlet Oak Blvd.
St. Louis, MO 63122-6606
800-325-3878
636-861-0364
fax 636-861-9109
e-mail sales@kepro.com
web www.kepro.com

Kilo-Tec
PO Box 10
Oak View, CA 93022
805-646-9645 (voice and fax)

Kirby
298 West Carmel Dr
Carmel, IN 46032
317-843-2212

Kooltronic
1700 Morse Ave
Ventura, CA 93003
805-642-8521
fax 805-658-2901
web www.kooltronic.com/

K2AW's Silicon Alley
175 Friends Ln
Westbury, NY 11590
516-334-7024
fax 516-334-7024

Lashen Electronics, Inc
21 Broadway
Denville, NJ 07834
800-552-7436
973-627-3783
fax 973-625-9501
e-mail sales@lashen.com
web www.lashen.com/

Roy Lewallen, W7EL
PO Box 6658
Beaverton, OR 97007
503-646-2885
fax 503-671-9046
e-mail w7el@eznec.com
web www.eznec.com

Lodestone Pacific
4769 E. Wesley Dr
Anaheim, CA 92807
   800-694-8089
714-970-0900
fax 714-970-0800
web www.lodestonepacific.com

The Longwave Club of America
45 Wildflower Rd
Levittown, PA 19057
215-945-0543
e-mail naswa1@aol.com
web anarc.org/lwca/

M/A-COM, Inc (an AMP
Company)
1011 Pawtucket Blvd
PO Box 3295
Lowell, MA 01853-3295
800-366-2266
978-442-5000
fax 978-442-5167
web www.macom.com/

M² Antenna Systems
7560 North Del Mar Ave
Fresno, CA 93711
559-432-8873
fax 559-432-3059
e-mail m2inc@m2inc.com
web www.m2inc.com/

MAI/Prime Parts
5736 N Michigan Rd
Indianapolis, IN 46208
317-257-6811
fax 317-257-1590
e-mail mai@iquest.net
web www.websitea.com/mai/
index.html

The Manual Man
27 Walling St
Sayreville, NJ 08872-1818
732-238-8964
fax 732-238-8964

Marlin P. Jones & Associates,
Inc
PO Box 12685
Lake Park, FL 33403-0685
800-652-6733 (Orders)
561-848-8236 (Tech)
fax 800-432-9937
e-mail mpja@mpja.com
web www.mpja.com/

MARS
Chief Air Force MARS
HQ AFCA/GCWM (MARS)
203 W. Losey St, Room 3065
Scott AFB, IL 62225-5222
618-229-5958
e-mail
   USAF.MARS@scott.af.mil
web public.afca.scott.af.mil/
public/mars/mars1.htm

Navy-Marine Corps MARS
Chief US Navy-Marine Corps
Military Affiliate Radio System
(MARS)—Bldg 13
NAVCOMMU WASHINGTON
Washington, DC 20397-5161
web www.navymars.org/

Army MARS
HQ US ARMY SIGNAL
COMMAND
ATTN: AFSC-OPE-MA (ARMY
MARS)
Ft Huachuca, AZ 85613-5000
web www.asc.army.mil/mars/

Maxim Integrated Products
120 San Gabriel Dr
Sunnyvale, CA 94086
408-737-7600
fax 408-737-7194
web www.maxim-ic.com/

Richard Measures, AG6K
6455 LaCumbre Rd
Somis, CA 93066
805-386-3734
e-mail 2@vcnet.com
web www.vcnet/measures/

Mendelsohn Electronics Co, Inc
(MECI)
340 E First St
Dayton, OH 45402
800-344-4465
937-461-3525
fax 800-344-6324
fax 937-461-3391
web www.meci.com

Metal and Cable Corp, Inc
9337 Ravenna Rd, Unit C
PO Box 117
Twinsburg, OH 44087
330-425-8455
fax 330-963-7246
web www.metal-cable.com/

MFJ Enterprises
PO Box 494
Mississippi State, MS 39762
662-323-5869
800-647-1800
fax 662-323-6551
e-mail mfj@mfjenterprises.com
web www.mfjenterprises.com/

Microchip Technology
2355 W Chandler Blvd
Chandler, AZ 85224-6199
480-792-7966
fax 480-792-4338
web www.microchip.com/

Microcraft Corp
PO Box 513Q
Thiensville, WI 53092
262-241-8144

Microwave Components of
   Michigan
PO Box 1697
Taylor, MI 48180
313-753-4581 (evenings)

Microwave Filter Co, Inc
6743 Kinne St
E Syracuse NY 13057
800-448-1666
315-438-4700
fax 888-411-8860
fax 315-463-1467
e-mail
   mfcsales@microwavefilter.com
web www.mwfilter.com/

Mini Circuits Labs
PO Box 350166
Brooklyn, NY 11235-0003
800-654-7949
718-934-4500
fax 718-332-4661
web www.minicircuits.com/

Mirage Communications
300 Industrial Park Road
Starkville, MS 39759
662-323-8287
fax 662-323-6551
web www.mirageamp.com/

Model Aviation
5151 East Memorial Dr
Muncie, IN 47302
765- 288-4899
fax 765-289-4248
web modelaircraft.org/mag/
index.htm

Morse Telegraph Club, Inc
Grand Secretary: Derek Cohn
8141 Stratford Dr
Clayton, MO 63105-3707
e-mail
   vibroplex@mindspring.com
web members.tripod.com/
morse_telegraph_club/

Motorola Semiconductor
Products, Inc
5005 East McDowell Rd
Phoenix, AZ 85008
512-891-2030
512-891-3773
web www.mot.com/

Mouser Electronics
1000 N Main St
Mansfield, TX 76063
800-346-6873
   fax 817-804-3899
e-mail sales@mouser.com
web www.mouser.com/

Multi-Tech Industries, Inc.
64 South Main Street
P.O. Box 159
Marlboro, NJ 07746-0159
800-431-3223
fax 732-409-6695
e-mail multitech@sprynet.com
web www.multi-tech-
industries.com/

National Electronics
PO Box 15417
Shawnee Mission, KS 66285
800-762-5049 (orders)
e-mail sales@national-
electronics.com
web www.national-
electronics.com/

National Fire Protection
Association
1 Batterymarch Park
PO Box 9101
Quincy, MA 02269-9101
800-344-3555
617 770-3000
fax 617 770-0700
web www.nfpa.org/

National Semiconductor Corp
PO Box 58090
Santa Clara, CA 95052-8090
800-272-9959
408-721-5000
fax 800-432-9672
web www.national.com/

National Technical Information
Service
5285 Port Royal Rd
Springfield, VA 22161
800-553-6847
703-605-6000 (sales desk)
703-487-4639 (TDD - for the
hearing impared)
fax 703-605-6900
web www.ntis.gov/

The New RTTY Journal
PO Box 236
Champaign, IL 61824-0236
217-367-7373
fax 217-367-1701
web www.rttyjournal.com/

New Sensor Corp
20 Cooper Station
New York, NY 10003
212-529-0466
800-633-5477 (orders)
fax 212-529-0486
web www.sovtek.com/

Newark Electronics
4801 N. Ravenswood Ave
Chicago, IL 60640-4496
800-463-9275
773-784-5100
fax 773-907-5339
web www.newark.com/

Noble Publishing Corp
630 Pinnacle Court
Norcross, GA 30071
770-449-6774
fax 770-448-2839
web www.noblepub.com/

NOISE/COM Co
E 64 Midland Ave
Paramus, NJ 07652
201-261-8797
fax 201-261-8339
e-mail info@noisecom.com.
web www.noisecom.com/

Northern Lights Software
P O Box 321
Canton, NY 13617
315-379-0161
fax 315-379-0161
e-mail nlsa@nlsa.com
web www.nlsa.com/

Nuts & Volts Magazine
430 Princeland Court
Corona, CA 92879
800-783-4624 (orders)
909-371-8497
fax 909-371-3052
e-mail subscribe@nutsvolts.com
web www.nutsvolts.com/

Oak Hills Research
(div of Millstone Technologies)
2460 S Moline Way
Aurora, CO 80014
800-238-8205 (orders)
303-752-3382
fax 303-745-6792
e-mail qrp@ohr.com
web www.ohr.com/

Ocean State Electronics
P. O. Box 1458
6 Industrial Drive
Westerly, RI 02891
401-596-3080
800-866-6626
fax 401-596-3590
e-mail ose@oselectronics.com
web www.oselectronics.com

Old Tech – Books & Things
498 Cross St.
Carlisle, MA 01741
978-371-2231

Osborne/McGraw-Hill
2600 10th St., 6th Floor
Berkeley, CA 94710
800-227-0900
web www.osborne.com

PacComm Packet Radio
   Systems, Inc.
7818-B Causeway Blvd.
Tampa, FL 33619-6574
800-486-7388 (Orders)
813-874-2980
fax 813-872-8696
e-mail info@paccomm.com
web www.paccomm.com

Palomar Engineers
P. O. Box 462222
Escondido, CA 92046
760-747-3343
fax 760-747-3346
e-mail Info@Palomar-
   Engineers.com
web www.Palomar-
   Engineers.com

Pasternak Enterprises
P. O. Box 16759
Irvine, CA 92623-6759
949-261-1920
fax 949-261-7451
e-mail sales@pasternak.com
web www.pasternak.com

PC Electronics
2522 Paxson Lane
Arcadia, CA 91007
626-447-4565
fax 626-447-0489
email tom@hamtv.com
web www.hamtv.com

Phillips Components
23142 Alcalde Drive, Suite A
Laguna Hills, CA 92653
949-855-4263
800-899-4263
fax 949-583-9337
e-mail
   info@phillipscomponents.net
web www.phillipscomponents.net

Phillips-Tech Electronics
P. O. Box 737
Trinidad, CA 95570
707-677-0159
fax 707-677-0934
e-mail samsphillips@cox.net
web www.phillips-tech.com

Bob Platts, G8OZP
43 Ironwalls Ln
Tutbury,
Strafordshire DE13 9NH
United Kingdom
+44-12-8381-3392
e-mail g8ozp@hotmail.com

PolyPhaser Corp.
P.O. Box 9000
Minden, NV 89423
800-325-7170
775-782-2511
fax 775-782-4476
e-mail info@polyphaser.com
web www.polyphaser.com

Popular Communications
(see CQ Communications)

Power Supply Components is
   now -
PSC Electronics
2304 Calle Del Mundo
Santa Clara, CA 95054
408-737-1333
e-mail jena@pscelex.com
web www.pscelex.com/
   index.html

Practical Wireless
Arrowsmith Court
Station Approach
Broadstone, Dorset BH18 8PW
United Kingdom
+44-1202-659910
fax +44-1202-659950
e-mail rob@pwpublishing.ltd.uk
web www.pwpublishing.ltd.uk/
   pw/index.html

Pro Distributors, Inc.
5135 A 69th St.
Lubbock, TX 79424
800-658-2027 (orders)
806-794-3692
fax 806-794-9699
web www.prodistributors.com

PSK31
web www.aintel.bi.ehu.es/
   psk31.html

QRP Quarterly (Subscriptions)
Mark Milburn, KQ0I
117 E. Philip St.
Des Moines, IA 50315-4114
e-mail kq0i@arrl.net
web www.arparci.org

Quantics
P. O. Box 2163
Nevada City, CA 95959-2163
e-mail dave@w9gr.com
web www.w9gr.com

R & L Electronics
1315 Maple Ave
Hamilton, OH 45011
800-221-7735
513-868-6399
fax 513-868-6574
e-mail sales@randl.com
web www.randl.com

Radio Adventures Corp.
RD #4, Box 240
Summit Drive
Franklin, PA 16323
814-437-5355
fax 814-437-5432
e-mail
   information@radioadv.com
web www.radioadv.com

Radio Amateur
   Telecommunications Society
c/o Brian Boccardi
203 Bishop Blvd
North Brunswick, NJ 08902
e-mail askrat@rats.org
web www.rats.org

Radio Bookstore and Radioware
P. O. Box 209
Rindge, NH 03461-0209
800-457-7373
603-899-6826
fax 603-899-6826
web www.radiobooks.com

RadioShack Corporation
100 Throckmorton St., Suite
   1800
Ft. Worth, TX 76102
817-415-3700
800-theshack
web www.radioshack.com

Radio Society of Great Britain
Lambda House
Cranborne Road
Potters Bar
Herts EN6 3JE
United Kingdom
+44-870-904-7373
fax +44-870-904-7374
e-mail postmaster@rsgb.org.uk
web www.rsgb.org

Radio Switch Corp.
(see Multi-Tech Industries, Inc.)

Radiokit
P. O. Box 973
Pelham, NH 03076
603-635-2235
fax 603-635-2943
e-mail km1h@juno.com

Ramsey Electronics, Inc.
793 Canning Parkway
Victor, NY 14564
585-924-4560
800-446-2295
fax 585-924-4886
e-mail sales@ramseymail.com
web www.ramseyelectronics.com

The Raymond Sarrio Company
6147 Via Serena St.
Alta Loma, CA 91701
800-413-1129 (orders)
fax 508-355-8261
e-mail sarrio@sarrio.com
web www.sarrio.com

Marius Rensen
e-mail mrensen@hffax.de
Web www.hffax.de

RF Parts Company
435 South Pacific St.
San Marcos, CA 92069
760-744-0700
800-737-2787 (orders)
fax 888-744-1943
e-mail rfp@rfparts.com
web www.rfparts.com

Rohn Industries, Inc.
6718 West Plank Road
Peoria, IL 61604
309-697-4400
fax 603-497-3244
e-mail mail@rohnnet.com
web www.rohnnet.com

S & S Associates
14102 Brown Rd.
Smithsburg, MD 21783
301-416-0661
fax 301-416-0963

Sentry Manufacturing Corp.
1201 Crystal Park
Chickasha, OK 73018-1766
405-224-6780
800-252-6780
fax 405-224-8808

SHF Microwave Parts Company
7102 West 500 South
La Porte, IN 43650
fax 219-785-4552
e-mail prutz@shfmicro.com
web www.shfmicro.com

Sky Publishing Corp.
49 Bay State Road
Cambridge, MA 02138-1200
800-253-0245
617-864-7360
fax 617-864-6117
e-mail skytel@skypub.com
web www.skypub.com

Skymoon
RR10, Box 27
Mt. Pleasant, TX 75455
web web.wt.net/~w5un/
   skymoon.htm

Skywave Technologies
17 Pine Knoll Road
Lexington, MA 02420
781-862-6742
e-mail skywavetec@aol.com
web members.aol.com/
   skywavetec/

Small Parts, Inc.
13980 NW 58th Ct
P. O. Box 4650
Miami Lakes, FL 33014-0650
800-220-4242 (Orders)
305-557-7955 (Customer
   Service)
fax 800-423-9009
e-mail parts@smallparts.com
web www.smallparts.com

Society of Wireless Pioneers Inc.
P. O. Box 86
Geyserville, CA 95441
e-mail k6dzy@direcpc.com
web www.sowp.org

Software Systems Consulting
615 South El Camino Real
San Clemente, CA 92682
949-498-5784
fax 949-498-0568

Solder-It Co.
P. O. Box 360
Chagrin Falls, OH 44022
440-247-6322
800-897-8989
fax 440-247-4630
e-mail fdoob@solder-it.com
web www.solder-it.com

Southern Electronics Supply
1909 Tulane Ave.
New Orleans, LA 70112
504-524-2343
800-447-0444
fax 504-523-1000
e-mail e-mail@southernele.com
web www.southernele.com

Sparrevohn Engineering
6911 E. 11th St.
Long Beach, CA 90815
652-799-1577
e-mail zsmrtfred@aol.com
web www.members.aol.com/
zsmrtfred

SPEC-COM Journal
PO Box 1002
Dubuque, IA 52004-1002

Spectrum International, Inc
PO Box 1084
Concord, MA 01742
978-263-2145
fax 978-263-7008

Star Circuits
PO Box 94917
Las Vegas, NV 89193

SunLight Energy Systems
955 Manchester Ave SW
N Lawrence, OH 44666
330-832-3114
fax 330-832-4161
e-mail prosolar@sssnet.com
web www.seslogic.com/

Surplus Sales of Nebraska
1502 Jones St
Omaha, NE 68102-3112
800-244-4567 (orders)
402-346-4750
fax 402-346-2939
e-mail grinnell@surplussales.com
web www.surplussales.com/

Svetlana Electron Devices
8200 S. Memorial Parkway
Huntsville, AL 35802
256-882-1344
800-239-6900
fax 256-880-8077
e-mail sales@svetlana.com
web www.svetlana.com/

TAB/McGraw-Hill
Blue Ridge Summit, PA 17214-
0850
800-822-8158

Tandy National Parts
(see RadioShack Corporation)

TE Systems
RLS Electronics - Distributor

1710 East Parkway
Russellville, AR 72802
888-315-7388
e-mail rlselect@mail.cswnet.com
web www.rlselectronics.com/
ampframe.html

Teletec Corp
10101 North Blvd
Wake Forest, NC 27587
909-556-7800

Telex Communications, Inc
12000 Portland Ave South
Burnsville, MN 55337
952-884-4051
fax 952-884-0043
e-mail info@telex.com
web www.telex.com

Tempo Research Corp [see AEA]

Ten-Tec, Inc
1185 Dolly Parton Pkwy
Sevierville, TN 37862
865-453-7172
fax 865-428-4483
e-mail sales@tentec.com
web www.tentec.com/

Texas Towers
1108 Summit Ave, Suite 4
Plano, TX 75074
800-272-3467
972-422-7306 (Tech)
fax 972-881-0776
e-mail sales@texastowers.com
web www.texastowers.com/

Timewave Technology Inc
501 W. Lawson Ave.
St Paul MN 55117
651-489-5080
fax 651-489-5066
e-mail sales@timewave.com
web www.timewave.com

Toroid Corporation of Maryland
202 Northwood Dr
Salisbury, MD 21801
410-860-0300
fax 410-860-0302
e-mail sales@toroid.com
web www.toroid.com

Tri-Ex Tower Corp
7182 Rasmussen Ave
Visalia, CA 93291
800-328-2393 (orders)
209-651-7850
fax 209-651-5157

Trinity Software
James L. Tonne
7801 Rice Dr
Rowlett, TX 75088
972-475-7132

Tucson Amateur Packet Radio
8987-309 E Tanque Verde Rd,
#337
Tucson, AZ 85749-9399
972-671-8277
fax 971-671-8716
e-mail tapr@tapr.org
web www.tapr.org

TX RX Systems, Inc
8625 Industrial Pky
Angola, NY 14006
716-549-4700
fax 716-549-4772
e-mail sales@txrx.com
web www.txrx.com

Typetronics
PO Box 8873
Fort Lauderdale, FL 33310-8873
954-583-1340
fax 954-583-0777

Unified Microsystems
PO Box 133-W
Slinger, WI 53086
262-644-9036
fax 262-644-9036
e-mail w9xt@qth.com
web www.qth.com/w9xt

United Nations Bookshop
UN General Assembly Building,
Room 32B
New York, NY 10017
e-mail bookshop@un.org
web www.un.org/Pubs/bookshop/
bookshop.htm

Universal Manufacturing Co
43900 Groesbeck Hwy
Clinton Township, MI 48036
586-463-2560
fax 586-463-2964

US Electronics (Port Jefferson,
NY)
Acquired by Communication
Dynamics Inc.
325 Laudermilch Rd.
Hershey, PA 17033
717-312-1159

US Government Printing Office -
Bookstore
202-512-1800
866-512-1800 (toll free)
fax 202-512-2250
e-mail orders@gpo.gov
web www.bookstore.gpo.gov/

US Plastic Corp
1390 Neubrecht Rd
Lima, OH 45801-3196
800-809-4217
fax 800-854-5498
e-mail usp@usplastic.com
web www.usplastic.com

US Tower Corp
1220 Marcin St
Visalia, CA 93291-9288
559-733-2438
fax 559-733-7194
e-mail sales@ustower.com
web www.ustower.com

VHF PAK
Bob Mobile, K1SIX
33 Kimball Hill Road
Hillsboro, NH 03244

VK3UM EME Planner
Doug McArthur
Tikaluna
26 Old Murrindindi Road
Glenburn, VIC 3717
Australia
Download: www.qsl.net/sm2cew/
download.htm

W&W Manufacturing Co
800 South Broadway
Hicksville, NY 11801-5017
800-221-0732
516-942-0011
fax 516-942-1944
web www.ww-manufacturing.com/

The W5YI Group
PO Box 565101
Dallas, TX 75356
800-669-9594 (orders)
817-274-0400
fax 817-548-9594
e-mail w5yi@w5yi.org
web www.w5yi.org/

W6EL Software
11058 Queensland St
Los Angeles, CA 90034-3029
310-473-7322
e-mail ad363@lafn.org

W7FG Vintage Manuals
402731 West 2155 Drive
Bartlesville, OK 74006
800-807-6146 (orders)
918-333-3754
fax 918-774-9180
e-mail w7fg@w7fg.com
web www.w7fg.com/

Ed Wetherhold, W3NQN
1426 Catlyn Pl
Annapolis, MD 21401-4208
410-268-0916
fax 410-268-4779

Wilderness Radio
PO Box 734
Los Altos, CA 94023-0734
650-494-3806
e-mail qrpbob@datatamers.com
web www.fix.net/jparker/wild.html

Winegard
3000 Kirkwood St
Burlington, IA 52601-1007
800-288-8094
319-754-0600
fax 319-754-0787
web www.winegard.com/

The Wireman Inc
261 Pittman Rd
Landrum, SC 29356-9544
800-727-WIRE (800-727-9473)
Orders only
864-895-4195 Technical
fax 864-895-5811
e-mail info@thewireman.com
web www.thewireman.com/

Worldradio
2120 28th St
Sacramento, CA 95818
916-457-3655
877 472-8643 (subscriptions)
e-mail editor@wr6wr.com
web www.wr6wr.com/

Wyman Research, Inc
8339 South, 850 West
Waldron, IN 46182-9644
765-525-6452
e-mail wyman@svs.net
web www.svs.net/wyman

Yaesu U.S.A.
Vertex Standard
10900 Walker St
Cypress, CA 90630
714-827-7600
fax 714-827-8100
e-mail
amateursales@vxstdusa.com
web www.vxstdusa.com/

E.H. Yost and Company
Mr. NiCd's Batteries America
2211-D Parview Rd
Middleton, WI 53562
800-308-4805 Orders only
fax 608-831-1082
e-mail ehyost@chorus.net
web www.batteriesamerica.com/

Zero Surge Inc
889 State Rte 12
Frenchtown NJ 08825
800-996-6696
908-996-7700
fax 908-996-7773
e-mail info@zerosurge.com
web www.zerosurge.com/

73 Amateur Radio Today
70 Route 202 N
Peterborough, NH 03458-1107
800-274-7373 (subscriptions)
603-924-0058
fax 603-924-8613

Index

NOTES

NOTES

NOTES

FEEDBACK

Please use this form to give us your comments on this book and what you'd like to see in future editions, or e-mail us at **pubsfdbk@arrl.org** (publications feedback). If you use e-mail, please include your name, call, e-mail address and the book title, edition and printing in the body of your message. Also indicate whether or not you are an ARRL member.

Where did you purchase this book?
☐ From ARRL directly ☐ From an ARRL dealer

Is there a dealer who carries ARRL publications within:
☐ 5 miles ☐ 15 miles ☐ 30 miles of your location? ☐ Not sure.

License class:
☐ Novice ☐ Technician ☐ Technician Plus ☐ General ☐ Advanced ☐ Amateur Extra

---

Name _____

ARRL member? ☐ Yes ☐ No

Call Sign _____

Daytime Phone ( ) _____ Age _____

Address _____

City, State/Province, ZIP/Postal Code _____ E-mail:_____

If licensed, how long? _____

Other hobbies _____

For ARRL use only		H&K
Edition		16 17 18 19 20
Printing	1 2 3 4 5 6 7 8 9 10 11 12	

Occupation _____

From _____

_____

_____

EDITOR, HINTS & KINKS
ARRL—THE NATIONAL ASSOCIATION FOR
 AMATEUR RADIO
225 MAIN STREET
NEWINGTON CT 06111-1494

— — — — — — — — — — — — — — — — — please fold and tape — — — — — — — — — — — — — — — — — — —